T0191579

Lecture Notes in Computer Science   13271

Founding Editors

Gerhard Goos
Karlsruhe Institute of Technology, Karlsruhe, Germany

Juris Hartmanis
Cornell University, Ithaca, NY, USA

Editorial Board Members

Elisa Bertino
Purdue University, West Lafayette, IN, USA

Wen Gao
Peking University, Beijing, China

Bernhard Steffen ⓘ
TU Dortmund University, Dortmund, Germany

Moti Yung ⓘ
Columbia University, New York, NY, USA

More information about this series at https://link.springer.com/bookseries/558

Maurice H. ter Beek · Marjan Sirjani (Eds.)

Coordination Models and Languages

24th IFIP WG 6.1 International Conference, COORDINATION 2022
Held as Part of the 17th International Federated Conference
on Distributed Computing Techniques, DisCoTec 2022
Lucca, Italy, June 13–17, 2022
Proceedings

 Springer

Editors
Maurice H. ter Beek 🆔
ISTI-CNR
Pisa, Italy

Marjan Sirjani 🆔
Mälardalen University
Västerås, Sweden

ISSN 0302-9743   ISSN 1611-3349 (electronic)
Lecture Notes in Computer Science
ISBN 978-3-031-08145-3   ISBN 978-3-031-08143-9 (eBook)
https://doi.org/10.1007/978-3-031-08143-9

© IFIP International Federation for Information Processing 2022
This work is subject to copyright. All rights are reserved by the Publisher, whether the whole or part of the material is concerned, specifically the rights of translation, reprinting, reuse of illustrations, recitation, broadcasting, reproduction on microfilms or in any other physical way, and transmission or information storage and retrieval, electronic adaptation, computer software, or by similar or dissimilar methodology now known or hereafter developed.
The use of general descriptive names, registered names, trademarks, service marks, etc. in this publication does not imply, even in the absence of a specific statement, that such names are exempt from the relevant protective laws and regulations and therefore free for general use.
The publisher, the authors and the editors are safe to assume that the advice and information in this book are believed to be true and accurate at the date of publication. Neither the publisher nor the authors or the editors give a warranty, expressed or implied, with respect to the material contained herein or for any errors or omissions that may have been made. The publisher remains neutral with regard to jurisdictional claims in published maps and institutional affiliations.

This Springer imprint is published by the registered company Springer Nature Switzerland AG
The registered company address is: Gewerbestrasse 11, 6330 Cham, Switzerland

Foreword

The 17th International Federated Conference on Distributed Computing Techniques (DisCoTec 2022) took place in Lucca from June 13 to June 17, 2022. It was organized by the IMT School for Advanced Studies Lucca. The DisCoTec series is one of the major events sponsored by the International Federation for Information Processing (IFIP), the European Association for Programming Languages and Systems (EAPLS), and the Microservices Community. It comprises three conferences:

- COORDINATION, the IFIP WG 6.1 24th International Conference on Coordination Models and Languages
- DAIS, the IFIP WG 6.1 22nd International Conference on Distributed Applications and Interoperable Systems
- FORTE, the IFIP WG 6.1 42nd International Conference on Formal Techniques for Distributed Objects, Components and Systems

Together, these conferences cover a broad spectrum of distributed computing subjects, ranging from theoretical foundations and formal description techniques to systems research issues. As is customary, the event also included several plenary sessions in addition to the individual sessions of each conference, which gathered attendees from the three conferences. These included joint invited speaker sessions and a joint session for the best papers from the three conferences.

DisCoTec 2022 featured the following invited speakers:

- Muffy Calder, University of Glasgow, UK
- Maarten van Steen, University of Twente, The Netherlands
- Luca Viganò, King's College London, UK

Associated with the federated event, five satellite events took place:

- BlockTEE 2022: Workshop on Blockchain Technologies and Trusted Execution Environments
- CoMinDs 2022: Workshop on Collaborative Mining for Distributed Systems
- FOCODILE 2022: Workshop on the Foundations of Consensus and Distributed Ledgers
- ICE 2022: Workshop on Interaction and Concurrency Experience
- REMV 2022: Workshop on Robotics, Electronics and Machine Vision

Moreover, we also had a number of short tutorials on hot topics:

- An Introduction to Spatial Logics and Spatial Model Checking by Vincenzo Ciancia
- A Gentle Adventure Mechanising Message Passing Concurrency Systems by David Castro-Perez, Francisco Ferreira, Lorenzo Gheri, and Martin Vassor

- Smart Contracts in Bitcoin and BitML by Massimo Bartoletti and Roberto Zunino
- The ΔQ Systems Development Paradigm by Neil Davies, Seyed Hossein Haeri, Peter Thompson, and Peter Van Roy
- ChorChain: a Model-driven Approach for Trusted Execution of Multi-party Business Processes on Blockchain by Alessandro Marcelletti

Of course, all of this could not be done without the precious work of the members of the Program Committees of the three main conferences and of the five workshops, and of the Steering Committee and Advisory Boards. Many thanks to all of them, they are too many to mention. However, I would like to thank personally the Program Committee chairs of the main conferences, namely Maurice ter Beek and Marjan Sirjani (for COORDINATION), David Eyers and Spyros Voulgaris (for DAIS), and Mohammad Mousavi and Anna Philippou (for FORTE). They have managed to select an excellent set of research papers.

The organization of DisCoTec 2022 was only possible thanks to the dedicated work of the Organizing Committee, including Marinella Petrocchi, Simone Soderi, Francesco Tiezzi (Workshops and Tutorials Chair) and Giorgio Audrito (Publicity Chair). But a special thanks has to go to Letterio Galletta, the Chair of the Local Organizing Committee, who, in many cases, because of my absence, acted also as General Chair. Finally, I would like to thank IFIP WG 6.1, EAPLS, and the Microservices Community for sponsoring this event, Springer's Lecture Notes in Computer Science team for their support and sponsorship, EasyChair for providing the reviewing framework, and the IMT School for providing the support and the infrastructure to host the event.

June 2022   Rocco De Nicola

Preface

This volume contains the papers presented at the 24th International Conference on Coordination Models and Languages (COORDINATION 2022) held in beautiful Lucca, Italy, hosted by the IMT School for Advanced Studies Lucca, as part of the 17th International Federated Conference on Distributed Computing Techniques (DisCoTec 2022).

Modern information systems rely increasingly on combining concurrent, distributed, mobile, adaptive, reconfigurable, and heterogeneous components. New models, architectures, languages, and verification techniques are necessary to cope with the complexity induced by the demands of today's software development. Coordination languages have emerged as a successful approach, in that they provide abstractions that cleanly separate behavior from communication, thereby increasing modularity, simplifying reasoning, and ultimately enhancing software development. COORDINATION provides a well-established forum for the growing community of researchers interested in models, languages, architectures, and implementation techniques for coordination.

COORDINATION 2022 solicited high-quality contributions in five different categories: (1) regular long papers describing thorough and complete research results and experience reports; (2) regular short papers describing research in progress or opinion papers on past COORDINATION research, on the current state of the art, or on prospects for the years to come; (3) short tool papers describing technological artefacts in the scope of the research topics of COORDINATION; (4) long tool papers describing technological artefacts in the scope of the research topics of COORDINATION; and (5) survey papers describing important results and success stories that originated in the context of COORDINATION. Furthermore, to enable cross-fertilization with other research communities in computer science or in other engineering or scientific disciplines, COORDINATION sought contributions for a dedicated session on the special topic of microservices organized by Ivan Lanese and Fabrizio Montesi.

The Program Committee (PC), with members from 15 different countries spread over four continents, originally received a total of 32 abstract submissions distributed over all five categories, which eventually resulted in 22 paper submissions: 16 regular long papers, four long tool papers, one regular short paper, and one short tool paper. We were pleased to receive submissions from authors based in 11 different countries in Europe along with the USA. Each submission went through a rigorous review process in which all papers were reviewed by at least three PC members, with the help of some external reviewers. Tool papers were selected according to an account of the tool's functionality and practical capabilities and a short video demonstration. Notably, a lightweight rebuttal was used during the reviewing phase, allowing reviewers to ask for a quick rebuttal in the case of a clearly identifiable issue that seemed decisive for the review outcome and which could likely be quickly clarified by the authors. This phase was followed by a short yet very intense discussion phase. The decision to accept or reject a paper was based not only on the review reports and scores but also, and in particular, on these in-depth discussions. In the end, the PC of COORDINATION 2022 selected 12 papers for presentation during the conference and inclusion in these proceedings: seven regular long papers, four long tool papers, and one short tool paper. This amounts to an acceptance rate of 55% (independent of whether or not the short papers are included in the calculation).

To credit the effort of tool developers, this edition of COORDINATION introduced for the first time EAPLS artefact badging. The Artefact Evaluation Committee, chaired by the tool track chair Ferruccio Damiani, received six submissions and worked hard to run sometimes complex tools and long experiments. All artefacts achieved the available badge, while five artefacts of particularly good quality were awarded the functional and reusable badge.

The conference featured a keynote by Luca Viganò (King's College London, UK) entitled "Formal Methods for Socio-Technical Security (Formal and Automated Analysis of Security Ceremonies)". We hereby heartily thank our invited speaker.

We are grateful to all involved in COORDINATION 2022. In particular, all PC members and external reviewers for their accurate and timely reviewing, all authors for their submissions, and all attendees for their participation. We also thank all chairs and committees, itemized on the following pages, and the excellent local organization committee chaired by Rocco De Nicola and Letterio Galletta.

We are very grateful to the organizations which sponsored the conference: EAPLS (European Association for Programming Languages and Systems), IFIP (International Federation for Information Processing) WG 6.1, Microservices Community, and Springer.

Finally, we thank Springer for publishing these proceedings in their LNCS and LNPSE book series in cooperation with IFIP, and for facilitating the EAPLS artefact badges on the papers, and we kindly acknowledge the support from EasyChair in assisting us in managing the complete process from submissions through these proceedings to the program.

We hope you enjoyed the conference!

April 2022

Maurice H. ter Beek
Marjan Sirjani

Organization

General Chair

Rocco De Nicola   IMT School for Advanced Studies Lucca, Italy

Program Committee Chairs

Maurice H. ter Beek   ISTI–CNR, Italy
Marjan Sirjani   Mälardalen University, Sweden

Tool Track Chair

Ferruccio Damiani   University of Turin, Italy

Program Committee

Erika Ábrahám	RWTH Aachen University, Germany
Davide Basile	ISTI–CNR, Italy
Simon Bliudze	Inria, France
Marcello Bonsangue	Leiden University, The Netherlands
Ornela Dardha	University of Glasgow, UK
Patricia Derler	National Instruments, USA
Adrian Francalanza	University of Malta, Malta
Vashti Galpin	University of Edinburgh, UK
Fatemeh Ghassemi	University of Tehran, Iran
Einar Broch Johnsen	University of Oslo, Norway
Christine Julien	University of Texas at Austin, USA
Narges Khakpour	Linnaeus University, Sweden
Eva Kühn	Vienna University of Technology, Austria
Ivan Lanese	University of Bologna, Italy
Alberto Lluch Lafuente	Technical University of Denmark, Denmark
Michele Loreti	University of Camerino, Italy
Mieke Massink	ISTI–CNR, Italy
Hernán Melgratti	University of Buenos Aires, Argentina
Fabrizio Montesi	University of Southern Denmark, Denmark
José Proença	Polytechnic Institute of Porto, Portugal
Rosario Pugliese	University of Florence, Italy
Cristina Seceleanu	Mälardalen University, Sweden

Meng Sun	Peking University, China
Carolyn Talcott	SRI International, USA
Hugo Torres Vieira	Evidence Srl, Italy
Emilio Tuosto	Gran Sasso Science Institute, Italy
Mirko Viroli	University of Bologna, Italy

Artefact Evaluation Committee

Gianluca Aguzzi	University of Bologna, Italy
Giorgio Audrito	University of Turin, Italy
Roberto Casadei	University of Bologna, Italy
Guillermina Cledou	University of Minho, Portugal
Giovanni Fabbretti	Inria, France
Fabrizio Fornari	University of Camerino, Italy
Danilo Pianini	University of Bologna, Italy
Lorenzo Rossi	University of Camerino, Italy
Larisa Safina	Inria, France
Alceste Scalas	Technical University of Denmark, Denmark

Steering Committee

Gul Agha	University of Illinois Urbana-Champaign, USA
Farhad Arbab	CWI and Leiden University, The Netherlands
Simon Bliudze	Inria, France
Laura Bocchi	University of Kent, UK
Ferruccio Damiani	University of Turin, Italy
Ornela Dardha	University of Glasgow, UK
Wolfgang De Meuter	Vrije Universiteit Brussel, Belgium
Rocco De Nicola	IMT School for Advanced Studies Lucca, Italy
Giovanna di Marzo Serugendo	University of Geneva, Switzerland
Tom Holvoet	KU Leuven, Belgium
Jean-Marie Jacquet	University of Namur, Belgium
Christine Julien	University of Texas at Austin, USA
Eva Kühn	Vienna University of Technology, Austria
Alberto Lluch Lafuente	Technical University of Denmark, Denmark
Michele Loreti	University of Camerino, Italy
Mieke Massink (Chair)	ISTI–CNR, Italy
José Proença	Polytechnic Institute of Porto, Portugal
Rosario Pugliese	University of Florence, Italy
Hanne Riis Nielson	Technical University of Denmark, Denmark
Marjan Sirjani	Mälardalen University, Sweden
Carolyn Talcott	SRI International, USA
Emilio Tuosto	Gran Sasso Science Institute, Italy

Vasco T. Vasconcelos	University of Lisbon, Portugal
Mirko Viroli	University of Bologna, Italy
Gianluigi Zavattaro	University of Bologna, Italy

Organizing Committee

Giorgio Audrito (Publicity Chair)	University of Turin, Italy
Letterio Galletta (Chair)	IMT School for Advanced Studies Lucca, Italy
Marinella Petrocchi	IIT–CNR, Italy
Simone Soderi	IMT School for Advanced Studies Lucca, Italy
Francesco Tiezzi (Workshop and Tutorial Chair)	University of Florence, Italy

Additional Reviewers

Gianluca Aguzzi	Rudolf Schlatte
Roberto Casadei	Charilaos Skandylas
Simon Fowler	Gianluca Turin
Geri Joskowicz	Uraz Türker
Eduard Kamburjan	A. Laura Voinea
Weibin Ma	Xiyue Zhang

Contents

Runtime Verification and Monitor Synthesis

Microservices

Invited Presentation

Formal Methods for Socio-technical Security
(Formal and Automated Analysis of Security Ceremonies)

Luca Viganò[(✉)] [ID]

Department of Informatics, King's College London, London, UK
`luca.vigano@kcl.ac.uk`

Abstract. Software engineers and analysts traditionally focus on cyber systems as technical systems, which are built only from software processes, communication protocols, crypto algorithms, etc. They often neglect, or choose not, to consider the human user as a component of the system's security as they lack the expertise to fully understand human factors and how they affect security. However, humans should not be designed out of the security loop. Instead, we must deal with security assurance as a true socio-technical problem rather than a mere technical one, and consider cyber systems as socio-technical systems with people at their hearts. The main goal of this short paper, which accompanies my keynote talk at the 24th International Conference on Coordination Models and Languages (COORDINATION 2022), is to advocate the use of formal methods to establish the security of socio-technical systems, and to discuss some of the most promising approaches, including those that I have helped develop.

1 Introduction

A recent study by IBM revealed that 95% of cyber-attacks are due to human error [35]. This is not surprising as, in a landscape where the security threats and attacks are in continuous evolution and high-value private information can be lost or manipulated, there is an increasing number of cyber systems (for communication, commerce, business, voting, industrial processes, critical infrastructures, etc.) whose security depends intrinsically on human users.[1] However, software engineers and analysts traditionally focus on cyber systems as *technical systems*, which are built only from software processes, communication protocols, crypto algorithms, etc. They often neglect, or choose not, to consider the human user as a component of the system's security as they lack the expertise to fully understand human factors and how they affect security. Humans should not be

---

[1] A *cyber system* is a system of interlinked computers forming part of cyberspace. More specifically, a cyber system is any combination of facilities, equipment, personnel, procedures, and communications integrated to provides cyber services. Information and communication technology (ICT) systems and cyber-physical systems (CPS) are examples of cyber systems. See, e.g., [49] for some useful definitions and discussions.

© IFIP International Federation for Information Processing 2022
M. H. ter Beek and M. Sirjani (Eds.): COORDINATION 2022, LNCS 13271, pp. 3–14, 2022.
https://doi.org/10.1007/978-3-031-08143-9_1

designed out of the security loop [29]: we must deal with security assurance as a true socio-technical problem rather than a mere technical one, and consider cyber systems as *socio-technical systems (STSs)* with people at their hearts.

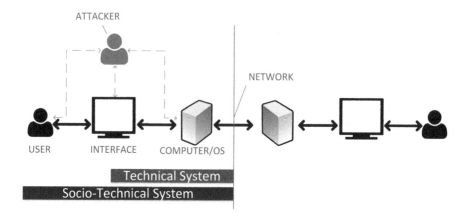

Fig. 1. Socio-technical system vs. technical system

Figure 1 shows the differences between a technical system and an STS: the technical system consists of a machine that communicates over a network with another machine, whereas the STS extends outwards, including user interfaces and actual users. The attacker can interfere in any of the communicating entities (i.e., user, user-interface, computer/OS). In fact, the security requirements of an STS don't simply derive from the system's technical layers, such as those of the OSI model, but also from the non-technical layers surrounding them. Here, humans often follow peculiar paths of practice due to diverse societal/personal reasons and to physical/social contexts wherein humans liaise with the technology. These paths may differ from those written on the system's user manual, or get consolidated out of day-to-day experience because no manual exists. We must seek to better understand how the two components of an STS, the *technical component* and the *social component* (e.g., user interaction processes and user behavior), interoperate to achieve (or not!) overall security. This requires extending the technical analysis/testing approaches with a mature understanding of human behavior. We need to develop appropriate *formal methods* that are up to this task.

Experience over the last 30+ years has namely shown that the design of systems for cyber security is highly error-prone and that conventional analysis techniques based on informal/semi-formal arguments and/or standard testing approaches fail to discover a large number of attacks. Formal methods for modeling and analysis aim at guaranteeing that a system satisfies certain properties of interest. This is typically achieved by developing a logico-mathematical model of the system (i.e., its structure and behavior) and of the desired properties, and an analysis algorithm that checks whether the model of the system satisfies the properties.

The main goal of this short paper, which accompanies my keynote talk at the 24th International Conference on Coordination Models and Languages (COORDINATION 2022), is to advocate the use of formal methods to establish the security of socio-technical systems, and to discuss some of the most promising approaches. Please, note that, despite the general-sounding title, this paper is by no means a comprehensive and up to date survey of the state of the art in socio-technical security (such a survey would be most welcome, though, so I hope that others will be able to provide one soon). On the contrary, I will focus mainly on security ceremonies as a specific example of socio-technical systems and on the approaches that I helped develop as specific examples of formal and automated methods.

2 From Technical to Socio-technical Security

Traditionally, security has been established technically, by means of implementations of crypto algorithms, security protocols, intrusion detection systems, firewalls, dedicated hardware, etc. [15], but there has always been awareness of the human risk of *mistakes* (i.e., the user's failure to do what she intends to do), *slips* (i.e., momentary lapses that see the user take unintended actions), or *noncompliance* (i.e., the user's possibly deliberate failure to do what the system intended of the user). Until recently, this risk was mitigated by means of user manuals, but manuals have disappeared today when the technology is a computer or a mobile device exposing browsers and apps. Modern users are bound, for instance, to access their on-line bank account through a browser (but using also their smartphone in those cases in which multi-factor authentication is foreseen) without having studied, on a manual and beforehand, what to do. This contributed to inspiring research in *usable security* [30] to assess the ease with which users can learn the behavior that they are expected to take while operating security-sensitive technology. However, humans are complicated and nothing guarantees that, even if they learned how to operate a technology, either from a manual or through its use, they will comply with what they learned. Reasons include cognitive biases, fallacies, ignorance, distraction, laziness, curiosity of different uses, insufficient awareness of the security sensitivity of their behavior, etc.

Much effort has been devoted to the technical analysis of the security of cyber systems. As a concrete example, consider security protocols. A *security protocol*, sometimes also called *cryptographic protocol*, is essentially a communication protocol (an agreed sequence of actions performed by two or more communicating entities in order to accomplish some mutually desirable goals) that makes use of cryptographic techniques, allowing the communicating entities to satisfy one or more security properties (such as authentication, confidentiality of data or integrity of data).

Several formal methods and automated tools (e.g., [2, 3, 5, 8, 16, 21–23, 28, 40, 42]) have been developed to analyze security protocols to check whether they do indeed satisfy the security properties they were designed for. These approaches rely on symbolically modeling the agents involved in the protocol along with an attacker who is trying to subvert the protocol's security. There are thus two types of agents:

- *honest agents*, who behave only according to what the protocol specifies (encrypting, decrypting and sending and receiving messages as specified by the protocol), and
- the *attacker*, a dishonest agent who can behave as he wishes, including following the protocol steps.

The attacker is often modeled using the *Dolev-Yao attacker model* [26], which allows him to send, read, encrypt and decrypt any message as long as he possesses the corresponding cryptographic keys.[2] In other words, cryptography is assumed to be perfect.[3]

Testing approaches have also been put forward to analyze security protocol implementations rather than their specifications (e.g., [25,33,44,53]). Even though these approaches are often limited in the strength of the protocols that can be considered, model-based testing approaches in which the formal analysis of a protocol specification is used to generate test cases for the protocol code have proven to be quite successful.

In contrast to formal analysis and testing of security protocols, for which a plethora of mature approaches and tools exist, socio-technical security is a discipline still in its childhood, with no widely recognized methodologies or comprehensive tools mature enough to take into full account human behavioral and cognitive aspects in their relation with "machine" security, and thus reason with the breadth and depth that is required by real-life STSs.

3   Formal and Automated Analysis of Security Ceremonies

Most of the research efforts on formal methods for socio-technical security have focused on security ceremonies as concrete, relevant, and timely examples of STSs (e.g., [6,7,9,10,12,19,20,24,31,36,38,39,45–47,50,51]).

The term *ceremony* was coined by Jesse Walker [37] to describe the interaction between a user and computing devices. The use of the term in the area of information/cyber security is due to Ellison [27]: a *security ceremony* expands a

---

[2] One can show that in the presence of such a powerful attacker it is enough to consider only one attacker [4], whereas in other scenarios (e.g., where movement of the agents or where different devices are considered), one might need to model attackers that have different capabilities and collaborate to carry out an attack.

[3] In addition to symbolic approaches, there are also a number of cryptographically-faithful approaches in which the perfect cryptography assumption is relaxed and the properties of the employed crypto algorithms are considered explicitly, e.g., [17,48]. I will not consider them here as the focus is on the human users of the protocols and ceremonies.

security protocol with everything that is considered out-of-band to it. More precisely: "Ceremonies include all protocols, as well as all applications with a user interface, all workflow and all provisioning scenarios" [27]. Therefore, the innovative stance of security ceremonies is to include human nodes alongside computer nodes, with communication links that comprise user interfaces, human-to-human communication and transfers of physical objects that carry data.

Security ceremonies are essentially "rituals" with finely orchestrated actions being carried out in a prescribed order by the agents involved in the ceremony. Works in the socio-technical security field typically use the term security ceremony to refer to an extension of a security protocol in which human agents and software-based agents exchange encrypted messages to achieve certain goals. Other kinds of ceremonies are key-signing ceremonies such as those required for DNSSEC [34], which are somewhat more akin to "a public or religious occasion that includes a series of formal or traditional actions" (which is one of the meanings of "ceremony" according to the Oxford English Dictionary). Another meaning is related to the secure key generation process that constitutes the initialisation phase of the wallet infrastructure and private keys in the realm of crypto-currencies [32]. In this paper, I take the socio-technical security view and focus on the first meaning.

As technology progresses in any area, human beings are increasingly surrounded by, and immersed in, such security ceremonies during their everyday lives. They carry out security tasks that occur through a virtually infinite range of scenarios interposing people's: (i) professional activities, such as logging into their employer's computer systems using two-factor authentication, (ii) business or leisure activities, such as taking a flight which involves getting through airport security, and (iii) chores, such as paying for their shopping with a debit card. As a concrete example, consider the sequence diagram shown in Fig. 2, in which a human user carries out a two-factor authentication security ceremony by interacting with an interface to exchange messages with a device and a database.

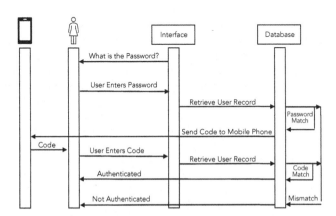

Fig. 2. A sequence diagram of a two-factor authentication security ceremony

Although many of the works cited at the beginning of this section are quite preliminary studies, and a mature and systematic approach is still missing, some formal methods and automated tools have been successfully extended to analyze a number of real-life security ceremonies. For instance, Bella and Coles-Kemp [9] defined a layered model of socio-technical protocols between a user persona and a computer interface, and used the Isabelle theorem prover to analyze a ceremony that allows Internet users to register with a service provider; Basin et al. [6,7] provided a formal account on human error in front of basic authentication properties and described how to analyze security ceremonies such as MP-Auth using the Tamarin tool; Giustolisi [31] used Tamarin to analyze the security of mobile tickets used in public transport ceremonies in Denmark; Martimiano and Martina [38] showed how a popular security ceremony for remote file sharing could be made fail-safe assuming a weaker threat model than normally considered in formal analysis and compensating for that with usability; Bella, Giustolisi and Lenzini carried out a socio-technical formal analysis of TLS certificate validation in modern browsers [10] and provided a novel protocol for secure exams that they formally analyzed using the tool ProVerif [11]; Bella, Giustolisi and Schürmann [12] used Tamarin to analyze two deposit-return systems currently deployed in Denmark and a variant that they designed to strengthen them.

As I mentioned above, the vast majority of the approaches for the formal analysis of security protocols adopt the Dolev-Yao attacker model, and most of the works on the formal analysis of security ceremonies extend this model to capture different socio-technical aspects. However, Sempreboni, Bella, Giustolisi and I remarked in [51] that in the case of security ceremonies such an attacker provides an inherent "flattening" that likely makes one miss relevant threat scenarios, and thus we advocated that for security ceremonies we need an approach that provides a birds-eye view, an "overview" that allows one to consider what are the different threats and where they lie, with the ultimate aim of finding novel attacks. Our main contribution in [51] is the systematic definition of an encompassing method to build the *full threat model chart* for security ceremonies from which one can conveniently reify the threat models of interest for the ceremony under consideration. To demonstrate the relevance of the chart, we formalized this threat model using Tamarin and analyzed three real-life ceremonies that had already been considered, albeit at different levels of detail and analysis, in the literature: MP-Auth [7], Opera Mini [47], and the Danish Mobilpendlerkort ceremony [31]. The full threat model chart suggested some interesting threats that hadn't been investigated although they are well worth of scrutiny. In particular, we found out that the Danish Mobilpendlerkort ceremony is vulnerable to the combination of an attacking third party and a malicious phone of the ticket holder. The threat model that leads to this vulnerability had not been considered before and arose thanks to our charting method.

One of most promising approaches for the formal and automated analysis of security ceremonies is the *mutation-based approach* that Sempreboni and I proposed in [52], which allows security analysts to model possible mistakes by human users as mutations with respect to the behavior that the ceremony originally specified for such users. In security ceremonies humans are (and should be considered to be) first-class actors, so it is not enough to take the "black&white" view of security protocol analysis, in which there is a Dolev-Yao attacker (the black agent) against a set of honest agents (the white agents). It is not enough to model human users as "honest processes" or as attackers, because they are neither. Modeling a person's behavior is not simple and requires formalizing the human "shades of gray". It requires modeling the way humans interact with the protocols, their behavior and the mistakes they may make, independent of attacks and, in fact, possibly independent of the presence of an attacker. In other words, when considering the mistakes that human users might make when interacting in a security ceremony, attacks may occur even without the presence of an attacker.

In [52] and the journal version that we are currently working on, we formalize four main human mutations of a ceremony:

- skipping one or more of the actions that the ceremony expects the human user to carry out (such as sending or receiving a message),
- adding an action (e.g., sending a message twice),
- replacing a message with another one (e.g., forgetting to include some information in a message and thus sending a shorter message than expected, or sending an altogether different message),
- neglecting to adhere to one or more inner behaviors expected by the ceremony (e.g., neglecting to carry out a check on the contents of a message).

Given a specification of a ceremony and its goals, our approach generates a mutated specification that models possible behaviors of a human user, along with mutations in the behavior of the other agents of the ceremony to match the human-induced mutations. This allows for the analysis of the original ceremony specification and its possible mutations, which may include the way in which the ceremony has actually been implemented. We have automated our approach by implementing a tool called *X-Men*, which builds on top of Tamarin.[4] As a proof of concept, we have applied our approach to three real-life case studies, uncovering a number of concrete vulnerabilities.

Similar to what happens for the formal analysis of security protocols, if the tool terminates[5] and verifies the model under consideration, then we can provide a security guarantee. Our approach allows us to provide such guarantee not only for the original ceremony but also for its mutations for which Tamarin's analysis terminates with a proof.

To some extent, this applies also when X-Men's/Tamarin's analysis of a security ceremony times out without a proof or without having discovered an attack, since, if the timeout is large enough, it can provide some degree of guarantee that an attack is unlikely. Still, an attack might be possible: even if a tool is

---

[4] The name X-Men was chosen to suggest that it considers human mutations.

[5] The analysis of security protocols in the presence of an active attacker is an undecidable problem, so protocol analysis tools might not terminate, unless one introduces some restrictions and bounds to force the analysis to complete.

not able to find an attack in, say, 10 min, nothing guarantees that the attack would not have been discovered if only one had allowed the tool to run for a couple more minutes. To tame the complexity of the search for an attack in case of security ceremonies and their mutations, we will consider adapting *compositionality* results like those of [1,41,43], which identify conditions that allow one to split a complex composed protocol into its subprotocols that can be analyzed independently with the guarantee that also their composition is secure.

If the analysis of a security protocol model instead terminates with the discovery of an attack, typically the attack trace can be used to distill a fix to the protocol specification; one would also usually wish to check whether the attack on the model also applies for the concrete implementation (assuming that it is available), so the attack trace can also be used to devise test cases for the implementation (see, e.g., [33,44,53]). The same applies in the case of our mutated ceremonies and we plan to extend X-Men to generate test cases similar to mutation-based testing [18,25].

Given the presence of human users, one can also aim to use the attack trace to distill recommendations and guidelines for the users of the ceremony so that they interact with it in a way that does not endanger security. The rules of [7] that restrict how the human can deviate from the protocol specification are a good example for such guidelines. In future work, we aim to investigate if and how recommendations and guidelines could be generated (semi-)automatically from the analysis of security ceremonies and their mutations (similar to the generation of test cases), and how they could be communicated to human users in an effective way. To that end, we plan to exploit also our works on how to provide security explanations to laypersons [54–58] and on how to beautify security ceremonies [13,14] and thus make their secure use more appealing to human users.

Acknowledgments. Thanks to Giampaolo Bella, Rosario Giustolisi, Jacques Ophoff, Karen Renaud, Diego Sempreboni for their invaluable contributions to our joint works on socio-technical security. Thanks also to Lynne Coventry and Gabriele Lenzini for many interesting discussions. I acknowledge funding from the UKRI Trustworthy Autonomous Systems Hub (EP/V00784X/1).

References

1. Almousa, O., Mödersheim, S., Modesti, P., Viganò, L.: Typing and compositionality for security protocols: a generalization to the geometric fragment. In: Pernul, G., Ryan, P.Y.A., Weippl, E. (eds.) ESORICS 2015. LNCS, vol. 9327, pp. 209–229. Springer, Cham (2015). https://doi.org/10.1007/978-3-319-24177-7_11
2. Armando, A., et al.: The AVANTSSAR platform for the automated validation of trust and security of service-oriented architectures. In: Flanagan, C., König, B. (eds.) TACAS 2012. LNCS, vol. 7214, pp. 267–282. Springer, Heidelberg (2012). https://doi.org/10.1007/978-3-642-28756-5_19

3. Armando, A., et al.: The AVISPA Tool for the Automated Validation of Internet Security Protocols and Applications. In: Etessami, K., Rajamani, S.K. (eds.) CAV 2005. LNCS, vol. 3576, pp. 281–285. Springer, Heidelberg (2005). https://doi.org/10.1007/11513988_27
4. Basin, D.A., Caleiro, C., Ramos, J., Viganò, L.: Distributed temporal logic for the analysis of security protocol models. Theor. Comput. Sci. **412**(31), 4007–4043 (2011). https://doi.org/10.1016/j.tcs.2011.04.006
5. Basin, D.A., Cremers, C., Meadows, C.: Model checking security protocols. In: Handbook of Model Checking, pp. 727–762. Springer, Cham (2018). https://doi.org/10.1007/978-3-319-10575-8_22
6. Basin, D.A., Radomirović, S., Schläpfer, M.: A complete characterization of secure human-server communication. In: Proceedings of the 28th IEEE Computer Security Foundations Symposium (CSF 2015), pp. 199–213. IEEE (2015). https://doi.org/10.1109/CSF.2015.21
7. Basin, D.A., Radomirović, S., Schmid, L.: Modeling human errors in security protocols. In: Proceedings of the 29th IEEE Computer Security Foundations Symposium (CSF 2016), pp. 325–340. IEEE (2016). https://doi.org/10.1109/CSF.2016.30
8. Bella, G.: Formal Correctness of Security Protocols. Springer, Berlin (2007). https://doi.org/10.1007/978-3-540-68136-6
9. Bella, G., Coles-Kemp, L.: Layered analysis of security ceremonies. In: Gritzalis, D., Furnell, S., Theoharidou, M. (eds.) SEC 2012. IAICT, vol. 376, pp. 273–286. Springer, Heidelberg (2012). https://doi.org/10.1007/978-3-642-30436-1_23
10. Bella, G., Giustolisi, R., Lenzini, G.: Socio-technical formal analysis of TLS certificate validation in modern browsers. In: Castella-Roca, J. et al. (ed.), Proceedings of the 11th International Conference on Privacy, Security and Trust (PST 2013), pp. 309–316. IEEE Press (2013). https://doi.org/10.1109/PST.2013.6596067
11. Bella, G., Giustolisi, R., Lenzini, G.: Invalid certificates in modern browsers: a socio-technical analysis. J. Comput. Secur. **26**(4), 509–541 (2015). https://doi.org/10.3233/JCS-16891
12. Bella, G., Giustolisi, R., Schürmann, C.: Modelling human threats in security ceremonies. J. Comput. Secur. (2022, to appear)
13. Bella, G., Renaud, K., Sempreboni, D., Viganò, L.: An investigation into the "beautification" of security ceremonies. In: Proceedings of the 16th International Conference on Security and Cryptography, pp. 125–136. Scitepress Digital Library (2019). https://doi.org/10.5220/0007921501250136
14. Bella, G., Viganò, L.: Security is beautiful. In: Christianson, B., Švenda, P., Matyáš, V., Malcolm, J., Stajano, F., Anderson, J. (eds.) Security Protocols 2015. LNCS, vol. 9379, pp. 247–250. Springer, Cham (2015). https://doi.org/10.1007/978-3-319-26096-9_25
15. Bishop, M.: Computer Security: Art and Science. 2d edition, Addison-Wesley Professional, Boston (2019)
16. Blanchet, B.: An efficient cryptographic protocol verifier based on prolog rules. In: Proeedings of the IEEE Computer Society Foundations Workshop (CSFW 2001), IEEE CS Press (2001). https://doi.org/10.1109/CSFW.2001.930138
17. Blanchet, B.: A computationally sound mechanized prover for security protocols. In: Proceedings of the IEEE Symposium on Security and Privacy, pp. 140–154. IEEE (2006). https://doi.org/10.1109/SP.2006.1
18. Büchler, M., Oudinet, J., Pretschner, A.: Security mutants for property-based testing. In: Gogolla, M., Wolff, B. (eds.) TAP 2011. LNCS, vol. 6706, pp. 69–77. Springer, Heidelberg (2011). https://doi.org/10.1007/978-3-642-21768-5_6

19. Carlos, M.C., Martina, J.E., Price, G., Custódio, R.F.: A proposed framework for analysing security ceremonies. In: Proceedings of the International Conference on Security and Cryptography - Volume 1: SECRYPT (ICETE 2012), pp. 440–445. INSTICC, Scitepress Digital Library (2012). https://doi.org/10.5220/0004129704400445
20. Carlos, M.C., Martina, J.E., Price, G., Custódio, R.F.: An updated threat model for security ceremonies. In: Proceedings of SAC 2013, pp. 1836–1845. ACM (2013). https://doi.org/10.1145/2480362.2480705
21. Cortier, V., Kremer, S.: Formal models and techniques for analyzing security protocols: a tutorial. Found. Trends Program. Lang. **1**(3), 151–267 (2014). https://doi.org/10.1561/2500000001
22. Cortier, V., Kremer, S.: Formal models for analyzing security protocols: some lecture notes. In: Dependable Software Systems Engineering, volume 45 of NATO Science for Peace and Security Series – D: Information and Communication Security, pp. 33–58. IOS Press (2016). https://doi.org/10.3233/978-1-61499-627-9-33
23. Cremers, C.J.F.: The Scyther tool: verification, falsification, and analysis of security protocols. In: Gupta, A., Malik, S. (eds.) CAV 2008. LNCS, vol. 5123, pp. 414–418. Springer, Heidelberg (2008). https://doi.org/10.1007/978-3-540-70545-1_38
24. Curzon, P., Rukšėnas, R., Blandford, A.: An approach to formal verification of human-computer interaction. Formal Aspects Comput. **19**(4), 513–550 (2007). https://doi.org/10.1007/s00165-007-0035-6
25. Dadeau, F., Héam, P.-C., Kheddam, R., Maatoug, G., Rusinowitch, M.: Model-based mutation testing from security protocols in HLPSL. Softw. Test. Verification Reliab. **25**(5–7), 684–711 (2015). https://doi.org/10.1002/stvr.1531
26. Dolev, D., Yao, A.: On the security of public-key protocols. IEEE Trans. Inf. Theor. **29**(2), 198–208 (1983). https://doi.org/10.1109/TIT.1983.1056650
27. Ellison, C.M.: Ceremony design and analysis. IACR Cryptology ePrint Archive **399**, 1–17 (2007)
28. Escobar, S., Meadows, C., Meseguer, J.: Maude-NPA: cryptographic protocol analysis modulo equational properties. In: Aldini, A., Barthe, G., Gorrieri, R. (eds.) FOSAD 2007-2009. LNCS, vol. 5705, pp. 1–50. Springer, Heidelberg (2009). https://doi.org/10.1007/978-3-642-03829-7_1
29. Flechais, I., Riegelsberger, J., Sasse, M.A.: Divide and conquer: the role of trust and assurance in the design of secure socio-technical systems. In: Proceedings of the 2005 Workshop on New Security Paradigms (NSPW), pp. 33–41. ACM (2005). https://doi.org/10.1145/1146269.1146280
30. Garfinkel, S., Lipford, H.R.: Usable Security: History, Themes, and Challenges. Morgan & Claypool, San Rafael (2014)
31. Giustolisi, R.: Free rides in Denmark: lessons from improperly generated mobile transport tickets. In: Lipmaa, H., Mitrokotsa, A., Matulevičius, R. (eds.) NordSec 2017. LNCS, vol. 10674, pp. 159–174. Springer, Cham (2017). https://doi.org/10.1007/978-3-319-70290-2_10
32. CVA Cybersecurity Working Group. Trusted Key Ceremony Guidelines – Guidelines for Generating Digital Asset Secrets (2020). https://d1c2gz5q23tkk0.cloudfront.net/assets/uploads/2956620/asset/CVA_Trusted_Key_Ceremony_Guidelines.pdf?1594131972
33. Pierre-Cyrille, H., Dadeau, F., Kheddam, R., Maatoug, G., Rusinowitch, M.: A model-based testing approach for security protocols. In: Proceedings of the 2016 IEEE International Conference on Computational Science and Engineering (CSE)

and IEEE International Conference on Embedded and Ubiquitous Computing (EUC) and 15th International Symposium on Distributed Computing and Applications for Business Engineering (DCABES), pp. 553–556. IEEE (2016). https://doi.org/10.1109/CSE-EUC-DCABES.2016.240

34. Internet Assigned Numbers Authority (IANA). Key Signing Ceremonies (2022). https://www.iana.org/dnssec/ceremonies

35. IBM Global Technology Services (Managed Security Services). IBM Security Services 2014 Cyber Security Intelligence Index (2014)

36. Johansen, C., Jøsang, A.: Probabilistic modelling of humans in security ceremonies. In: Garcia-Alfaro, J., et al. (eds.) DPM/QASA/SETOP -2014. LNCS, vol. 8872, pp. 277–292. Springer, Cham (2015). https://doi.org/10.1007/978-3-319-17016-9_18

37. Lortz, V.B., Walker, J.R., Hegde, S.S., Kulkarni, A.A., Tai, T.Y.C.: Device introduction and access control framework, Google Patents US Patent 8,146,142 (2012)

38. Martimiano, T., Martina, J.E.: Daemones non operantur nisi per artem. In: Matyáš, V., Švenda, P., Stajano, F., Christianson, B., Anderson, J. (eds.) Security Protocols 2018. LNCS, vol. 11286, pp. 96–105. Springer, Cham (2018). https://doi.org/10.1007/978-3-030-03251-7_11

39. Martimiano, T., Martina, J.E., Olembo, M.M., Carlos, M.C.: Modelling user devices in security ceremonies. In: Proceedings of the Workshop on Socio-Technical Aspects in Security and Trust, pp. 16–23 (2014). https://doi.org/10.1109/STAST.2014.11

40. Meier, S., Schmidt, B., Cremers, C., Basin, D.: The TAMARIN prover for the symbolic analysis of security protocols. In: Sharygina, N., Veith, H. (eds.) CAV 2013. LNCS, vol. 8044, pp. 696–701. Springer, Heidelberg (2013). https://doi.org/10.1007/978-3-642-39799-8_48

41. Mödersheim, S., Viganò, L.: Secure pseudonymous channels. In: Backes, M., Ning, P. (eds.) ESORICS 2009. LNCS, vol. 5789, pp. 337–354. Springer, Heidelberg (2009). https://doi.org/10.1007/978-3-642-04444-1_21

42. Mödersheim, S., Viganò, L.: The open-source fixed-point model checker for symbolic analysis of security protocols. In: Aldini, A., Barthe, G., Gorrieri, R. (eds.) FOSAD 2007-2009. LNCS, vol. 5705, pp. 166–194. Springer, Heidelberg (2009). https://doi.org/10.1007/978-3-642-03829-7_6

43. Mödersheim, S., Viganò, L.: Sufficient conditions for vertical composition of security protocols. In: Proceedings of the 9th ACM Symposium on Information, Computer and Communications Security (ASIA CCS 2014), pp. 435–446. ACM (2014). https://doi.org/10.1145/2590296.2590330

44. Peroli, M., De Meo, F., Viganò, L., Guardini, D.: MobSTer: a model-based security testing framework for web applications. Softw. Test. Verification Reliab. **28**(8), e1685 (2018). https://doi.org/10.1002/stvr.1685

45. Probst, C.W., Kammüller, F., Hansen, R.R.: Formal modelling and analysis of socio-technical systems. In: Probst, C.W., Hankin, C., Hansen, R.R. (eds.) Semantics, Logics, and Calculi. LNCS, vol. 9560, pp. 54–73. Springer, Cham (2016). https://doi.org/10.1007/978-3-319-27810-0_3

46. Radke, K., Boyd, C.: Security proofs for protocols involving humans. Comput. J. **60**(4), 527–540 (2017). https://doi.org/10.1093/comjnl/bxw066

47. Radke, K., Boyd, C., Gonzalez Nieto, J., Brereton, M.: Ceremony analysis: strengths and weaknesses. In: Camenisch, J., Fischer-Hübner, S., Murayama, Y., Portmann, A., Rieder, C. (eds.) SEC 2011. IAICT, vol. 354, pp. 104–115. Springer, Heidelberg (2011). https://doi.org/10.1007/978-3-642-21424-0_9

48. Ramsdell, J.D.: Cryptographic protocol analysis and compilation using CPSA and Roletran. In: Dougherty, D., Meseguer, J., Mödersheim, S.A., Rowe, P. (eds.) Protocols, Strands, and Logic. LNCS, vol. 13066, pp. 355–369. Springer, Cham (2021). https://doi.org/10.1007/978-3-030-91631-2_20

49. Refsdal, A., Solhaug, B., Stølen, K.: Cyber-risk management. In: Cyber-Risk Management. SCS, pp. 33–47. Springer, Cham (2015). https://doi.org/10.1007/978-3-319-23570-7_5

50. Rukšėnas, R., Curzon, P., Blandford, A.: Modelling and analysing cognitive causes of security breaches. Innov. Syst. Softw. Eng. **4**, 143–160 (2008). https://doi.org/10.1007/s11334-008-0050-7

51. Sempreboni, D., Bella, G., Giustolisi, R., Viganò, L.: What are the threats? (Charting the threat models of security ceremonies). In: Proceedings of the 16th International Joint Conference on e-Business and Telecommunications, ICETE – Volume 2: SECRYPT, pp. 161–172. Scitepress Digital Library (2019). https://doi.org/10.5220/0007924901610172

52. Sempreboni, D., Viganò, L.: X-Men: a mutation-based approach for the formal analysis of security ceremonies. In: Proceedings of the 5th IEEE European Symposium on Security and Privacy (EuroS&P), pp. 87–104. IEEE (2020). https://doi.org/10.1109/EuroSP48549.2020.00014

53. Viganò, L.: The SPaCIoS Project: Secure Provision and Consumption in the Internet of Services. In: Proceedings of the IEEE Sixth International Conference on Software Testing, Verification and Validation (ICST), pp. 497–498. IEEE (2013). https://doi.org/10.1109/ICST.2013.75

54. Viganò, L.: Explaining cybersecurity with films and the arts. In: Imagine Math 7, pp. 297–309. Springer, Cham (2020). https://doi.org/10.1007/978-3-030-42653-8_18

55. Viganò, L.: Nicolas Cage is the center of the cybersecurity universe. In: Ardito, C., et al. (eds.) INTERACT 2021. LNCS, vol. 12932, pp. 14–33. Springer, Cham (2021). https://doi.org/10.1007/978-3-030-85623-6_3

56. Viganò, L.: Don't tell me the cybersecurity moon is shining... (Cybersecurity show and tell). In: Emmer, M. (ed.), Imagine Math 8. Springer, Cham (to appear)

57. Viganò, L., Magazzeni, D.: Explainable security. CoRR (2018). http://arxiv.org/abs/1807.04178

58. Viganò, L., Magazzeni, D.: Explainable security. In: IEEE European Symposium on Security and Privacy Workshops, EuroS&P Workshops 2020, pp. 293–300. IEEE (2020). A preliminary version appeared as [58]. https://doi.org/10.1109/EuroSPW51379.2020.00045

Timed and Probabilistic Systems

MIMOS: A Deterministic Model for the Design and Update of Real-Time Systems

Wang Yi[1]([envelope]), Morteza Mohaqeqi[1], and Susanne Graf[2]

[1] Uppsala University, Uppsala, Sweden
{wang.yi,morteza.mohaqeqi}@it.uu.se
[2] Univ Grenoble Alpes, CNRS, Grenoble, France
susanne.graf@imag.fr

Abstract. Inspired by the pioneering work of Gilles Kahn on concurrent systems, we model real-time systems as a network of software components each of which is specified to compute a collection of functions according to given timing constraints. The components communicate with each other and their environment via two types of channels: (1) FIFO queues for buffering data, and (2) Registers for sampling time-dependent data streams from sensors or output streams of other components executed at different rates. We present a fixed-point semantics for this model which shows that each system function of a network computes for a given set of input (timed) streams, a unique (timed) output stream. Thanks to the deterministic semantics, a model-based approach is enabled for not only building systems but also updating them after deployment, allowing model-in-the-loop simulation to verify the complete behaviour of the resulting system.

1 Motivation

Today, a large part of the functionality of Cyber-Physical Systems such as cars, airplanes, and medical devices is implemented by software, as an (embedded) real-time system. The current trend is that traditionally mostly closed and single-purpose Cyber-Physical Systems will become open platforms. They will allow integration of an expanding number of software components over their life-time, e.g., in order to customize and enhance their functionality according to the varying needs of individual users. To enable this, we must design and build systems that allow for updates after deployment. Furthermore, it must be guaranteed that the resulting systems not only preserve the original as well as the extended functionality, but also stay safe after updates. Unfortunately, current design methodologies for real-time systems, in particular safety-critical systems, offer only limited or no support for modifications and extensions on systems after deployment without demanding re-designing the whole system.

This paper develops a semantic model for real-time systems that can be updated in a model-based and incremental manner. We model such systems as a network of real-time software components connected by communication channels in the style of Kahn Process Networks (KPN) [15], allowing asynchronous data exchange. We present a

This work is partially supported by the projects: ERC CUSTOMER and KAW UPDATE.

© IFIP International Federation for Information Processing 2022
M. H. ter Beek and M. Sirjani (Eds.): COORDINATION 2022, LNCS 13271, pp. 17–34, 2022.
https://doi.org/10.1007/978-3-031-08143-9_2

simple but expressive model, MIMOS, to formalize such abstract network models. In designing the model and its semantics, we adopt the following principles:

Determinism. In a model-based approach to software design and update, using deterministic model is crucial to ensure that any property validated on a system model holds also on the final implementation i.e. executable code generated from the model. For safety-critical systems, future software updates may have to be validated and deployed based on the system model modified according to the intended updates. For example, to update the software of a pacemaker in-operated in a human body, safety properties of the intended updates may be validated and tested in a model-based approach instead of testing directly on human body, which may risk human life.

Separation of Functionality and Timing. The model of a system should allow to specify and to reason about the system functions independently of their implementation that may be subject to timing and resource constraints. This gives the advantage that the functional correctness can be validated efficiently without taking into account the complex timing behavior of the implementation. When the system inputs (e.g., sampled data from sensors) are time-dependent, the system output is also time-dependent. In such cases, we need to reason about streams of reals (called here, time streams), representing time points at which sensor data are sampled or outputs are written. Time streams are simply another type of input and output streams for the system functions. In fact, time streams are generated by the system scheduler, and in turn used to sample the input and output streams computed by the system functions.

Separation of Computation and Communication. We assume non-blocking data exchange between system components, implemented by either asynchronous FIFO channels for buffering system inputs and outputs, or registers for storing sampled time-dependent data. This allows system components to be specified as *independent real-time tasks*, whose timing behaviours can be analyzed efficiently. In particular, the underlying schedulability analysis for deployment will be greatly simplified compared with the case for dependent real-time tasks. More importantly, it enables the component-wise construction of systems avoiding interference between the original system and newly integrated components in case of updates.

Updatability (Avoidance of Interference). The model of a system should allow for modifications by integrating new components to implement new system functions or replacing the existing components with refined ones, without changing the existing system functions determined by the original model. The separation of computation and communication by asynchronous data exchange avoids inter-component interference when new components are integrated. We require that new components may read but never write to the existing components via FIFOs or registers unless writing operations by the new components fulfill given requirements (specified using e.g. contracts [12]), which is essential for future updates to preserve the original system functionality. Even though protocols may be needed to coordinate data exchange among the components (e.g. to avoid race conditions in register reading and writing), the components may operate autonomously or independently from each other even when some of them stopped functioning correctly.

2   Contributions and Related Work

One of the main challenges in embedded real-time systems design is to ensure that the resulting system has deterministic input-output and predictable timing behavior (typically with deterministic input-to-output latency or known time bounds) even when multiple system functions are integrated and co-execute on a platform with limited resources. The deterministic semantics allows model-in-the-loop simulation using successful tools like Simulink/Stateflow to simulate and verify the complete system behavior. Over the past decades, numerous approaches to address this challenge have been devised by research communities in hardware, software, control, and communication. Several, including the *synchronous approach*, embodied by the languages Esterel, Lustre, and Signal [13], and the time-triggered paradigm promoted by Kopetz [17], ensure deterministic behavior by scheduling computation and communication among components at pre-determined time points. This results in highly reliable and predictable systems, but severely restricts the possibility to modify or update systems after deployment. The reason is that new components must fit exactly into the already determined time schedules, and components may perturb each others' timing via shared resources. In recent years, software updates of real-time systems after deployment have attracted increasing interest. A model-based approach to the design and updates for cyber-physical systems is proposed in [25]. The work of [10] demonstrates that autonomous systems in operation can be updated through contract negotiation and run-time enforcement of contracts.

Contributions. We present a semantic model for real-time systems which on one hand, ensures the deterministic input-output and predictable timing behaviors of a system, and on the other hand supports incremental updates after deployment without re-designing the whole system. In this model, a real-time system is described as a network of software components connected by communication channels. We provide a simple but expressive model named MIMOS to formalize such networks where each component is designed to compute a collection of functions over data streams and the communication channels can be of two types: FIFO queues for buffering inputs and outputs, and registers for sampling time-dependent data from sources such as sensors or streams that are written and read at different rates. The components are further specified as real-time tasks to enforce that they read inputs, compute, and write outputs at time points satisfying certain time constraints. A fixed-point semantics is developed for the model, showing that it enjoys two desired properties: (1) such a network of real-time software components computes a set of functions over data streams such that each of them, for a given set of (timed) input streams, defines a unique (timed) output stream; furthermore (2) the network can be modified by integrating new components for adding new system functions or replacing the existing components with refined ones (e.g. for better performance or security patches) without re-designing the whole system or changing the original system functions.

Related Work. An example of a time-triggered language developed for real-time systems is Giotto [14] A Giotto program is a set of periodic tasks that communicate through ports. Giotto implements the synchronous semantics, preserving timing determinism and also value-determinism by restricting to periodic tasks where reading from and writing to ports is fixed and performed at deterministic time points. It does not allow asynchronous communication via FIFO channels as MIMOS. This limits the possibility of updating a system in operation. A more recent work addressing the quasi-synchronous semantics of [7] is presented in [5]. The work also proposes to use multiple periodic tasks to implement the synchronous semantics on parallel and distributed architectures. It remains in the category of synchronous approaches to real-time programming without addressing issues related to dynamic updates. MIMOS can be viewed as a timed extension of Kahn Process Networks (KPN) [15]. In the literature, there have been various extensions to KPN. A special case of KPNs is dataflow process networks (DPN) [20]. A DPN is a general dataflow model where each process is specified as repeated firings of a node. A node becomes enabled for execution according to a set of *firing rules*. However, no time constraints are specified in the firing rules. An implementation of KPN with bounded-size buffers is proposed in [9]. In this work, a composition approach preserving the Kahn semantics is presented for components whose production and consumption rate are the same in the long run. The work, however, is confined within the synchronous programming model. Related to the communication channels of KPN, a time-aware implementation of C, called *Timed C*, has been proposed in [22]. In Timed C, a program consists of a set of tasks communicating through two types of channels: *FIFO* and *Latest Value (LV)*. Analogous to KPN, reading from FIFO is blocking while writing is non-blocking. In contrast, reading and writing of LV channels are non-blocking. This communication model is similar to that of MIMOS. However, while Timed C is a general programming language without a guaranteed determinism, we focus on both functional and timing determinism, and study these properties in a well-defined formal semantics. A standardized software architecture for automotive domain is developed by AUTOSAR [3]. Based on this, an application is organized as a collection of software components which perform data communication through a sender/receiver model. Data is processed by a receiver using a *queue* or a *last-is-best* policy. Our model can be thought of as a specialization of this approach which has a formal and deterministic semantics. Due to the known fact that AUTOSAR is only a reference model for automotive software architecture with various implementations and without a formal semantics, any formal proof is impossible.

3   The MIMOSModel

In this section, we present MIMOS based on Kahn Process Network (KPN) [15]. A KPN is an abstract model of a parallel system consisting of a collection of processes connected by FIFO queues for data exchange. We view real-time systems as such a network where the computations as well as the respective input and outputs of the processes must meet given time constraints. Our model can be viewed as a timed version of KPN whose nodes are extended with timing constraints, and edges with registers for sampling time-dependent inputs in addition to FIFO queues.

As KPN, MIMOS is essentially a simple model to formalize system models. In this section, we present the main primitives and informal semantics of MIMOS. A fixed-point semantics is given in Sect. 4.

3.1 Preliminaries on KPN

This subsection reviews the original notion of KPN, and its main properties. A KPN is a set of stand-alone processes, called nodes, which communicate through a set of *FIFO* channels. A node accesses channels through two operations: **read** and **write**.

Definition 1 (KPN). *A Kahn Process Network $\mathcal{N}$ is a set of processes, called nodes, and a set of FIFO queues, called* channels. *Nodes behave according to the following rules.*

- *Each node has a set of inputs and a set of outputs, and it computes a set of functions, one for each output. For a set of input sequences, each of the functions defines a unique output sequence. A node may have memory which cannot be accessed by other nodes.*
- *Channels are of unbounded capacity. A channel connects exactly one writer node to exactly one reader node. However, multiple channels may be connected to single output.*
- **read** *from a channel is blocking, that is, a node can only execute if all its input channels contain enough data. This means that a node cannot test the emptiness of channels;* **write** *to a channel is non-blocking.*

□

A node of KPN can be implemented with a set of local variables and a procedure, repeated indefinitely. The procedure may be specified in any conventional programming language such as C.

Example 1. Listing 1 shows a program representing an example KPN. Nodes are defined by `process` keyword. The procedure executed by a node is written in a `Repeat` block. The structure of this program is shown in Fig. 1, where arrows represent FIFO channels.

□

```
process f(int out V) {
  Repeat {    write 1 on V;    }
}
process g(int in U; int threshold; int out V) {
  int count = 0;         // local variable
  Repeat {
    read(U);             // read from a channel
    count = count + 1;
    if count == threshold
      write 1 on V;       // write to a channel
      count = 0;
  }
}
int channel X, Y;
f(X) || g(X, 5, Y);      // concurrent execution
```

Listing 1. A sample KPN program.

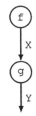

Fig. 1. Structure of the program in Listing 1.

A KPN can be seen as a parallel program computing a set of functions from a set of input streams to a set of output streams obtained by computing node functions in an arbitrary order [15].

An essential property of KPNs is their *determinism*. It is guaranteed under any sufficiently fair scheduler, i.e., schedulers which do not postpone a process indefinitely.

Theorem 1 (Functional Determinism [15]). *Given a set of input streams (histories on input edges), the set of output streams computed by a KPN is uniquely defined.*   □

Theorem 1 states that implementation aspects, such as execution order, scheduling, and platform speed do not affect the functional behavior of a system implementing a KPN model.

3.2   Timed Kahn Process Networks

The order- and speed-independent functional determinism of KPN leads to a natural function preserving extension of KPN to timed versions of KPN which allow to represent real-time systems as KPN in which each node is executed according to some *release pattern*—that is, a sequence of time points—and a deadline for each release.

Definition 2 (Timed KPN (TKPN)). *A timed KPN, denoted $\mathcal{N}_T$, is obtained by associating with each node n of KPN $\mathcal{N}$ a release pattern and a deadline, represented by positive integer.*   □

As *release pattern* one may choose any reoccurring real-time task model [24], such as periodic tasks [21], generalized multiframe [4], or DRT [23] and timed automata [11] as long as they are deterministic.

A TKPN is a KPN, that is each node computes a tuple of functions on streams, one for each output channel. One may generalize this model by allowing the definition of a different deadline for each output of a node.

Note also that in Definition 2, the internal structure and resource requirement for the nodes of a TKPN and the scheduling algorithm to be adopted in the implementation are left open. Only the time constraints (i.e. the release patterns and deadlines for the executions of nodes) are specified.

Informally, the operational behavior of a node in $\mathcal{N}_T$ is defined as follows. At each release time point, if all needed inputs are available, the node computes and delivers the resulting outputs within the specified deadline. In order to achieve timing determinism, a node reads at the release time and delivers outputs at the given deadline. This read-execute-write approach is similar to the *implicit* communication model of AUTOSAR [1].

Because a TKPN is also a KPN, and the execution rates assigned to nodes only restrict more explicitly the computation order of eligible nodes, the behaviour of a TKPN enjoys the desired functional determinism, which follows directly from Theorem 1. Furthermore, as nodes read and write at deterministically defined time points, it enjoys also the timing determinism. In order to formulate these properties, we need to consider *timed* event histories or streams, as the time-points at which the outputs are delivered depends on the time-points at which the inputs become available.

Theorem 2 (Functional and Timing Determinism of TKPN). *For any given set of timed input streams (histories of inputs values and the time-point at which the values are available), the set of timed output streams computed by a TKPN is uniquely defined.*

The result is established in Proposition 1 of Sect. 4.   □

3.3 MIMOS: TKPN with Registers

In real-time applications, value streams produced by the environment may be time-dependent. In Cyber-Physical Systems, typical examples would be values from sensors capturing physical phenomena. The system usually does not need all values produced by a sensor but at any time, it would use the newest available value. Additionally, the refresh rate of the sensor is not necessarily compliant with the execution rate of the node(s) reading the sensor. In this case, using a FIFO would typically lead to memory overflow. Or, a too slow sensor could block the system. Neither situation is desirable. In such cases, it is useful to have a communication channel which keeps always the most recently written value. We extend TKPN with such channels, called *register*.

Definition 3 (MIMOS: TKPN with registers). *TKPN extended by registers is TKPN where some channels can be a register instead of a FIFO. We call this extension of TKPN MIMOS.*   □

The operations to access registers are syntactically the same as the ones to access FIFOs. We adopt the "last-is-best" semantics of [3]: **write** to a register over-writes the current value, and **read** from a register is non-blocking and reads the current value. When both **read** and **write** occur at the same time, the current value is updated by **write** before **read**.

Example 2. Listing 2 shows the program in Listing 1 extended with a register and time constraints. The program structure is illustrated by Fig. 2, where FIFO channels are represented by solid-line arrows, and registers by dashed arrows.   □

In this example, using a register instead of a FIFO to carry the *threshold* values has the advantage to (1) always use the most recent value, and (2) guarantee absence of buffer overflow regardless of the speed at which these values are produced and read.

Theorem 3 (Functional and Timing Determinism of MIMOS). *For any given set of timed input streams (histories of inputs values and the time-point at which the values are available), the set of timed output streams computed by a TKPN with registers is uniquely defined.*

This result is established by Proposition 2 of Sect. 4.   □

```
process f(int out V) { ... }          //
    unchanged

process h(int out V) {
  Repeat {     write 6 on V;   }
}
process g(int in U; int in C; int out V) {
  int count = 0;
  int threshold;
  Repeat {
    read(U);              // reading (from FIFO)
    count = count + 1;
    threshold = read(C); // reading (from
    register)
    if count >= threshold then
      write 1 on V;
      count = 0;
  }
}
// Instantiating and connecting the components.
int channel FIFO X, Y;
int channel register Z;
f.timings = periodic(10, 10);   // period=
    deadline=10
g.timings = periodic(10, 10);
h.timings = periodic(10, 10);
f(X) || h(Z) || g(X, Z, Y);
```

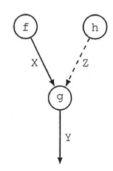

Fig. 2. The structure of the program in Listing 2. Dashed arrow indicates a *register*.

Listing 2. A sample MIMOS program.

3.4 Design and Update with MIMOS

A model-based approach can be sketched as follows[1]. First, to build a new system, a set of system functions to be implemented must be specified in terms of functional and timing requirements on their inputs and outputs as well as the respective end-to-end latency (see Sect. 5). A MIMOS model may be constructed, verified to satisfy the given requirements and compiled into code executable on the target platform to compute these functions. Prior to any update over the life cycle of the system, its original MIMOS model may be extended (i.e., updated) by connecting the outputs of the existing components to the new ones. Additionally, existing components may be replaced also by new ones fulfilling given requirements. Thanks to the independence of reading from/writing to channels, the added (or updated) system functions will not interfere with the existing ones. Thanks also to the deterministic semantics, it can be verified based on the updated model that the resulting system satisfies the functional and timing requirements. Further, it must be verified that the platform is able to provide enough resources to meet the resource requirements of the new components by schedulability analysis and analysis of memory usage (see Sect. 5). If all verification steps are successful, the new components can be deployed (or installed). Otherwise, the update is rejected.

[1] Addressing the different steps in details, including specification, modelling, verification and compilation is not in the scope of this paper.

4 Fixed-Point Semantics

In this section, we present a formal semantics for MIMOS. We use the notations introduced in [15] to prove the order and time independent determinism of KPNs of Definition 1. The notion of *timed stream* is introduced to define the semantics of TKPNs of Definition 2 and to show their timing determinism.

4.1 Preliminaries on KPN [15]

We recall the basic notations from [15]. The function **F** associated with each node of a KPN is represented as a function from a set of input streams to a set of output streams.

We now formally define streams and functions. We consider streams of elements from a generic domain $\mathbb{D}$ which may be instantiated by any data domain. To ensure generality, we consider the time domain to be reals $\mathbb{R}$.

Definition 4 (Streams, time streams and timed streams). *Let the stream domain $\mathbb{S}$ be the set of finite and infinite sequences in $\mathbb{D}^\infty$. The domain of time streams $\mathbb{T}$ is the set of finite and infinite sequences of time points in $\mathbb{R}^\infty$ consisting of (not necessarily strictly) increasing time points. Infinite time streams must diverge.*

The domain of timed streams $\mathbb{S} \times \mathbb{T}$ are finite and infinite sequences in $(\mathbb{D} \times \mathbb{R})^\infty$.

Note that a tuple of streams (of the same length) can also be seen as a stream of tuples, and conversely. We alternate freely between these views. In particular, a timed stream may either be denoted as $S \times T$ for two appropriate streams of the same length or as a single stream of appropriate pairs.

Sometimes, we want to view a stream of $\mathbb{S}$ explicitly as a stream of finite "segments", such that a segment is now considered an "element". We denote by Σ the domain of finite segments of $\mathbb{D}$, and by $\mathbb{S}^\Sigma$ the domain of streams of Σ.[2]

We use $\sqsubseteq$ to stand for the standard prefix order on sequences, λ for the empty sequence, and "•" for concatenation. Denote ϵ the "empty element", the neutral element for concatenation. □

Node functions **F** are built from the following basic functions mapping (tuples of) streams to (tuples of) streams.

Definition 5 (Functions on streams).

1. *Data transformations: functions $\mathbf{F}^{\mathbb{D}} : \mathbb{D}^n \mapsto \mathbb{D}^m$ applied to elements of streams. We call $\mathbf{F}$ the corresponding function lifted to streams:*
   $\mathbf{F}(a_1 \bullet S_1, \dots a_k \bullet S_n) = \mathbf{F}^{\mathbb{D}}(a_1, \dots a_n) \bullet \mathbf{F}(S_1, \dots S_n)$.
2. *Standard order preserving stream manipulating functions "first", "remainder" and "append" as in [15]:*
   - $\mathbf{first}(a \bullet S) = a$ *(sometimes $\mathbf{f}$ for short)*.
   - $\mathbf{R}(a \bullet S) = S$ *(skips the first element of a stream)*.
   - $\mathbf{app}(\text{ini}, S) = \text{ini} \bullet S$ *(adds an initial element and pushes S to the right)*. □

---

[2] Note that a stream in $\mathbb{S}^\Sigma$ is also a stream in $\mathbb{S}$ (for an appropriate Data domain).

Example 3 (Illustrating Example). Consider node g of Fig. 1 (Example 1) with input X and output Y. We present here the definitions of all output streams using the functions of Definition 5. Node g has a local variable *count* which gives rise to two streams: C_M, the previously stored values used as input of g, and C, the new value produced by g. We treat threshold as a parameter Th, a—possibly constant and infinite—stream. Function G associated with node g is a pair (G_Y, G_c), and the memory C_M is defined by function G_M. They are (recursively) defined by the following equations[3]

$$G_Y(X, C_M, Th) = G_Y^D(\mathbf{f}(X), \mathbf{f}(C_M), \mathbf{f}(Th)) \bullet G_Y(\mathbf{R}(X), \mathbf{R}(C_M), \mathbf{R}(Th))$$
$$\text{with } G_Y^D(x, c, th) = \text{if } (c + 1 \geq th) \text{ then } 1 \text{ else } \epsilon$$
$$G_C(X, C_M, Th) = G_C^D(\mathbf{f}(X), \mathbf{f}(C_M), \mathbf{f}(Th)) \bullet G_C(\mathbf{R}(X), \mathbf{R}(C_M), \mathbf{R}(Th))$$
$$\text{with } G_C^D(x, c, th) = \text{if } (c + 1 < th) \text{ then } (c + 1) \text{ else } 0$$
$$G_M(C) = 0 \bullet C \text{ (initially 0, then } C \text{ "shifted to the right")}$$

One may observe that node g applies a data transformation to the first elements of the inputs, produces an output element, or alternatively produces nothing[4], and then is applied recursively to the remainder of the input streams. Note also that here, the values of the output Y do not depend on input X; but X determines the length of Y. "Memories" such as C_M are defined by an initial element followed by the input stream which they "memorize" (this is the meaning of function G_M).

In the general case, a function may in each recursion step read zero or more elements from its input streams, and write zero or more elements to its outputs. That is, we can write any function $\mathbf{F} : \mathbb{S}^n \mapsto \mathbb{S}^m$ (other than the simpler memory functions) in the form:

$$\mathbf{F}(X) = \mathbf{Data_F}(\mathbf{Read_F}(X)) \bullet \mathbf{F}(\mathbf{Rem_F}(X)) \tag{1}$$

Thus, the functions $\mathbf{Read_F}$, $\mathbf{Data_F}$ and $\mathbf{Rem_F}$ fully characterize $\mathbf{F}$, where

- $\mathbf{Read_F} : \mathbb{S}^n \mapsto (\Sigma^n - \{\lambda\})$ extracts the (non-empty) initial input segments to be transformed by $\mathbf{Data_F}$
- $\mathbf{Data_F} : \Sigma^n \mapsto \Sigma^m$ the "data transformation" or "step" function of $\mathbf{F}$ (which in the general case transforms segments to segments) and defines the segments appended to the output streams.
- $\mathbf{Rem_F} : \mathbb{S}^n \mapsto \mathbb{S}^n$ defines which suffix to be considered for the recursive application of $\mathbf{F}$. Very often, we have $\mathbf{Read_F}(X) \bullet \mathbf{Rem_F}(X) = X$, that is exactly the inputs "read" by $\mathbf{Read_F}$ are "consumed" from the input streams at each "step"
- all these functions must be definable by basic functions of Definition 5.

The semantics of a KPN is defined by the union of the equation systems of its nodes. Kahn's results [15] stating that such an equation system has a unique solution, that is, a KPN defines a function on streams, is formulated in Theorem 1.

---

[3] where for readability reasons, instead of notation $\mathbf{app}(a, X)$, we use its definition $a \bullet X$.

[4] such as G_Y which produces element "1" only if $c + 1 \geq th$ otherwise produces nothing, that is, ϵ.

4.2   Semantics of Timed KPN

We define now the semantics of a timed node with a release pattern $P \in \mathbb{T}$ and a deadline δ. In order to do so, we show that we can extend a node function $\mathbf{F}$ on data streams (the node's semantic function) to a function $\mathbf{F}_\delta$ on timed streams, such that: (1) $\mathbf{F}_\delta = (\mathbf{F}, \mathbf{F}^T)$ defines a tuple of streams consisting of the data streams defined by $\mathbf{F}$, and the corresponding time streams defining the time points at which each data element is written into its destination FIFO[5]. (2) $\mathbf{F}_\delta$ is a Kahn function if time streams are interpreted as particular data streams. (3) The time extension expresses the intuition of release pattern P and the output delay δ of Definition 2. That is, the computation of F is divided into "steps" defined by the activation pattern, where the necessary data are read at activation, and the result of computation written out at the deadline. We now state the proposition which in turn proves Theorem 2 of Sect. 3. The remainder of the subsection is dedicated to its proof.

Proposition 1. *The semantics of a TKPN is a function from Timed input streams to Timed output streams defined by a set of node functions $\mathbf{F}_\delta$ which are Kahn functions on Timed Streams and enjoy the three above mentioned properties.*

Proof: We consider for each node a fixed deadline δ^6, and we prove this proposition by constructing for any function $\mathbf{F} : \mathbb{S}^n \mapsto \mathbb{S}^m$ an appropriate function $\mathbf{F}_\delta : \mathbb{S}^n \times \mathbb{T}^{n+1} \mapsto \mathbb{S}^m \times \mathbb{T}^m$ of the form $(\mathbf{F}, \mathbf{F}^T)$, with $\mathbf{F}^T : \mathbb{S}^n \times \mathbb{T}^{n+1} \mapsto \mathbb{T}^m$.

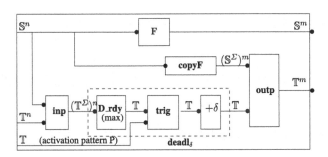

Fig. 3. Graphical representation of F_δ

Figure 3 illustrates the structure of $\mathbf{F}_\delta$ which we explain while introducing the auxiliary functions f required for the definition of $\mathbf{F}^T$. Most functions f are presented in the form of Eq. 1, that is, defined by functions $\mathbf{Read}_f$, $\mathbf{Data}_f$ and $\mathbf{Rem}_f$, where here $\mathbf{Rem}_f(X)$ is always the function consuming $\mathbf{Read}_f(X)$ from X. If $\mathbf{Read}_f(X)$ is "trivial" (reads the first element of all its inputs), we may not mention it.

1. Function **inp** reads the appropriate prefix from the timed input streams of $\mathbf{F}_\delta$ and outputs them in the form of a tuple of segments. If $\mathbf{Read}_\mathbf{F}$ is data independent, then

---

[5] in a corresponding TKPN implementation.

[6] Making δ an input which may vary over time is straightforward.

$\mathbf{Read}_{inp} = \mathbf{Read_F}$. Otherwise, it is a function that extends $\mathbf{Read_F}$ by simultaneously reading the timed input streams in the same way, so that also in this case, the tuple of segments read from the data streams and from the time streams have an identical structure (size). $\mathbf{Data}_{inp}$ is simply the projection on the tuple of time segments.

2. The *deadline*, that is, the time point at which the output of $\mathbf{F}$ is written is calculated by a composition of three functions on time streams: the first one, $\mathbf{D\_rdy}$, produces the time points at which the inputs of $\mathbf{F}$ are ready (all required data are available), the second one, $\mathbf{trig}$, uses the activation pattern P to produce the time points at which $\mathbf{F}$ is triggered, and the third one, $+\delta$, produces the time points at which the outputs of $\mathbf{F}$ are written into their destination streams:

3. Function $\mathbf{D\_rdy}$ reads the first tuple of segments of its input time streams, and $\mathbf{Data}_{D\_rdy}$ calculates the maximum of all available time points, that is, the latest date at which on of the corresponding data items has been written.

4. Function $\mathbf{trig}$ reads the first element from its input stream (produced by $\mathbf{D\_rdy}$), a time point t, and reads the smallest prefix $p_1 \bullet ... \bullet p_k$ of P such that $p_k \geq t$[7] because, according to Sect. 3.2, once all input data are available (time point t), the execution of $\mathbf{F}$ must be triggered at the earliest possible activation time point of the activation pattern (p_k). This function can be defined as follows:
$\mathbf{trig}(T, P)$ = if $(\mathbf{f}(T) \leq \mathbf{f}(P))$ then $\mathbf{f}(P) \bullet \mathbf{trig}(\mathbf{R}(T), \mathbf{R}(P))$ else $\mathbf{trig}(T, \mathbf{R}(P))$

5. Function $+\delta$ reads a time point from its input and adds δ to it. This is the desired time point of writing for all data items written by $\mathbf{F}$ at the corresponding "step".

6. Function $\mathbf{outp}$ makes sure that for each data item appended by $\mathbf{F}$ to one of the output streams at some step, the time point of writing is appended at the corresponding position of the time streams. Its first input comes from a modified version of $\mathbf{F}$ that presents the output of $\mathbf{F}$ explicitly as a tuple of segments[8]. $\mathbf{Read}_{outp}$ reads such a segment tuple and a time point t (the time point of writing) from its second input. $\mathbf{Data}_{outp}$ replaces every data element of this tuple by t.[9]

It is easy to see that all these functions can be written in terms of the basic functions of Definition 5, and therefore are Kahn functions. Finally, it satisfies also the third condition, as it clearly defines the intended meaning of activation pattern and deadline of Definition 2. This completes the proof.   □

Example 4 (Illustrating example, continued). Consider again function g of Fig. 1. Now, g is executed with a periodic activation pattern p, and has a global output delay dl .

As the function(s) $\mathbf{F}$ on data remain untouched, we only need to add new equations defining $\mathbf{F}^T$, that is the time streams Y^T, C^T and C_M^T associated with Y, C and C_M. The situation here is a bit simpler than the general case: (1) we know that at each step exactly one item is read from each input, implying that function $\mathbf{Read}_{inp} \equiv \mathbf{first}$, and (2) function G_Y may or may not output a data item, whereas G_C

---

[7] which must exist.

[8] it may use a strongly abstracted version of $\mathbf{F}$ which only preserves the structure of the output.

[9] E.g., if $\mathbf{F}$ produces one element on each output stream, that is an m-tuple $(d_1...d_m)$, then it produces the m-tuple $(t...t)$.

and G_M always produce one item. Therefore $\mathbf{Data}_{outp}(x, c, th, t) = $ if $(c + 1 \geq th)$ then (t, t, t) else (ϵ, t, t)[10]. Furthermore, we suppose that the activation pattern is "well chosen", that is, at every activation time point there is indeed sufficient data available[11]. This allows to easily write the corresponding equations, where we abbreviate $\mathbf{deadl}_\delta(\mathbf{f}(X^T, C_M^T, Th^T), \mathbf{f}(P))$ by D, and $\mathbf{R}(X^T, C_M^T, Th^T, P)$ by $\mathbf{Rem}$. Note that only Y^T depends on the data streams)

- $G_Y^T((X, C_M, Th), (X^T, C_M^T, Th^T, P)) =$
  $\qquad$ [if $\mathbf{f}(C_M) + 1 \geq \mathbf{f}(Th)$ then D else $\epsilon] \bullet G_Y^T(\mathbf{Rem})$
- $G_C^T(X^T, C_M^T, Th^T, P) = D \bullet G_C^T(\mathbf{Rem})$
- $G_M^T(C^T) = 0 \bullet C^T$

$\qquad\qquad\qquad\qquad\qquad\qquad\qquad\qquad\qquad\qquad\qquad\qquad\qquad\qquad$ □

4.3 Adding Registers to Timed KPN

Finally, we provide the semantic underpinning for the full MIMOS model where some of the channels are registers. At the semantic level, a register is a node whose function transforms the timed stream produced by the source node into the timed stream read by the target node depending on a time stream representing the time points at which the register is read[12].

As the function of a register node is time dependent, we do not define time and function separately. The function $\mathbf{Reg}$ reads a value t from the trigger input, and the smallest prefix of the timed stream that contains a pair with a time value $> t$[13]. It appends to the output the last pair of this prefix with time value $\leq t$, and leaves for the recursive application the suffix including the element it has output. Therefore, the output stream defines for each trigger time point the (timed) value at the register input. We do not define the functions $\mathbf{Read}$, $\mathbf{Data}$ and $\mathbf{Rem}$ for Reg, to avoid too much repetition but we define $\mathbf{Reg}$ directly[14].

Definition 6 (Stream transformation for a register). *Let be* (S, T) *a timed stream, and* $\mathbf{Tr}$ *the time stream of trigger points. The function* $\mathbf{Reg} : (\mathbb{S} \times \mathbb{T}) \times \mathbb{T} \mapsto \mathbb{S} \times \mathbb{T}$ *is defined by the following fixpoint equation, where* $\mathbf{2nd}(X)$ *is an abbreviation for* $\mathbf{f}(\mathbf{R}(X))$:

$\mathbf{Reg}((S, T), \mathbf{Tr}) =$
$\qquad$ *if* $\mathbf{f}(S, T) = \mathbf{f}(\mathbf{Tr})$ *then*
$\qquad\qquad$ *if* $\mathbf{2nd}(S, T) > \mathbf{f}(\mathbf{Tr})$ *then* $\mathbf{f}(S, T) \bullet \mathbf{Reg}((S, T), \mathbf{R}(\mathbf{Tr}))$ *% output 1st*
$\qquad\qquad$ *else % that is* $\mathbf{2nd}(S, T) = \mathbf{f}(\mathbf{Tr})$

---

[10] G_M has the same deadline as G, meaning that the data put in the "memory" is immediately available.

[11] In the general case, the equations are more complicated as a variable length segment is to be read from P as indicated by the definition of function $\mathbf{trig}$.

[12] which is the trigger time of the node reading the register.

[13] which must exist if the stream is infinite. If it is finite, the definition of $\mathbf{Reg}$ is a bit more complicated, but it is easy to see that this can be fixed.

[14] Note some similarity with the definition of function $\mathbf{trig}$.

$$\text{Reg}(\text{R}(S,T), \textsf{Tr}) \text{ \% eliminate 1st}$$
$$else \text{ \% that is } \textbf{f}(S,T) < \textbf{f}(\textsf{Tr})$$
$$if \; \textbf{2nd}(S,T) \le \textbf{f}(\textsf{Tr}) \; then \; \text{Reg}(\text{R}(S,T), \textsf{Tr}) \text{ \% eliminate 1st}$$
$$else \text{ \% that is } \textbf{2nd}(S,T) > \textbf{f}(\textsf{Tr})$$
$$\textbf{f}(S,T)\bullet\text{Reg}((S,T), \text{R}(\textsf{Tr})) \text{ \% output 1st}$$

Clearly, this function outputs a youngest pair $\le$ the trigger time. If there are several pairs with the same date, the latest written is chosen. If initially the first value of $\textbf{T}$ is 0, then it is guaranteed that $(\textbf{S}, \textbf{T})$ contains always an "old" pair, that is one with a time value $\le$ the first value of $\textsf{Tr}$. The reason is that the last output pair is reused in the next step. The definition gives also the expected result if the sequence of trigger time points is not strictly increasing—even if this usually is not expected.

If the register is rarely updated, and the date of the "next" data element is much larger than the "current", the same element may be read over and over again, according to the intuition of a register.

Note that a node function $\textbf{F}_\delta$ could be ill defined in the case that $\textbf{Read}_\textbf{F}$ depends on a value read from a register, because then there could be a circular dependency between the value read and trigger time point. We call a function $\textbf{F}$ with register inputs *well defined* it is not ill defined in that sense.

We illustrate the effect of replacing a FIFO by a register input on $\textbf{F}_\delta$ on hand of our running example which is clearly *well defined* because none of its $\textbf{Read}$ functions is data dependent.

Example 5 (Illustrating example, continued). Again, consider function g from the previous example. Now, input Th read from a register. This affects both time and data.

- As a register holds a valid data at any time, Th^T does not affect the trigger time point. Therefore, it is not anymore an input of the functions G^T. The new equations for G^T are obtained from those in Ex. 4 by eliminating Th^T from the inputs. This may allow the functions to be triggered earlier and more often.
- The value read from Th is now time dependent. The equations for G_Y and G_C are obtained from those of Ex. 3 by replacing Th by the register value read at the trigger time points, that is by $\textbf{Reg}((Z, Z^T), \textbf{trig}(\textbf{D\_rdy}(\textbf{f}(X^T, C_M^T)), P))$. This is a sequence of values obtained from Th by over- and under-sampling, depending on the activation pattern P.[15]   □

We now formulate the proposition which guarantees Theorem 3. It is very similar to Prop. 1, but the function on data streams is not time independent anymore.

Proposition 2. *The semantics of a TKPN with* well defined *nodes including registers is a function from timed input streams to timed output streams defined by the set of (new) node functions* $\textbf{F}_\delta$. *The function* $\textbf{Reg}$ *associated with a register is a Kahn function and expresses well the informal semantics of Sect. 3.*

Proof: as $\textbf{Reg}$ is defined using the functions of Definition 5, we stay within Kahn's framework. This guarantees that the entire network defines unique function. We have already argued that The functions $\textbf{Reg}$ express well the intuition of a register as

---

[15] in fact, due to our simplifying assumptions in Example 4, only oversampling.

described Sect. 3. In particular, the fact that the value read at time t is always the last one written up to t (including t), reflects the "write over read precedence mentioned there. This completes the proof.   □

Note that the semantics of the function reading a register can be expressed within the framework of Kahn. Nevertheless, as one can see from Definition 6, this is done at the price of some "look a head" into future time points, necessary to make sure to choose the "latest value written up to t". It might be difficult to implement this semantics, in particular in a distributed setting or in the presence of even minimal jitter. We envisage two solutions for preserving determinism in this case. (1) approximation, that is determinism up to some ϵ[16], and (2) adapting the solution of [8], which consists in reading old enough data, that can be guaranteed to be present, despite possible jitter.

5   Analysis Problems

To enable that a MIMOS model can be compiled into a program executable on a platform with limited resources, the model should be verified to meet expected requirements. There are two principle ones: (1) the memory requirements must be bounded and (2) timing requirements on the system functions must be satisfied, in particular for safety-critical applications. In general, these verification problems are undecidable. However, with proper assumptions and restrictions, there are efficient solutions for practical purposes [2,18]. Thanks to the determinism of MIMOS, verified properties on a MIMOS model will be preserved by the execution of code generated in compilation.

First, it is vital to know that the required memory never exceeds the available memory. In the execution of a MIMOS (program), the consumed memory depends on the buffer size required by the FIFOs, which can be specified as follows.

Definition 7 (Required buffer size (RBS)). *Assume that the data written to and read from a FIFO buffer are specified by timed streams* $(a_1, t_1)(a_2, t_2)...$ *and* $(a_1, t_1')(a_2, t_2')...,$ *respectively. Also, let* $\omega(t) \equiv \max\{i | t_i \leq t\}$ *and* $\gamma(t) \equiv \max\{i | t_i' < t\}$. *The FIFO's required buffer size (RBS) is defined as* $\max\{\omega(t) - \gamma(t) | t \geq 0\}$.   □

In words, $\omega(t)$ is the total number of items written to a FIFO up to (including) time t, and $\gamma(t)$ is the total number of items read from the FIFO strictly before t. Based on this, the RBS of a FIFO denotes the maximum number of items which can simultaneously exist in the queue. Indeed, computing RBS in a *process network* has been shown undecidable [6]. Despite this, the measure is computable for some subsets of KPN. For instance, if for each node the number of produced and consumed items is fixed in all firings, as is the case in synchronous data flow (SDF) [19], the problem has efficient solutions [19]. Further, for those KPNs in which data producing/consuming pattern of the nodes is periodic (except for a bounded initial time), it is shown that the required capacity for a FIFO is bounded if and only if writing and reading rates are *asymptotically* the same [9].

The RBS of a MIMOS model depends on the release pattern of the nodes, the pattern by which input data arrives, and also the data consumption pattern. According to these

---

[16] note that registers are used for reading continuous data streams.

factors, a variety of instances of the problem of computing (a bound on) RBS can be defined, which is not our current focus. Here, we just provide some initial observation.

A fairly direct consequence of Definition 7 is that the RBS of a FIFO in a MIMOS model is bounded if and only if there exists a constant c for which $\forall t \geq 0 : \omega(t) - \gamma(t) \leq c$. Based on this, we conjecture that: *The RBS of a FIFO is bounded if and only if reading and writing rates are asymptotically the same, i.e.,* $\lim_{t\to\infty}\{\omega(t)/\gamma(t)\} = 1$

The other measure to be analyzed is *end-to-end latency*, which essentially reflects the responsiveness of a system. It is important that when the input changes, the system provides a response (or react) with a bounded delay. The response should be observable on an output channel. We define the end-to-end latency for each output channel of the system with respect to an influencing input.

Definition 8 (Worst-case end-to-end latency, e2e(i)). *Assume that the behavior of a MIMOS model is determined by a k-ary function $\mathbf{F}$ on streams. Let $(I_1, \ldots I_k)$ be a set of (possibly infinite) external input timed streams for which $\mathbf{F}(I_1, \ldots I_k) = (Y^D, Y^T)$. Consider now, for some i, $1 \leq i \leq k$, a modified version of I_i, called I_i', which is obtained by changing the j-th entry of I_i from (a, t) to (b, t). Assume $\mathbf{F}(I_1, \ldots, I_i', \ldots I_k) = (Y'^D, Y'^T)$. Let $j' = \min\{m | Y_m'^D \neq Y_m^D \text{ or } Y_m'^T \neq Y_m^T\}$, where X_m denotes the m-th element of a stream X. We define $delay(I_1, \ldots I_k, i, j, b) = Y_{j'}'^T - t$. Accordingly, we define $delay(I_1, \ldots I_k, i) = \max\{delay(I_1, \ldots I_k, i, j, b) | \forall j, b\}$. The worst-case end-to-end latency for the i-th input line is then $\mathbf{e2e}(i) = \max\{delay(I_1, \ldots I_k, i) | \forall (I_1, \ldots I_k)\}$.*

Computing end-to-end latency can be studied with respect to the release patterns of the nodes in a MIMOS model. For instance, for a set of periodic tasks communicating through some registers, which can be viewed as a special case of MIMOS, the problem is explored in [16], where a worst-case analysis method with exponential time complexity is proposed. Also, a polynomial-time approach is provided for computing an upper bound. Both methods are limited to task sets scheduled with a fixed-priority policy on a single processor. Investigating the problem in MIMOS for different release patterns and target platforms such as multi-core and distributed architectures is left to future work.

6 Conclusions

The MIMOS model presented in this paper is to enable a model-based approach for not only systems design but also dynamic updates on systems after deployment (or in operation). It is deterministic: for a given set of (timed) input streams, the set of (timed) output streams determined by a MIMOS model are unique. The determinism allows that the complete behavior of the resulting system can be verified by simulation prior to the implementation and any intended update. Differently from the semantic model for the family of synchronous programming languages such as Lustre for real-time programming, MIMOS adopts asynchronous communications via FIFO channels and registers. MIMOS allows integration of new components on a system after deployment for new functions without re-designing the whole system or interfering with the existing system functionality. Additionally, existing components may be replaced also by new ones fulfilling given requirements.

As future work, MIMOS will be further developed to be a modelling and programming language for embedded systems design and update. A compiler will be developed to generate executable code from MIMOS models for both simulation and final implementation on a given target platform.

References

1. AUTOSAR - Specification of RTE Software (2019)
2. Abdullah, J., Dai, G., Yi, W.: Worst-case cause-effect reaction latency in systems with non-blocking communication. In: Design, Automation Test in Europe Conference Exhibition (DATE), pp. 1625–1630 (2019)
3. AUTOSAR. AUTomotive Open System ARchitecture. https://www.autosar.org
4. Baruah, S., Chen, D., Gorinsky, S., Mok, A.: Generalized multiframe tasks. Real-Time Syst. **17**(1), 5–22 (1999)
5. Baudart, G.: A synchronous approach to quasi-periodic systems. Phd dissertation, PSL Research University, March 2017
6. Buck, J.T., Lee, E.A.: Scheduling Dynamic Dataflow Graphs with Bounded Memory Using the Token Flow Model. PhD thesis, University of California, Berkeley (1993). AAI9431898
7. Caspi, P.: The quasi-synchronous approach to distributed control systems. Technical report, Technical Report CMA/009931, Verimag, CrysisProject "The Cooking Book" (2000)
8. Caspi, P., Mazuet, C., Paligot, N.R.: About the design of distributed control systems: the quasi-synchronous approach. In: Voges, U. (ed.) SAFECOMP 2001. LNCS, vol. 2187, pp. 215–226. Springer, Heidelberg (2001). https://doi.org/10.1007/3-540-45416-0_21
9. Cohen, A., Duranton, M., Eisenbeis, C., Pagetti, C., Plateau, F., Pouzet, M.: N-synchronous Kahn networks: a relaxed model of synchrony for real-time systems. ACM SIGPLAN Not. **41**(1), 180–193 (2006)
10. Dörflinger, A., et al.: Demonstrating controlled change for autonomous space vehicles. In: NASA/ESA Conference on Adaptive Hardware and Systems, AHS, Colchester, UK, July 22–24, pp. 95–102. IEEE (2019)
11. Fersman, E., Krcal, P., Pettersson, P., Yi, W.: Task automata: schedulability, decidability and undecidability. Inf. Comput. **205**(8), 1149–1172 (2007)
12. Graf, S., Quinton, S., Girault, A., Gössler, G.: Building correct cyber-physical systems: why we need a multiview contract theory. In: Howar, F., Barnat, J. (eds.) FMICS 2018. LNCS, vol. 11119, pp. 19–31. Springer, Cham (2018). https://doi.org/10.1007/978-3-030-00244-2_2
13. Halbwachs, N.: Synchronous Programming of Reactive Systems. Springer, US (2013)
14. Henzinger, T.A., Horowitz, B., Kirsch, C.M.: Giotto: a time-triggered language for embedded programming. Proc. IEEE **91**(1), 84–99 (2003)
15. Kahn, G.: The semantics of a simple language for parallel programming. Inf. Process. **74**, 471–475 (1974)
16. Kloda, T., Bertout, A., Sorel, Y.: Latency upper bound for data chains of real-time periodic tasks. J. Syst. Arch. **109**, 101824 (2020)
17. Kopetz, H., Bauer, G.: The time-triggered architecture. Proc. IEEE **91**(1), 112–126 (2003)
18. Krcal, P., Yi, W.: Communicating timed automata: the more synchronous, the more difficult to verify. In: Ball, T., Jones, R.B. (eds.) CAV 2006. LNCS, vol. 4144, pp. 249–262. Springer, Heidelberg (2006). https://doi.org/10.1007/11817963_24
19. Lee, E.A., Messerschmitt, D.G.: Synchronous data flow. Proc. IEEE **75**(9), 1235–1245 (1987)
20. Lee, E.A., Parks, T.M.: Dataflow process networks. Proc. IEEE **83**(5), 773–801 (1995)

21. Liu, C.L., Layland, J.W.: Scheduling algorithms for multiprogramming in a hard-real-time environment. J. ACM (JACM) **20**(1), 46–61 (1973)
22. Natarajan, S., Broman, D.: Timed C: An extension to the C programming language for real-time systems. In: 2018 IEEE Real-Time and Embedded Technology and Applications Symposium (RTAS), pp. 227–239. IEEE (2018)
23. Stigge, M., Ekberg, P., Guan, N., Yi, W.: The digraph real-time task model. In: 2011 17th IEEE Real-Time and Embedded Technology and Applications Symposium, pp. 71–80. IEEE (2011)
24. Stigge, M., Yi, W.: Graph-based models for real-time workload: a survey. Real-Time Syst. **51**(5), 602–636 (2015). https://doi.org/10.1007/s11241-015-9234-z
25. Yi, Wang: Towards customizable CPS: composability, efficiency and predictability. In: Duan, Zhenhua, Ong, Luke (eds.) ICFEM 2017. LNCS, vol. 10610, pp. 3–15. Springer, Cham (2017). https://doi.org/10.1007/978-3-319-68690-5_1

A Sound Up-to-n, δ Bisimilarity for PCTL

Massimo Bartoletti[1](✉), Maurizio Murgia[2,3,4], and Roberto Zunino[2]

[1] Università Degli Studi di Cagliari, Cagliari, Italy
`bart@unica.it`
[2] Università degli Studi di Trento, Trento, Italy
[3] Università degli Studi di Bologna, Bologna, Italy
[4] Gran Sasso Science Institute, L'Aquila, Italy

Abstract. We tackle the problem of establishing the soundness of approximate bisimilarity with respect to PCTL and its relaxed semantics. To this purpose, we consider a notion of bisimilarity similar to the one introduced by Desharnais, Laviolette, and Tracol, which is parametric with respect to an approximation error δ, and to the depth n of the observation along traces. Essentially, our soundness theorem establishes that, when a state q satisfies a given formula up-to error δ and steps n, and q is bisimilar to q' up-to error δ' and enough steps, we prove that q' also satisfies the formula up-to a suitable error δ'' and steps n. The new error δ'' is computed from δ, δ' and the formula, and only depends linearly on n. We provide a detailed overview of our soundness proof.

Keywords: PCTL · Probabilistic processes · Approximate bisimulation

1 Introduction

The behaviour of many real-world systems can be formally modelled as probabilistic processes, e.g. as discrete-time Markov chains. Specifying and verifying properties on these systems requires probabilistic versions of temporal logics, such as PCTL [25]. PCTL allows to express probability bounds using the formula $\mathsf{Pr}_{\geq \pi}[\psi]$, which is satisfied by those states starting from which the path formula ψ holds with probability $\geq \pi$. A well-known issue is that real-world systems can have tiny deviations from their mathematical models, while logical properties, such as those written in PCTL, impose sharp constraints on the behaviour. To address this issue, one can use a *relaxed* semantics for PCTL, as in [21]. There, the semantics of formulae is parameterised over the error $\delta \geq 0$ one is willing to tolerate. While in the standard semantics of $\mathsf{Pr}_{\geq \pi}[\psi]$ the bound $\geq \pi$ is *exact*, in relaxed PCTL this bound is weakened to $\geq \pi - \delta$. So, the relaxed semantics generalises the standard PCTL semantics of [25], which can be obtained by choosing $\delta = 0$. Instead, choosing an error $\delta > 0$ effectively provides a way to measure "how much" a state satisfies a given formula: some states might require only a very small error, while others a much larger one.

© IFIP International Federation for Information Processing 2022
M. H. ter Beek and M. Sirjani (Eds.): COORDINATION 2022, LNCS 13271, pp. 35–52, 2022.
https://doi.org/10.1007/978-3-031-08143-9_3

When dealing with temporal logics such as PCTL, one often wants to study some notion of state equivalence which preserves the semantics of formulae: that is, when two states are equivalent, they satisfy the same formulae. For instance, probabilistic bisimilarities like those in [16,19,29] preserve the semantics of formulae for PCTL and other temporal logics. Although *strict* probabilistic bisimilarity preserves the semantics of relaxed PCTL, it is not *robust* against small deviations in the probability of transitions in Markov chains [24]. A possible approach to deal with this issue is to also relax the notion of probabilistic bisimilarity, by making it parametric with respect to an error δ [21]. Relaxing bisimilarity in this way poses a choice regarding which properties of the strict probabilistic bisimilarity are to be kept. In particular, transitivity is enjoyed by the strict probabilistic bisimilarity, but it is *not* desirable for the relaxed notion. Indeed, we could have three states q, q' and q'' where the behaviour of q and q' is similar enough (within the error δ), the behaviour of q' and q'' is also similar enough (within δ), but the distance between q and q'' is larger than the allowed error δ. At best, we can have a sort of "triangular inequality", where q and q'' can still be related but only with a larger error $2 \cdot \delta$.

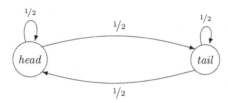

Fig. 1. A Markov chain modelling repeated tosses of a fair coin.

Bisimilarity is usually defined by coinduction, essentially requiring that the relation is preserved along an arbitrarily long sequence of moves. Still, in some settings, observing the behaviour over a very long run is undesirable. For instance, consider the PCTL formula $\phi = \Pr_{\geq 0.5}[\text{true } U^{\leq n} \text{ a}]$, which is satisfied by those states from which, with probability ≥ 0.5, a is satisfied within n steps. In this case, a behavioural equivalence relation that preserves the semantics of ϕ can neglect the long-run behaviour after n steps. More generally, if all the until operators are *bounded*, as in $\phi_1 U^{\leq k} \phi_2$, then each formula has an upper bound of steps n after which a behavioural equivalence relation can ignore what happens next. Observing the behaviour after this upper bound is unnecessarily strict, and indeed in some settings it is customary to neglect what happens in the very long run. For instance, a real-world player repeatedly tossing a coin is usually considered equivalent to a Markov chain with two states and four transitions with probability 1/2 (see Fig. 1), even if in the long run the real-world system will diverge from the ideal one (e.g., when the player dies).

Another setting where observing the long-term behaviour is notoriously undesirable is that of cryptography. When studying the security of systems modelling cryptographic protocols, two states are commonly considered equivalent when their behaviour is similar (up to a small error δ) in the short run, even when in the long run they diverge. For instance, a state q could represent an ideal system where no attacks can be performed by construction, while another state q' could represent a real system where an adversary can try to disrupt the cryptographic protocol. In such a scenario, if the protocol is secure, we would like to have q and q' equivalent, since the behaviour of the real system is close to the one of the ideal system. Note that in the real system an adversary can repeatedly try to guess the secret cryptographic keys, and break security in the very long run, with very high probability. Accordingly, standard security definitions require that the behaviour of the ideal and real system are within a small error, but only for a *bounded* number of steps, after which their behaviour could diverge.

Contributions. To overcome the above mentioned issues, in this work we introduce a bounded, approximate notion of bisimilarity $\sim_\delta^n$, that only observes the first n steps, and allows for an error δ. Unlike standard bisimilarity, our relation is naturally defined by *induction* on n. We call this looser variant of bisimilarity an *up-to-n, δ* bisimilarity. We showcase up-to-n, δ bisimilarity on a running example (Examples 1, 2 and 4), comparing an ideal combination padlock against a real one which can be opened by an adversary guessing its combination. We show that the two systems are bisimilar up-to-n, δ, while they are not bisimilar according to the standard coinductive notion. We then discuss how the two systems satisfy a basic security property expressed in PCTL, with suitable errors. To make our theory amenable to reason about infinite-state systems, such as those usually found when modelling cryptographic protocols, all our results apply to Markov chains with countably many states. In this respect, our work departs from most literature on probabilistic bisimulations [21,33] and bisimilarity distances [7,9,13,22,34–36], which usually assume finite-state Markov chains. In Example 3 we exploit infinite-state Markov chains to compare a biased random bit generator with an ideal one.

Our main contribution is a soundness theorem establishing that, when a state q satisfies a PCTL formula ϕ (up to a given error), any bisimilar state $q' \sim q$ must also satisfy ϕ, at the cost of a slight increase of the error. More precisely, if ϕ only involves until operators bounded by $\leq n$, state q satisfies ϕ up to some error, and bisimilarity holds for enough steps and error δ, then q' satisfies ϕ with an *additional* asymptotic error $O(n \cdot \delta)$.

This asymptotic behaviour is compatible with the usual assumptions of computational security in cryptography. There, models of security protocols include a security parameter η, which affects the length of the cryptographic keys and the running time of the protocol: more precisely, a protocol is assumed to run for $n(\eta)$ steps, which is polynomially bounded w.r.t. η. As already mentioned above, cryptographic notions of security do not observe the behaviour of the systems after this bound $n(\eta)$, since in the long run an adversary can surely guess the secret keys by brute force. Coherently, a protocol is considered to be secure if (roughly) its actual behaviour is *approximately* equivalent to the ideal one for $n(\eta)$ steps and up to an error $\delta(\eta)$, which has to be a negligible function, asymptotically approaching zero faster than any rational function. Under these bounds on n and δ, the asymptotic error $O(n \cdot \delta)$ in our soundness theorem is negligible in η. Consequently, if two states q and q' represent the ideal and actual behaviour, respectively, and they are bisimilar up to a negligible error, they will satisfy the same PCTL formulae with a negligible error.

We provide a detailed overview of the proof of our soundness theorem, explaining the techniques that we used. Due to space limitations, we present the full proofs of our results in [5].

Related Work. There is a well-established line of research on establishing soundness and completeness of probabilistic bisimulations against various kinds of probabilistic logics [19,23,26,29,31,32].

The work closest to ours is that of D'Innocenzo, Abate and Katoen [21], which addresses the model checking problem on relaxed PCTL. Their relaxed PCTL differs from ours in a few aspects. First, their syntax allows for an individual bound for each until operator $U^{\leq k}$, while we assume all such bounds are equal. This difference does not seem to affect our results, which could be extended to cover the general case. Second, their main result shows that bisimilar states up-to a given error ϵ satisfy the same formulae ψ, provided that ψ ranges over the so-called ϵ-robust formulae. Instead, our soundness result applies to *all* PCTL formulae, and ensures that when moving from a state satisfying ϕ to a bisimilar one, ϕ is still satisfied, but at the cost of slightly increasing the error. Third, their relaxed semantics differs from ours. In ours, we relax all the probability bounds by the same amount δ. Instead, the relaxation in [21] affects the bounds by a different amount which depends on the error ϵ, the until bound k, and the underlying DTMC.

Desharnais, Laviolette and Tracol [20] use a coinductive approximate probabilistic bisimilarity, up-to an error δ. Using such coinductive bisimilarity, [20] establishes the soundness and completeness with respect to a Larsen-Skou logic [29] (instead of PCTL). In [20], a bounded, up-to n, δ version of bisimilarity is only briefly used to derive a decision algorithm for coinductive bisimilarity under the assumption that the state space is finite. In our work, instead, the bounded up-to n, δ bisimilarity is the main focus of study. In particular, our soundness result only assumes n, δ bisimilarity, which is strictly weaker than coinductive bisimilarity. Another minor difference is that [20] considers a labelled Markov process, i.e. the probabilistic variant of a labelled transition system, while we instead focus on DTMCs having labels on states.

Bian and Abate [6] study bisimulation and trace equivalence up-to an error ϵ, and show that ϵ-bisimilar states are also ϵ'-trace equivalent, for a suitable ϵ' which depends on ϵ. Furthermore, they show that ϵ-trace equivalent states satisfy the same formulae in a bounded LTL, up-to a certain error. In our work, we focus instead on the branching logic PCTL.

A related research line is that on *bisimulation metrics* [7,8,10]. Some of these metrics, like our up-to bisimilarity, take approximations into account [12,17]. Similarly to our bisimilarity, bisimulation metrics allow to establish two states equivalent up-to a certain error (but usually do not take into account the bound on the number of steps). Interestingly, Castiglioni, Gebler and Tini [12] introduce a notion of distance between Larsen-Skou formulae, and prove that the bisimulation distance between two processes corresponds to the distance between their mimicking formulae. De Alfaro, Majumdar, Raman and Stoelinga [2] elegantly characterise bisimulation metrics with a quantitative μ-calculus. Such logic allows to specify interesting properties such as maximal reachability and safety probability, and the maximal probability of satisfying a general ω-regular specification, but not full PCTL. Mio [30] characterises a bisimulation metric based on total variability with a more general quantitative μ-calculus, dubbed Łukasiewicz μ-calculus, able to encode PCTL. Both [2] and [30] do not take the number of steps into account, therefore their applicability to the analysis of security protocols is yet to be investigated.

Metrics with discount [1,3,9,15,18] are sometimes used to relate the behaviour of probabilistic processes, weighing less those events that happen in the far future compared to those happening in the first steps. Often, in these metrics each step causes the probability of the next events to be multiplied by a constant factor $c < 1$, in order to diminish their importance. Note that this discount makes it so that after η steps, this diminishing factor becomes c^η, which is a negligible function of η. As discussed before, in cryptographic security one needs to consider as important those events happening within polynomially many steps, while neglecting the ones after such a polynomial threshold. Using an exponential discount factor c^η after only η steps goes against this principle, since it would cause a secure system to be at a negligible distance from an insecure one which can be violated after just η steps. For this reason, instead of using a metric with discount, in this paper we resort to a bisimilarity that is parametrized over the number of steps n and error δ, allowing us to obtain a notion which distinguishes between the mentioned secure and insecure systems.

Several works develop algorithms to decide probabilistic bisimilarity, and to compute metrics [11,13,22,34–36]. To this purpose, they restrict to finite-state systems, like e.g. probabilistic automata. Our results, instead, apply also to infinite-state systems.

2   PCTL

Assume a set $\mathcal{L}$ of labels, ranged over by l, and let δ, π range over non-negative reals. A *discrete-time Markov chain* (DTMC) is a standard model of probabilistic systems. Throughout this paper, we consider a DTMC having a countable, possibly infinite, set of states q, each carrying a subset of labels $\ell(q) \subseteq \mathcal{L}$.

Definition 1 (Discrete-Time Markov Chain). *A (labelled) DTMC is a triple* $(Q, \Pr, \ell)$ *where:*

- Q *is a countable set of states;*
- $\Pr : Q^2 \to [0, 1]$ *is a function, named transition probability function;*
- $\ell : Q \to \mathcal{P}(\mathcal{L})$ *is a labelling function*

Given $q \in \mathcal{Q}$ *and* $Q \subseteq \mathcal{Q}$, *we write* $\Pr(q, Q)$ *for* $\sum_{q' \in \mathcal{Q}} \Pr(q, q')$ *and we require that* $\Pr(q, \mathcal{Q}) = 1$ *for all* $q \in \mathcal{Q}$.

A *trace* is an infinite sequence of states $t = q_0 q_1 \cdots$, where we write $t(i)$ for q_i, i.e. the i-th element of t. A *trace fragment* is a finite, non-empty sequence of states $\tilde{t} = q_0 \cdots q_{n-1}$, where $|\tilde{t}| = n \geq 1$ is its length. Given a trace fragment $\tilde{t}$ and a state q, we write $\tilde{t}q^\omega$ for the trace $\tilde{t}qqq \cdots$.

It is well-known that, given an initial state q_0, the DTMC induces a σ-algebra of measurable sets of traces T starting from q_0, i.e. the σ-algebra generated by cylinders. More in detail, given a trace fragment $\tilde{t} = q_0 \cdots q_{n-1}$, its cylinder $Cyl(\tilde{t}) = \{t \mid \tilde{t} \text{ is a prefix of } t\}$ is given probability $\Pr(Cyl(\tilde{t})) = \prod_{i=0}^{n-2} \Pr(q_i, q_{i+1})$. As usual, if $n = 1$ the product is empty and evaluates to 1. Closing the family of cylinders under countable unions and complement we obtain the family of measurable sets. The probability measure on cylinders then uniquely extends to all the measurable sets.

Given a set of trace fragments $\tilde{T}$, all starting from the same state q_0 and having the same length, we let $\Pr(\tilde{T}) = \Pr(\bigcup_{\tilde{t} \in \tilde{T}} Cyl(\tilde{t})) = \sum_{\tilde{t} \in \tilde{T}} \Pr(Cyl(\tilde{t}))$. Note that using same-length trace fragments ensures that their cylinders are disjoint, hence the second equality holds.

Below, we define PCTL formulae. Our syntax is mostly standard, except for the *until* operator. There, for the sake of simplicity, we do not bound the number of steps in the syntax $\phi_1 \cup \phi_2$, but we do so in the semantics. Concretely, this amounts to imposing the same bound to *all* the occurrences of $\cup$ in the formula. Such bound is then provided as a parameter to the semantics. We foresee no problems in relaxing this restriction, which we make only to simplify our treatment.

Definition 2 (PCTL syntax). *The syntax of PCTL is given by the following grammar, defining* state formulae ϕ *and* path formulae ψ:

$$\phi ::= l \mid \mathsf{true} \mid \neg\phi \mid \phi \wedge \phi \mid \mathsf{Pr}_{\rhd \pi}[\psi] \qquad where \rhd \in \{>, \geq\}$$
$$\psi ::= \mathsf{X}\,\phi \mid \phi \cup \phi$$

As syntactic sugar, we write $\mathsf{Pr}_{<\pi}[\psi]$ *for* $\neg\mathsf{Pr}_{\geq\pi}[\psi]$, *and* $\mathsf{Pr}_{\leq\pi}[\psi]$ *for* $\neg\mathsf{Pr}_{>\pi}[\psi]$.

Given a PCTL formula ϕ, we define its maximum X-nesting $\mathsf{X}_{max}(\phi)$ and its maximum U-nesting $\mathsf{U}_{max}(\phi)$ inductively as follows:

Definition 3 (Maximum nesting). *For* $\circ \in \{\mathsf{X}, \mathsf{U}\}$, *we define:*

$$\circ_{max}(l) = 0 \qquad \circ_{max}(\mathsf{true}) = 0 \qquad \circ_{max}(\neg\phi) = \circ_{max}(\phi)$$
$$\circ_{max}(\phi_1 \wedge \phi_2) = \max(\circ_{max}(\phi_1), \circ_{max}(\phi_2)) \qquad \circ_{max}(\mathsf{Pr}_{\rhd \pi}[\psi]) = \circ_{max}(\psi)$$
$$\circ_{max}(\mathsf{X}\phi) = \circ_{max}(\phi) + \begin{cases} 1 & \textit{if } \circ = \mathsf{X} \\ 0 & \textit{otherwise} \end{cases}$$
$$\circ_{max}(\phi_1 \cup \phi_2) = \max(\circ_{max}(\phi_1), \circ_{max}(\phi_2)) + \begin{cases} 1 & \textit{if } \circ = \mathsf{U} \\ 0 & \textit{otherwise} \end{cases}$$

We now define a semantics for PCTL where the probability bounds $\rhd\pi$ in $\mathsf{Pr}_{\rhd\pi}[\psi]$ can be relaxed or strengthened by an error δ. Our semantics is parameterized over the *until* bound n, the error $\delta \in \mathbb{R}^{\geq 0}$, and a direction $r \in \{+1, -1\}$. Given the parameters, the semantics associates each PCTL state formula with the set of states satisfying it. Intuitively, when $r = +1$ we relax the semantics of the formula, so that increasing δ causes more states to satisfy it. More precisely, the probability bounds $\rhd\pi$ in positive occurrences of $\mathsf{Pr}_{\rhd\pi}[\psi]$ are decreased by δ, while those in negative occurrences are increased by δ. Dually, when $r = -1$ we strengthen the semantics, modifying $\rhd\pi$ in the opposite direction.

Definition 4 (PCTL semantics). *The semantics of PCTL formulas is given below. Let $n \in \mathbb{N}$, $\delta \in \mathbb{R}^{\geq 0}$ and $r \in \{+1, -1\}$.*

$$
\begin{aligned}
[\![l]\!]^n_{\delta,r} &= \{q \in \mathcal{Q} \mid l \in \ell(q)\} \\
[\![\mathsf{true}]\!]^n_{\delta,r} &= \mathcal{Q} \\
[\![\neg\phi]\!]^n_{\delta,r} &= \mathcal{Q} \setminus [\![\phi]\!]^n_{\delta,-r} \\
[\![\phi_1 \wedge \phi_2]\!]^n_{\delta,r} &= [\![\phi_1]\!]^n_{\delta,r} \cap [\![\phi_2]\!]^n_{\delta,r} \\
[\![\mathsf{Pr}_{\rhd\pi}[\psi]]\!]^n_{\delta,r} &= \{q \in \mathcal{Q} \mid \mathrm{Pr}(Cyl(q) \cap [\![\psi]\!]^n_{\delta,r}) + r \cdot \delta \rhd \pi\} \\
[\![\mathsf{X}\phi]\!]^n_{\delta,r} &= \{t \mid t(1) \in [\![\phi]\!]^n_{\delta,r}\} \\
[\![\phi_1 \mathsf{U} \phi_2]\!]^n_{\delta,r} &= \{t \mid \exists i \in 0..n.\; t(i) \in [\![\phi_2]\!]^n_{\delta,r} \wedge \forall j \in 0..i-1.\; t(j) \in [\![\phi_1]\!]^n_{\delta,r}\}
\end{aligned}
$$

The semantics is mostly standard, except for $\mathsf{Pr}_{\rhd\pi}[\psi]$ and $\phi_1 \mathsf{U} \phi_2$. The semantics of $\mathsf{Pr}_{\rhd\pi}[\psi]$ adds $r \cdot \delta$ to the probability of satisfying ψ, which relaxes or strengthens (depending on r) the probability bound as needed. The semantics of $\phi_1 \mathsf{U} \phi_2$ uses the parameter n to bound the number of steps within which ϕ_2 must hold.

Our semantics enjoys monotonicity. The semantics of state and path formulae is increasing w.r.t. δ if $r = +1$, and decreasing otherwise. The semantics also increases when moving from $r = -1$ to $r = +1$.

Lemma 1 (Monotonicity). *Whenever $\delta \leq \delta'$, we have:*

$$[\![\phi]\!]^n_{\delta,+1} \subseteq [\![\phi]\!]^n_{\delta',+1} \qquad [\![\phi]\!]^n_{\delta',-1} \subseteq [\![\phi]\!]^n_{\delta,-1} \qquad [\![\phi]\!]^n_{\delta,-1} \subseteq [\![\phi]\!]^n_{\delta,+1}$$

$$[\![\psi]\!]^n_{\delta,+1} \subseteq [\![\psi]\!]^n_{\delta',+1} \qquad [\![\psi]\!]^n_{\delta',-1} \subseteq [\![\psi]\!]^n_{\delta,-1} \qquad [\![\psi]\!]^n_{\delta,-1} \subseteq [\![\psi]\!]^n_{\delta,+1}$$

Note that monotonicity does *not* hold for the parameter n, i.e. even if $n \leq n'$, we can *not* conclude $[\![\phi]\!]^n_{\delta,+1} \subseteq [\![\phi]\!]^{n'}_{\delta,+1}$. As a counterexample, let $\mathcal{Q} = \{q_0, q_1\}$, $\ell(q_0) = \emptyset$, $\ell(q_1) = \{a\}$, $\mathrm{Pr}(q_0, q_1) = \mathrm{Pr}(q_1, q_1) = 1$, and $\mathrm{Pr}(q, q') = 0$ elsewhere. Given $\phi = \mathsf{Pr}_{\leq 0}[\mathsf{true}\ \mathsf{U}\ a]$, we have $q_0 \in [\![\phi]\!]^0_{0,+1}$ since in $n = 0$ steps it is impossible to reach a state satisfying a. However, we do *not* have $q_0 \in [\![\phi]\!]^1_{0,+1}$ since in $n' = 1$ steps we always reach q_1, which satisfies a.

Example 1. We compare an ideal combination padlock to a real one from the point of view of an adversary. The ideal padlock has a single state q_{ok}, representing a closed padlock that can not be opened. Instead, the real padlock is under attack from the adversary who tries to open the padlock by repeatedly guessing its 5-digit PIN. At each step the adversary generates a (uniformly) random

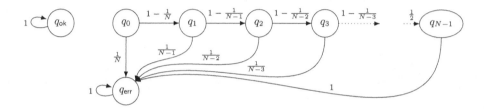

Fig. 2. A Markov chain modelling an ideal (left) and a real (right) padlock.

PIN, different from all the ones which have been attempted so far, and tries to open the padlock with it. The states of the real padlock are $q_0, \ldots, q_{N-1}$ (with $N = 10^5$), where q_i represents the situation where i unsuccessful attempts have been made, and an additional state q_{err} that represents that the padlock was opened.

Since after i attempts the adversary needs to guess the correct PIN among the $N - i$ remaining combinations, the real padlock in state q_i moves to q_{err} with probability $1/(N - i)$, and to q_{i+1} with the complementary probability.

Summing up, we simultaneously model both the ideal and real padlock as a single DTMC with the following transition probability function (see Fig. 2):

$$\begin{aligned}
&\Pr(q_{ok}, q_{ok}) = 1 \\
&\Pr(q_{err}, q_{err}) = 1 \\
&\Pr(q_i, q_{err}) = 1/(N - i) && 0 \le i < N \\
&\Pr(q_i, q_{i+1}) = 1 - 1/(N - i) && 0 \le i < N - 1 \\
&\Pr(q, q') = 0 && \text{otherwise}
\end{aligned}$$

We label the states with labels $\mathcal{L} = \{\}err$ by letting $\ell(q_{err}) = \{\}err$ and $\ell(q) = \emptyset$ for all $q \ne q_{err}$.

The PCTL formula $\phi = \Pr_{\le 0}[\text{true U err}]$ models the expected behaviour of an unbreakable padlock, requiring that the set of traces where the padlock is eventually opened has zero probability. Formally, ϕ is satisfied by state q when

$$\begin{aligned}
q \in [\![\phi]\!]^n_{\delta,+1} &\iff q \in [\![\neg\Pr_{>0}[\text{true U err}]]\!]^n_{\delta,+1} \\
&\iff q \notin [\![\Pr_{>0}[\text{true U err}]]\!]^n_{\delta,-1} \\
&\iff \neg(\Pr(Cyl(q) \cap [\![\text{true U err}]\!]^n_{\delta,-1}) - \delta > 0) \\
&\iff \Pr(Cyl(q) \cap [\![\text{true U err}]\!]^n_{\delta,-1}) \le \delta \qquad (1)
\end{aligned}$$

When $q = q_{ok}$ we have that $Cyl(q_{ok}) \cap [\![\text{true U err}]\!]^n_{\delta,-1} = \emptyset$, hence the above probability is zero, which is surely $\le \delta$. Consequently, ϕ is satisfied by the ideal padlock q_{ok}, for all $n \ge 0$ and $\delta \ge 0$.

By contrast, ϕ is not always satisfied by the real padlock $q = q_0$, since we have $q_0 \in [\![\phi]\!]^n_{\delta,+1}$ only for some values of n and δ. To show why, we start by considering some trivial cases. Choosing $\delta = 1$ makes Eq. (1) trivially true for all n. Furthermore, if we choose $n = 1$, then $Cyl(q_0) \cap [\![\text{true U err}]\!]^n_{\delta,-1} = \{q_0 q_{err}^\omega\}$

is a set of traces with probability $1/N$. Therefore, equation (1) holds only when $\delta \geq 1/N$. More in general, when $n \geq 1$, we have

$$Cyl(q_0) \cap [\![\text{true U err}]\!]_{\delta, -1}^n = \{q_0 q_{\text{err}}^\omega, \, q_0 q_1 q_{\text{err}}^\omega, \, q_0 q_1 q_2 q_{\text{err}}^\omega, \, \ldots, \, q_0 \cdots q_{n-1} q_{\text{err}}^\omega\}$$

The probability of the above set is the probability of guessing the PIN within n steps. The complementary event, i.e. not guessing the PIN for n times, has probability

$$\frac{N-1}{N} \cdot \frac{N-2}{N-1} \cdots \frac{N-n}{N-(n-1)} = \frac{N-n}{N}$$

Consequently, (1) simplifies to $n/N \leq \delta$, suggesting the least value of δ (depending on n) for which q_0 satisfies ϕ. For instance, when $n = 10^3$, this amounts to claiming that the real padlock is secure, up to an error of $\delta = n/N = 10^{-2}$.

3   Up-to-n, δ Bisimilarity

We now define a relation on states $q \sim_\delta^n q'$ that intuitively holds whenever q and q' exhibit similar behaviour for a bounded number of steps. The parameter n controls the number of steps, while δ controls the error allowed in each step. Note that since we only observe the first n steps, our notion is *inductive*, unlike unbounded bisimilarity which is co-inductive, similarly to [12].

Definition 5 (Up-to-n, δ Bisimilarity). *We define the relation $q \sim_\delta^n q'$ as follows by induction on n:*

1. *$q \sim_\delta^0 q'$ always holds*
2. *$q \sim_\delta^{n+1} q'$ holds if and only if, for all $Q \subseteq \mathfrak{Q}$:*
    (a) $\ell(q) = \ell(q')$
    (b) $\Pr(q, Q) \leq \Pr(q', \sim_\delta^n (Q)) + \delta$
    (c) $\Pr(q', Q) \leq \Pr(q, \sim_\delta^n (Q)) + \delta$

where $\sim_\delta^n (Q) = \{q' \mid \exists q \in Q. \, q \sim_\delta^n q'\}$ is the image of the set Q according to the bisimilarity relation.

We now establish two basic properties of the bisimilarity. Our notion is reflexive and symmetric, and enjoys a triangular property. Furthermore, it is monotonic on both n and δ.

Lemma 2. *The relation $\sim$ satisfies:*

$$q \sim_\delta^n q \qquad q \sim_\delta^n q' \implies q' \sim_\delta^n q \qquad q \sim_\delta^n q' \wedge q' \sim_{\delta'}^n q'' \implies q \sim_{\delta+\delta'}^n q''$$

Proof. Straightforward induction on n.   □

Lemma 3 (Monotonicity).

$$n \geq n' \wedge \delta \leq \delta' \wedge p \sim_\delta^n q \implies p \sim_{\delta'}^{n'} q$$

Example 2. We use up-to-n, δ bisimilarity to compare the behaviour of the ideal padlock q_{ok} and the real one, in any of its states, when observed for n steps. When $n = 0$ bisimilarity trivially holds, so below we only consider $n > 0$.

We start from the simplest case: bisimilarity does not hold between q_{ok} and q_{err}. Indeed, q_{ok} and q_{err} have distinct labels ($\ell(q_{ok}) = \emptyset \neq \{err\} = \ell(q_{err})$), hence we do not have $q_{ok} \sim_\delta^n q_{err}$, no matter what $n > 0$ and δ are.

We now compare q_{ok} with any q_i. When $n = 1$, both states have an empty label set, i.e. $\ell(q_{ok}) = \ell(q_i) = \emptyset$, hence they are bisimilar for any error δ. We therefore can write $q_{ok} \sim_\delta^1 q_i$ for any $\delta \geq 0$.

When $n = 2$, we need a larger error δ to make q_{ok} and q_i bisimilar. Indeed, if we perform a move from q_i, the padlock can be broken with probability $1/(N - i)$, in which case we reach q_{err}, thus violating bisimilarity. Accounting for such probability, we only obtain $q_{ok} \sim_\delta^2 q_i$ for any $\delta \geq 1/(N - i)$.

When $n = 3$, we need an even larger error δ to make q_{ok} and q_i bisimilar. Indeed, while the first PIN guessing attempt has probability $1/(N - i)$, in the second move the guessing probability increases to $1/(N-i-1)$. Choosing δ equal to the largest probability is enough to account for both moves, hence we obtain $q_{ok} \sim_\delta^3 q_i$ for any $\delta \geq 1/(N - i - 1)$. Technically, note that the denominator $N - i - 1$ might be zero, since when $i = n - 1$ the first move always guesses the PIN, and the second guess never actually happens. In such case, we instead take $\delta = 1$.

More in general, for an arbitrary $n \geq 2$, we obtain through a similar argument that $q_{ok} \sim_\delta^n q_i$ for any $\delta \geq 1/(N - i - n + 2)$. Intuitively, $\delta = 1/(N-i-n+2)$ is the probability of guessing the PIN in the last attempt (the n-th), which is the attempt having the highest success probability. Again, when the denominator $N - i - n + 2$ becomes zero (or negative), we instead take $\delta = 1$.

Note that the DTMC of the ideal and real padlocks (Example 1) has finitely many states. Our bisimilarity notion and results, however, can also deal with DTMCs with a countably infinite set of states, as we show in the next example.

Example 3. We consider an ideal system which randomly generates bit streams in a fair way. We model such a system as having two states $\{q_a, q_b\}$, with transition probabilities $\Pr(x, y) = 1/2$ for any $x, y \in \{q_a, q_b\}$, as in Fig. 1. We label state q_a with label a denoting bit 0, and state q_b with label b denoting bit 1.

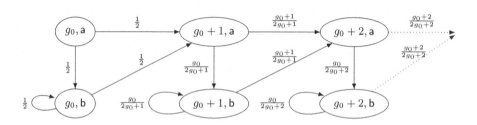

Fig. 3. A Markov chain modelling an unfair random generator of bit streams.

We compare this ideal system with a real system which generates bit streams in an unfair way. At each step, the real system draws a ball from an urn, initially having g_0 a-labelled balls and g_0 b-labelled balls. After each drawing, the ball is placed back in the urn. However, every time an a-labelled ball is drawn, an additional a-labelled ball is put in the urn, making the next drawings more biased towards a.

We model the real system using the infinite[1] set of states $\mathbb{N} \times \{a, b\}$, whose first component counts the number of a-labelled balls in the urn, and the second component is the label of the last-drawn ball. The transition probabilities are as follows, where $g_0 \in \mathbb{N}^+$ (see Fig. 3):

$$\Pr((g, x), (g + 1, a)) = g/(g + g_0)$$
$$\Pr((g, x), (g, b)) \quad = g_0/(g + g_0)$$
$$\Pr((g, x), (g', x')) \quad = 0 \qquad\qquad \text{otherwise}$$

We label each such state with its second component.

We now compare the ideal system to the real one. Intuitively, the ideal system, when started from state q_a, produces a sequence of states whose labels are uniform independent random values in $\{a, b\}$. Instead, the real system slowly becomes more and more biased towards label a. More precisely, when started from state (g_0, a), in the first drawing the next label is uniformly distributed between a and b, as in the ideal system. When the sampled state has label a, this causes the component g to be incremented, increasing the probability $g/(g + g_0)$ of sampling another a in the next steps. Indeed, the value g is always equal to g_0 plus the number of sampled a-labelled states so far.

Therefore, unlike the ideal system, on the long run the real system will visit a-labelled states with very high probability, since the g component slowly but steadily increases. While this fact makes the two systems *not* bisimilar according to the standard probabilistic bisimilarity [28], if we restrict the number of steps to $n \ll g_0$ and tolerate a small error δ, we can obtain $q_a \sim_\delta^n (g_0, a)$.

For instance, if we let $g_0 = 1000$, $n = 100$ and $\delta = 0.05$ we have $q_a \sim_\delta^n (g_0, a)$. This is because, in n steps, the first component g of a real system (g, x) will at most reach 1100, making the probability of the next step to be $(g + 1, a)$ to be at most $1100/2100 \simeq 0.523$. This differs from the ideal probability 0.5 by less than δ, hence bisimilarity holds.

4   Soundness

Our soundness theorem shows that, if we consider any state q satisfying ϕ (with steps n and error δ'), and any state q' which is bisimilar to q (with enough steps and error δ), then q' must satisfy ϕ, with the same number n of steps, at the cost of suitably increasing the error. For a fixed ϕ, the "large enough" number of steps and the increase in the error depend linearly on n.

---

[1] Modelling this behaviour inherently requires an *infinite* set of states, since each number of a-labelled balls in the urn leads to a unique transition probability function.

Theorem 1 (Soundness). *Given a formula ϕ, let $k_X = X_{max}(\phi)$ be the maximum X-nesting of ϕ, and let $k_U = U_{max}(\phi)$ be the maximum U-nesting of ϕ. Then, for all n, δ, δ' we have:*

$$\sim_\delta^{\bar{n}} \left(\llbracket \phi \rrbracket_{\delta',+1}^n\right) \subseteq \llbracket \phi \rrbracket_{\bar{n}\cdot\delta+\delta',+1}^n \qquad \text{where } \bar{n} = n \cdot k_U + k_X + 1$$

Example 4. We now apply Theorem 1 to our padlock system in the running example. To do so, we take the same formula $\phi = \mathsf{Pr}_{\leq 0}[\text{true U err}]$ of Example 1 and choose $n = 10^3$ and $\delta' = 0$. Since ϕ has only one until operator and no next operators, the value $\bar{n}$ in the statement of the theorem is $\bar{n} = 10^3 \cdot 1 + 0 + 1 = 1001$. Therefore, from Theorem 1 we obtain, for all δ:

$$\sim_\delta^{1001} \left(\llbracket \phi \rrbracket_{0,+1}^{1000}\right) \subseteq \llbracket \phi \rrbracket_{1001\cdot\delta,+1}^{1000}$$

In Example 1 we discussed how the ideal padlock q_{ok} satisfies the formula ϕ for any number of steps and any error value. In particular, choosing 1000 steps and zero error, we get $q_{\mathsf{ok}} \in \llbracket \phi \rrbracket_{0,+1}^{1000}$.

Moreover, in Example 2 we observed that states q_{ok} and q_0 are bisimilar with $\bar{n} = 1001$ and $\delta = 1/(N - 0 - \bar{n} + 2) = 1/99001$, i.e. $q_{\mathsf{ok}} \sim_\delta^{\bar{n}} q_0$.

In such case, the theorem ensures that $q_0 \in \llbracket \phi \rrbracket_{1001/99001,+1}^{1000}$, hence the real padlock can be considered unbreakable if we limit our attention to the first $n = 1000$ steps, up to an error of $1001/99001 \approx 0.010111$. Finally, we note that such error is remarkably close to the least value that would still make q_0 satisfy ϕ, which we computed in Example 1 as $n/N = 10^3/10^5 = 0.01$.

In the rest of this section, we describe the general structure of the proof in a top-down fashion, leaving the detailed proof for [5].

We prove the soundness theorem by induction on the state formula ϕ, hence we also need to deal with path formulae ψ. Note that the statement of the theorem considers the image of the semantics of the state formula ϕ w.r.t. bisimilarity (i.e., $\sim_\delta^{\bar{n}} (\llbracket \phi \rrbracket_{\delta',+1}^n)$). Analogously, to deal with path formulae we also need an analogous notion on sets of traces. To this purpose, we consider the set of traces in the definition of the semantics: $T = Cyl(p) \cap \llbracket \psi \rrbracket_{\delta,r}^n$. Then, given a state q bisimilar to p, we define the set of *pointwise bisimilar traces* starting from q, which we denote with $\tilde{R}_{\delta,q}^n(T)$. Technically, since ψ can only observe a finite portion of a trace, it is enough to define $\tilde{R}_{\delta,q}^n(\tilde{T})$ on sets of *trace fragments* $\tilde{T}$.

Definition 6. *Write $F_{q_0}^n$ for the set of all trace fragments of length n starting from q_0. Assuming $p \sim_\delta^n q$, we define $\tilde{R}_{\delta,q}^n() : \mathcal{P}(F_p^n) \to \mathcal{P}(F_q^n)$ as follows:*

$$\tilde{R}_{\delta,q}^n(\tilde{T}) = \{\tilde{u} \in F_q^n \mid \exists \tilde{t} \in \tilde{T}. \forall 0 \leq i < n. \; \tilde{t}(i) \sim_\delta^{n-i} \tilde{u}(i)\}$$

The key inequality we exploit in the proof (Lemma 4) compares the probability of a set of trace fragments $\tilde{T}$ starting from p to the one of the related set of trace fragments $\tilde{R}_{\delta,q}^m(\tilde{T})$ starting from a q bisimilar to p. We remark that the component $\bar{n}\delta$ in the error that appears in Theorem 1 results from the component $m\delta$ appearing in the following lemma.

Lemma 4. *If $p \sim_\delta^n q$ and $\tilde{T}$ is a set of trace fragments of length m, with $m \leq n$, starting from p, then:*
$$\Pr(\tilde{T}) \leq \Pr(\tilde{R}_{\delta,q}^m(\tilde{T})) + m\delta$$

Lemma 4 allows $\tilde{T}$ to be an infinite set (because the set of states $\mathcal{Q}$ can be infinite). We reduce this case to that where $\tilde{T}$ is finite. We first recall a basic calculus property: any inequality $a \leq b$ can be proved by establishing instead $a \leq b + \epsilon$ for all $\epsilon > 0$. Then, since the probability distribution of trace fragments of length m is discrete, for any $\epsilon > 0$ we can always take a finite subset of the infinite set $\tilde{T}$ whose probability differs from that of $\tilde{T}$ less than ϵ. It is therefore enough to consider the case where $\tilde{T}$ is finite, as done in the following lemma.

Lemma 5. *If $p \sim_\delta^n q$ and $\tilde{T}$ is a finite set of trace fragments of length $n > 0$ starting from p, then:*
$$\Pr(\tilde{T}) \leq \Pr(\tilde{R}_{\delta,q}^n(\tilde{T})) + n\delta$$

We prove Lemma 5 by induction on n. In the inductive step, we partition the traces according to their first move, i.e., on their next state after p (for the trace fragments in T) or q (for the bisimilar counterparts). A main challenge here is caused by the probabilities of such moves being weakly connected. Indeed, when p moves to p', we might have several states q', bisimilar to p', such that q moves to q'. Worse, when p moves to another state p'', we might find that some of the states q' we met before are also bisimilar to p''. Such overlaps make it hard to connect the probability of p moves to that of q moves.

To overcome these issues, we exploit the technical lemma below. Let set A represent the p moves, and set B represent the q moves. Then, associate to each set element $a \in A, b \in B$ a value $(f_A(a), f_B(b)$ in the lemma) representing the move probability. The lemma ensures that each $f_A(a)$ can be expressed as a weighted sum of $f_B(b)$ for the elements b bisimilar to a. Here, the weights $h(a, b)$ make it possible to relate a p move to a "weighted set" of q moves. Furthermore, the lemma ensures that no $b \in B$ has been cumulatively used for more than a unit weight ($\sum_{a \in A} h(a, b) \leq 1$).

Lemma 6. *Let A be a finite set and B be a countable set, equipped with functions $f_A : A \to \mathbb{R}_0^+$ and $f_B : B \to \mathbb{R}_0^+$. Let $g : A \to 2^B$ be such that $\sum_{b \in g(a)} f_B(b)$ converges for all $a \in A$. If, for all $A' \subseteq A$:*

$$\sum_{a \in A'} f_A(a) \leq \sum_{b \in \bigcup_{a \in A'} g(a)} f_B(b) \qquad (2)$$

then there exists $h : A \times B \to [0, 1]$ such that:

$$\forall b \in B : \sum_{a \in A} h(a, b) \leq 1 \qquad (3)$$

$$\forall A' \subseteq A : \sum_{a \in A'} f_A(a) = \sum_{a \in A'} \sum_{b \in g(a)} h(a, b) f_B(b) \qquad (4)$$

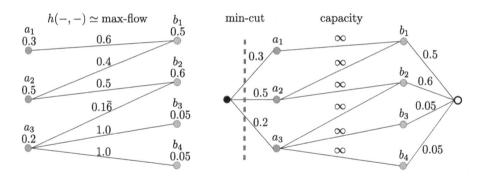

Fig. 4. Graphical representation of Lemma 6 (left) and its proof (right).

We visualize Lemma 6 in Fig. 4 through an example. The leftmost graph shows a finite set $A = \{a_1, a_2, a_3\}$ where each a_i is equipped with its associated value $f_A(a_i)$ and, similarly, a finite set $B = \{b_1, \ldots, b_4\}$ where each b_i has its own value $f_B(b_i)$. The function g is rendered as the edges of the graph, connecting each a_i with all $b_j \in g(a_i)$.

The graph satisfies the hypotheses, as one can easily verify. For instance, when $A' = \{a_1, a_2\}$ inequality (2) simplifies to $0.3 + 0.5 \leq 0.5 + 0.6$. The thesis ensures the existence of a weight function $h(-, -)$ whose values are shown in the graph on the left over each edge.

These values indeed satisfy (3): for instance, if we pick $b = b_2$ the inequality reduces to $0.5 + 0.1\bar{6} \leq 1$. Furthermore, (4) is also satisfied: for instance, taking $A' = \{a_2\}$ the equation reduces to $0.5 = 0.4 \cdot 0.5 + 0.5 \cdot 0.6$, while taking $A' = \{a_3\}$ the equation reduces to $0.2 = 0.1\bar{6} \cdot 0.6 + 1.0 \cdot 0.05 + 1.0 \cdot 0.05$.

The rightmost graph in Fig. 4 instead sketches how our proof devises the desired weight function h, by constructing a network flow problem, and exploiting the well-known min-cut/max-flow theorem [14], following the approach of [4]. We start by adding a source node to the right (white bullet in the figure), connected to nodes in B, and a sink node to the left, connected to nodes in A. We write the capacity over each edge: we use $f_B(b_i)$ for the edges connected to the source, $f_A(a_i)$ for the edges connected to the sink, and $+\infty$ for the other edges in the middle.

Then, we argue that the leftmost cut C shown in the figure is a min-cut. Intuitively, if we take another cut C' not including some edge in C, then C' has to include other edges making C' not any better than C. Indeed, C' can surely not include any edge in the middle, since they have $+\infty$ capacity. Therefore, if C' does not include an edge from some a_i to the sink, it has to include all the edges from the source to each $b_j \in g(a_i)$. In this case, hypothesis (2) ensures that doing so does not lead to a better cut. Hence, C is indeed a min-cut.

From the max-flow corresponding to the min-cut, we derive the values for $h(-, -)$. Thesis (3) follows from the flow conservation law on each b_i, and the fact that the incoming flow of each b_j from the source is bounded by the capacity of the related edge. Finally, thesis (4) follows from the flow conservation law on each a_i, and the fact that the outgoing flow of each a_i to the sink is exactly the capacity of the related edge, since the edge is on a min-cut.

5   Conclusions

In this paper we studied how the (relaxed) semantics of PCTL formulae interacts with (approximate) probabilistic bisimulation. In the regular, non relaxed case, it is well-known that when a state q satisfies a PCTL formula ϕ, then all the states that are probabilistic-bisimilar to q also satisfy ϕ ([19]). Theorem 1 extends this to the relaxed semantics, establishing that when a state q satisfies a PCTL formula ϕ up-to n steps and error δ, then all the states that are approximately probabilistic bisimilar to q with error δ' (and enough steps) also satisfy ϕ up-to n steps and suitably increased error. We provide a way to compute the new error in terms of n, δ, δ'.

Our results are a first step towards a novel approach to the security analysis of cryptographic protocols using probabilistic bisimulations. Ideally, when one is able to prove that a real-world specification of a cryptographic protocol is bisimilar to an ideal one, with an error that is asymptotically negligible as long as the number of steps is kept polynomial, then one can invoke Theorem 1 and claim that the two models satisfy the same PCTL formulae (with negligible error and a polynomial number of steps), essentially reducing the security proof of the cryptographic protocol to verifying the ideal model. A relevant line for future work is to study the applicability of our theory in this setting. Related to this, one would like to investigate proof techniques for establishing approximate bisimilarity and refinement [27].

Another possible line of research would be devising algorithms for approximate bisimilarity, along the lines of [11,13,22,34–36]. This direction, however, would require restricting our theory to finite-state systems, which contrasts with our general motivation coming from cryptographic security. Indeed, in the analysis of cryptographic protocols, security is usually to be proven against an arbitrary adversary, hence also against infinite-state ones. Hence, model-checking of finite-state systems would not directly be applicable in this setting.

Acknowledgements. Massimo Bartoletti is partially supported by Conv. Fondazione di Sardegna & Atenei Sardi projects F74I19000900007 *ADAM* and F75F21001220007 *ASTRID*. Maurizio Murgia and Roberto Zunino are partially supported by MIUR PON *Distributed Ledgers for Secure Open Communities*.

References

1. de Alfaro, L., Henzinger, T.A., Majumdar, R.: Discounting the future in systems theory. In: Baeten, J.C.M., Lenstra, J.K., Parrow, J., Woeginger, G.J. (eds.) ICALP 2003. LNCS, vol. 2719, pp. 1022–1037. Springer, Heidelberg (2003). https://doi.org/10.1007/3-540-45061-0_79
2. de Alfaro, L., Majumdar, R., Raman, V., Stoelinga, M.: Game refinement relations and metrics. Log. Methods Comput. Sci. 4(3), 1–28 (2008)

3. Bacci, G., Bacci, G., Larsen, K.G., Mardare, R., Tang, Q., van Breugel, F.: Computing probabilistic bisimilarity distances for probabilistic automata. Log. Methods Comput. Sci. **17**(1), 9:1-9:36 (2021)
4. Baier, C.: Algorithmic verification methods for probabilistic systems. Habilitation Thesis, Universität Mannheim (1998). https://www.inf.tu-dresden.de/content/institutes/thi/algi/publikationen/texte/15_98.pdf
5. Bartoletti, M., Murgia, M., Zunino, R.: A sound up-to-n,δ bisimilarity for PCTL. CoRR abs/2111.03117 (2021)
6. Bian, G., Abate, A.: On the relationship between bisimulation and trace equivalence in an approximate probabilistic context. In: Esparza, J., Murawski, A.S. (eds.) FoSSaCS 2017. LNCS, vol. 10203, pp. 321–337. Springer, Heidelberg (2017). https://doi.org/10.1007/978-3-662-54458-7_19
7. van Breugel, F.: Probabilistic bisimilarity distances. ACM SIGLOG News **4**(4), 33–51 (2017)
8. van Breugel, F., Hermida, C., Makkai, M., Worrell, J.: An accessible approach to behavioural pseudometrics. In: Caires, L., Italiano, G.F., Monteiro, L., Palamidessi, C., Yung, M. (eds.) ICALP 2005. LNCS, vol. 3580, pp. 1018–1030. Springer, Heidelberg (2005). https://doi.org/10.1007/11523468_82
9. van Breugel, F., Sharma, B., Worrell, J.: Approximating a behavioural pseudometric without discount for probabilistic systems. Log. Methods Comput. Sci. **4**(2) (2008). https://doi.org/10.2168/LMCS-4(2:2)2008
10. van Breugel, F., Worrell, J.: A behavioural pseudometric for probabilistic transition systems. Theor. Comput. Sci. **331**(1), 115–142 (2005). https://doi.org/10.1016/j.tcs.2004.09.035
11. van Breugel, F., Worrell, J.: The complexity of computing a bisimilarity pseudometric on probabilistic automata. In: van Breugel, F., Kashefi, E., Palamidessi, C., Rutten, J. (eds.) Horizons of the Mind. A Tribute to Prakash Panangaden. LNCS, vol. 8464, pp. 191–213. Springer, Cham (2014). https://doi.org/10.1007/978-3-319-06880-0_10
12. Castiglioni, V., Gebler, D., Tini, S.: Logical characterization of bisimulation metrics. In: Workshop on Quantitative Aspects of Programming Languages and Systems (QAPL), EPTCS, vol. 227, pp. 44–62 (2016). https://doi.org/10.4204/EPTCS.227.4
13. Chen, D., van Breugel, F., Worrell, J.: On the complexity of computing probabilistic bisimilarity. In: Birkedal, L. (ed.) FoSSaCS 2012. LNCS, vol. 7213, pp. 437–451. Springer, Heidelberg (2012). https://doi.org/10.1007/978-3-642-28729-9_29
14. Dantzig, G.B., Fulkerson, D.R.: On the Max Flow Min Cut Theorem of Networks. RAND Corporation, Santa Monica, CA (1955)
15. Deng, Y., Chothia, T., Palamidessi, C., Pang, J.: Metrics for action-labelled quantitative transition systems. Electron. Notes Theor. Comput. Sci. **153**(2), 79–96 (2006). https://doi.org/10.1016/j.entcs.2005.10.033
16. Desharnais, J., Edalat, A., Panangaden, P.: Bisimulation for labelled Markov processes. Inf. Comput. **179**(2), 163–193 (2002). https://doi.org/10.1006/inco.2001.2962
17. Desharnais, J., Gupta, V., Jagadeesan, R., Panangaden, P.: Metrics for labeled Markov systems. In: Baeten, J.C.M., Mauw, S. (eds.) CONCUR 1999. LNCS, vol. 1664, pp. 258–273. Springer, Heidelberg (1999). https://doi.org/10.1007/3-540-48320-9_19
18. Desharnais, J., Gupta, V., Jagadeesan, R., Panangaden, P.: Metrics for labelled Markov processes. Theor. Comput. Sci. **318**(3), 323–354 (2004). https://doi.org/10.1016/j.tcs.2003.09.013

19. Desharnais, J., Gupta, V., Jagadeesan, R., Panangaden, P.: Weak bisimulation is sound and complete for pCTL*. Inf. Comput. **208**(2), 203–219 (2010). https://doi.org/10.1016/j.ic.2009.11.002

20. Desharnais, J., Laviolette, F., Tracol, M.: Approximate analysis of probabilistic processes: Logic, simulaiton and games. In: Quantitative Evaluaiton of Systems (QEST), pp. 264–273. IEEE Computer Society (2008). https://doi.org/10.1109/QEST.2008.42

21. D'Innocenzo, A., Abate, A., Katoen, J.: Robust PCTL model checking. In: Dang, T., Mitchell, I.M. (eds.) Hybrid Systems: Computation and Control (HSCC), pp. 275–286. ACM (2012). https://doi.org/10.1145/2185632.2185673

22. Fu, H.: Computing game metrics on Markov decision processes. In: Czumaj, A., Mehlhorn, K., Pitts, A., Wattenhofer, R. (eds.) ICALP 2012. LNCS, vol. 7392, pp. 227–238. Springer, Heidelberg (2012). https://doi.org/10.1007/978-3-642-31585-5_23

23. Furber, R., Mardare, R., Mio, M.: Probabilistic logics based on riesz spaces. Log. Methods Comput. Sci. **16**(1) (2020). https://doi.org/10.23638/LMCS-16(1:6)2020

24. Giacalone, A., Jou, C., Smolka, S.A.: Algebraic reasoning for probabilistic concurrent systems. In: Broy, M., Jones, C.B. (eds.) Programming concepts and methods: Proceedings of the IFIP Working Group 2.2, 2.3 Working Conference on Programming Concepts and Methods, pp. 443–458. North-Holland (1990)

25. Hansson, H., Jonsson, B.: A logic for reasoning about time and reliability. Formal Aspects Comput. **6**(5), 512–535 (1994). https://doi.org/10.1007/BF01211866

26. Hermanns, H., Parma, A., Segala, R., Wachter, B., Zhang, L.: Probabilistic logical characterization. Inf. Comput. **209**(2), 154–172 (2011). https://doi.org/10.1016/j.ic.2010.11.024

27. Jonsson, B., Larsen, K.G.: Specification and refinement of probabilistic processes. In: IEEE Symp. on Logic in Computer Science (LICS), pp. 266–277. IEEE Computer Society Press (1991)

28. Larsen, K.G., Skou, A.: Bisimulation through probabilistic testing. In: ACM Symposium on Principles of Programming Languages (POPL), pp. 344–352. ACM Press (1989). https://doi.org/10.1145/75277.75307

29. Larsen, K.G., Skou, A.: Bisimulation through probabilistic testing. Inf. Comput. **94**(1), 1–28 (1991). https://doi.org/10.1016/0890-5401(91)90030-6

30. Mio, M.: Upper-expectation bisimilarity and Łukasiewicz μ-calculus. In: Muscholl, A. (ed.) FoSSaCS 2014. LNCS, vol. 8412, pp. 335–350. Springer, Heidelberg (2014). https://doi.org/10.1007/978-3-642-54830-7_22

31. Mio, M.: Riesz modal logic with threshold operators. In: Dawar, A., Grädel, E. (eds.) ACM/IEEE Symposium on Logic in Computer Science (LICS), pp. 710–719. ACM (2018). https://doi.org/10.1145/3209108.3209118

32. Mio, M., Simpson, A.: Łukasiewicz μ-calculus. Fundam. Informaticae **150**(3–4), 317–346 (2017). https://doi.org/10.3233/FI-2017-1472

33. Song, L., Zhang, L., Godskesen, J.C., Nielson, F.: Bisimulations meet PCTL equivalences for probabilistic automata. Logical Methods Comput. Sci. **9**(2) (2013). https://doi.org/10.2168/LMCS-9(2:7)2013

34. Tang, Q., van Breugel, F.: Computing probabilistic bisimilarity distances via policy iteration. In: International Conference on Concurrency Theory (CONCUR). LIPIcs, vol. 59, pp. 22:1–22:15. Schloss Dagstuhl - Leibniz-Zentrum für Informatik (2016). https://doi.org/10.4230/LIPIcs.CONCUR.2016.22

35. Tang, Q., van Breugel, F.: Algorithms to compute probabilistic bisimilarity distances for labelled markov chains. In: International Conference on Concurrency Theory (CONCUR). LIPIcs, vol. 85, pp. 27:1–27:16. Schloss Dagstuhl - Leibniz-Zentrum für Informatik (2017). https://doi.org/10.4230/LIPIcs.CONCUR.2017.27
36. Tang, Q., van Breugel, F.: Deciding probabilistic bisimilarity distance one for labelled Markov chains. In: Chockler, H., Weissenbacher, G. (eds.) CAV 2018. LNCS, vol. 10981, pp. 681–699. Springer, Cham (2018). https://doi.org/10.1007/978-3-319-96145-3_39

Collective Adaptive Systems and Aggregate Computing

Extensible 3D Simulation of Aggregated Systems with FCPP

Giorgio Audrito$^{(\boxtimes)}$ ⓘ, Luigi Rapetta, and
Gianluca Torta ⓘ

Università Degli Studi di Torino,
Torino, Italy
{giorgio.audrito,
gianluca.torta}@unito.it,
luigirapetta@libero.it

Abstract. Programming massively distributed systems in unreliable
environments poses several non-trivial challenges. Such systems need
to be able to adapt and self-organise, and special algorithms need to
be developed for this purpose. In particular, simulators provide an irre-
placeable tool for the development process.

Among other tools for programming self-organizing systems, the
FieldCalc++ (FCPP, implementing the field calculus in C++) library
stands out for its efficiency, portability and extensibility, and its support
for aggregate programs. On the other hand, the simulator's output was
limited up to now to numeric statistical information, reducing the user's
ability to understand and interact with the system under simulation.

In this paper, we present a novel graphical user interface for FCPP,
allowing for a real-time, interactive and three-dimensional visualization
of the simulated system. Through this interface, the user can control the
simulation flow, visualize summary information of the network at a single glance, and inspect detailed information via auxiliary windows. The
interface is designed to require minimal effort from the end user for its
setup, and can be further extended for increased interaction.

Keywords: Distributed computing · Aggregate computing ·
Toolchains

1 Introduction

Human environments are increasingly populated by situated and mobile computing devices (phones, watches, vehicles, sensors, smart home appliances), and the
problem of their coordination into meaningful distributed systems is therefore
growing in importance as well as in complexity.

Implementing such distributed systems by individual programming of every
single node has become prohibitively costly and error prone, driving the search
for solutions increasing the autonomy of computing systems while reducing their

© IFIP International Federation for Information Processing 2022
M. H. ter Beek and M. Sirjani (Eds.): COORDINATION 2022, LNCS 13271, pp. 55–71, 2022.
https://doi.org/10.1007/978-3-031-08143-9_4

overall complexity. In particular, the class of *Collective Adaptive Systems* (CAS), which are able to autonomously adapt their internal structure and function in response to external events, has the potential to meet the coordination challenges outlined above.

However, programming CAS in an effective way is in itself a non-trivial task. *Aggregate Programming* (AP) [10] is drawing an increasing attention as an effective approach to program distributed, situated CAS, based on the functional composition of reusable blocks of collective behaviour, with the goal of effectively achieving resilient complex behaviours in dynamic networks, integrating and surpassing traditional multi-agent planning techniques [3,4]. Functional composition is key in enabling the study of properties like self-stabilisation [25] and density independence [11] on complex CAS starting from simple building blocks (e.g., broadcast, collective distance estimation and data aggregation).

Few different implementations of the AP paradigm exist: the Java external DSL Protelis [23], the Scala library Scafi [26] and the C++ library FieldCalc++ (FCPP) [2]. Among them, the latter stands out for its portability and high efficiency, obtained without sacrificing ease of use and extensibility. The main strenghts of FCPP are its component-based architecture, which enables extensibility, the widespread support for C++ on target architectures, which allows deployments on most systems (including microcontrollers), and its speed and memory requirements compared to the other JVM-based implementations.

A shortcoming of the simulation support of FCPP has been up to now the lack of a graphical interface. While it was possible to configure scenarios with hundreds of nodes, and run an AP program on each of them while keeping track of aggregate statistics on resulting node attributes, the dynamic evolution of such systems could not be visualized. However, such a visualization is often very important to get an intuitive idea of the system behavior, especially for debugging and spotting unexpected global emergent behaviors.

In this paper, we present an extension to FCPP defining new components for the 3D visualization of simulations, also providing a basic support to the simulation of environments with obstacles. Through the new interface, the user can control the simulation flow, visualize summary information of the network at a single glance, and inspect detailed information via auxiliary windows. Interestingly, as we shall demonstrate below, the new components perfectly fit within the existing architecture, showing that the component-based approach adopted for FCPP does indeed make it easier to extend it with new functionalities. To showcase the possible applications, we conclude the paper presenting four new case studies that have been added to the FCPP sample project to demonstrate the new features. In order to increase the accessibility of the tool, a video demo of the FCPP GUI has been recently made available,[1] together with a quick-start guide[2] and other resources.[3]

---

[1] https://www.youtube.com/watch?v=zWsNqJMVxKs.

[2] https://github.com/fcpp/fcpp-exercises#readme.

[3] Accessible starting from: https://fcpp.github.io.

The paper is structured as follows. Section 2 presents the background, including the FCPP and OpenGL libraries. Section 3 discusses the extension of FCPP for 3D simulations. Section 4 shows four case studies demonstrating the new features. Finally, Sect. 5 concludes with plans of future development.

2 Background

2.1 Collective Adaptive Systems

Collective Adaptive Systems (CAS) are collections of intelligent agents able to automatically change their internal structure (i.e., the connections between their components) and/or their function in response to external inputs.

Due to such characteristics, programming CAS presents peculiar challenges, that must be addressed in ways that depend on the given context and goals. At a sufficient level of abstraction, the various approaches can be classified in four categories [9]:

- methods that abstract devices and/or networks, such as TOTA [20] and MapReduce [16];
- methods that provide geometrical or topological pattern languages, such as the *self-healing geometries* in [18];
- methods that provide languages for information retrieval and routing, such as TinyLime [15];
- general space-time computing models, such as StarLisp [19] and Aggregate Programming [10].

2.2 Aggregate Programming

Among the approaches previously mentioned, in this paper we focus on *Aggregate Programming* (AP). AP is characterized by the definition of a single program that is executed asynchronously in each node of a whole network. The networked system is thus modelled as a single aggregate machine, which manipulates collections of distributed data called *computational fields*.

Communication between devices is realised at low level through proximity-based broadcasts, which at a higher level generate *neighbouring fields*, i.e., maps from neighbour device identifiers to their relative values. Neighbouring fields cannot be accessed directly; instead, they are manipulated through "map" operations that produce a new field, and "fold" operations that synthesize a single value from a field.

Such aggregate computations can be expressed using the *Field Calculus* (FC) [8], which is a minimal universal language based on the functional paradigm. FC provides the necessary mechanism to express and functionally compose distributed computations neglecting low-level aspects such as synchronisation, delivery of messages between devices, and even the number and physical positions of the devices in the network. An FC program P running on every device δ of the network, executes the following steps periodically:

- the device perceives contextual information, i.e.:
  - data provided by local sensors,
  - local (state) information stored in the previous round,
  - messages received from neighbours after the previous round.
  As said above, the latter are made available to the program P as a *neighbouring field* ϕ;
- the device evaluates the program P considering as input the contextual information gathered as described above. Note, therefore, that P is not only executed by each device, but also at each round: when needed, different behaviors are obtained by branching statements in P based on the input context;
- the result of the local computation is stored locally (as local state), sent to neighbours and may produce outputs fed to local actuators.

The above steps, executed across space by different devices, and across time at different rounds, give rise to a global behaviour at the overall network-level [25] that can thus be viewed as a single aggregate machine.

While the neighbouring relation is usually based on physical spatial proximity, it is perfectly possible to define it as a logical relationship, for example as a master-slave relationship among devices independently of their position.

2.3   FCPP

FCPP (FieldCalc++) is a library written in the C++ language that implements the Field Calculus (FC). Given the goal of being able to deploy FCPP on as many platforms as possible, C++ has been chosen as the implementation language not only for its power and efficiency, but also because it can target most platforms, from microcontrollers to GPUs. Beside providing an internal DSL for expressing FC programs within C++, the library provides several features:

- a component-based software architecture, suitable to be extended and customised for different application scenarios, such as deployments on IoT devices, simulation, and HPC;
- an efficient implementation exploiting compile-time optimisations through advanced template programming [1];
- support for parallel execution of a simulated system or self-organising cloud application;
- tools for executing FC programs on simulations of distributed systems.

The only scenario that is currently fully supported by the implemented components of FCPP is the simulation of distributed systems. Compared to the alternative implementations of FC (Protelis [23] and Scafi [26]), it features additional simulation capabilities (3D environments, basic physics, probabilistic wireless connection models), with a significant reduction of the simulation cost, and a corresponding speedup of the development and test of new distributed algorithms. Moreover, thanks to the extensible architecture, it is much easier to address additional scenarios than with previous FC implementations. Two such scenarios are of particular practical interest:

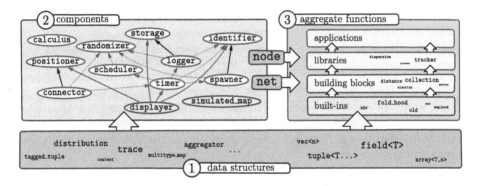

Fig. 1. Representation of the software architecture of FCPP as the combination of three main layers: *data structures* for both other layers, and *components* which provide node and network abstractions to *aggregate functions*. Components are categorized as general purpose (cyan), used across different domains, and simulation-specific (violet), with variations for different domains. The new *displayer* and *simulated map* (simulation-specific) components are highlighted in magenta. Dependencies between them can be either *hard* (solid), for which the pointed component is required as an ancestor of the other; or *soft* (dotted), for which the pointed component is not required, but if present, it should be an ancestor of the other component.

- deployments on microcontroller-based systems typically used in IoT applications, which have limited computing power and memory;
- deployments as self-organising cloud applications, which require fine-grained parallelism in order to be able to scale with the resources allocated in the cloud.

Prototype components addressing these scenarios are currently under development, and are already available in the main FCPP distribution.

Figure 1 shows the architecture of the FCPP library, partitioned in three main conceptual layers:

1. *C++ data structures of general use.* Some are needed by the components of the second layer either for internal implementation or for the external specification of their options; other data structures are designed for implementing the aggregate functions of the third layer.
2. *components.* They define the abstractions for representing single devices (*nodes*) and the overall network (*net*), which is fundamental in scenarios where there is no physical network, such as simulations and cloud-oriented applications. It is worth noting that, in an application based on FCPP, the two types node and net are obtained through template programming by combining a chosen sequence of components [21], each of them providing a needed functionality, in a *mixin*-like fashion [12,13]. The role of the component system is thus that of enabling the reuse of specific functionalities across different application scenarios.

3. *aggregate functions.* Actual implementations of FC programs, as templated functions with a `node` parameter; note that also these functions are partitioned in several layers, starting from the built-ins that implement the core of FC, up to the applications written by the users of the FCPP library.

Figure 1 shows the dependencies between components, i.e., whether a component needs another component as its ancestor in the mixin composition. The number of such dependencies has been kept as low as possible, and it is always possible to substitute a "required" component for another offering an analogous interface in the composition.

2.4 OpenGL

OpenGL is an API standard for the development and maintenance of real-time graphical applications. As a standard, it defines the high-level output of a set of functions with a given signature, related to graphical rendering and processing of the relevant data structures. The implementations reside into the graphical drivers, developed for a specific set of GPUs.

Internally, OpenGL is structured as a state machine whose state is called *context*, and consists of a set of variables and settings influencing the rendering output. The standard offers both functions for modifying the context, and others relying on it. OpenGL applications can define and maintain multiple contexts, possibly assigning them to different threads: one thread can be bound to only one context at a time. Allocated resources can be bound to a context.

The rendering process in OpenGL is defined by a pipeline, with the main goals of *(i)* transforming a set of vertex coordinates from a 3D space to a 2D one; and *(ii)* transforming such 2D coordinates into actual pixels displayed on the screen. The steps of the pipeline consist of small programs called *shaders*, which can be executed in parallel SIMD[4] steps on the GPU. The programmer can define the behaviour of three shaders of the pipeline: *(i)* vertex shader; *(ii)* geometry shader; *(iii)* fragment shader. The first and the third are crucial for defining the behaviour of an OpenGL application, while the second one is optional. The vertex shader transforms 3D vertex coordinates through several coordinate spaces applying transformation matrices. The geometry shader processes a geometric primitive to be rendered (e.g., a triangle) by injecting additional vertices into it, generating additional primitives. Then, the *rasterization* process maps the transformed vertices into pixels to display: such process generates *fragments*, data collections representing the output of (part of) the associated pixels. The fragment shader processes these generated fragments by calculating their output colors, inducing the final colors of the corresponding pixels.

---

[4] Acronym for *Same Instruction, Multiple Data.*

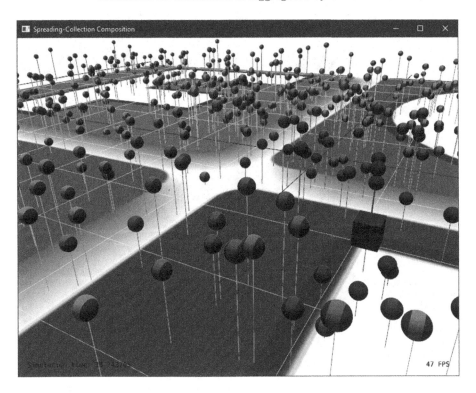

Fig. 2. Screenshot of the "spreading-collection" case study.

3 Extending FCPP with a Graphical User Interface

3.1 Features

FCPP as presented in [2] already supported the execution of simulated networks with 3D physics and running aggregate programs. However, the simulation results were only made available through statistical summaries of numerical values across the network, in the form of text data files, that could then be turned into plots. This limited the possible user interactions with the system, making tasks such as algorithm design and bug detection harder.

The introduction of the three-dimensional GUI drastically improves the interaction between the final user and FCPP's simulation toolset. The interface allows the user to visualize the simulated state of the network as a 3D scene (Fig. 2 and 3), that the user can navigate, zoom and rotate through. The 3D scene updates in real-time with the progress of the simulation, always displaying its current state. The GUI also allows for the tuning of the simulation speed, which can be paused, sped up or slowed down. Additional information is displayed within the main rendering window, such as the elapsed simulation time and the current

Fig. 3. Screenshot of the "channel-broadcast" case study. The grid and the pins are toggled off, while links to neighbours are displayed.

FPS^5 value. The three-dimensional scene displays two main actors: *(i)* the grid plane; *(ii)* the nodes.

The grid plane is included to provide a reliable spatial reference, and consists of a plane placed along the x and y axes with a grid pattern of lines, possibly customized with a texture providing an additional spatial reference for the nodes to be compared with.[6] The texture information can also be accessed within the simulated program, to model interaction with obstacles thereby depicted. The grid is automatically calibrated so that the step represents a power of 10 and a reasonable amount of lines are drawn, and can be toggled off (Fig. 3) in order to suppress visual noise if needed.

The nodes are a graphical representation of the devices forming the distributed network, with an appearance that represents summary information on the distributed computation, allowing to get a sense of the status of the whole network in a single glance. Nodes are characterized by a position along the three

---

[5] Acronym for *Frames Per Second.*

[6] For instance, while simulating the flying patterns of a group of drones, a top-view of a city could be applied on the grid plane in order to compare the positions of the drones with the city blocks.

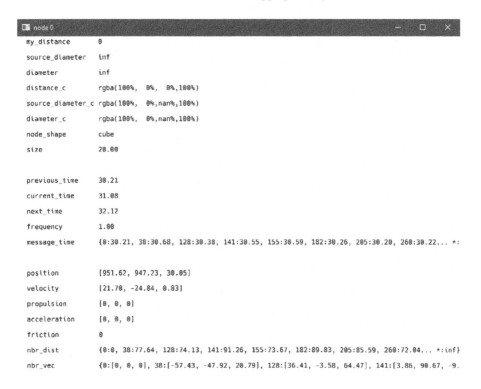

Fig. 4. Screenshot of a monitoring window.

orthogonal axes, colored sections, a shape and a size. The position along the z axis can be emphasized by a pin starting from the center of the node and ending on the grid plane (Fig. 2). A node can support up to three colored sections (Fig. 2), each displaying a custom color defined by the programmer, which can change during the simulation. The node's shape is taken from a predefined set of three-dimensional models, which are scaled by the node's size value, and also both the shape and size can be set by the programmer and can change in real-time. Additionally, the GUI allows to toggle the visualization of the links of a node with its own neighbours (Fig. 3), explicating the network topology induced by message exchanges among devices.

The summary information given by the grid and nodes is complemented by the possibility of accessing detailed information for any particular node. By clicking on a node of choice, the user opens a new monitoring window (Fig. 4) displaying a customizable list of values for the selected node (defined through the *storage* component of FCPP). The list updates in real-time, allowing the user to monitor the evolution of such values together with the overall graphical representation. Hovered or selected nodes are emphasized, and any number of nodes can be selected at once. Selection of nodes can be toggled off, informing the user of the deactivation by changing the cursor's shape.

Overall, the presented features allow the programmer to better test and debug distributed applications, therefore promoting a better design process through an enhanced human-computer interaction. Furthermore, as we shall see in the next section, the introduction of the GUI into FCPP projects comes with a minimal cost for the end-user.

3.2   Architecture

The 3D GUI is managed by the *displayer* component, which is dedicated to update the rendering window, to regulate simulation speed and to manage user's input and monitoring windows. As shown in Fig. 1, the displayer component (violet) has hard dependencies with other simulation-specific components: *(i)* positioner (to access positions to be represented); *(ii)* storage (to access detailed values for nodes); *(iii)* timer (to access time information); *(iv)* identifier (to access the nodes themselves). Just by adding a displayer component into an FCPP project (a one-word edit), the GUI is immediately available and already able to show the nodes' positions, connections and detailed information. With minimal effort, the representation can then be enhanced by adding a few lines to regulate the colors, shape and sizes of nodes into the program run by the nodes.

In case interaction with obstacles depicted in the texture is needed, a further *simulated map* component is provided, which provides nodes with information on their surroundings (in terms of obstacle presence, closest obstacles and empty spaces). This information can be used by library aggregate functions to mimic repulsive elastic forces, preventing nodes from crossing obstacles.

During an FCPP simulation, simulated actions are processed as *events* issued by the various components at given simulated times. The displayer follows the general execution path, by defining periodic update events which first initialize necessary attributes, and then handle: *(i)* finding the node under the cursor through auxiliary raycast operations; *(ii)* rendering the nodes, the plane and 2D information text; *(iii)* managing input events; *(iv)* managing monitoring windows; *(v)* swapping framebuffers.[7] The displayer component makes use of a few auxiliary classes: *(i)* *renderer* (abstraction of a rendering window which can be invoked to render on the relative window); *(ii)* *info_window* (abstraction of a monitoring window); *(iii)* *camera* (needed to define and manipulate the point of view from which the scene is rendered).

A renderer object has at its disposal both shared and window-specific resources. Among the latter there are a camera object and the context related to the window. The displayer owns an instance of the renderer and, since such renderer is the first one to get created, it allocates all the shared resources. Thus, such renderer is considered *master*, while other *slave* renderers will need to access the shared resources through the master. When clicking on a node, the displayer creates a new *info_window* instance which is handled by a secondary thread. An *info_window* object owns a (slave) renderer as well, which accesses the shared resources through the master renderer.

---

[7] The *framebuffer* is a buffer storing frames to be rendered, and swapping such buffer basically means to display its content on screen.

3.3 Technical Challenges

While realising the GUI for FCPP, several challenges were identified that needed to be addressed:

1. The graphic libraries used should be as *portable* as possible, in order not to reduce the overall portability of the FCPP tool;
2. The graphical representation should be sufficiently *performing*, lightweight and optimised to be able to process in real-time even large-scale simulated networks, minimising the overhead on the simulation itself;
3. The GUI code should *integrate* into the FCPP component structure, so that the mere addition and removal of a dedicated displayer component should enable and disable the user interface, without further actions needed on user code;
4. The *representation* should allow the recognition of high-level patterns in the whole network, as well as detailed data on individual nodes;
5. The interface should allow *interaction* with the simulation flow;
6. The GUI should be compatible with 2D as well as 3D spaces, and be compatible with spaces with obstacles as well.

In order to address portability (1), efficiency (2) and 3D readiness (6), OpenGL was chosen as reference graphical library, due to its low-level and portable nature (through the CMake build tool, as well as WebGL-WebAssembly for browser applications). Significant effort was spent on optimising the performances, with a strong impact, using strategies such as adaptive frame-rates (for the main window based on CPU availability, and for info windows based on the updates of the corresponding node), multi-threading (between the main window and info windows) and indexing/buffering of shapes of general use. Such fine-grained optimisation would not have been possible with higher-level frameworks such as the *Unreal Engine*. With the optimisations, the GUI feels responsive and efficient, though still coming with a non-negligible overhead. On a reference computer,[8] the GUI is able to smoothly process in real-time up to ≈ 20 rounds/sec of the *spreading collection* case study; while a batch execution is able to process up to ≈ 45 rounds/sec of the same code.

In order to address integration (3), a displayer component was developed, with a minimal node structure (caching node positions before draws, updating some display information after rounds, managing node highlight, and offering a draw method), and a more complex net structure (managing frame refreshes, keyboard and mouse inputs, and auxiliary windows). The data to be displayed was obtained through the existing *positioner* (for node positions) and *storage* (for node data) components, in order to further the integration with existing code. In order to allow the representation (4) requirements on whole networks, while preserving integration (3), options were provided to specify storage fields where node color, shape and size information could be written by aggregate programs and then read by the displayer component. Similarly, for individual nodes a fully

---

[8] MacBook Pro, 2.4GHz intel Core i9 8-core, 32GB RAM, Intel UHD Graphics 630.

template-based introspection mechanism was written to automatically extract a readable representation of all storage contents in info windows.

Finally, in order to address interaction (5), keyboard shortcuts were defined to regulate the simulation flow, inspired from video playback applications, along further shortcuts to regulate space navigation (also assisted by mouse input). In order to address the presence of obstacles (6), we included the possibility of loading a custom texture for the environment, while also providing an additional *simulated map* component to access texture information and detect nearby obstacles.

3.4   Comparison with Protelis and Scafi

The other two languages for the development of AP systems, Protelis [23] and Scafi [26], both rely on the external simulator Alchemist [22] for their simulation capabilities. Alchemist supports a number of features similar to the ones developed into the new graphical interface for FCPP: the control of the simulation flow, a graphical visualization of the status of the overall network through colors and shapes, and access to detailed information on nodes through separate windows. However, Alchemist is only restricted to 2D simulations, and no support for physics is available. Furthermore, the performance increase of FCPP can be seen in the graphical interface as well: larger networks can be visualized in real-time, given the performance limits of a machine at hand.

It is worth noting that several multi-robot simulators exist, that support features such as the ones described here, and possibly more, e.g. [17,24]. Such tools, however, lack the integration with the FCPP library that allows the simulation of Aggregate Programming systems.

4   Case Studies

The FCPP distribution comes with a sample project,[9] as a reference to ease the setup of new projects. With the introduction of the GUI, the build system had to be moved from Bazel to CMake, and two additional graphical simulations were added to the sample project (which previously consisted of a single batch simulation), described in the following. In both simulations, devices move through waypoints randomly chosen in a parallelepiped area, and the connection topology is driven by the physical distance between the devices.

4.1   Composition of Spreading and Collection Blocks

The first example is an implementation of a typical monitoring application in aggregate computing. Such an application is designed by functionally combining few basic steps, which are provided by the FCPP coordination library: *(i)*

---

[9] https://github.com/fcpp/fcpp-sample-project, non-retractable version evaluated with this paper: https://doi.org/10.5281/zenodo.6480037.

```
MAIN() {
  // random walk into a given rectangle with given speed
  rectangle_walk(CALL, make_vec(0,0,0), make_vec(side,side,height),
                       node.storage(tags::speed{}), 1);
  // selects a different source every 50 simulated seconds
  bool is_source = select_source(CALL, 50);
  // calculate distances from the source
  double dist = abf_distance(CALL, is_source);
  // collect maximum finite distance (diameter) back towards the source
  double sdiam = mp_collection(CALL,dist,dist,0.0,[](double x, double y){
    x = isfinite(x) ? x : 0;
    y = isfinite(y) ? y : 0;
    return max(x, y);
  }, [](double x, int){
    return x;
  });
  // broadcast the diameter computed in the source to the whole network
  double diam = broadcast(CALL, dist, sdiam);
  // store relevant values in the node storage
  node.storage(tags::calc_distance{}) = dist;
  ...
}
```

Fig. 5. Code snippet of the *spreading collection* case study.

distance computation from a selected source device; *(ii)* aggregation of the data distributed across the network, through paths of communication descending the distances previously computed; *(iii)* broadcasting the overall result computed in the source device to the whole network. In this specific example, the aggregation was set to approximate the network diameter. Figure 5 presents a code snippet of this simple aggregate program.

In this example, a common header file defines the aggregate program, together with general simulation settings. This same file is included by three different execution targets: one running a single batch execution, another running a single GUI execution, and the last running a batch of multiple simulations. In particular, the single GUI execution only differs from the batch execution by substituting `batch_simulator` with `interactive_simulator` in line 14 of the relevant cpp files, demonstrating how the GUI can be easily integrated into existing FCPP projects.

Figure 2 presents a screenshot of this application. The source node is highlighted by representing it as a larger cube. Other nodes are displayed as spheres with bands of color: the hue of the central band displays the distance approximated at step *(i)*, while the hue of the lateral bands displays the estimated diameter resulting from step *(iii)*. Note that central bands of the nodes closer to the source are more reddish, becoming more yellowish (then greenish, etc.) as they are farther.

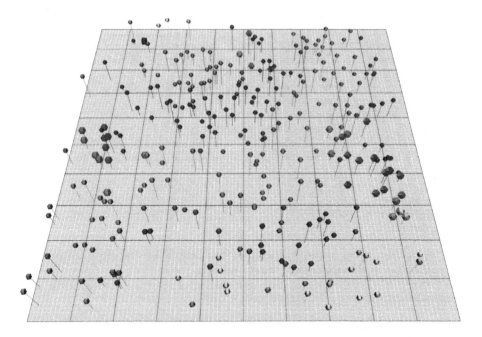

Fig. 6. Screenshot of the "message-dispatch" case study.

4.2 Broadcast Through a Self-organising Channel

The second example presents another typical aggregate routine: selection of a communication channel between a source and a destination, and broadcast of data through it. The channel is selected using the definition of ellipse as a locus of points, so that: *(i)* distances d_{is}, d_{id} from the source and destination devices are computed in every device i; *(ii)* the distance d_{ds} between source and destination is made available in the network through a broadcast; *(iii)* the channel area is then defined as those devices i such that $d_{is} + d_{id} \leq d_{ds} + w$, where w is a width parameter tuning the minor axis of the ellipse; *(iv)* data can then be broadcast in this restricted selected area. As before, all of these basic steps are available in the FCPP coordination library.

Figure 3 presents a screenshot of this application. The source and destination devices are highlighted as larger tetrahedra. Devices outside of the communication channel are represented as white spheres, and the channel itself is visualised as colored icosahedra, with the color hue tuned to represent their distance from the source and destination.

4.3 Peer-to-peer Message Dispatch

The third example presents a further archetypal task in distributed systems: peer-to-peer dispatch of messages. This is accomplished through *aggregate processes* [14], that expand guided by an adaptive spanning tree structure. Figure 6

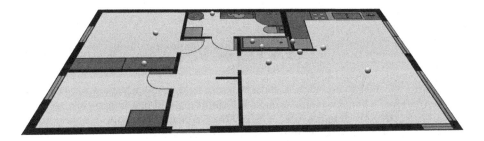

Fig. 7. Screenshot of the "apartment-walk" case study.

presents a screenshot of this application. The root of the spanning tree is represented as a larger cube (top-left). Nodes are colored according to their distance from the root in their central band. Nodes involved in message exchanges are larger, and their sides are colored with a color generated from the message. Three messages are currently being dispatched: one in light blue (right), another in red (top), and a last one in dark blue (left).

4.4   Random Walk in an Apartment

The fourth and last example presents a minimal scenario with obstacle avoidance. Figure 7 presents a screenshot of this application. In this scenario, 10 people (tan pins) are randomly moving through rooms in an apartment, while bouncing off walls (black areas), furniture (dark grey areas), and other people; being restricted to the free floor area (light blue).

5   Conclusion

In this paper, we presented a graphical user interface for the FCPP simulator. The GUI allows to control the simulation flow and to visualize both summary information of the network, through colors and shapes, and detailed information of individual devices, through auxiliary windows. The interface is implemented as a component that can be added to the others already available in FCPP, requiring minimal effort from the end user for its setup. Multiple case studies are available as a sample project, to allow quick-start of several common aggregate programming patterns. Further examples are available from published works using the FCPP GUI in its preliminary versions [5–7,27].

Future work may enhance the GUI with additional customisation options, support for loading general 3D models for nodes, and the support to multiple simultaneous visualizations of the same network. The possibilities for the user to affect the system under simulation may also be extended, by allowing to modify the detailed information of a node, or to drag-and-drop nodes to different locations. Also the possibility of filtering the displayed nodes based on their properties could be useful for the exploration of the system behavior, especially in 3D scenarios.

References

1. Abrahams, D., Gurtovoy, A.: C++ Template Metaprogramming: Concepts, Tools, and Techniques from Boost and Beyond (C++ in Depth Series). Addison-Wesley Professional, Boston (2004)
2. Audrito, G.: FCPP: an efficient and extensible field calculus framework. In: IEEE International Conference on Autonomic Computing and Self-Organizing Systems, ACSOS 2020, Washington, DC, USA, 17–21 August 2020, pp. 153–159. IEEE (2020). https://doi.org/10.1109/ACSOS49614.2020.00037
3. Audrito, G., Casadei, R., Torta, G.: Fostering resilient execution of multi-agent plans through self-organisation. In: IEEE International Conference on Autonomic Computing and Self-Organizing Systems, ACSOS 2021, Companion Volume, Washington, DC, USA, September 27 - October 1 2021, pp. 81–86. IEEE (2021). https://doi.org/10.1109/ACSOS-C52956.2021.00076
4. Audrito, G., Casadei, R., Torta, G.: Towards integration of multi-agent planning with self-organising collective processes. In: IEEE International Conference on Autonomic Computing and Self-Organizing Systems, ACSOS 2021, Companion Volume, Washington, DC, USA, September 27 - October 1 2021, pp. 297–298. IEEE (2021). https://doi.org/10.1109/ACSOS-C52956.2021.00042
5. Audrito, G., et al.: RM for users' safety and security in the built environment. In: VORTEX 2021: Proceedings of the 5th ACM International Workshop on Verification and mOnitoring at Runtime EXecution, Virtual Event, Denmark, 12 July 2021, pp. 13–16. ACM (2021). https://doi.org/10.1145/3464974.3468445
6. Audrito, G., Damiani, F., Stolz, V., Torta, G., Viroli, M.: Distributed runtime verification by past-ctl and the field calculus. J. Syst. Softw. **187**, 111251 (2022). https://doi.org/10.1016/j.jss.2022.111251
7. Audrito, G., Torta, G.: Towards aggregate monitoring of spatio-temporal properties. In: VORTEX 2021: Proceedings of the 5th ACM International Workshop on Verification and mOnitoring at Runtime EXecution, Virtual Event, Denmark, 12 July 2021, pp. 26–29. ACM (2021). https://doi.org/10.1145/3464974.3468448
8. Audrito, G., Viroli, M., Damiani, F., Pianini, D., Beal, J.: A higher-order calculus of computational fields. ACM Trans. Comput. Log. **20**(1), 5:1–5:55 (2019). https://doi.org/10.1145/3285956
9. Beal, J., Dulman, S., Usbeck, K., Viroli, M., Correll, N.: Organizing the aggregate: Languages for spatial computing. In: Formal and Practical Aspects of Domain-Specific Languages: Recent Developments, pp. 436–501. IGI Global (2013)
10. Beal, J., Pianini, D., Viroli, M.: Aggregate programming for the internet of things. IEEE Comput. **48**(9), 22–30 (2015). https://doi.org/10.1109/MC.2015.261
11. Beal, J., Viroli, M., Pianini, D., Damiani, F.: Self-adaptation to device distribution in the internet of things. ACM Trans. Autonom. Adapt. Syst. **12**(3), 12:1–12:29 (2017). https://doi.org/10.1145/3105758
12. Bracha, G., Cook, W.R.: Mixin-based inheritance. In: International Conference on Object-Oriented Programming Systems, Languages, and Applications (OOPSLA) / European Conference on Object-Oriented Programming (ECOOP), pp. 303–311. ACM (1990). https://doi.org/10.1145/97945.97982
13. Cannon, H.I.: Flavors: A non-hierarchical approach to object-oriented programming. Technical Report, Artificial Intelligence Laboratory, MIT, USA (1979)
14. Casadei, R., Viroli, M., Audrito, G., Pianini, D., Damiani, F.: Engineering collective intelligence at the edge with aggregate processes. Eng. Appl. Artif. Intell. **97**, 104081 (2021). https://doi.org/10.1016/j.engappai.2020.104081

15. Curino, C., Giani, M., Giorgetta, M., Giusti, A., Murphy, A.L., Picco, G.P.: Mobile data collection in sensor networks: the tinyLime. Pervasive Mobile Comput. **1**(4), 446–469 (2005). https://doi.org/10.1016/j.pmcj.2005.08.003

16. Dean, J., Ghemawat, S.: Mapreduce: simplified data processing on large clusters. Commun. ACM **51**(1), 107–113 (2008). https://doi.org/10.1145/1327452.1327492

17. Koenig, N., Howard, A.: Design and use paradigms for gazebo, an open-source multi-robot simulator. In: IEEE/RSJ International Conference on Intelligent Robots and Systems, pp. 2149–2154. Sendai, Japan, September 2004

18. Kondacs, A.: Biologically-inspired self-assembly of two-dimensional shapes using global-to-local compilation. In: 18th International Joint Conference on Artificial Intelligence (IJCAI), pp. 633–638. Morgan Kaufmann (2003)

19. Lasser, C., Massar, J., Miney, J., Dayton, L.: Starlisp Reference Manual. Thinking Machines Corporation (1988)

20. Mamei, M., Zambonelli, F.: Programming pervasive and mobile computing applications: the TOTA approach. ACM Trans. Softw. Eng. Methodol. **18**(4), 15:1–15:56 (2009). https://doi.org/10.1145/1538942.1538945

21. McIlroy, M.D., Buxton, J., Naur, P., Randell, B.: Mass-produced software components. In: 1st International Conference on Software Engineering, pp. 88–98 (1968)

22. Pianini, D., Montagna, S., Viroli, M.: Chemical-oriented simulation of computational systems with ALCHEMIST. J. Simul. **7**(3), 202–215 (2013). https://doi.org/10.1057/jos.2012.27

23. Pianini, D., Viroli, M., Beal, J.: Protelis: practical aggregate programming. In: 30th ACM Symposium on Applied Computing (SAC), pp. 1846–1853. ACM (2015). https://doi.org/10.1145/2695664.2695913

24. Pinciroli, C., et al.: ARGoS: a modular, parallel, multi-engine simulator for multi-robot systems. Swarm Intell. **6**(4), 271–295 (2012)

25. Viroli, M., Audrito, G., Beal, J., Damiani, F., Pianini, D.: Engineering resilient collective adaptive systems by self-stabilisation. ACM Trans. Model. Comput. Simul. **28**(2), 16:1–16:28 (2018). https://doi.org/10.1145/3177774

26. Viroli, M., Casadei, R., Pianini, D.: Simulating large-scale aggregate mass with alchemist and scala. In: Federated Conference on Computer Science and Information Systems (FedCSIS). Annals of Computer Science and Information Systems, vol. 8, pp. 1495–1504. IEEE (2016). https://doi.org/10.15439/2016F407

27. Zainab, H., Audrito, G., Dasgupta, S., Beal, J.: Effect of monotonic filtering on graph collection dynamics. In: IEEE International Conference on Autonomic Computing and Self-Organizing Systems, ACSOS 2021, Companion Volume, Washington, DC, USA, September 27 - October 1 2021, pp. 68–73. IEEE (2021). https://doi.org/10.1109/ACSOS-C52956.2021.00036

Towards Reinforcement Learning-based Aggregate Computing

Gianluca Aguzzi$^{(\boxtimes)}$, Roberto Casadei, and Mirko Viroli

Alma Mater Studiorum - Università di Bologna, Cesena, Italy
{gianluca.aguzzi,roby.casadei,mirko.viroli}@unibo.it

Abstract. Recent trends in pervasive computing promote the vision of Collective Adaptive Systems (CASs): large-scale collections of relatively simple agents that act and coordinate with no central orchestrator to support distributed applications. Engineering global behaviour out of local activity and interaction, however, is a difficult task, typically addressed by try-and-error approaches in simulation environments. In the context of Aggregate Computing (AC), a prominent functional programming approach for CASs based on field-based coordination, this difficulty is reflected in the design of versatile algorithms preserving efficiency in a variety of environments. To deal with this complexity, in this work we propose to apply Machine Learning techniques to automatically devise local actions to improve over manually-defined AC algorithms specifications. Most specifically, we adopt a Reinforcement Learning-based approach to let a collective learn local policies to improve over the standard gradient algorithm—a cornerstone brick of several higher-level self-organisation algorithms. Our evaluation shows that the learned policies can speed up the self-stabilisation of the gradient to external perturbations.

Keywords: Collective adaptive system · Aggregate computing · Reinforcement learning · Collective intelligence

1 Introduction

The pervasiveness of computing and networking fosters applications backed by large-scale cyber-physical collectives—cf. edge-fog-cloud infrastructures, robot swarms, and smart ecosystems. Combined with the *autonomic computing* vision [18], which promotes autonomy and self-* capabilities in engineered systems, there is an increasing trend towards Collective Adaptive Systems (CASs) and their engineering [9,31]. CASs are characterised by a multitude of agents that can produce globally coherent results (*emergents* [43]), and collective-level adaptivity to environment change via local decision-making and decentralised interaction. The *engineering of CASs* is an open research problem [19,31] of significance, tightly linked with the problems of "steering" self-organisation and "controlling" emergence to promote desired while avoiding undesired emergents [29]. In

© IFIP International Federation for Information Processing 2022
M. H. ter Beek and M. Sirjani (Eds.): COORDINATION 2022, LNCS 13271, pp. 72–91, 2022.
https://doi.org/10.1007/978-3-031-08143-9_5

general, when dealing with CASs, there are two distinct problems: (i) given an initial system state and local behavioural rules, predicting what global outcomes will be produced (*forward*, *prediction*, or *local-to-global problem*); and (ii) what local behavioural rules must be assigned to the system devices to achieve certain global outcomes (*inverse*, *control*, or *global-to-local problem*). These two problems provide corresponding perspectives for *designing* CASs. In particular, the latter perspective has promoted research on *spatial* and *macro-programming* [7,10] aiming at expressing programs in terms of the desired global outcome and leaving the underlying platform to deal with the global-to-local mapping.

In this work, we consider *Aggregate Computing (AC)* [8], a prominent *field-based coordination* approach [41] promoting macro-programming by capturing CAS behaviours as functions operating on *computational fields* [41], in a system model of neighbour-interacting devices operating in asynchronous sense-compute-interact rounds. A computational field is a macro-abstraction that maps a set of devices over time to computational values. AC is based on the *Field Calculus (FC)* [41], or variants thereof, that define constructs for manipulating and evolving fields. So, CAS behaviour can be expressed by a single *aggregate program* (global perspective) that also defines what processing and communication activities must be performed by each individual device (local perspective).

Besides the programming model and its implications, a significant portion of research on AC [41] has focussed on design and analysis of *coordination algorithms* expressed in FC for efficiently carrying out self-organising behaviours like, e.g., computing fields of minimum distances from sources (*gradients*) [4,24,30], electing leaders [27], or distributed summarisation [3]. However, devising self-organising coordination algorithms is not easy; especially difficult is identifying solutions that are efficient across environment assumptions, configurations, and perturbations. The difficulty lies in determining, for a current context, the local decisions of each device, in terms e.g. of processing steps and communication acts, producing output fields that quickly converge to the correct solution.

In this work, we start what we consider a key future research thread of field-based coordination, i.e., the study of Machine Learning techniques to improve existing AC coordination algorithms. Specifically, we adopt a *Reinforcement Learning (RL)-based approach*—where an agent learns from experience how to behave in order to maximise delayed cumulative rewards [38]. We devise a general methodology that somewhat resembles the notion of *sketching* in program synthesis [36]: a template program is given and *holes* are filled with actions determined through search. In our case, the program is the AC specification of a coordination algorithm, and holes are filled with actions of a policy learnt through Hysteretic Q-Learning [25]. We consider the case of the classic gradient algorithm, a paradigmatic and key building block of self-organising coordination [7,10,41]: we show via simulations that the system, after sufficient training, learns an improved way to compute and adjust gradient fields to network perturbations.

In the rest of the paper: Sect. 2 offers background on AC and RL; Sect. 3 discusses the integration of RL and AC, and the use of the approach to improve the basic gradient algorithm; Sect. 4 provides an experimental evaluation of the proposed approach; Sect. 5 summarises results and future research.

2   Background

In this work, we contribute to *field-based coordination* [23,24,40,41,45], a well-known nature-inspired approach [32] to coordination that exploits computational mechanisms inspired by the force fields of physics. Use of *artificial force fields* for navigation and obstacle avoidance has been explored since the 90s [45]. In *co-fields* [24], fields produced by agents or the environment are used to drive the activities of agent swarms. In TOTA (Tuples on the air) [23], tuples spread over the network to model dynamic distributed data. In Aggregate Computing [8,41], the field-based coordination approach we consider in this work, fields are used as an abstraction for functionally expressing CAS behaviour.

We recap Aggregate Computing in Sect. 2.1. Then, we review RL in Sect. 2.3, to prepare the ground for our contribution, *Reinforcement Learning-based Aggregate Computing* (Sect. 3).

2.1   Aggregate Computing

Aggregate Computing [8,41] is a paradigm for CAS programming. The approach generally assumes a system model of *neighbour-interacting devices* that work at asynchronous *rounds* of *sense-compute-act* steps. On such an execution model, self-organising collective behaviour is expressed in terms of functional manipulations of *computational fields* [41]: maps from devices to values. A field can denote, e.g., what different devices sense from the environment, or the outputs of their computations. The *Field Calculus (FC)* [41] is a core functional language that captures the key constructs needed to properly manipulate fields in order to express collective adaptive computations; they cover state evolution, communication, and computation branching. The main benefit of AC/FC is its *compositionality*: the ability to abstract collective adaptive behaviours into reusable functions that can be composed together to build more complex behaviours.

The FC is implemented by aggregate programming languages such as *ScaFi* (**Sca**la **Fi**elds) [14]. So, in practice, developing a CAS using this paradigm amounts to: (i) writing an *aggregate program* using e.g. ScaFi; (ii) setting up an AC middleware (for simulation or concrete distributed systems) to handle the scheduling of computations and communications; (iii) deploying and configuring the middleware and the program on a network of nodes. The approach has proven effective to implement various kinds of coordination services [15] and self-* applications in domains like crowd management [8], swarm robotics [11], and smart cities [12]—see [41] for a recent review.

In the following, we summarise the computation model and the FC/ScaFi language, which are essential to understand the contribution and case study.

System Model. For an aggregate program to yield collective adaptive behaviour, *ongoing* computation and communication are needed. An individual atomic step of a device is called a *round* and consists of the following:

1. *context acquisition*: the device collects information from the sensors, and the most recent messages received from each neighbour (including the device itself—to model state);
2. *program evaluation*: the aggregate program is evaluated against the acquired context, yielding an *export*, namely a message to be sent to neighbours for coordination purposes and that is implied by the use of communication constructs in the aggregate program;
3. *export sharing*: the export is sent to the neighbours;
4. *actuations*: the export also includes information that can be used to drive actuators in the local node.

Rounds execution is completely asynchronous: there is no global clock or barrier to coordinate the aggregate. Scheduling of rounds might be periodic or reactive [34], and messages from neighbours are assumed to be retained for some configurable amount time. Such asynchrony, combined with local interaction, promotes scalability. The combination of the aggregate program logic and such a collective and periodical execution promotes the emergence of globally coherent results.

Field Calculus. The main constructs that capture the essential aspects for programming self-organising systems with FC are:

- *Stateful field evolution* — expression `rep(e₁) {(x) => e₂}` describes a field evolving in time. e_1 is the initial field value and the function $(x) => e_2$ defines how the field changes round by round substituting (x) with the value of the previous computed field (at the beginning $(x) = e_1$).
- *Neighbour interaction* — expression `nbr{e}` involves evaluation of e, sharing of the corresponding local value with neighbours, and observation of the neighbours' evaluations of e. Then, `*hood` operators can be used to locally reduce such neighbouring fields to values. For instance, for a device, `minHood` returns the minimum value of e found in its neighbourhood.
- *Domain partitioning* — expression `branch(e₀){e₁}{e₂}` splits the computational field into two non-communicating domains hosting isolated sub-computations: e_1 where e_0 is true, and e_2 where e_0 is false.

Full coverage of FC/ScaFi is beyond the scope of this paper. A more comprehensive presentation is given in [41]. As a key example, we introduce the gradient algorithm, which will be considered Sect. 3 and 4.

2.2 The Gradient Building Block

A *gradient* [4,24,30] is a field mapping each device in the system with its minimum distance from the closest *source* device. A *(self-healing) gradient algorithm* is one that computes a gradient field and automatically adjusts it after changes in the source set and the connectivity network. This algorithm is important as it often recurs as part of higher-level self-organising algorithms, such as information flows [44], distributed data collection [3], and regional network partitioning [13]. A simple implementation, which we call *classic gradient*, can be expressed in FC as follows:

```
def gradient(source, metric) { // source is a Boolean field
  rep(infinity) {
    g => mux(source) { 0 } { minHoodPlus(nbr(g) + metric())}
  }
}
```

where `metric` is 0-ary function that evaluates the distance between two neighbours; `mux(c){e1}{e2}` is a conditional expression selector which evaluates all its arguments and selects `e1` if `c` is true or `e2` otherwise; and `minHoodPlus` selects the minimum of its argument across the neighbourhood without considering the contribution of the device itself. A repeated evaluation of this program will self-stabilise to the field of minimum distances from the sources, i.e., it will eventually converge to the ideal gradient field once the inputs and topology stop changing.

Though working and self-stabilising, this algorithm suffers some problems [4]. One is the *rising value problem* (also known as *count to infinity*): due to the repeated minimisation of all the contributions, the system handles well the situations when the output needs to drop (e.g. a new source enters the system) but it instead reacts slowly when the output needs to rise (e.g. a source node turns off). In literature, several heuristics are proposed to tackle the problems of the classical gradient [4]. One of them is CRF (Constraint and Restoring Force) [6]. Its goal is to deal with the problem by enforcing a constant rising speed when nodes recognise a local slow rising of the gradient field. To this end, each node is affected by a set of constraints (i.e. nodes that have a lower gradient value). If a node finds that it is slowly rising (i.e. there are no more constraints) then it increases its output at a fixed velocity, ignoring its neighbours. Otherwise, the output of the gradient follows the classical formula.

2.3   Reinforcement Learning

Reinforcement Learning [38] is a generic framework used to structure *control problems*. The focus is on *sequential* interactions between *agents* (i.e. entity able to act) and an *environment* (i.e. anything outside the control of agents). At each discrete time step t, an agent observes the current environment *state* s_t (i.e. the information perceivable by an agent) and selects an *action* a_t through a *policy* π (i.e. a probabilistic mapping between state and action). Partly as a consequence of its action, at the next time step $t + 1$ the agent finds itself in state s_{t+1} and receives a *reward* r_{t+1}, i.e. a scalar signal quantifying how good the action was against the given environment configuration. The goal of RL is to *learn* a policy π^* that maximises the long-term return G (i.e. the cumulative reward) through a *trial-and-error* process. Different problems can be devised in these settings, like video games [2], robotics [20], routing [22], etc.

This general framework is supported by Markov Decision Process (MDP), a mathematical model that describes the environment evolution in sequential decision problems. A MDP consists of a tuple $< \mathcal{S}, \mathcal{A}, \mathcal{P}, \mathcal{R} >$ in which:

- $\mathcal{S}$ denotes the set of states;
- $\mathcal{A}$ is the set of actions;
- $\mathcal{P}(s_{t+1}|s_t, a_t)$ define the probability to reach some state s_{t+1} starting from s_t and performing a_t (i.e. transition probability function);
- $\mathcal{R}(s_t, a_t, s_{t+1})$ devise a probabilistic reward function.

In MDP, $\mathcal{R}$ is memory-less, namely the next environment state depends only on the current state. Typically, in RL problems, agents do not have access to $\mathcal{R}$ or $\mathcal{P}$ but they can rely only on the experience (s_t, a_t, r_t) sampled at a time step. Therefore, G is defined as the discounted sum of reward a possible future trajectory τ (i.e. a sequence of time steps):

$$G_t = r_t + \gamma r_{t+1} + \gamma^2 r_{t+2} + \cdots + \gamma^T r_{t+T} = \sum_{k=t}^{T} \gamma^{k-t} r_k \tag{1}$$

where $0 \leq \gamma \leq 1$ is the *discount factor*, that is how much the future reward impacts the long-term return. Finally, the RL goal can be expressed as the maximisation of the *expected* long-term return following a policy π:

$$J = \mathbb{E}_\pi \left[G_t \right] = \mathbb{E}_\pi \left[\sum_{k=t}^{T} \gamma^{t-k} r_k \right] \tag{2}$$

The RL algorithms classification depends on how we derive the π^* (i.e. the optimal policy) according to J. In particular, *value-based* methods learn one further function (Q^π or V^π) to derive π^*. V^π is the value function that evaluates how good (or bad) a *state* is according to the long-term return following the policy π (*expected value*). It is defined as:

$$V(s)^\pi = \mathbb{E}_\pi \left[G_t | s_t = s \right] \tag{3}$$

Q^π is the corresponding value fuction that evaluates *state-action* pairs:

$$Q(s, a)^\pi = \mathbb{E}_\pi \left[G_t | s_t = s, a_t = a \right] \tag{4}$$

Policies could be defined through value functions. In particular, a greedy policy based on Q function is the one that always chooses the action with the highest value in a certain state: $\pi(s) = \arg \max_a (Q(s, a))$.

Q-Learning [42] is one of the most famous value-based algorithms. It aims at finding the Q^* (i.e. the Q function associated with π^*) by incrementally refining a Q table directly sampling from an unknown environment. Particularly, this is done through a temporal difference update performed at each time step:

$$Q(s_t, a_t) = Q(s_t, a_t) + \alpha * [r_t + \gamma * \arg\max_a (Q(s_{t+1}, a)) - Q(s_t, a_t)] \quad (5)$$

where α is the learning rate (i.e. how much new information will influence the learned Q at each update). The agent typically follows a ϵ-greedy policy (*behavioural* policy, the function chooses a random action with a ϵ probability) to balance the *exploitation* and *exploration* trade-off. Using Q^* we could extract the π^* greedy policy (*target* policy).

Nowadays, Q-Learning is applied in various fields, ranging from robotics to wireless sensor networks and smart grids [17]. However, one of the most challenging settings in which Q-Learning could be applied is when the learning process has to deal with multiple concurrent learners, namely a multi-agent system.

Multi-agent Reinforcement Learning. RL was originally proposed as a framework to control a *single* agent. However, in CASs we are interested in *many* agents that interact in a common environment. The study of learning in these settings is known as Multi-Agent Reinforcement Learning (MARL) [39].

A straightforward way to apply RL algorithms to multi-agent settings, called *independent learning* (IL) approach [39], consists in deploying a learning process *for each* agent and considering other agents as *part* of the environment. However, applying single-agent algorithms as-is would probably lead to bad results, due to the non-stationarity of the environment induced by concurrent learning , and stochasticity [26]. Therefore, different algorithms are proposed to handle those issues in IL settings, such as Hysteretic Q-Learning [25] and Distributed Q-Learning (DQL) [21]. Hysteretic Q-Learning (HQL) aims at managing the stochasticity problems exploiting an *optimistic* heuristic.The idea is to give more importance to good actions than bad actions – more frequent due to the concurrent learning – reducing the policies oscillation during the learning. To this aim, HQL introduces two learning rates (α and β) to weigh the increase and decrease of Q values. The update equation becomes:

$$\delta(t) = r_t + \gamma \arg\max_a (Q(s_{t+1}, a)) - Q(s_t, a_t) \quad (6)$$

$$Q(s_t, a_t) = \begin{cases} Q(s_t, a_t) + \alpha\,\delta(t) & \text{if } \delta \geq 0 \\ Q(s_t, a_t) + \beta\,\delta(t) & \text{else} \end{cases} \quad (7)$$

In this study (cf. Sect. 4), we use HQL as reference RL algorithm since it has a strong empirical track for cooperative multi-agent systems [5,26,46]. Moreover, although structurally similar to DQL, it can be used in non-deterministic MDPs—a typical setting for CASs. Indeed, DQL is a particular case of HQL where $\beta = 0$. However, in doing so, the agents tend to overestimate the Q value due to the optimistic settings because they do not consider the environment noise.

RL could also be used in multi-agent settings through a central controller that learns exploiting system-wide information. The learning problem thus becomes a single agent one in which the agent consists of the Cartesian product of all the system nodes. However, this solution cannot be applied to CASs, due to the many-agent settings, openness, and the lack of a central entity. Novel approaches are structured in between independent learners and centralised learners techniques—the so-called Centralised Training Decentralised Execution (CTDE) [16]. In CTDE, a central agent performs the learning process and generates distributed controllers, one for each agent. CTDE is typically applied in offline learning through the use of simulations. This way, it is possible to leverage global information at simulation time, but then the controllers are completely independent of this central authority. So, when the learner finds a good policy, it can be removed from the system.

Although CTDE allows RL to be used in environments with many agents, the learner must consider a large population of agents at simulation time, leading to sample inefficient algorithms. A solution to this problem in similar CASs (e.g. swarm robotics [37]) is to add another constraint, namely the agents' homogeneous and cooperative behaviour [33]. With this assumption, the learner only has to find a single strategy that applies to the whole system.

3 Reinforcement Learning-based Aggregate Computing

3.1 On Integrating Machine Learning and Aggregate Computing

As anticipated in Sect. 2.1, the behaviour of an aggregate system depends on the interplay of three main ingredients: (i) the aggregate program, expressing conceptually the global behaviour of the entire system, and concretely the local behaviour of each individual node in terms of local processing and data exchange with neighbours; and (ii) the aggregate execution model, promoting a certain dynamics of the system in terms of topology management (e.g., via neighbour discovery), execution of rounds, scheduling of communications; and (iii) the environment dynamics. While the latter cannot be controlled, the importance of the first element is reflected by research on the design of novel algorithms (cf. [4,41]), while the second element is studied w.r.t. the possibility of tuning and adaptivity according to available technology and infrastructure or the dynamics of the environment. Since tuning programs or execution details to specific environments or adapting those to changing environments can be burdensome, it makes sense to consider the use of Machine Learning techniques to let a system *learn* effective strategies for unfolding collective adaptive behaviour.

3.2 Aggregate Programs Improvement Through RL

In this work, we focus on *improving aggregate programs* by learning effective local actions within a given algorithmic schema—an approach similar to the *sketching* technique for program synthesis [36]. As a learning framework, we use

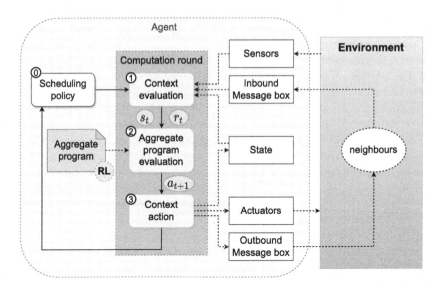

Fig. 1. Integration of RL within the AC control architecture [11]. The RL state and reward concepts build upon the context, given by environment and neighbour data. The designer configures action points where learning can improve the aggregate computation. The actions selected by the learned policies will then affect the environment (via actuators) and neighbours (via outbound messages).

RL as we deal with systems of agents performing ongoing activities by interacting with one another and the environment. From a local viewpoint, an AC device is an agent acting based on the local context it perceives (sensor readings, device state, and messages from neighbours), and this matches the RL execution model very well.

So, our long-term goal is to integrate RL into the AC "stack" (i.e., across the platform, language, and library levels) to improve the collective behaviour defined by ScaFi aggregate programs in terms of *efficiency* (i.e., reducing the resource usage maintaining the same functional interface), *efficacy* (i.e., synthesising more stable and faster converging behaviours) and *adaptability* (i.e., the same program works against different environments).

As a first contribution, summarised in Fig. 1, in this work we integrate RL within the AC control architecture in order to support learning of good collective behaviour sketched by a given aggregate program. Specifically, we focus on improving AC building blocks (such as the gradient algorithm covered in Sect. 2.2) through learning, leading toward a so-called *Reinforcement Learning-based Aggregate Computing*. Learning, thus, does not replace the AC methodology for defining the programs but it is best understood as a technique that supports and improves the AC algorithm design process.

3.3   Building Blocks Refinement

A major advantage of AC as a programming model is its *compositionality*: complex collective behaviours (e.g., the maintenance of a multi-hop connectivity channel) can be expressed through a combination of building blocks capturing simpler collective behaviours (e.g., gradients). Since building blocks are fundamental bricks of behaviour that often recur in programs, their bad and good qualities (cf., convergence speed, stability, etc.) tend to amplify and affect behaviours that depend on them. Therefore, research tends to investigate refined variants of building blocks that provide the same functionality but are more effective or efficient under specific assumptions or contexts (e.g., high mobility, situations where stability is more important than precision, etc.) [3,4]. With a library of algorithms, the designer can choose the best combination of building blocks that are well-fitted for a given environment, and even substitute a building block with a variant implementation without substantially affecting the application logic. In general, a building block can be seen as a black box (function) that takes a set of input fields (e.g. metric, perception fields, constant fields, etc.) and yields an output field. To increase its flexibility, such a function could leverage a *refinement policy* able to affect the behaviour of the building block over time or in a certain situation. This policy could be a feedback loop, hysteresis, or custom logic to solve a specific problem. We aim at structuring the learning of refinement policies through RL [1]. Our idea is that it should not be the designer who codes a particular block to be used, but that it is the learning algorithm that understands, given a global policy to be optimised following a utility function, what actions need to be activated.

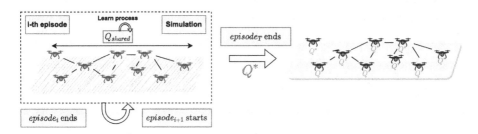

Fig. 2. Reinforcement learning schema used in our simulations. The learning algorithm is applied at simulation time (for T episodes) improving a shared Q table. At the deployment time then, the agents exploit a local copy of the optimal Q^* table found by learning.

However, using Machine Learning to improve AC programs exposes several non-trivial challenges:

- *scale-free behaviours*: the learned policy should work in small networks as well as in large networks as fostered by the AC abstractions;

- the state typically depends on *continuous* value as computational fields are often associated with continuous data (e.g. temperature or distance fields);
- *multi-agent credit assignment problem*: it is not easy to adequately reward and credit local actions for their contribution to the eventual convergence to the "target" field denoting the desired, emergent, collective result.

The AC system model is based on *cooperative* and *homogeneous* behaviour. Indeed, when a node participates in an aggregate system, it has to execute an aggregate program shared within the whole system, which yields different outcomes according to the contexts on which it gets evaluated. This leads to handling homogeneous MARL, hence our goal will be to find one policy for the entire ensemble, partially solving the scale-free behaviour problem, since the learned policy will not depend on the system's size.

The continuous and variable state problems are typically tackled using Deep Learning to learn the right state representation for a given problem [28]. In this case, instead, we used a handcraft feature engineering process since we are more interested in devising a general design process.

Concerning the *multi-agent credit assignment problem*, we decided to use offline learning in a typical CTDE setting (Fig. 2). This way, we assess the influence of an individual in comparison to the entire system, which cannot be done in online learning due to the difficulty of achieving global snapshots of the system in a reasonable time.

Learning Schema. The learning algorithm is seen as a state (s_t) evolution function in which the nodes try to apply a correction factor (`update`) following a policy (π_{target}^Q or $\pi_{behavioral}^Q$) refined by learning. The state is built from a neighbourhood field of the building block generic output (o_t) passed as input. Listing 1.1 exemplifies the general program structure used to combine RL with AC for improving building blocks. The branching operator (`branch`) on `learn` condition makes it possible to use the CTDE schema since when the `learn` is `false` there is no need for a central entity (`simulation`). The Q table is gathered using `sense`, a ScaFi operator used to query sensors and collect data from them. At simulation time, Q is a shared object, but at runtime each agent owns a local table.

```
def optBlock(o_{t-1}) { // learning as a field that evolves in time
  rep((s_0,a_0, o_0)) { // s_0, a_0 context dependent
    case (s_{t-1},a_{t-1}, _) => {
      val Q = sense("Q") // global during training, local during execution
      val o_t = update(o_{t-1}, a_{t-1}) // local action
      // state from the neighbourhood field program output
      val s_t = state(nbr(o_t))
      val a_t = branch(learn) { // actions depends on learn condition
        val r_{t-1} = reward(o_t, simulation) // simulation is a global object
        simulation.updateQ(Q, s_{t-1}, a_{t-1}, r_{t-1}, s_t) // Q update
        ~ π_{behavioural}^Q(s_t) // sample from a probabilistic distribution
      } {
        π_{target}^Q(s_t) // greedy policy, no sampling is needed
      }
```

```
    }
    (s_t, a_t, o_t)
  }._3 // select the output from the tuple
}
```

Listing 1.1. ScaFi-like pseudocode description (implemented in the simulation) for value-based RL algorithm applied AC. `state`, `update`, `reward` are block specific.

Finally, the produced o_t is returned to the caller.

In this case, we encoded the learning process with AC itself. Though we could have extracted the learning process from the AC program, we took this decision because: (i) it allows us to extend learning by exploiting neighbourhood Q table fields – so we can think of doing non-homogeneous learning in different areas of the system; (ii) the scheme for taking state and choosing actions is the same as the one we would need for learning, so the only difference is in the branch; and (iii) it can simply be extended to online learning.

3.4 Reinforcement Learning-based Gradient Block

The gradient block (cf. Sect. 2.2) could be generalised as follows:

```
def gradientOpt(source, metric, opt) {
  rep(infinity) { g => mux(source) { 0 } { opt(g, metric)) } }
}
```

where `opt` is a function that determines how to evolve the gradient based on the field of current gradient values `g` and current `metric` (estimation of distances to neighbours). In this article, we consider `opt` as a *hole* that a RL algorithm will fill through raw experience with actions aiming at incrementally constructing a gradient field, hopefully mitigating the *rising-value* issue (cf. Sect. 2.2). To frame our learning problem, we adopt the above-described general schema (Fig. 2). The state and action functions are inspired by the CRF algorithm. The `state` function must hold enough information to know when agents should speed up the local rising of values. In this case, we encode the state as the difference between the output perceived by a node and the minimum and maximum gradient received by its neighbours: $s_t = (|min_t - o_t|, |max_t - o_t|)$. These data have to be discretised; otherwise, the search space would be too big and the solution could suffer from overfitting. The discretisation is ruled by two variables, *maxBound* and *buckets*. The former constrains the output to be between $-radius * maxBound$ and $radius * maxBound$ (where *radius* is the maximum communication range of the nodes). The values outside that range will be considered as the same state. The *buckets* variable rules the division count of the given range. Finally, we stack two time steps in order to encode history inside the agent state: $h_t = [(s_{t-1}, s_t)]$. h_t is used as the state function for our RL algorithm. Hence, the cardinality of the state space of $|s_t| * |s_t| = buckets^4$. The action space is divided into two action types: `ConsiderNeighborhood` is the action that will produce the classic gradient evaluation, while `Ignore(velocity)` ignores the neighbour data and increases the gradient at a given `velocity`. So, the `update` function is defined as:

```
def update(o_{t-1}, a_{t-1}, metric) { // o_{t-1} is the previous gradient output
  val g_classic = minHoodPlus(nbr(o_{t-1}) + metric())
  match a_{t-1} { // scala-like pattern matching
    case ConsiderNeighborhood => g_classic
    case Ignore(velocity) => o_t + velocity * deltaTime()
  }
}
```

Table 1. Summary of the simulation variables. A simulation is identified by a quadruple (i, j, k, l) of indexes for each variable.

Name	Values
(γ)	$[0.4 - 0.7 - 0.9]$
(ϵ_0, θ)	$[(0.5,200) - (0.01,1000) - (0.05,400) - (0.02,500)]$
(β, α)	$[(0.5,0.01) - (0.5,0.1) - (0.3,0.05) - (0.2,0.03) - (0.1,0.01)]$
(buckets, maxBound)	$[(16,4) - (32,4) - (64,4)]$

Finally, the **reward** function is described as follows:

```
def reward(o_t, simulation) {
  if(o_t - simulation.rightValueFor(mid()) ~= 0) { 0 } { -1 }
}
```

where mid returns the field of node identifiers. The idea is to push the nodes to produce an output that is very close to the ideal, correct gradient value as provided by an oracle (simulation.rightValuefor()). When this is the case, we provide a value equals to 0; instead, when the value is different from the expected one, we provide a small negative reward, -1, in order to push the nodes to quickly seek the situation where the actual and ideal value match.

4   Evaluation

To evaluate our approach, we run a set of simulated experiments and verify that an aggregate system can successfully learn an improved way to compute a gradient field (cf. the gradient block described in Sect. 2.2). To this purpose, we adopt Alchemist [35], a flexible simulator for pervasive and networked systems that comes with a support for aggregate systems programmed with ScaFi [14]. The source code, data, and instructions for running the experiments have been made fully available at a public repository[1], to promote reproducibility of results.

---

[1] https://github.com/cric96/experiment-2022-coordination.

4.1   Simulation Setup

The simulated system consists of N devices deployed in a grid. We use two kinds of grid-like environments. They both have the same width (200 m) and distance between nodes (5 m), but they differ in the row count. In one case, only one row exists (so the nodes are placed in a line). In the other case, there are five rows. The total number (N) of agents is then defined as $200/5 * rows$. So in the first case, we have a total of 40 agents, in the second case we have 200 agents. Each node asynchronously fires the round evaluation at 1 Hz. The leftmost and the rightmost agents are marked as source nodes. Each simulated episode lasts 85 s (T). For simulating the slow rising problem, we drop the left source at 35 s (C_s), and so the left part of the system starts to rise until eventually stabilising to the correct computational field. An entire simulation lasts $N_E = 1200$ episodes, in which in the first $N_L = 1000$ the system uses RL to improve a shared Q table, and then in the last $N_T = 200$, the system deploys the Q table found in each agent. In these last runs, the agents act following the greedy policy.

As learning algorithm, we used Hysteretic Q-Learning (cf. Sect. 2.3). As behavioural policy, we use an ϵ-greedy with an exponential decay to balance the exploration-exploitation. We make this choice because without using the decay the policy found tends to be not optimised (i.e. the exploration is preferred w.r.t exploitation). At each episode i, the ϵ value is updated as $\epsilon_i = \epsilon_0 \cdot e^{i/\theta}$.

Several variables are used, summarised in Table 1, so we perform a grid search to find the optimal combination. To evaluate a particular configuration, we verified the total error performed in the last N_T episodes. This is calculated from the error performed by each node i at each time step t:

$$error_i^t = |gradient_i^t - simulated_i^t| \tag{8}$$

Then for each time step t, we evaluate the average system error as:

$$error_t = \frac{1}{n} \sum_{i=0}^{N} error_i^t \tag{9}$$

And finally, the error of each episode is evaluated as:

$$error_{episode} = \sum_{t=0}^{T} error_t \tag{10}$$

We choose the configuration by observing the box plots (Fig. 3a) and taking the lowest average error in the last N_T episodes.

4.2   Results and Discussion

Figure 3 shows the performance of our Reinforcement Learning-based gradient algorithm. Figure 3a was used to choose which configuration was the best. Figuer 3b shows the error trend as the episodes change. The second row shows the trend

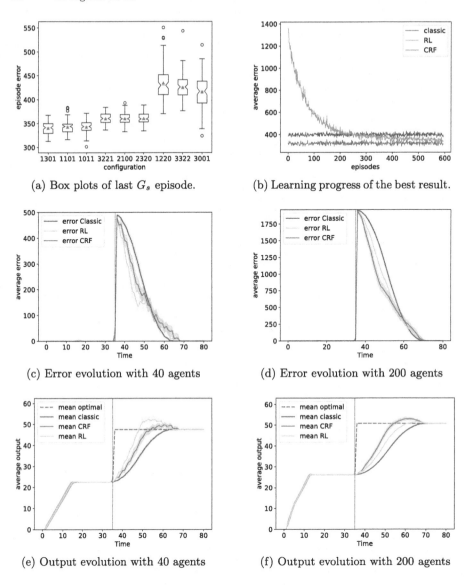

(a) Box plots of last G_s episode.

(b) Learning progress of the best result.

(c) Error evolution with 40 agents

(d) Error evolution with 200 agents

(e) Output evolution with 40 agents

(f) Output evolution with 200 agents

Fig. 3. Performance of our RL-based gradient algorithm with `velocity = 20`.

of the mean error over the last N_T episodes. The coloured area under the curve defines the standard deviation. The dashed vertical line is the time at which the source change occurs. Finally, the last row shows the average output of the various algorithms. In the following we discuss the result reached with the best configuration, that has $\gamma = 0.9$, $\epsilon_0 = 0.5$, $\theta = 200$, $\alpha = 0.3$ and $\beta = 0.05$.

Our goal was to create a solution that outperforms the classic gradient against the rising-value problem. In fact, the system eventually learns how to speed up the gradient rising: observing the Figure 3b the $error_{episode}$ of the new algorithm is lower than the error produced by the standard solution. In particular, this means that the agents learn the moment when they should ignore their neighbourhood and increase the output with a certain velocity (i.e. using the Ignore action).

This intuition is enforced by Fig. 3c to 3f. In particular, in Fig. 3e and 3e the behaviour is more evident due to the reduced number of agents: when the error is maximised (due to the source that disappears), the error decreased faster than the naive gradient (and, consequently, the output is faster growing). Furthermore, we can also observe that the overall algorithm behaviour is comparable with the CRF handcrafted solution for the rising problem. Indeed, both have a phase of speed up followed by another phase of overestimation (i.e. the system-wide output is greater than the true gradient field output) that eventually brings the system to slowly reaches the correct value. Moreover, not only the RL-based solution has similar behaviour to CRF, but also it has comparable performance – it means that the aggregate reaches a near-optimal policy with these state-action-reward settings.

We want also to underline that the policy learned is *one* and shared with the whole system. Thereby, the policy can be easily scaled in deployments with different node counts. In this case, the *same* function outperforms our baseline in a system with different nodes and deployment configurations.

Finally, we want to stress that the nodes do not fire synchronously, and thus there is not any kind of global and shared clock: any node round evaluation order reaches the same behaviour in our test deployments. This, again, makes it possible to use the same policy in different scenarios due to the unknown local aggregate programs evaluation order.

5 Conclusion

This paper discusses the integration of Aggregate Computing – a programming approach for Collective Adaptive Systems – and Reinforcement Learning, with the goal of fostering the design of collective adaptive behaviour. In particular, we propose to use RL as a means to improve building block AC algorithms. Our approach is applied to improving the gradient algorithm, one of the key AC algorithms, where learning is performed through Hysteretic Q-Learning. We evaluate the approach through synthetic experiments comparing the reactivity of different gradient algorithms in dealing with the rising value problem.

This work is the first effort towards Reinforcement Learning-based Aggregate Computing. In fact, there are still many aspects that need to be analysed in detail both at the conceptual and practical levels. First of all, the approach could be tuned to learn gradient strategies for smoothness or maximal reactivity in highly variable scenarios, and compared with state-of-the-art algorithms like BIS and ULT [4]. Secondly, the approach could be systematically applied to other building blocks as well [41]. Very interesting would also be the application of Machine Learning at the aggregate execution platform level, e.g. to improve the round frequency to reduce power consumption, reduce the amount of data exchanged between neighbours, or support opportunistic re-configuration of aggregate system deployments.

Acknowledgements. This work has been supported by the MIUR FSE REACT-EU PON R&I 2014–2022 (CCI2014IT16M2OP005).

References

1. Aguzzi, G.: Research directions for aggregate computing with machine learning. In: IEEE International Conference on Autonomic Computing and Self-Organizing Systems, ACSOS 2021, Companion Volume, pp. 310–312. IEEE (2021). https://doi.org/10.1109/ACSOS-C52956.2021.00078
2. Arulkumaran, K., Deisenroth, M.P., Brundage, M., Bharath, A.A.: Deep reinforcement learning: a brief survey. IEEE Signal Process. Mag. **34**(6), 26–38 (2017). https://doi.org/10.1109/MSP.2017.2743240
3. Audrito, G., Casadei, R., Damiani, F., Pianini, D., Viroli, M.: Optimal resilient distributed data collection in mobile edge environments. Comput. Electr. Eng. **96**(Part), 107580 (2021). https://doi.org/10.1016/j.compeleceng.2021.107580
4. Audrito, G., Casadei, R., Damiani, F., Viroli, M.: Compositional blocks for optimal self-healing gradients. In: 11th IEEE International Conference on Self-Adaptive and Self-Organizing Systems, SASO 2017, pp. 91–100. IEEE Computer Society (2017). https://doi.org/10.1109/SASO.2017.18
5. Barbalios, N., Tzionas, P.: A robust approach for multi-agent natural resource allocation based on stochastic optimization algorithms. Appl. Soft Comput. **18**, 12–24 (2014). https://doi.org/10.1016/j.asoc.2014.01.004
6. Beal, J., Bachrach, J., Vickery, D., Tobenkin, M.M.: Fast self-healing gradients. In: Proceedings of the 2008 ACM Symposium on Applied Computing (SAC), pp. 1969–1975. ACM (2008). https://doi.org/10.1145/1363686.1364163
7. Beal, J., Dulman, S., Usbeck, K., Viroli, M., Correll, N.: Organizing the aggregate: languages for spatial computing. In: Formal and Practical Aspects of Domain-Specific Languages: Recent Developments, pp. 436–501. IGI Global (2013)
8. Beal, J., Pianini, D., Viroli, M.: Aggregate programming for the internet of things. Computer **48**(9), 22–30 (2015). https://doi.org/10.1109/MC.2015.261
9. Bucchiarone, A., et al.: On the social implications of collective adaptive systems. IEEE Technol. Soc. Mag. **39**(3), 36–46 (2020). https://doi.org/10.1109/MTS.2020.3012324
10. Casadei, R.: Macroprogramming: concepts, state of the art, and opportunities of macroscopic behaviour modelling. CoRR **abs/2201.03473** (2022)
11. Casadei, R., Aguzzi, G., Viroli, M.: A programming approach to collective autonomy. J. Sens. Actuator Networks **10**(2), 27 (2021). https://doi.org/10.3390/jsan10020027
12. Casadei, R., Pianini, D., Placuzzi, A., Viroli, M., Weyns, D.: Pulverization in cyber-physical systems: engineering the self-organizing logic separated from deployment. Future Internet **12**(11), 203 (2020). https://doi.org/10.3390/fi12110203
13. Casadei, R., Pianini, D., Viroli, M., Natali, A.: Self-organising coordination regions: a pattern for edge computing. In: Riis Nielson, H., Tuosto, E. (eds.) COORDINATION 2019. LNCS, vol. 11533, pp. 182–199. Springer, Cham (2019). https://doi.org/10.1007/978-3-030-22397-7_11

14. Casadei, R., Viroli, M., Audrito, G., Damiani, F.: FSCAFI: a core calculus for collective adaptive systems programming. In: Margaria, T., Steffen, B. (eds.) ISoLA 2020. LNCS, vol. 12477, pp. 344–360. Springer, Cham (2020). https://doi.org/10.1007/978-3-030-61470-6_21

15. Casadei, R., Viroli, M., Ricci, A., Audrito, G.: Tuple-based coordination in large-scale situated systems. In: Damiani, F., Dardha, O. (eds.) COORDINATION 2021. LNCS, vol. 12717, pp. 149–167. Springer, Cham (2021). https://doi.org/10.1007/978-3-030-78142-2_10

16. Foerster, J.N.: Deep multi-agent reinforcement learning. Ph.D. thesis, University of Oxford, UK (2018)

17. Jang, B., Kim, M., Harerimana, G., Kim, J.W.: Q-learning algorithms: a comprehensive classification and applications. IEEE Access 7, 133653–133667 (2019). https://doi.org/10.1109/ACCESS.2019.2941229

18. Kephart, J.O., Chess, D.M.: The vision of autonomic computing. Computer 36(1), 41–50 (2003). https://doi.org/10.1109/MC.2003.1160055

19. Kernbach, S., Schmickl, T., Timmis, J.: Collective adaptive systems: Challenges beyond evolvability. CoRR abs/1108.5643 (2011)

20. Kober, J., Bagnell, J.A., Peters, J.: Reinforcement learning in robotics: a survey. Int. J. Robot. Res. 32(11), 1238–1274 (2013). https://doi.org/10.1177/0278364913495721

21. Lauer, M., Riedmiller, M.A.: An algorithm for distributed reinforcement learning in cooperative multi-agent systems. In: Langley, P. (ed.) Proceedings of the Seventeenth International Conference on Machine Learning (ICML 2000), Stanford University, Stanford, CA, USA, June 29 - July 2, 2000, pp. 535–542. Morgan Kaufmann (2000)

22. Luong, N.C., et al.: Applications of deep reinforcement learning in communications and networking: a survey. IEEE Commun. Surv. Tutorials 21(4), 3133–3174 (2019). https://doi.org/10.1109/COMST.2019.2916583

23. Mamei, M., Zambonelli, F.: Programming pervasive and mobile computing applications: the TOTA approach. ACM Trans. Softw. Eng. Methodol. 18(4), 15:1–15:56 (2009). https://doi.org/10.1145/1538942.1538945

24. Mamei, M., Zambonelli, F., Leonardi, L.: Co-fields: a physically inspired approach to motion coordination. IEEE Pervasive Comput. 3(2), 52–61 (2004). https://doi.org/10.1109/MPRV.2004.1316820

25. Matignon, L., Laurent, G.J., Fort-Piat, N.L.: Hysteretic q-learning : an algorithm for decentralized reinforcement learning in cooperative multi-agent teams. In: 2007 IEEE/RSJ International Conference on Intelligent Robots and Systems, pp. 64–69. IEEE (2007). https://doi.org/10.1109/IROS.2007.4399095

26. Matignon, L., Laurent, G.J., Fort-Piat, N.L.: Independent reinforcement learners in cooperative markov games: a survey regarding coordination problems. Knowl. Eng. Rev. 27(1), 1–31 (2012). https://doi.org/10.1017/S0269888912000057

27. Mo, Y., Beal, J., Dasgupta, S.: An aggregate computing approach to self-stabilizing leader election. In: 2018 IEEE 3rd International Workshops on Foundations and Applications of Self* Systems (FAS*W), Trento, Italy, September 3–7, 2018, pp. 112–117. IEEE (2018). https://doi.org/10.1109/FAS-W.2018.00034

28. Mousavi, S.S., Schukat, M., Howley, E.: Deep reinforcement learning: An overview. CoRR abs/1806.08894 (2018)

29. Müller-Schloer, C., Sick, B.: Controlled emergence and self-organization. In: Organic Computing. UCS, pp. 81–103. Springer, Heidelberg (2009). https://doi.org/10.1007/978-3-540-77657-4_4

30. Nagpal, R., Shrobe, H., Bachrach, J.: Organizing a global coordinate system from local information on an Ad Hoc sensor network. In: Zhao, F., Guibas, L. (eds.) IPSN 2003. LNCS, vol. 2634, pp. 333–348. Springer, Heidelberg (2003). https://doi.org/10.1007/3-540-36978-3_22

31. De Nicola, R., Jähnichen, S., Wirsing, M.: Rigorous engineering of collective adaptive systems: special section. Int. J. Softw. Tools Technol. Transf. **22**(4), 389–397 (2020). https://doi.org/10.1007/s10009-020-00565-0

32. Omicini, A.: Nature-inspired coordination for complex distributed systems. In: Intelligent Distributed Computing VI - Proceedings of the 6th International Symposium on Intelligent Distributed Computing - IDC 2012. Studies in Computational Intelligence, vol. 446, pp. 1–6. Springer, Cham (2012). https://doi.org/10.1007/978-3-642-32524-3_1

33. Panait, L., Luke, S.: Cooperative multi-agent learning: the state of the art. Auton. Agents Multi Agent Syst. **11**(3), 387–434 (2005). https://doi.org/10.1007/s10458-005-2631-2

34. Pianini, D., Casadei, R., Viroli, M., Mariani, S., Zambonelli, F.: Time-fluid field-based coordination through programmable distributed schedulers. Logical Methods Comput. Sci. **17**(4) (2021). https://doi.org/10.46298/lmcs-17(4:13)2021

35. Pianini, D., Montagna, S., Viroli, M.: Chemical-oriented simulation of computational systems with ALCHEMIST. J. Simulation **7**(3), 202–215 (2013). https://doi.org/10.1057/jos.2012.27

36. Solar-Lezama, A.: Program Synthesis by Sketching. University of California, Berkeley (2008)

37. Sosic, A., KhudaBukhsh, W.R., Zoubir, A.M., Koeppl, H.: Inverse reinforcement learning in swarm systems. In: Larson, K., Winikoff, M., Das, S., Durfee, E.H. (eds.) Proceedings of the 16th Conference on Autonomous Agents and MultiAgent Systems, AAMAS 2017, São Paulo, Brazil, May 8–12, 2017, pp. 1413–1421. ACM (2017)

38. Sutton, R.S., Barto, A.G.: Reinforcement Learning: An Introduction. MIT Press, Cambridge (2018)

39. Tan, M.: Multi-agent reinforcement learning: independent versus cooperative agents. In: Utgoff, P.E. (ed.) Machine Learning, Proceedings of the Tenth International Conference, University of Massachusetts, Amherst, MA, USA, June 27–29, 1993, pp. 330–337. Morgan Kaufmann (1993). https://doi.org/10.1016/b978-1-55860-307-3.50049-6

40. Trzec, K., Lovrek, I.: Field-based coordination of mobile intelligent agents: an evolutionary game theoretic analysis. In: Apolloni, B., Howlett, R.J., Jain, L. (eds.) KES 2007. LNCS (LNAI), vol. 4692, pp. 198–205. Springer, Heidelberg (2007). https://doi.org/10.1007/978-3-540-74819-9_25

41. Viroli, M., Beal, J., Damiani, F., Audrito, G., Casadei, R., Pianini, D.: From distributed coordination to field calculus and aggregate computing. J. Log. Algebraic Methods Program. **109**, 100486 (2019). https://doi.org/10.1016/j.jlamp.2019.100486

42. Watkins, C.J.C.H., Dayan, P.: Technical note q-learning. Mach. Learn. **8**, 279–292 (1992). https://doi.org/10.1007/BF00992698

43. De Wolf, T., Holvoet, T.: Emergence versus self-organisation: different concepts but promising when combined. In: Brueckner, S.A., Di Marzo Serugendo, G., Karageorgos, A., Nagpal, R. (eds.) ESOA 2004. LNCS (LNAI), vol. 3464, pp. 1–15. Springer, Heidelberg (2005). https://doi.org/10.1007/11494676_1

44. Wolf, T.D., Holvoet, T.: Designing self-organising emergent systems based on information flows and feedback-loops. In: Proceedings of the First International Conference on Self-Adaptive and Self-Organizing Systems, SASO 2007, Boston, MA, USA, July 9–11, 2007, pp. 295–298. IEEE Computer Society (2007). https://doi.org/10.1109/SASO.2007.16

45. Xiao, D., Hubbold, R.J.: Navigation guided by artificial force fields. In: Atwood, M.E., Karat, C., Lund, A.M., Coutaz, J., Karat, J. (eds.) Proceeding of the CHI 1998 Conference on Human Factors in Computing Systems, pp. 179–186. ACM (1998). https://doi.org/10.1145/274644.274671

46. Xu, Y., Zhang, W., Liu, W., Ferrese, F.T.: Multiagent-based reinforcement learning for optimal reactive power dispatch. IEEE Trans. Syst. Man Cybern. Part C **42**(6), 1742–1751 (2012). https://doi.org/10.1109/TSMCC.2012.2218596

Sibilla: A Tool for Reasoning about Collective Systems

Nicola Del Giudice, Lorenzo Matteucci, Michela Quadrini, Aniqa Rehman, and Michele Loreti

University of Camerino, Camerino, Italy
{nicola.delgiudice,lorenzo.matteucci,
michela.quadrini,aniqa.rehman,
michele.loreti}@unicam.it

Abstract. Sibilla is a Java framework designed to support the analysis of Collective Adaptive Systems. These are systems composed by a large set of interactive agents that cooperate and compete to reach local and global goals. Sibilla is thought of container where different tools supporting specification and analysis of concurrent and distributed large scaled systems can be integrated. In this paper, a brief overview of Sibilla features is provided together with a simple example showing some of the tool's practical capabilities.

Keywords: Collective systems · Specification languages · Property specification and verification

1 Sibilla in a Nutshell

Sibilla[1] is a modular tool, developed in Java, to support quantitative analysis of Collective Adaptive Systems (CAS). This tool is thought of as a container where new components can be easily added to integrate new analysis techniques and specification languages. In this section, we first provide an overview of Sibilla back end. Then the specification languages that are currently available in our tool are presented. Finally, the user interfaces provided by Sibilla are described.

1.1 Sibilla Back End

Sibilla back end consists of four components: *Models*, *Simulation*, *Tools* and *Runtime*.

---

[1] The tool is available on GitHub at https://github.com/quasylab/sibilla and on *Software Heritage* with id swh:1:dir:fe015fb0a6fb6f5ee7cd6c58d446ab14168f39d4.

This research has been partially supported by Italian PRIN project "IT-MaTTerS" n, 2017FTXR7S, and by POR MARCHE FESR 2014–2020, project "MIRACLE", CUP B28I19000330007.

© IFIP International Federation for Information Processing 2022
M. H. ter Beek and M. Sirjani (Eds.): COORDINATION 2022, LNCS 13271, pp. 92–98, 2022.
https://doi.org/10.1007/978-3-031-08143-9_6

Models. This component provides interfaces and classes that can be used to describe a *Stochastic Process* [14]. This is a collection of *random variables* $\{X(t)|t \in T \subseteq \mathbb{R}_{\geq 0}\}$. These random variables take values on a *measurable set* S representing the *state space* of the stochastic process. Random variable $X(t)$ describes the state of the process at time unit $t \in T$. Different types of stochastic processes can be considered depending on the index set T (*discrete time* vs *continuous time*) or the properties of the considered process (such as *Markovian Processes*). The classes provided in the *Models* permits describing these processes together with some utility classes for their analysis (such as *transient analysis* of *Markov Chains*). These classes provide the base on top of which different *specification languages* can be implemented (see Sect. 1.2).

Simulation. When one considers a system composed of a large number of entities, exact numerical analysis of stochastic processes is often hard or even impossible to be used. This is mainly due to the problem of *state space explosion*. For this reason, Sibilla provides a set of classes that permits supporting simulation of stochastic processes. First of all, these classes permit sampling a *path* from a model. This represents a possible computation/behaviour that can be experienced in the model. Classes to extract *measures* from a *path* and to collect statistical information are also provided. The classes for simulation samplings and statistical analyses rely on the *The Apache Commons Mathematics*[2].

Sometimes, even simulation can require a remarkable computational effort. For this reason, in Sibilla a framework has been integrated that permits supporting simulation to follow a *multi-threading* approach. The framework, based on *Java Concurrency API*, supports the execution of *simulation tasks* according to different *scheduling policies* that can be tailored to fit with the *parallelism* of the hosting architecture. Currently, a framework that permits dispatching simulation tasks over multiple hosts is under development.

Tools. This component provides a set of tools that can be used to analyse the data collected from Sibilla simulator. Currently the following tools are available: computation of *first-passage-time* and *reachability analysis*.

The *first-passage-time* is used to estimate the average amount of time needed by a model to reach a given *condition*. The latter consists of a *predicate* on the states of the considered process. *Reachability analysis* permits estimating the probability that a given set of states (identified by a *condition*) can be reached within a given amount of time by passing through states satisfying a given predicate. We will see in Sect. 1.2 how the specific syntax and format of used conditions depend on the used *specification language*.

The above mentioned tools strongly rely on *statistical inference techniques*. Note that, thanks to the Sibilla modularity, other tools can be easily integrated.

Runtime. Sibilla runtime provides the classes that permit access to all the features provided by our tool. The runtime in fact plays the role of the *controller* in

---

[2] https://commons.apache.org/proper/commons-math/.

the standard *Model-View-Controller* pattern [13] and it is used by the Sibilla user interfaces (see Sect. 1.3). Sibilla runtime is structured in *modules*. Each module is associated with a *specification language*. When a module is *selected*, the runtime environment will start working with the corresponding language.

1.2   Sibilla Specification languages

In this section, a brief overview of the specification languages currently included in Sibilla is provided. These languages permit describing stochastic processes with different features and using different primitives. As we have already remarked, one of the main features of Sibilla is that the tool is not focused on a specific language, but it can be extended to consider many formalism. This feature is useful whenever one is interested in the study languages that are equipped with constructs and primitives thought to model specific application domains (see for instance [2,11,12]).

Currently, in Sibilla three specification languages are fully integrated: *Language of Interactive Objects*, *Language of Population Model*, and *Simple Language for Agent Modeling*.

Language of Interactive Objects (LIO). This is a formalism introduced in [8] where a *system* consists of a population of N identical interacting objects. At any step of computation, each object can be in any of its finitely many states. Objects evolve following a *clock-synchronous* computation. Each member of the population must either execute one of the transitions that are enabled in its current state (by executing an *action*), or remain in such a state. This choice is performed according to a probability distribution that depends on the whole system state. The stochastic process associated with a LIO specification is a *Discrete Time Markov Chain* (DTMC) whose states consists of a vector of counting variables associating each state with the number of agents in this state. LIO models have been used to describe a number of case studies in different application domains [6–8].

Language of Population Models (LPM). A *Population Model* [4] consists of a set of agents belonging to given set of *species*. A system evolves by means of *reaction rules* describing how the number of elements of the different species changes. Rules are applied with a *rate*, which is a positive *real value*, that depends on the number of agents in the different species. The stochastic process associated with a LPM specification is a *Continuous Time Markov Chain*. Those models have been widely used to model different kinds of systems in different application domains ranging from ecology and epidemics to cyber-physical systems.

Simple Language for Agent Modelling (SLAM). This is an agent-oriented specification language. A system consists of a set of agents that interact in order to reach *local* and *global goals*. Each agent is equipped with a set of *attributes*. Some of these attributes are under the control of the agent and are updated during its evolution, while others depend on the environment where the agent operates, and their values are updated as the time is passing. The latter are used in particular to model the fact that an agent is able to *sense* its environment. In SLAM, agents interact via explicit message passing via *attribute based communication primitives* [1,9,10]: an agent sends messages to other agents satisfying a given predicate. The stochastic process associated with a SLAM specification is a *Timed Process* where actions and activities may have a duration sampled by generic distributions.

1.3   Sibilla front ends

To simplify the integration of Sibilla has several interpreters to allow smooth interaction between user and tool. For each specification language there is its own interpreter that allows simple creation of models so that the user can create his own model without necessarily knowing Java technicality. Then the user can easily perform analyses and interact with its own model in different ways, for example, by using the shell provided. The user can also use Sibilla by coding in Python, thus allowing the use of web-based interactive development environment like Google Colaboratory or Jupyter Notebook (see Subsect. 1.3). The current version of the tool allows to execute simulations in two ways: either via command line tool (denominated Sibilla shell), via Python scripts. Moreover, a Docker image is available to simplify deployment of the tool.

Sibilla *Shell.* This is a *command line interpreter* that can be used to interact with the Sibilla core modules and permits performing all the analysis outlined in the previous section. This front end can be either used interactively[3] or in a *batch mode* to execute saved scripts.

Python Front End. Python is one of the easiest to learn and versatile language, and it has been established as one of the most used languages, especially in the context of *data analysis*. For these reasons, Sibilla also provides a *Python front end* that permits interacting with Sibilla back end from Python programs. This front end relies on the *Pyjnius* library [15] that simplifies the interaction between Python and Java classes. The use of this front end permits using many of the available Python libraries likes, for instance, Matplotlib[4] that simplifies data visualisation. Moreover, Sibilla can be used within a web-based IDE such as Jupyter notebook/lab [5] and in Google Colaboratory [3]. This significantly increases the portability of the tool which can then be used without the need to install anything on the local machine.

Docker. Sibilla can be built by using Gradle. However, this needs some familiarity with the Java ecosystem. To simplify the deployment of Sibilla, a docker image is provided for creating containers that already have all the needed dependencies, and that can be easily executed in the Docker framework.

---

[3] The full list of shell commands is available at the Sibilla web site.

[4] https://matplotlib.org.

2 Sibilla at Work

In this section, we use a simple example to show how Sibilla can be used to support analysis of a simple scenario[5]. We consider a classical epidemic example based on the *Language of Population Model*: the *SEIR Model*. The goal of the model is to represent the spread of an infection disease. The model, whose specification is reported in Listing 1.1, consists of four species (or compartments): S, an individual that is susceptible; E, an individual that has been exposed to the virus but is not yet infected; I, an individual that is infected; R, an individual that is immune.

```
param lambdaMeet = 10.0; /* Meeting rate */
param probInfection = 1.00; /* Probability of Infection */
param incubationRate = 2.00; /* rate of Infection */
param lambdaRecovery = 0.5; /* rate of recovery */
param scale = 1.0;

const startS = 99; /* Initial number of S agents */
const startI = 1; /* Initial number of I agents */

species S;
species E;
species I;
species R;

rule exposure {
    S|I -[ #S*%I*lambdaMeet*probInfection ]-> E|I
}
rule infection {
    E -[ #E*lambdaInfection ]-> I
}
rule recovered {
    I -[ #I*lambdaRecovery ]-> R
}

system init = S<startS*scale>|I<startI*scale>;

predicate allRecovered = (#S+#E+#I==0) ;
```

Listing 1.1. SEIR model in SIBILLA

We can observe that a specification can contain a set of *parameters*. These are *real values* that can be changed after the model is loaded. The parameters considered in our model are the agent meeting rate (lambdaMeet), the probability of infection (probInfection), the rate of incubation (incubationRate) and the recovery rate (recoverRate).

A set of rules are used to describe system dynamics. The simper form of the rule is the following:

```
rule <rulename> {
    <species>(|<species>)* -[ <exp> ]->  <species>(|<species>)*
}
```

---

[5] Detailed Sibilla documentation is available at https://github.com/quasylab/sibilla/wiki.

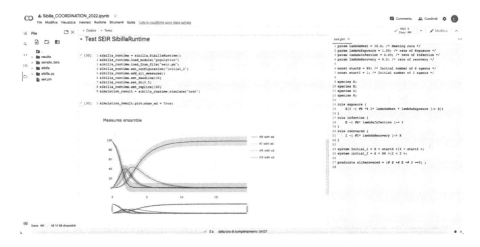

Fig. 1. Sibilla running at Google colaboratory

where `<rulename>` is the name of the rule, `<species>` is a species name and `<exp>` is the expression used to compute the rule rates. Expressions are build by using standard mathematical operators and the two special operators `%X` and `#X`: the former returns the *fraction of agents of species* `X` while the latter amounts to the *number of agents of species* `X`. In our SEIR scenario, such operators are used in the rule `exposure`:

```
rule exposure {
    S|I -[ #S*%I*lambdaMeet*probInfection ]-> E|I
}
```

The initial configurations of a system are described in the form

```
system <name> = <species>(|<species>)*;
```

When multiple copies of the same species `X` are in the system, the form `X<n>` can be used, where n is a numerical value.

In Fig. 1 the analysis of the SEIR model with Sibilla is performed in Google Colaboratory. We can observe how results of the simulation are represented as a plot. Moreover, we can also compute the average time needed to eradicate the infection. This can be obtained in terms of the *first passage time* of the condition `#E+#I=0`, namely when then number agents that are either *exposed* or *infected* is 0. At the same time, reachability can be used to compute the probability that in a given time unit t 90% of the agents *recovered* while never happens that more than 10% of agents are infected.

3 Concluding Remarks

In this paper, a brief overview of the framework Sibilla has been provided. Sibilla is a Java framework designed to support the analysis of Collective Adaptive

Systems. It is thought of as a container where different tools supporting specification and analysis of concurrent and distributed large scaled systems can be integrated. A simple example has been used to show basic features of Sibilla.

As future work, we will plan to integrate in Sibilla a *Graphical User Interface*. The goal is to improve the usability of our tool for users that are not familiar with formal methods. Moreover, we plan to extend the analysis tools available in Sibilla in order to consider model checking tools in the spirit of [6]. Finally, we plan to integrate an optimization module that, by relying on machine learning-assisted inference tools, permits identifying the best parameters that maximize/minimize given goal functions.

References

1. Alrahman, Y.A., Nicola, R.D., Loreti, M.: Programming interactions in collective adaptive systems by relying on attribute-based communication. Sci. Comput. Program. **192**, 102428 (2020)
2. Bettini, L., et al.: The Klaim project: theory and practice. In: Priami, C. (ed.) GC 2003. LNCS, vol. 2874, pp. 88–150. Springer, Heidelberg (2003). https://doi.org/10.1007/978-3-540-40042-4_4
3. Bisong, E.: Google Colaboratory, pp. 59–64. Apress, Berkeley, CA (2019)
4. Bortolussi, L., Hillston, J., Latella, D., Massink, M.: Continuous approximation of collective system behaviour: a tutorial. Perform. Eval. **70**(5), 317–349 (2013)
5. Kluyver, T., et al.: Jupyter notebooks - a publishing format for reproducible computational workflows. In: Loizides, F., Schmidt, B. (eds.), Positioning and Power in Academic Publishing: Players, Agents and Agendas, pp. 87–90. IOS Press (2016)
6. Latella, D., Loreti, M., Massink, M.: On-the-fly PCTL fast mean-field approximated model-checking for self-organising coordination. Sci. Comput. Program. **110**, 23–50 (2015)
7. Latella, D., Loreti, M., Massink, M.: FlyFast: a mean field model checker. In: Legay, A., Margaria, T. (eds.) TACAS 2017. LNCS, vol. 10206, pp. 303–309. Springer, Heidelberg (2017). https://doi.org/10.1007/978-3-662-54580-5_18
8. Le Boudec, J.-Y., McDonald, D., Mundinger, J.: A generic mean field convergence result for systems of interacting objects. In: Fourth international conference on the quantitative evaluation of systems (QEST 2007), pp. 3–18. IEEE (2007)
9. Loreti, M., Hillston, J.: Modelling and analysis of collective adaptive systems with CARMA and its tools. In: Bernardo, M., De Nicola, R., Hillston, J. (eds.) SFM 2016. LNCS, vol. 9700, pp. 83–119. Springer, Cham (2016). https://doi.org/10.1007/978-3-319-34096-8_4
10. Nicola, R.D., Duong, T., Loreti, M.: Provably correct implementation of the ABC calculus. Sci. Comput. Program. **202**, 102567 (2021)
11. Nicola, R.D., Latella, D., Loreti, M., Massink, M.: MarCaSPiS: a markovian extension of a calculus for services. Electron. Notes Theoret. Comput. Sci. **229**(4), 11–26 (2009)
12. Nicola, R.D., Loreti, M., Pugliese, R., Tiezzi, F.: A formal approach to autonomic systems programming. ACM Trans. Autonom. Adapt. Syst. **9**(2), 1–29 (2014)
13. Reenskaug, T., Wold, P., Lehne, O.A., et al.: Working with objects: the OOram software engineering method, chapter 9.3.2, pp. 333–338. Citeseer (1996)
14. Ross, S.M., et al.: Stochastic processes, vol. 2. Wiley, New York (1996)
15. K. Team and other contributors. pyjnius. https://github.com/kivy/pyjnius

Space-Fluid Adaptive Sampling:
A Field-Based, Self-organising Approach

Roberto Casadei[1]([✉])[iD], Stefano Mariani[2][iD], Danilo Pianini[1][iD],
Mirko Viroli[1][iD], and Franco Zambonelli[2][iD]

[1] Alma Mater Studiorum—Università Bologna,
Cesena, Italy
{roby.casadei,danilo.pianini,
mirko.viroli}@unibo.it
[2] Università di Modena e Reggio Emilia,
Reggio Emilia, Italy
{stefano.mariani,
franco.zambonelli}@unimore.it

Abstract. A recurrent task in coordinated systems is managing (estimating, predicting, or controlling) signals that vary in space, such as distributed sensed data or computation outcomes. Especially in large-scale settings, the problem can be addressed through decentralised and situated computing systems: nodes can locally sense, process, and act upon signals, and coordinate with neighbours to implement collective strategies. Accordingly, in this work we devise distributed coordination strategies for the estimation of a spatial phenomenon through collaborative adaptive sampling. Our design is based on the idea of dynamically partitioning space into regions that compete and grow/shrink to provide accurate aggregate sampling. Such regions hence define a sort of virtualised space that is "fluid", since its structure adapts in response to pressure forces exerted by the underlying phenomenon. We provide an adaptive sampling algorithm in the field-based coordination framework. Finally, we verify by simulation that the proposed algorithm effectively carries out a spatially adaptive sampling.

Keywords: Field-based coordination · Distributed leader election · Aggregate processes · Fluidware · Space-fluid computation

1 Introduction

A recurrent problem in engineering is dealing with (e.g., estimating, predicting, or controlling) phenomena that vary in space. Examples include the displacement of waste in a city, the pollution in a geographical area, the temperature in a large building. The problem can be addressed by deploying sensors and actuators in space, processing collected data, and possibly planning actuations [31]. In many settings, the computational activity can (or have to) be performed *in-network* [5] in a *decentralised* way: in such systems, nodes locally sense, process,

© IFIP International Federation for Information Processing 2022
M. H. ter Beek and M. Sirjani (Eds.): COORDINATION 2022, LNCS 13271, pp. 99–117, 2022.
https://doi.org/10.1007/978-3-031-08143-9_7

and act upon the environment, and coordinate with *neighbour* nodes to collectively self-organise their activity. However, in general there exists a trade-off between performance and efficiency, that suggests to concentrate the activities on few nodes, or to endow systems with the capability of autonomously adapt the *granularity* of computation [32].

In this work, we focus on sampling signals that vary in space. Specifically, we would like to sample a spatially distributed signal through device coordination and self-organisation such that the samples accurately reflect the original signal and the least amount of resources is used to do so. In particular, we push forward a vision of space-fluid computations, namely computations that are fluid, i.e. change seamlessly, in space and – like fluids – adapt in response to pressure forces exerted by the underlying phenomenon. We reify the vision through an algorithm that handles the shape and lifetime of leader-based "regional processes" (cf. [21]), growing/shrinking as needed to sample a phenomenon of interest with a (locally) maximum level of accuracy and minimum resource usage. For instance, we would like to sample more densely those regions of space where the spatial phenomenon under observation has high variance, to better reflect its spatial dynamics. On the contrary, in regions where variance is low, we would like to sample the phenomenon more sparsely, so as to, e.g., save energy, communication bandwidth, etc. while preserving the same level of accuracy.

Accordingly, we consider the *field-based coordination* framework of *aggregate computing* [2,29], which has proven to be effective in modelling and programming self-organising behaviour in situated networks of devices interacting asynchronously. On top of it, we devise a solution that we call *aggregate sampling*, inspired by the approaches of self-stabilisation [28] and density-independence [3], that maps an input field representing a signal to be sampled into a regional partition field where each region provides a single sample; then, we characterise the aggregate sampling error based on a distance defined between stable snapshots of regional partition fields, and propose that an *effective* aggregate sampling is one that is locally optimal w.r.t. an error threshold, meaning that the regional partition cannot be improved simply by merging regions. In summary, we provide the following contributions:

- we define a model for distributed collaborative adaptive sampling and characterise the corresponding problem in the field-based coordination framework;
- we implement an algorithmic solution to the problem that leverages self-organisation patterns like gradients [6,28] and coordination regions [21] as well as *aggregate processes* [4];
- we experimentally validate the algorithm to verify interesting trade-offs between sparseness of the sampling and its error.

The rest of the paper is organised as follows. Section 2 covers motivation and related work. Section 3 provides a model for distributed sampling and the problem statement. Section 4 describes an algorithmic solution to the problem of sampling a distributed signal using the framework of aggregate computing. Section 5 performs an experimental validation of the proposed approach. Finally, Sect. 6 provides conclusive thoughts and delineates directions for further research.

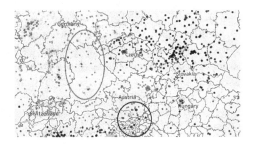

Fig. 1. Air quality statistics map taken from https://archive.ph/dMJO2. There are areas where the underlying phenomenon does not vary significantly in space (light-grey oval), hence sampling could be "sparsified" with tolerable loss of accuracy in modelling the observed phenomenon. In others (darker circle) variance is high, requiring a more detailed spatial sampling.

2 Motivation and Related Work

Consider a wireless sensor network (WSN) of any topology deployed across a geographical area to monitor a spatially-distributed phenomenon, such as, for instance, air quality, as depicted in Fig. 1. We want to dynamically and adaptively find a partitioning that minimises the number and maximises the size of regions, while preserving as much as possible the underlying information. Hence, in areas with low variance, we want our regions to be larger, as many samples will report similar values. Conversely, in areas with high spatial variance, smaller regions are necessary as even proximal samples may have very different values.

There are several approaches in the literature that attempt to solve similar problems, in different research areas and with different techniques. In *adaptive sampling* [17,27] the goal is to extend or reduce the set of samples drawn depending on temporal dynamics or across space. There, most of the literature is about designing fixed strategies for sensor placement (at design-time), sensor selection (at run-time), or so-called sampling designs, that is, how the sampling process may be adaptive to either network-level measures (energy consumption, communication costs, sensor distance, etc.) or domain-level measures (information gain, entropy, correlation, etc.). Our approach fundamentally differs in core aspects, such as full distribution of computations, and full self-adaptiveness to the observed phenomenon without any a-priori knowledge.

Other research focuses on *mobile* sensors, e.g., robots [7,8,15,25], hence the goal is to move them to the most informative sensing locations. Some work aims to adapt the sampling process to cope with *spatial* (and, often, temporal) phenomena, preserving some spatial properties of the WSN or the phenomenon under observation [9,12,26]. These pursue a goal similar to the one of this work, but with different techniques: we leverage a programmable, adaptive, and self-organising approach based on the field calculus and aggregate programming, whereas they adopt heterogeneous tools rooted in geometric frameworks (such as Voronoi tessellation), information theory, and optimisation.

Finally, there are approaches explicitly relying on adaptive and spatial *clustering* techniques [13,14,30], where device partitioning is meant to improve energy efficiency or reduce communication costs by electing leaders that perform sampling on behalf of the whole cluster. These approaches are mostly driven by network-level metrics, whereas we rely on any arbitrary univariate statistics of the phenomenon under observation.

In [30], the proposed approach combines distance measurements, connectivity, and density information of sensors (not the underlying phenomenon) to define clusters with similar deployment density that group devices in close proximity. The objective is to produce better deployments of sensors whose aggregate measurements can benefit energy consumption. On the contrary, our objective is to create irregularities in the device network to better represent the phenomenon under observations, with a trade-off about not wasting resources while doing so. Accordingly, we do clustering through leader election as in [30], but based on univariate statistics of the observed phenomenon, rather than on network-related information. With this respect, the work in [14] groups together sensors with similar readings, hence is similar to ours in how clusters are formed. However, the authors attempt to build clusters with minimal variance in size, that is contrary to our goal of adaptively shape clusters with different sizes so as to better sample the underlying spatial phenomenon. Finally, the work in [12] is a rare example of an adaptive algorithm that is also concerned with up-scaling sampling when is needed, whereas most efforts go in the direction of down-scaling for energy saving purposes. In this it is similar to our own proposal. However, they exploit the assumption there measures coming from sensors in close proximity are highly correlated, whereas we specifically focus on those domains where the opposite may be true.

3   Distributed Aggregate Sampling: Model

In order to define the problem and characterise our approach, we leverage the event structure framework [1].

3.1   Computational Model

We consider a computational model where a set of *devices* compute at discrete steps called *computation rounds* and interact with *neighbour devices* by exchanging messages. Executions of such systems can be modelled through *event structures* [18]. Following the general approach in [1], we enrich the event structure with information about the devices where events occur.

Definition 1 (Situated event structure). *A* situated event structure *(ES) is a pair* $\langle E, \rightsquigarrow, d \rangle$ *where*

- *E is a countable set of* **events***,*
- $\rightsquigarrow \subseteq E \times E$ *is a* **messaging** *relation from a* **sender** *event to a* **receiver** *event (these are also called* **neighbour** *events),*

- $d : E \rightarrow \Delta$, where Δ is finite, maps an event to the device where it occurs,

such that:

- the transitive closure of $\rightsquigarrow$ forms an irreflexive partial order $< \subseteq E \times E$, called **causality** relation (an event ϵ is in the **past** of another event ϵ' if $\epsilon < \epsilon'$, in the **future** if $\epsilon' < \epsilon$, or **concurrent** otherwise);
- for any $\delta \in \Delta$, the projection of the ES to the set of events $E_\delta = \{\epsilon \in E \mid d(\epsilon) = \delta\}$ forms a well-order, i.e., a sequence $\epsilon_0 \rightsquigarrow \epsilon_1 \rightsquigarrow \epsilon_2 \rightsquigarrow \ldots;$

We also define:

- Notation $recvs(\epsilon) = \{\delta \in \Delta \mid \delta = d(\epsilon') \implies \epsilon \rightsquigarrow \epsilon'\}$ to denote the set of receivers of ϵ, i.e., the devices receiving a message from ϵ.
- Notation $T_{\epsilon_0}^- = \{\epsilon : \epsilon < \epsilon_0\}$ to denote the past event cone of ϵ_0 (finite set).
- Notation $T_{\epsilon_0}^+ = \{\epsilon : \epsilon_0 < \epsilon\}$ to denote the future event cone of ϵ_0.
- Notation $X|_{E'}$ to denote the projection of a set, function, or ES thereof X to the set of events $E' \subseteq E$. Note that the projection of an event structure to the future event cone of an event is still a well-formed ES.

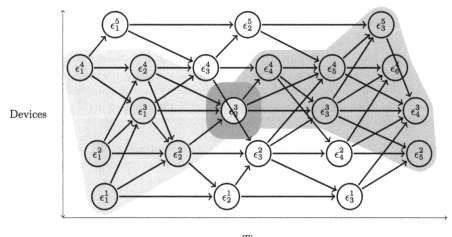

Devices

Time

Fig. 2. Example of an event structure. In the node labels, superscripts denote device identifiers, while subscripts are progressive numbers denoting subsequent rounds at the same device. The blue (resp. green) background denotes the future (resp. past) of a reference event denoted with a yellow background. (Color figure online)

An example of ES is given in Fig. 2, events denote computation rounds. Note that self-messages (i.e., messages from an event to the next on the same device) model persistence of *state* over time. In the computation model we consider, based on [1], each event ϵ represents the execution of a program taking all incoming messages, and producing an outgoing message (sent to all neighbours) and a result value associated with ϵ. Such "map" of result values across all events defines a computational field, as follows.

Definition 2 (Computational field). *Let* $\mathbf{E} = \langle E, \rightsquigarrow, d \rangle$ *be an event structure. A* computational field *on* $\mathbf{E}$ *is a function* $f : E \rightarrow \mathbb{V}$ *that maps every event* ϵ *in* E *(also called the* domain *of the field) to some value in a value set* $\mathbb{V}$.

Computational fields are essentially the "distributed values" which our model deals with; hence computation is captured by the following definition.

Definition 3 (Field computation). *Let* $\mathbf{E} = \langle E, \rightsquigarrow, d \rangle$ *be an event structure, and* $\mathbb{F}_{E,\mathbb{V}}$ *be the set of fields on domain* E *with range* $\mathbb{V}$, *i.e.*, $\mathbb{F}_{E,\mathbb{V}} = \{f_i : E \rightarrow \mathbb{V}\}$. *A* field computation *over* $\mathbf{E}$ *is a function* $\Phi_{\mathbf{E}} : \mathbb{F}_{E,\mathbb{V}} \rightarrow \mathbb{F}_{E,\mathbb{V}}$ *mapping an input field to an output field on the same domain of* $\mathbf{E}$.

This definition naturally extends to the case of zero or multiple input fields.

Definition 4 (Field operator). *A* field operator *(or* field program*) is denoted as the result of computation on any possible environment, hence it is a function* P *taking an ES and yielding the field computation that would occur on it, namely* $P(\mathbf{E}) = \Phi_{\mathbf{E}}$.

3.2 Self-stabilisation

We now provide the definitions necessary to model *self-stabilisation* following the approach in [28]. Namely, the following definitions capture the idea of *adaptiveness* whereby as the environment of computation stabilises, then the result of computation stabilises too, and such a result does not depend on previous transitory changes.

Definition 5 (Static environment). *An event structure* $\mathbf{E} = \langle E, \rightsquigarrow, d \rangle$ *is said to be a* static environment *if it has stable topology, namely all events of a given device always share the same set of receivers, i.e.,* $\forall \epsilon, \epsilon', d(\epsilon) = d(\epsilon') \Rightarrow recvs(\epsilon) = recvs(\epsilon')$.

Definition 6 (Stabilising environment). *An event structure* $\mathbf{E} = \langle E, \rightsquigarrow, d \rangle$ *is said to be a* stabilising environment *if it is eventually static, i.e.,* $\exists \epsilon_0 \in E$ *such that* $\mathbf{E}|_{T_{\epsilon_0}^+} = \langle E|_{T_{\epsilon_0}^+}, \rightsquigarrow |_{T_{\epsilon_0}^+}, d|_{T_{\epsilon_0}^+} \rangle$ *is static. In this case we say it is static since event* ϵ_0.

Definition 7 (Stabilising field). *Let event structure* $\mathbf{E} = \langle E, \rightsquigarrow, d \rangle$ *be a stabilising environment, static since event* ϵ_0. *A field* $f : E \rightarrow \mathbb{V}$ *is said stabilising if it eventually provides stable output, i.e.,* $\exists \epsilon > \epsilon_0$ *such that* $\forall \epsilon' > \epsilon$ *it holds that* $d(\epsilon) = d(\epsilon') \implies f(\epsilon) = f(\epsilon')$.

Definition 8 (Stabilising computation). *A field computation* $\Phi_{\mathbf{E}} = \mathbb{F}_{E,\mathbb{V}} \rightarrow \mathbb{F}_{E,\mathbb{V}}$ *is said* stabilising *if, when applied to a stabilising input field, it yields a stabilising output field.*

Definition 9 (Self-stabilising operator). *A field operator (or program) P is said self-stabilising, if in any stabilising environment $\mathbf{E}$ it yields a stabilising computation $\Phi_{\mathbf{E}}$ such that, for any pair of input fields f_1, f_2 eventually equal, i.e. $f_1|_{T_\epsilon^+} = f_2|_{T_\epsilon^+}$ for some event ϵ, their ouput is eventually equal too, i.e., there exists a $\epsilon' > \epsilon$ such that $\Phi_{\mathbf{E}}(f_1)|_{T_{\epsilon'}^+} = \Phi_{\mathbf{E}}(f_2)|_{T_{\epsilon'}^+}$*

3.3 Problem Definition

We start by introducing the notion of *regional partition*, which is a finite set of non-overlapping contiguous clusters of devices: a notion that prepares the ground to that of an *aggregate sampling* which we introduce in this paper.

Definition 10 (Regional partition field). *Let $\mathbf{E} = \langle E, \rightsquigarrow, d \rangle$ be a stabilising environment static since event ϵ_0. A regional partition field is a stabilising field $f : E \rightarrow \mathbb{V}$ on $\mathbf{E}$ such that:*

- *(finiteness) the image $Img(f) = \{f(x) \mid x \in E\}$ is a finite set of values;*
- *(eventual contiguity) there exists an event $\epsilon_0' > \epsilon_0$ such that for any pair of events $\epsilon_1, \epsilon_n \in T_{\epsilon_0'}^+$ with $\epsilon_1 < \epsilon_n$, if $f(\epsilon_1) = f(\epsilon_n)$ then there exists a sequence of events (ϵ_i) connecting ϵ_1 to ϵ_n where $f(\epsilon_i) = f(\epsilon_1) = f(\epsilon_n)\ \forall n$.*

Note that the set of domains of regions induced by f is defined by $regions(f) = \{f^{-1}(v) : v \in Img(f)\}$.

An example of a regional partition field is shown in Fig. 3. Notice that for any pair of events in the same space-time region there exists a path of events entirely contained in that region. Also notice that, by this definition, different disjoint regions denoted by the same value r are not possible.

Definition 11 (Aggregate sampling). *An aggregate sampling is a stabilising computation $\Phi_S : \mathbb{F}_{E,\mathbb{V}} \rightarrow \mathbb{F}_{E,\mathbb{V}}$ that, given in input a field to be sampled, it outputs a regional partition field.*

Once we have defined an aggregate sampling process in terms of its inputs, outputs, and stabilising dynamics, we need a way to measure the error introduced by the aggregate sampling. To this purpose, we introduce the notion of a *stable snapshot*, namely a field consisting of a sample of one event per device from the stable portion of a stabilising field.

Definition 12 (Stable snapshot). *Let $\mathbf{E} = \langle E, \rightsquigarrow, d \rangle$ be an event structure, and $f : E \rightarrow \mathbb{V}$ be a stabilising field on $\mathbf{E}$ which provides stable output from $\epsilon_0 \in E$. We define a stable snapshot of field f as a field obtained by restricting f to a subset of events in the future event cone of ϵ_0 and with exactly one event per device, i.e., a field $f_S : E_S \rightarrow \mathbb{V}$ such that $E_S \subseteq T_{\epsilon_0}^+$, and $\forall \epsilon, \epsilon' \in E_S : d(\epsilon) = d(\epsilon') \implies \epsilon = \epsilon'$, and $\forall \epsilon \in T_{\epsilon_0}^+, \exists \epsilon' \in E_S : d(\epsilon') = d(\epsilon)$.*

Definition 13 (Spatial field distance). *A spatial field distance $\mu : \mathbb{F}_{E,\mathbb{V}} \times \mathbb{F}_{E,\mathbb{V}} \rightarrow \mathbb{R}_0^+$ is a function from pairs of spatial fields with the same domain to non-negative reals, such that:*

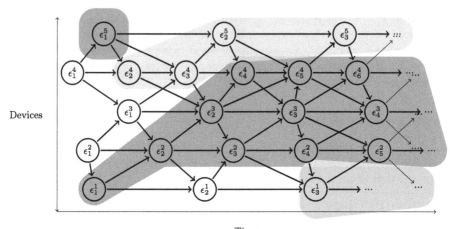

Time

Fig. 3. Example of a regional partition field with regions r_{blue}, r_{green}, r_{yellow}, r_{white} (the background is used to denote the output of the field). Notice that contiguity does not hold everywhere and anytime but only since event ϵ_2^3.

- (identity) $\mu(f, f') = 0 \iff f = f'$;
- (additivity) $\mu(f, f') \geq \mu(f|_{E'}, f'|_{E'})$ for any $E' \subseteq E$.

Definition 14 (Aggregate sampling error). *Let $\Phi_\mathbf{E} : \mathbb{F}_{E,\mathbb{V}} \to \mathbb{F}_{E,\mathbb{V}}$ be an aggregate sampling, and consider an input field $f_i : E \to \mathbb{V}$ and corresponding output regional partition $f_o : E \to \mathbb{V}$. We say that f_o samples f_i within error η according to distance μ, if the distance of stable snapshots of f_i and f_o in any region is not bigger then η, that is: let ϵ_0 be an event from which $\mathbf{E}$ is static and f_i and f_o are stable, let f_i^s and f_o^s be stable snapshots of f_i and f_o in the future cone of ϵ_0, then for any region $E' \in regions(f_o^s)$, we have $\mu(f_i^s|_{E'}, f_o^s|_{E'}) \leq \eta$.*

The aggregate sampling error provides a measure of *accuracy*, but in general we are also interested in *efficiency*, namely, in the ability of a regional partition to be accurate while relying on a small number of regions. Among the various possible definitions, we introduce the following notion of local optimality, stating that no region in the regional partition could be attached to an existing region without exceeding the desired error.

Definition 15 (Local optimality of a regional partition). *Let $\Phi_\mathbf{E} : \mathbb{F}_{E,\mathbb{V}} \to \mathbb{F}_{E,\mathbb{V}}$ be an aggregate sampling, and consider an input field f_i and corresponding output regional partition f_o such that f_o samples f_i within error η according to distance μ. We say that f_o is locally optimal under error η if for no pairs of contiguous regions $E', E'' \in regions(f_o)$ we have $\mu(f_i^s|_{E' \cup E''}, f_o^s|_{E' \cup E''}) \leq \eta$—with spatial fields f_i^s and f_o^s obtained as in Definition 14.*

Notice that, since our goal is to deal with dynamic phenomena and large-scale environments, we are not interested in finding globally optimal solutions, but rather heuristics for self-organising behaviour. So, we are now ready to define the goal operator for this paper.

Definition 16 (Effective sampling operator). *An effective sampling operator is a self-stabilising operator P_η, parametric in the error bound η, such that in any stabilising environment* **E** *and stabilising input f_i, a locally optimal regional partition within error η is produced.*

4 Aggregate Computing-Based Solution

In this section, we define an *effective aggregate sampling* within the framework of Aggregate Computing [2,29]. The approach is rooted in the idea that a system can be partitioned into regions by identifying *leader* devices (cf. algorithms for sparse-choice leader election [16]) associated with a set of devices expanding until the *aggregate sampling error* within the growing region is under some threshold—while ensuring there is no overlap with other regions (i.e., each device is associated with exactly one leader). More precisely:

1. each device announces its candidature for leader;
2. each device propagates to neighbours the candidature of the device it currently recognises as leader, fostering expansion of its corresponding region;
3. in a region, the *aggregate sampling error* is computed, which monotonically increases with the hop-distance from the leader;
4. devices discard candidatures whose errors exceed a threshold;
5. in case multiple valid candidatures (i.e., whose error is under the threshold) reach a device, one is selected based on a *competition policy*.

Competition and Leader Strength. Although competition among leaders could be realised in several ways, many techniques may lead to non-self-stabilising behaviour: for instance, if the winning leader is selected randomly in the set of those whose error is under threshold, regions may keep changing even in a static environment. In this work, we propose a simple strategy: every leader associates its candidature with the local value of a field that we call *leader strength*; in case of competing candidatures, the highest such value is selected as winner, breaking the symmetry. The leader strength can be of any orderable type, and its choice impacts the overall selection of the regions by imposing a selection priority over leaders (hence on region-generation points).

Region Expansion and Error Metric. Inspired by previous work on distributed systems whose computation is independent from device distribution [3], we accumulate an *error metric* along the path from the leader device towards other devices along a gradient [6], a distributed data structure proven to be self-stabilising [28]. We thus have two major drivers: 1. the leader strength affects the creation of the regions by influencing the positions of their source points; 2. the error metric influences the expansion in space of the region across all directions, mandating its size and (along with the interaction with other regions) its shape.

For instance, a metric could be the absolute value of the difference in the perceived signal between two devices: devices perceiving very different values would tend not to cluster together (even if spatially close), as they would perceive each other as farther away (leading to irregular shapes).

For the competition process to progress, we need that, in zones where multiple regions are expanding concurrently, multiple gradients run concurrently and overlapping [19]. This requires special handling in the aggregate computing framework, hence we modeled the expansion of each region as a separate aggregate process [4].

As the next section verifies through simulations, linking region expansion with the error metric enables to find locally optimal sampling regions, in the sense that all regions are necessary: be removing some region (e.g. merging it with a nearby region) less resources will be used, indeed, but accuracy would be compromised.

5   Evaluation

In this section, we validate the behaviour of the proposed effective aggregate sampling algorithm. The goals of the evaluation are the following:

- *stabilisation*: we expect the algorithm to be *self-stabilising*, and thus to behave in a self-stabilising way under different conditions (as per Definition 9);
- *high information (entropy)*: we expect the algorithm to split areas with different measurements, namely, to dynamically increase the number of regions on a per-need basis to minimise the *aggregate sampling error* (as per Definition 14);
- *error-controlled upscaling*: we expect the algorithm to not abuse of region creation, but to keep the minimum number of regions (hence of the largest size) required to maintain accuracy (as per Definition 15), intuitively, grouping together devices with similar measurements.

Clearly, upscaling and high information density are at odds: maximum information is achieved by maximising the number of regions, and thus assigning each device its unique region, but this would prevent any upscaling. On the other hand, the maximum possible upscaling would be achieved when all devices belong to the same region, thus minimising information. We want our regions to change in space "fluidly" and opportunistically tracking the situation at hand, achieving a trade-off between upscaling and amount of information (as per Definition 16).

5.1   Scenario

We challenge the proposed approach by letting the algorithm operate on different deployments of one thousand devices and different data sources. We deploy devices into a square arena with different topologies: *i) grid (regular grid)*: devices are regularly located in a grid; *ii) pgrid (perturbed/irregular grid)*: starting from a grid, devices' positions are perturbed randomly on both axes;

iii) uniform: positions are generated with a uniform random distribution; *iv)
exp (exponential random)*: positions are generated with a uniform random distribution on one axis and with an exponential distribution on the other, thus challenging device-distribution sensitivity. In all cases, we avoid network segmentation by forcing each device to communicate *at least* with the eight closest devices.

We simulate the system when sampling the following phenomena: *(i) Constant*: the signal is the same across the space, we expect the system to upscale as much as possible; *(ii) Uniform*: the signal has maximum entropy, each point in space has a random value, we thus expect the system to create many small regions; *(iii) Bivariate gaussian (gauss)*: the signal has higher value at the center of the network, and lower towards the borders, producing a gaussian curve whose expected value is located at the center of the network, we expect regions to be smaller where the data changes more quickly; *(iv) Multiple bivariate gaussian (multi-gauss)*: similar to the previous case, but the signal value is built by summing three bivariate gaussian whose expected value is one third of the previous gaussian, and whose expected values are located along the diagonal of the network (bottom-left corner, center, top-right corner); *(v) Dynamic*: the system cycles across the previous states, we use this configuration to investigate whether and how the proposed solution adapts to changes in the structure of the signal.

5.2   Parameters

The proposed solution can be tuned using three major knobs: the leader strength, the error tolerance, and the distance metric. In these experiments, we fix the error tolerance to a constant value throughout the board, while we try three different solutions for the leader strength and the distance metric.

For the former, we consider: *(i) value*: the local value of the tracked signal s; *(ii) mean*: the neighborhood-mean value of the tracked signal s, assuming N to be the set of neighbors (including the local device), and s_i to be the value of the tracked signal at device $i \in N$, the value is computed as: $M = \Sigma_{i \in N} s_i / |N|$; *(iii) variance*: the neighborhood-variance of the tracked signal s, assuming M_i to be the neighborhood-mean computed at device $i \in N$, the value is computed as: $\Sigma_{i \in N} (M_i - s_i)^2 / |N|$.

For the latter, we consider: *(i) distance*: the spatial distance is used as distance metric; *(ii) diff*: assuming that s_i is the value of the tracked signal at device i, the distance between two neighboring devices a and b is measured as: $e_{ab} = e_{ba} = min(\epsilon, |s_a - s_b|)$, where $\epsilon \in \mathbb{R}_+$, $\epsilon = 0$ iff $a = b$, $0 < \epsilon \ll 1$ otherwise, we bound the minimum value to preserve the triangle inequality; *(iii) mix*: we mix the two previous metrics so that both error and physical distance concur in the distance definition, assuming $\overline{ab}$ to be the spatial distance between devices a and b, we measure the mix metric as: *(iv)* $\overline{ab} \cdot e_{ab}$.

5.3 Metrics

We investigate the behaviour of the system through the following metrics, assuming, at any given time, a set of devices D partitioned into a set of regions $R = R_1 \cup \cdots \cup R_{|R|}$, where each R_r is a set of devices $\{D_1^r, \ldots, D_{|R_r|}^r\}$, and each device D_d^r reads the local value of the tracked signal s_d^r:

- *Region count $|R|$ (regions).* Counting the regions provides an indication about efficiency (Definition 15): more partitions should be present in contexts where the sampled signal has higher entropy;
- *Mean region size $\mu_R = \sum_{i=1}^{|R|} |R_i|/|R|$ (devices).* Ancillary to the region count, but density-sensitive: when devices are distributed irregularly (as in the **exp** deployment, see Sect. 5.1), we expect this metric to be less predictable;
- *Standard deviation of the mean of the signal in regions $\sigma(\mu_s)$ (same unit of the signal).* Proxy for inter-region difference, high values indicate large differences between different regions. The mean signal inside region R_r is computed as:

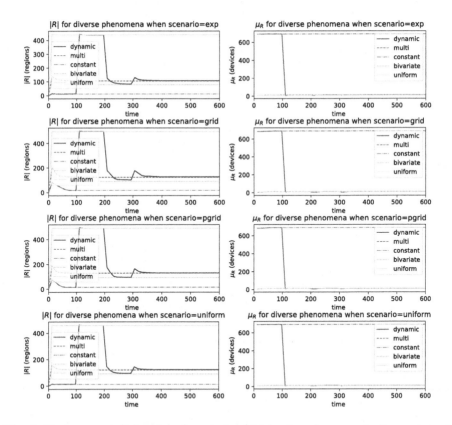

Fig. 4. Region count (left column) and size (right column) across deployments and scenarios. The system behaves very similarly regardless of the device disposition. As expected, the higher information density leads to more smaller regions. The dynamic scenario shows that the partitions change in response to changes in the signal.

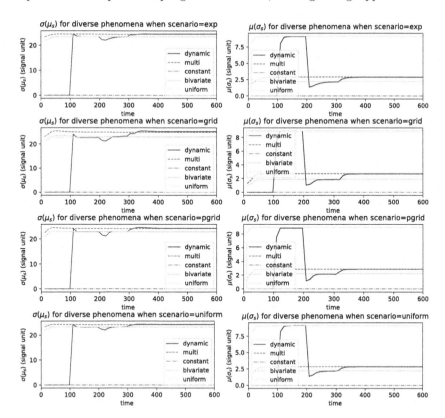

Fig. 5. Standard deviation of the mean region value (left) and mean standard deviation (right) across deployments and scenarios, indicating respectively how much the regions readings differ from each other (the higher the more different) and how the regions are internally similar (the lower the more homogeneous are regions). The constant and uniform random signals work as baselines: in the former case, very large areas gets formed, while in the latter most regions count a single device (as expected). In the other cases, inter-region differences is maximized (they get as high as the most extreme case) keeping internal consistency under control.

$\mu_s^{R_r} = \sum_{i=1}^{|R_r|} s_i^r / |R_r|$, the mean of the means of the signal is $\mu_s^R = \sum_{i=1}^{|R|} \mu_s^{R_i} / |R|$, thus $\sigma(\mu_s) = \sqrt{\frac{1}{|R|} \sum_{i=1}^{|R|} (\mu_s^{R_i} - \mu_s^R)^2}$;

- *Mean standard deviation of the signal in regions $\mu(\sigma_s)$ (same unit of the signal).* Proxy for intra-region error. The lower this value, the more similar are the signal readings inside regions, hence the lower the error induced by the grouping (Definition 14). The standard deviation of a the tracked signal inside region R_r is computed as: $\sigma_s^{R_r} = \sqrt{\frac{1}{|R_r|} \sum_{i=1}^{|R_r|} (s_i^r - \mu_s^{R_r})^2}$, thus $\mu(\sigma_s) = \sum_{i=1}^{|R|} \sigma_s^{R_i} / |R|$;

- *Standard deviation of the standard deviation of the signal in regions $\sigma(\sigma_s)$ (same unit of the signal).* Proxy metric for the consistency of partitioning. Higher values indicate that partitions have different internal error, hence behave differently (striving to satisfy Definition 16). Computed as: $\sigma(\sigma_s) = \sqrt{\frac{1}{|R|} \sum_{i=1}^{|R|} (\sigma_s^{R_r} - \mu(\sigma_s))^2}$.

5.4   Implementation and Reproducibility

We rely on a prototype implementation realised in the Protelis programming language [23]. The simulations were realised using Alchemist [22], the data analysis has been performed using Xarray [10] and matplotlib [11]. For each element in the cartesian product of the device deployment type, signal form, leader strength, and distance metric, an experiment was performed. Each simulation has been repeated 100 times with a different random seed; random seeds control both the evolution of the system (the order in which devices compute) and their position on the arena (except for the regular grid deployment, which is not randomised); the presented results are the average across all repetitions; when a chart does not mention some of the parameters, then the results that are presented are also averaged across all values the parameter may assume for the simulation set. The experiment has been open sourced, publicly released[1], documented, equipped with a continuous integration system to guarantee replicability, and published as a permanently available, reusable artifact [24].

5.5   Results

We present the major findings of our analysis, whose complete version counts 630 charts, available to the interested reader in the experiment repository. In Fig. 4,

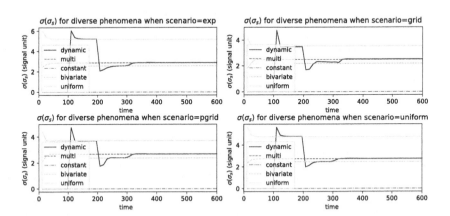

Fig. 6. Intra-region partitioning homogeneity, measured as the standard deviation across regions of the standard deviation of the signal inside regions. Higher values indicate that different regions are more heterogeneous, namely that some have more error than others.

---

[1] https://github.com/DanySK/Experiment-2022-Coordination-Space-Fluid.

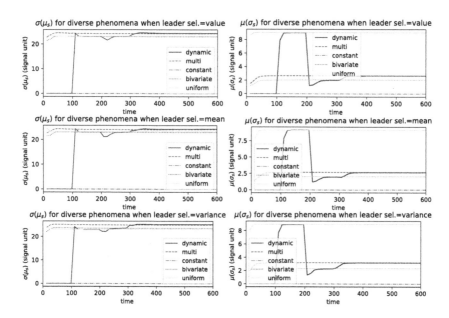

Fig. 7. Effect of different leader selection policies. The behaviour of the system is similar regardless of the way the region leader is selected.

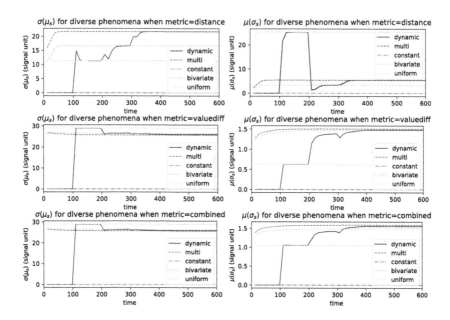

Fig. 8. Effect of different error measurement metrics. The system is very sensible to the metric used to accumulate error, which directly impacts the way distance is perceived, thus determining the maximum size and number of areas.

we show that our prototype implementation stabilises, as after a short transition all values become stable. Of course, in the dynamic case, these transitions are present throughout the experiment. As expected, the aggregate sampler defines a number of regions that differs depending on the underlying phenomenon under observation. From Fig. 5 and Fig. 6, we observe that the system tries indeed to maximise inter-region differences and minimise intra-region differences, thus effectively accounting or the tradeoff between *high information (entropy)* and *error-controlled upscaling* (as per Definition 16). Finally, Fig. 7 and Fig. 8 show how the algorithm responds to changing parameters. As expected, while modifying the leader selection policy has minimal impact on the behaviour of the system, changing the error metric modifies its behaviour greatly. In all cases, we observe that the driver signal with higher information entropy (uniform) generates more smaller regions than all other signals, while the one with lowest information entropy (constant) always produces few (usually one) large regions. The reason is that the leader selection impacts the originating point of a region, but it is its expansion (driven by the metric) that in the end determines both extension and shape.

6 Conclusions and Future Work

In this paper, we tackled the problem of defining an aggregate sampler sensitive to the spatial dynamics of the phenomenon under observation. In particular, we wanted to minimize the sampling error (minimum when all available sampling devices are used) while also minimising the regions count, two contrasting needs.

We formalised the problem within the framework of field calculus and aggregate computing, suitable to represent situated, large-scale, and dynamic computations. We thus designed a spatial adaptive aggregate sampler based on a leader election strategy that dynamically creates and grows/shrinks sampling clusters (or regions) based on error metric and leader strength. Through simulation, the sampler is shown to satisfy the mentioned tradeoff (*effective sampling*, Definition 16).

As measuring performance and efficiency of such an adaptive algorithm is far from trivial, we exploited several metrics to validate intended behaviour. However, as a follow-up work we would like to synthesize a single indicator able to measure both accuracy and efficiency, using information theory such as those derived from entropy (e.g. mutual information). Also, we are analyizing openly available air pollution datasets to design new simulations based on real-world data, so as to better emphasize the impact that our aggregate sampler could have for policy making based on spatial phenomena. Finally, future work will be devoted to investigating how space-fluid sampling can integrate with time-fluid aggregate computations [20].

Acknowledgements. This work has been supported by the MIUR PRIN 2017 Project "Fluidware" (N. 2017KRC7KT) and the MIUR FSE REACT-EU PON R&I 2014-2022 (N. CCI2014IT16M2OP005).

References

1. Audrito, G., Beal, J., Damiani, F., Viroli, M.: Space-time universality of field calculus. In: Serugendo, G.D.M., Loreti, M. (eds.) Coordination Models and Languages - 20th IFIP WG 6.1 International Conference, COORDINATION 2018, Held as Part of the 13th International Federated Conference on Distributed Computing Techniques, DisCoTec 2018, Madrid, Spain, 18–21 June 2018. Proceedings. LNCS, vol. 10852, pp. 1–20. Springer (2018). https://doi.org/10.1007/978-3-319-92408-3_1

2. Beal, J., Pianini, D., Viroli, M.: Aggregate programming for the internet of things. IEEE Comput. **48**(9), 22–30 (2015). https://doi.org/10.1109/MC.2015.261

3. Beal, J., Viroli, M., Pianini, D., Damiani, F.: Self-adaptation to device distribution in the internet of things. ACM Trans. Auton. Adapt. Syst. **12**(3), 12:1–12:29 (2017). https://doi.org/10.1145/3105758

4. Casadei, R., Viroli, M., Audrito, G., Pianini, D., Damiani, F.: Aggregate processes in field calculus. In: Riis Nielson, H., Tuosto, E. (eds.) COORDINATION 2019. LNCS, vol. 11533, pp. 200–217. Springer, Cham (2019). https://doi.org/10.1007/978-3-030-22397-7_12

5. Fasolo, E., Rossi, M., Widmer, J., Zorzi, M.: In-network aggregation techniques for wireless sensor networks: a survey. IEEE Wirel. Commun. **14**(2), 70–87 (2007). https://doi.org/10.1109/MWC.2007.358967

6. Fernandez-Marquez, J.L., Serugendo, G.D.M., Montagna, S., Viroli, M., Arcos, J.L.: Description and composition of bio-inspired design patterns: a complete overview. Nat. Comput. **12**(1), 43–67 (2013). https://doi.org/10.1007/s11047-012-9324-y

7. Garg, S., Ayanian, N.: Persistent monitoring of stochastic spatio-temporal phenomena with a small team of robots. In: Fox, D., Kavraki, L.E., Kurniawati, H. (eds.) Robotics: Science and Systems X, University of California, Berkeley, USA, July 12–16, 2014 (2014). https://doi.org/10.15607/RSS.2014.X.038. http://www.roboticsproceedings.org/rss10/p38.html

8. Graham, R., Cortés, J.: Cooperative adaptive sampling via approximate entropy maximization. In: Proceedings of the 48th IEEE Conference on Decision and Control, CDC 2009, Combined with the 28th Chinese Control Conference, 16–18 December 2009, Shanghai, China, pp. 7055–7060. IEEE (2009). https://doi.org/10.1109/CDC.2009.5400511

9. Hamouda, Y.E.M., Phillips, C.I.: Adaptive sampling for energy-efficient collaborative multi-target tracking in wireless sensor networks. IET Wirel. Sens. Syst. **1**(1), 15–25 (2011). https://doi.org/10.1049/iet-wss.2010.0059

10. Hoyer, S., Hamman, J.: xarray: N-D labeled arrays and datasets in Python. J. Open Res. Softw. **5**(1) (2017). https://doi.org/10.5334/jors.148

11. Hunter, J.D.: Matplotlib: a 2D graphics environment. Comput. Sci. Eng. **9**(3), 90–95 (2007). https://doi.org/10.1109/MCSE.2007.55

12. Lee, E.K., Viswanathan, H., Pompili, D.: SILENCE: distributed adaptive sampling for sensor-based autonomic systems. In: Schmeck, H., Rosenstiel, W., Abdelzaher, T.F., Hellerstein, J.L. (eds.) Proceedings of the 8th International Conference on Autonomic Computing, ICAC 2011, Karlsruhe, Germany, 14–18 June 2011, pp. 61–70. ACM (2011). https://doi.org/10.1145/1998582.1998594

13. Lin, Y., Megerian, S.: Sensing driven clustering for monitoring and control applications. In: 4th IEEE Consumer Communications and Networking Conference, CCNC 2007, Las Vegas, NV, USA, 11–13 January 2007, pp. 202–206. IEEE (2007). https://doi.org/10.1109/CCNC.2007.47

14. Liu, Z., Xing, W., Zeng, B., Wang, Y., Lu, D.: Distributed spatial correlation-based clustering for approximate data collection in WSNs. In: Barolli, L., Xhafa, F., Takizawa, M., Enokido, T., Hsu, H. (eds.) 27th IEEE International Conference on Advanced Information Networking and Applications, AINA 2013, Barcelona, Spain, 25–28 March 2013, pp. 56–63. IEEE Computer Society (2013). https://doi.org/10.1109/AINA.2013.26
15. Manjanna, S., Hsieh, A., Dudek, G.: Scalable multi-robot system for non-myopic spatial sampling. CoRR **abs/2105.10018** (2021). https://arxiv.org/abs/2105.10018
16. Mo, Y., Beal, J., Dasgupta, S.: An aggregate computing approach to self-stabilizing leader election. In: 2018 IEEE 3rd International Workshops on Foundations and Applications of Self* Systems (FAS*W), Trento, Italy, 3–7 September 2018, pp. 112–117. IEEE (2018). https://doi.org/10.1109/FAS-W.2018.00034
17. Mousavi, H.K., Sun, Q., Motee, N.: Space-time sampling for network observability. CoRR **abs/1811.01303** (2018). http://arxiv.org/abs/1811.01303
18. Nielsen, M., Plotkin, G.D., Winskel, G.: Petri nets, event structures and domains, part I. Theor. Comput. Sci. **13**, 85–108 (1981). https://doi.org/10.1016/0304-3975(81)90112-2
19. Pianini, D., Beal, J., Viroli, M.: Improving gossip dynamics through overlapping replicates. In: Lluch Lafuente, A., Proença, J. (eds.) COORDINATION 2016. LNCS, vol. 9686, pp. 192–207. Springer, Cham (2016). https://doi.org/10.1007/978-3-319-39519-7_12
20. Pianini, D., Casadei, R., Viroli, M., Mariani, S., Zambonelli, F.: Time-fluid field-based coordination through programmable distributed schedulers. Log. Methods Comput. Sci. **17**(4) (2021). https://doi.org/10.46298/lmcs-17(4:13)2021
21. Pianini, D., Casadei, R., Viroli, M., Natali, A.: Partitioned integration and coordination via the self-organising coordination regions pattern. Future Gener. Comput. Syst. **114**, 44–68 (2021). https://doi.org/10.1016/j.future.2020.07.032
22. Pianini, D., Montagna, S., Viroli, M.: Chemical-oriented simulation of computational systems with ALCHEMIST. J. Simul. **7**(3), 202–215 (2013). https://doi.org/10.1057/jos.2012.27
23. Pianini, D., Viroli, M., Beal, J.: Protelis: practical aggregate programming. In: Proceedings of the 30th Annual ACM Symposium on Applied Computing, Salamanca, Spain, 13–17 April 2015, pp. 1846–1853 (2015). https://doi.org/10.1145/2695664.2695913
24. Pianini, D., WhiteSource Renovate: Danysk/experiment-2022-coordination-space-fluid: 0.5.0-dev08+67e7add (2022). https://doi.org/10.5281/ZENODO.6473292
25. Rahimi, M.H., Hansen, M.H., Kaiser, W.J., Sukhatme, G.S., Estrin, D.: Adaptive sampling for environmental field estimation using robotic sensors. In: 2005 IEEE/RSJ International Conference on Intelligent Robots and Systems, Edmonton, Alberta, Canada, 2–6 August 2005, pp. 3692–3698. IEEE (2005). https://doi.org/10.1109/IROS.2005.1545070
26. Szczytowski, P., Khelil, A., Suri, N.: Asample: adaptive spatial sampling in wireless sensor networks. In: IEEE International Conference on Sensor Networks, Ubiquitous, and Trustworthy Computing, SUTC 2010 and IEEE International Workshop on Ubiquitous and Mobile Computing, UMC 2010, Newport Beach, California, USA, 7–9 June 2010, pp. 35–42. IEEE Computer Society (2010). https://doi.org/10.1109/SUTC.2010.37
27. Thompson, S.K.: Adaptive cluster sampling. J. Am. Stat. Assoc. **85**(412), 1050–1059 (1990). https://doi.org/10.1080/01621459.1990.10474975. https://www.tandfonline.com/doi/abs/10.1080/01621459.1990.10474975

28. Viroli, M., Audrito, G., Beal, J., Damiani, F., Pianini, D.: Engineering resilient collective adaptive systems by self-stabilisation. ACM Trans. Model. Comput. Simul. **28**(2), 1–28 (2018). https://doi.org/10.1145/3177774
29. Viroli, M., Beal, J., Damiani, F., Audrito, G., Casadei, R., Pianini, D.: From distributed coordination to field calculus and aggregate computing. J. Log. Algebraic Methods Program. **109**, 100486 (2019). https://doi.org/10.1016/j.jlamp.2019.100486
30. Virrankoski, R., Savvides, A.: TASC: topology adaptive spatial clustering for sensor networks. In: IEEE 2nd International Conference on Mobile Adhoc and Sensor Systems, MASS 2005, The City Center Hotel, Washington, USA, 7–10 November 2005, p. 10. IEEE Computer Society (2005). https://doi.org/10.1109/MAHSS.2005.1542850
31. Wu, F., Kao, Y., Tseng, Y.: From wireless sensor networks towards cyber physical systems. Pervasive Mob. Comput. **7**(4), 397–413 (2011). https://doi.org/10.1016/j.pmcj.2011.03.003
32. Yao, J.T., Vasilakos, A.V., Pedrycz, W.: Granular computing: perspectives and challenges. IEEE Trans. Cybern. **43**(6), 1977–1989 (2013). https://doi.org/10.1109/TSMCC.2012.2236648

Processes and Languages

Formal Choreographic Languages

Franco Barbanera[1], Ivan Lanese[2,3], and Emilio Tuosto[4(✉)]

[1] Department of Mathematics and Computer Science, University of Catania,
Catania, Italy
barba@dmi.unict.it
[2] Focus Team, University of Bologna, Bologna, Italy
ivan.lanese@gmail.com
[3] Focus Team, INRIA, Sophia Antipolis, France
[4] Gran Sasso Science Institute, L'Aquila, Italy
emilio.tuosto@gssi.it

Abstract. We introduce a meta-model based on formal languages, dubbed *formal choreographic languages*, to study message-passing systems. Our main motivation is to establish a framework for the comparison and generalisation of standard constructions and properties from the literature. In particular, we consider notions such as global view, local view, and projections from the former to the latter. The correctness of local views projected from global views is characterised in terms of a closure property. A condition is also devised to guarantee relevant communication properties such as (dead)lock-freedom. Formal choreographic languages capture existing formalisms for message-passing systems; we detail the cases of multiparty session types and choreography automata. Unlike many other models, formal choreographic languages can naturally model systems exhibiting non-regular behaviour.

1 Introduction

Choreographic models of message-passing systems are gaining momentum both in academia [8,12,13] and industry [10,27,34]. These models envisage the so-called *global* and *local* views of communicating systems. The former can be thought of as holistic descriptions of protocols that a number of participants should realise through some communication actions, the latter as descriptions of the contribution of single participants.

Research partly supported by the EU H2020 RISE programme under the Marie Skłodowska-Curie grant agreement No 778233. Work partially funded by MIUR project PRIN 2017FTXR7S *IT MATTERS* (Methods and Tools for Trustworthy Smart Systems). The first and second authors have also been partially supported by INdAM as members of GNCS (Gruppo Nazionale per il Calcolo Scientifico). The first author has also been partially supported by Progetto di Ateneo UNICT PIACERI. The authors thank the anonymous reviewers for their helpful comments, in particular one reviewer of a previous submission for suggesting the relation with Galois connections. The authors also thank Mariangiola Dezani-Ciancaglini for her support.

© IFIP International Federation for Information Processing 2022
M. H. ter Beek and M. Sirjani (Eds.): COORDINATION 2022, LNCS 13271, pp. 121–139, 2022.
https://doi.org/10.1007/978-3-031-08143-9_8

We propose *formal choreographic languages* (FCL) as a general framework to formalise message-passing systems; existing choreographic models can be conceived as specifications of FCLs. Specifically, we introduce *global* and *local* languages. Global languages (g-languages for short) are made of words built out of *interactions* of the form A→B:m, representing the fact that participant A sends message m to participant B, and participant B receives it. Local languages (l-languages for short) consist of words of *actions* of the forms A B?m and A B!m, respectively representing that participant B receives message m from A and that participant A sends message m to B.

Abstractly such languages consist of runs of a system described in terms of sequences of interactions at the global level and executed through message-passing at the local level. A word w in a global language represents then a possible run expected of a communicating system inducing an expected "local" behaviour on each participant A: the projection of w on A yields the sequence of *output* or *input* actions performed by A along the run w.

Our language-theoretic treatment is motivated mainly by the need for a general setting immune to syntactic restrictions. This naturally leads us to consider e.g., context-free choreographies (cf. Example 3.11). In fact, we strive for generality; basically *prefix-closure* is the only requirement we impose on FCL. The gist is that, if a sequence of interactions or of communications is an observable behaviour of a system, any prefix of the sequence should be observable as well. (We discuss some implications of relaxing prefix-closure in Sect. 8.) This allows us to consider partial executions as well as "complete" ones. We admit infinite words to account for diverging computations, ubiquitous in communication protocols.

Some g-languages cannot be faithfully executed by distributed components; consider { A→B:m, A→B:m·C→D:n } that specifies a system where, if occurring, the interaction between C and D has to follow the one between A and B. Clearly, this is not possible if the participants act concurrently because C and D are not aware of when the interaction between A and B takes place.

Contributions and Structure. We summarise below our main contributions. (Proofs and further material can be found in [7].)

Section 2 introduces FCL (g-languages in Definition 2.1, l-languages in Definition 2.2) and adapts standard constructions from the literature. We consider synchronous interactions; the asynchronous case, albeit interesting, is scope for future work (cf. Sect. 8). In particular, we render communicating systems as sets of l-languages (Definition 2.3), while we borrow projections from choreographies and multiparty session types.

Section 3 considers correctness and completeness. An immediate consequence of our constructions is the completeness of systems projected from g-languages (Corollary 3.2). Correctness is more tricky; for it, Definition 3.3 introduces *closure under unknown information* (CUI). Intuitively, a g-language is CUI if it contains extensions of words with a single interaction whose participants cannot distinguish the extended word from other words of the language. Theorem 3.7 characterises correctness of projected systems in terms of CUI.

Section 4 shows how FCLs capture many relevant communication properties in a fairly uniform way.

Section 5 proposes *branch-awareness* (Definition 5.3) to ensure the communication properties defined in Sect. 4 (Theorem 5.6). Intuitively, branch-awareness requires each participant to "distinguish" words where its behaviour differs. Notably, we separate the conditions for correctness from the ones for communication properties. Most approaches in the literature instead combine them into a single condition, which takes names such as well-branchedness or projectability [25]. Thus, these single conditions are stronger than each of CUI and branch-awareness.

Sections 6 and 7 illustrate the generality of FCLs on two case studies, respectively taken from multiparty session types [37] and choreography automata [6]. We remark that FCL can capture protocols that cannot be represented by regular g-languages such as the "task dispatching" protocol in Example 3.11. To the best of our knowledge this kind of protocols cannot be formalised in other approaches.

Section 8 draws some conclusions and discusses future work.

2   Formal Choreographic Languages

We briefly recall a few notions used through the paper. The sets of finite and infinite words on a given alphabet Σ are, respectively, denoted by Σ^* and Σ^ω, where an infinite word on Σ is a map from natural numbers to Σ (aka ω-word [38]). Let $\_\cdot\_$ be the concatenation operator on words and ε its neutral element. We write $a_0 \cdot a_1 \cdot a_2 \cdots$ for the word mapping i to $a_i \in \Sigma$ for all natural numbers i. A language L on Σ is a subset of $\Sigma^\infty = \Sigma^* \cup \Sigma^\omega$. The prefix-closure of $L \subseteq \Sigma^\infty$ is $\mathsf{pref}(L) = \{\, z \in \Sigma^\infty \mid \exists z' \in L : z \preceq z' \,\}$, where $\preceq$ is the prefix relation; L is *prefix-closed* if $L = \mathsf{pref}(L)$. A word z is *maximal* in a language $L \subseteq \Sigma^\infty$ if $z \preceq z'$ for $z' \in L$ implies $z' = z$. As usual we shall write $z \prec z'$ whenever $z \preceq z'$ and $z \neq z'$.

We shall deal with languages on particular alphabets, namely the alphabets of *interactions* Σ_{int} and of *actions* Σ_{act} whose definitions, borrowed from [6], are as follows[1]

$$\Sigma_{\text{int}} = \{\, \mathsf{A{\to}B{:}m} \mid \mathsf{A} \neq \mathsf{B} \in \mathfrak{P}, \mathsf{m} \in \mathfrak{M} \,\} \qquad \text{ranged over by } \alpha, \beta, \ldots$$
$$\Sigma_{\text{act}} = \{\, \mathsf{A\,B!m}, \mathsf{A\,B?m} \mid \mathsf{A} \neq \mathsf{B} \in \mathfrak{P}, \mathsf{m} \in \mathfrak{M} \,\} \qquad \text{ranged over by } \mathsf{a}, \mathsf{b}, \ldots$$

where $\mathfrak{P}$ is a fixed set of *participants* (or *roles*, ranged over by A, B, X, etc.) and $\mathfrak{M}$ is a fixed set of *messages* (ranged over by m, x, etc.); we take $\mathfrak{P}$ and $\mathfrak{M}$ disjoint. Let $\mathsf{msg}(\mathsf{A{\to}B{:}m}) = \mathsf{msg}(\mathsf{A\,B!m}) = \mathsf{m}$ and $\mathsf{ptp}(\mathsf{A{\to}B{:}m}) = \mathsf{ptp}(\mathsf{A\,B!m}) = \mathsf{ptp}(\mathsf{A\,B?m}) = \{\,\mathsf{A}, \mathsf{B}\,\}$. These functions extend homomorphically to (sets of) words. The *subject* of $\mathsf{A\,B!m}$ is the sender A and the subject of $\mathsf{A\,B?m}$ is the receiver B. Words on $\Sigma_{\text{int}}^\infty$ (ranged over by $w, w', \ldots$) are called *interaction*

---

[1] These sets may be infinite; formal languages over infinite alphabets have been studied, e.g., in [4].

words while those on Σ_{act}^{∞} (ranged over by $v, v', ...$) are called *words of actions*. Hereafter $z, z', ...$ range over $\Sigma_{int}^{\infty} \cup \Sigma_{act}^{\infty}$ and we use $\mathcal{L}$ and $\mathbb{L}$ to range over subsets of, respectively, Σ_{int}^{∞} and Σ_{act}^{∞}.

A *global language* specifies the expected interactions of a system while a *local language* specifies the communication behaviour of participants.

Definition 2.1 (Global language). *A global language (*g-language *for short) is a prefix-closed language $\mathcal{L}$ on Σ_{int}^{∞} such that $\mathsf{ptp}(\mathcal{L})$ is finite.*

Definition 2.2 (Local language). *A local language (*l-language *for short) is a prefix-closed language $\mathbb{L}$ on Σ_{act} such that $\mathsf{ptp}(\mathbb{L})$ is finite. An l-language is* A-local *if its words have all actions with subject* A.

As discussed in Sect. 1, l-languages give rise to *communicating systems*.

Definition 2.3 (Communicating system). *Let $\mathcal{P} \subseteq \mathfrak{P}$ be a finite set of participants. A (communicating) system over $\mathcal{P}$ is a map $S = (\mathbb{L}_A)_{A \in \mathcal{P}}$ assigning an* A-local language $\mathbb{L}_A \neq \{\varepsilon\}$ *such that $\mathsf{ptp}(\mathbb{L}_A) \subseteq \mathcal{P}$ to each participant* A $\in \mathcal{P}$.

By projecting a g-language $\mathcal{L}$ on a participant A we obtain the A-local language describing the sequence of actions performed by A in the interactions involving A in the words of $\mathcal{L}$.

Definition 2.4 (Projection). *The* projection on A *of an interaction* B→C:m *is computed by the function $\_ \downarrow\_ : \Sigma_{int} \times \mathfrak{P} \to \Sigma_{act} \cup \{\varepsilon\}$ defined by:*

$$(A{\to}B{:}m)\downarrow_A = A\,B!m \qquad (A{\to}B{:}m)\downarrow_B = A\,B?m \qquad (A{\to}B{:}m)\downarrow_C = \varepsilon$$

and extended homomorphically to interaction words and g-languages. The projection of a g-language $\mathcal{L}$, written $\mathcal{L}\downarrow$, is the communicating system $(\mathcal{L}\downarrow_A)_{A\in\mathsf{ptp}(\mathcal{L})}$.

Definition 2.4 recasts in our setting the notion of projection used, e.g., in [13,24].

Example 2.5. Let $\mathcal{L}$ = $\mathsf{pref}(\{\, C{\to}A{:}m \cdot A{\to}B{:}m,\ C{\to}B{:}m \cdot A{\to}B{:}m,\ C{\to}A{:}m \cdot C{\to}B{:}m \,\})$. By Definition 2.4, we have $\mathcal{L}\downarrow = (\mathcal{L}\downarrow_X)_{X \in \{A,B,C\}}$ where $\mathcal{L}\downarrow_A = \{\, \varepsilon,\ C\,A?m,\ C\,A?m \cdot A\,B!m,\ A\,B!m \,\}$, $\mathcal{L}\downarrow_B = \{\, \varepsilon,\ A\,B?m,\ C\,B?m,\ C\,B?m \cdot A\,B?m \,\}$, and $\mathcal{L}\downarrow_C = \{\, \varepsilon,\ C\,A!m,\ C\,B!m,\ C\,A!m \cdot C\,B!m \,\}$.   ◇

We consider a *synchronous* semantics of communicating systems, similarly to other choreographic approaches such as [12,13,15,37]. Intuitively, a choreographic word is in the semantics iff its projection on each participant A yields a word in the local language of A.

Definition 2.6 (Semantics). *Given a system S over $\mathcal{P}$, the set*

$$[\![S]\!] = \{\, w \in \Sigma_{int}^{\infty} \mid \mathsf{ptp}(w) \subseteq \mathcal{P} \ \wedge \forall A \in \mathcal{P}:\ w\downarrow_A \in S(A) \,\}$$

is the (synchronous) semantics *of S.*

Notice that the above definition coincides with the *join* operation in [18], used in realisability conditions for an asynchronous setting.

Example 2.7. The semantics $[\![\mathcal{L}\!\downarrow]\!]$ of the system $\mathcal{L}\!\downarrow$ in Example 2.5 is the prefix closure of $\{ \mathsf{C}{\rightarrow}\mathsf{A}{:}\mathsf{m}{\cdot}\mathsf{A}{\rightarrow}\mathsf{B}{:}\mathsf{m}, \ \mathsf{C}{\rightarrow}\mathsf{B}{:}\mathsf{m}{\cdot}\mathsf{A}{\rightarrow}\mathsf{B}{:}\mathsf{m}, \ \mathsf{C}{\rightarrow}\mathsf{A}{:}\mathsf{m}{\cdot}\mathsf{C}{\rightarrow}\mathsf{B}{:}\mathsf{m}{\cdot}\mathsf{A}{\rightarrow}\mathsf{B}{:}\mathsf{m} \}$.   ◇

Two interactions α and β are *independent* (in symbols $\alpha \parallel \beta$) when $\mathsf{ptp}(\alpha) \cap \mathsf{ptp}(\beta) = \emptyset$. Informally, independent interactions can be swapped. The concurrency closure on infinite words is delicate. One in fact has to allow infinitely many swaps while avoiding that they make an interaction disappear by pushing it infinitely far away. Technically, we consider Mazurkiewicz's traces [33] on Σ_{int} with independence relation $\alpha \parallel \beta$:

Definition 2.8 (Concurrency closure). *Let $\sim$ be the reflexive and transitive closure of the relation $\equiv$ on finite interaction words defined by $w\,\alpha\,\beta\,w' \equiv w\,\beta\,\alpha\,w'$ where $\alpha \parallel \beta$. Following [Def. 2.1][19], $\sim$ extends to Σ_{int}^{ω} by defining*

$$\text{for all } w, w' \in \Sigma_{int}^{\omega}: \qquad w \sim w' \quad \Longleftrightarrow \quad w \ll w' \quad \text{and} \quad w' \ll w$$

where $w \ll w'$ iff for each finite prefix w_1 of w there are a finite prefix w_1' of w' and a g-word $\hat{w} \in \Sigma_{int}^{*}$ such that $w_1 \cdot \hat{w} \sim w_1'$. A g-language $\mathcal{L}$ is concurrency closed (c-closed for short) if it coincides with its concurrency closure, namely $\mathcal{L} = \{ w \in \Sigma_{int}^{\infty} \mid \exists w' \in \mathcal{L} : w \sim w' \}$.

Semantics of systems are naturally c-closed since in a distributed setting independent events can occur in any order. Indeed

Proposition 2.9. *Let S be a system. Then $[\![S]\!]$ is c-closed.*

The intuition that g-languages, equipped with the projection and semantic functions of Definition 2.4 and Definition 2.6, do correspond to a natural syntax and semantics for the abstract notion of choreography, can be strengthened by showing that these functions form a Galois connection.

Let us define $\mathbb{G} = \{ \mathcal{L} \mid \mathcal{L} \text{ is a g-language} \}$ and $\mathbb{S} = \{ S \mid S \text{ is a system} \}$. Moreover, given $S, S' \in \mathbb{S}$, we define $S \subseteq S'$ if $S(\mathsf{A}) \subseteq S'(\mathsf{A})$ for each A.

Proposition 2.10. *The functions $\_\!\downarrow$ and $[\![\_]\!]$ form a (monotone) Galois connection between the posets $(\mathbb{G}, \subseteq)$ and $(\mathbb{S}, \subseteq)$, namely, $\_\!\downarrow$ and $[\![\_]\!]$ are monotone functions such that, given $\mathcal{L} \in \mathbb{G}$ and $S \in \mathbb{S}$:*

$$\mathcal{L}\!\downarrow \subseteq S \iff \mathcal{L} \subseteq [\![S]\!]$$

Notice that, by Proposition 2.10, $\mathcal{L}\!\downarrow \subseteq S$ can be understood as "$\mathcal{L}$ can be realized by S" according to the notion of realisability frequently used in the literature, namely that all behaviours of the choreography are possible for the system.

It is well-known that, given a Galois connection $(f_{\star}, f^{\star})$ the function $\mathsf{cl} = f^{\star} \circ f_{\star}$ is a closure operator namely, it is monotone ($x \leq y \implies \mathsf{cl}(x) \leq \mathsf{cl}(y)$), extensive ($x \leq \mathsf{cl}(x)$), and idempotent ($\mathsf{cl}(x) = \mathsf{cl}(\mathsf{cl}(x))$). In our setting $\mathsf{cl}(\_) = [\![\_\!\downarrow]\!]$, hence the above boils down to the following corollary:

Corollary 2.11. *For all g-languages* $\mathcal{L}, \mathcal{L}' \in \mathbb{G}$,

monotonicity: $\mathcal{L} \subseteq \mathcal{L}' \implies [\![\mathcal{L}\!\downarrow]\!] \subseteq [\![\mathcal{L}'\!\downarrow]\!]$,
extensiveness: $\mathcal{L} \subseteq [\![\mathcal{L}\!\downarrow]\!]$,
idempotency: $[\![\mathcal{L}\!\downarrow]\!] = [\![[\![\mathcal{L}\!\downarrow]\!]\!\downarrow]\!]$.

As we shall see, extensiveness coincides with completeness (Definition 3.1) and, together with monotonicity, implies *harmonicity* (Definition 4.1).

3 Correctness and Completeness

A g-language specifies the expected communication behaviour of a system made of several components. We now define properties relating a communicating system (i.e., a set of l-languages) with a specification (i.e., a g-language).

Definition 3.1 (Correctness and completeness). *A system S is* correct *(resp.* complete*) w.r.t. a g-language* $\mathcal{L}$ *if* $[\![S]\!] \subseteq \mathcal{L}$ *(resp.* $[\![S]\!] \supseteq \mathcal{L}$).

Correctness and completeness are related to existing notions. For instance, in the literature on multiparty session types (see, e.g., the survey [25]) correctness is analogous to *subject reduction* and completeness to *session fidelity*. Notice that by Proposition 2.10, we can interpret $\mathcal{L}\!\downarrow\,\subseteq S$ as a characterisation for completeness of S w.r.t. $\mathcal{L}$.

We discuss now how to ensure correctness and completeness "by construction". Completeness is trivial: it holds for any projected system and coincides with the extensiveness property of the closure operator associated to the Galois connection defined in Sect. 2.

Corollary 3.2. *The projection of a g-language* $\mathcal{L}$ *is complete w.r.t.* $\mathcal{L}$.

We show now how correctness can be characterised as a closure property.

Definition 3.3 (CUI). *A g-language* $\mathcal{L}$ *is* closed under unknown information *(in symbols* $cui(\mathcal{L})$*) if, for all finite words* $w_1 \cdot \alpha, w_2 \cdot \alpha \in \mathcal{L}$ *with the same final interaction* $\alpha = $ A→B:m $\in \Sigma_{int}$, $w \cdot \alpha \in \mathcal{L}$ *for all* $w \in \mathcal{L}$ *such that* $w\!\downarrow_A = w_1\!\downarrow_A$ *and* $w\!\downarrow_B = w_2\!\downarrow_B$.

Intuitively, participants cannot distinguish words with the same projection on their role. Hence, if two participants A and B find words w_1 and w_2 compatible with another word w, and interaction A→B:m can occur after both w_1 and w_2, then it should be enabled also after w. Indeed, A (resp. B) cannot know whether the current word is w or w_1 (resp. w_2), hence A and B are willing to take A→B:m, which can thus happen at the system level. Closure under unknown information (CUI for short) lifts this requirement at the level of g-language.

Example 3.4. The language $\mathcal{L}$ in Example 2.5 is not CUI because it contains the words

$$w_1 \cdot \alpha = \text{C→A:m·A→B:m} \qquad w_2 \cdot \alpha = \text{C→B:m·A→B:m} \qquad \text{and} \qquad w = \text{C→A:m·C→B:m}$$

and A cannot distinguish between w_1 and w while B cannot distinguish between w_2 and w; nonetheless $w \cdot \mathsf{A} {\rightarrow} \mathsf{B} {:} \mathsf{m} = \mathsf{C} {\rightarrow} \mathsf{A} {:} \mathsf{m} \cdot \mathsf{C} {\rightarrow} \mathsf{B} {:} \mathsf{m} \cdot \mathsf{A} {\rightarrow} \mathsf{B} {:} \mathsf{m} \notin \mathcal{L}$. Notice that $w \cdot \mathsf{A} {\rightarrow} \mathsf{B} {:} \mathsf{m} \in [\![\mathcal{L}{\downarrow}]\!]$, hence $\mathcal{L} \not\supseteq [\![\mathcal{L}{\downarrow}]\!]$. ◇

The language in Example 3.4 is not the semantics of any system, in fact languages obtained as semantics of a communicating system are always CUI.

Proposition 3.5 (Semantics is CUI). *For all systems S, $[\![S]\!]$ is CUI.*

The next property connects finite and infinite words in a language; it corresponds to the closure under the limit operation used in ω-languages [17,38].

Definition 3.6 (Continuity). *A language L on an alphabet Σ is continuous if $z \in L$ for all $z \in \Sigma^\omega$ such that $\mathsf{pref}(z) \cap L$ is infinite.*

This notion of continuity, besides being quite natural, is the most suitable for our purposes among the possible ones [36]. Intuitively, a language L is continuous if an ω-word is in L when infinitely many of its approximants (i.e., finite prefixes) are in L. A g-language $\mathcal{L}$ is *standard or continuous* (sc-language, for short) if either $\mathcal{L} \subseteq \Sigma^*_{\mathrm{int}}$ or $\mathcal{L}$ is continuous. Notice that for prefix-closed languages for all $z \in L^\omega$ we have that $\mathsf{pref}(z) \cap L$ is infinite iff $\mathsf{pref}(z) \subseteq L$.

Closure under unknown information characterises correct projected systems.

Theorem 3.7 (Characterisation of correctness). *If $\mathcal{L}{\downarrow}$ is correct w.r.t. $\mathcal{L}$ then $\mathsf{cui}(\mathcal{L})$ holds. If $\mathcal{L}$ is an sc-language and $\mathsf{cui}(\mathcal{L})$ then $\mathcal{L}{\downarrow}$ is correct w.r.t. $\mathcal{L}$.*

Notice that CUI is defined in terms of g-languages only, hence checking CUI does not require to build the corresponding system. Also, strengthening the precondition of Definition 3.3 with the additional requirement $w_1 = w_2$ would invalidate Theorem 3.7. Indeed, the language in Example 2.5 would become CUI but not correct. The next example shows that the continuity condition in Theorem 3.7 is necessary for languages containing infinite g-words.

Example 3.8 (Continuity matters). The CUI language

$$\mathcal{L} = \mathsf{pref}(\bigcup_{i \geq 0} \{\, \mathsf{A} {\rightarrow} \mathsf{B} {:} \mathsf{l} \cdot \mathsf{B} {\rightarrow} \mathsf{C} {:} \mathsf{n} \cdot (\mathsf{C} {\rightarrow} \mathsf{D} {:} \mathsf{n})^i \,\} \cup \{\, \mathsf{A} {\rightarrow} \mathsf{B} {:} \mathsf{r} \cdot \mathsf{B} {\rightarrow} \mathsf{C} {:} \mathsf{n} \cdot (\mathsf{C} {\rightarrow} \mathsf{D} {:} \mathsf{n})^\omega \,\})$$

does contain an infinite word but it is not continuous. The projection of $\mathcal{L}$ is not correct because its semantics contains the g-word $\mathsf{A} {\rightarrow} \mathsf{B} {:} \mathsf{l} \cdot \mathsf{B} {\rightarrow} \mathsf{C} {:} \mathsf{n} \cdot (\mathsf{C} {\rightarrow} \mathsf{D} {:} \mathsf{n})^\omega \notin \mathcal{L}$ since the projections of C and D can exchange infinitely many messages n due to the infinite g-word of $\mathcal{L}$ regardless whether A and B exchange l or r. ◇

Notice that, since $\mathcal{L} \subseteq [\![\mathcal{L}{\downarrow}]\!]$ always holds, Theorem 3.7 implies that $\mathsf{cui}(\mathcal{L})$ characterises the languages $\mathcal{L}$ such that $\mathcal{L} = [\![\mathcal{L}{\downarrow}]\!]$. Besides, the following corollary descends from Theorem 3.7.

Corollary 3.9. *For each sc-language $\mathcal{L}$, $\mathsf{cl}(\mathcal{L})$ is the smallest CUI sc-language containing $\mathcal{L}$.*

CUI ensures that continuous g-languages are c-closed.

Proposition 3.10. *If $\mathcal{L}$ is an sc-language and cui($\mathcal{L}$), then $\mathcal{L}$ is c-closed.*

Hence, an sc-language cannot be CUI unless it is c-closed.

As recalled before, in many choreographic formalisms (such as [5, 9, 14, 18, 25]) the correctness and completeness of a projected system, namely $\mathcal{L} = [\![\mathcal{L}\!\downarrow]\!]$ (together with some forms of liveness and deadlock-freedom properties), is guaranteed by *well-branchedness* conditions. Most of such conditions guarantee, informally, that participants reach consensus on which branch to take when choices arise. For instance, a well-branchedness condition could be that, at each choice, there is a unique participant deciding the branch to follow during a computation and that such participant informs each other participant. Such a condition is actually not needed to prove $\mathcal{L} = [\![\mathcal{L}\!\downarrow]\!]$. In fact the g-language obtained by adding the word w of Example 3.4 to the language of Example 2.5 is CUI, without being well-branched in the above sense. Indeed, after the interaction C→A:m, there is a branching in the projected system, since both the interactions C→B:m and A→B:m can be performed. However, these interactions do not have the same sender.

The next example exhibits a non-regular CUI g-language of finite words. By Theorem 3.7 and Corollary 3.2, the projected system is correct and complete.

Example 3.11 (Task dispatching). As soon as a server (S) communicates its availability (a), a dispatcher (D) sends a task (t) to S. The server either processes the task directly and sends back the resulting data (d) to D or sends the task to participant H for some pre-processing, aiming at resuming it later on. Indeed, after communicating a result to D, the server can resume (r) a previous task (if any) from H, process it, and send the result to D. The server eventually stops by sending s to both D and H; this can happen only when all dispatched tasks have been processed.

This protocol corresponds to the g-language $\mathcal{L} = \mathsf{pref}(\mathfrak{L})$, where $\mathfrak{L}$ is the (non-regular) language generated by the following context-free grammar.

$$S ::= S'\cdot\text{S→D:s}\cdot\text{S→H:s} \qquad S' ::= \text{S→D:a}\cdot\text{D→S:t}\cdot\text{S→H:t}\cdot S'\cdot\text{S→H:r}\cdot\text{H→S:r}\cdot\text{S→D:d}\cdot S'$$
$$\mid \text{S→D:a}\cdot\text{D→S:t}\cdot\text{S→D:d}\cdot S' \qquad \mid \varepsilon$$

Since S is involved in all the interactions of $\mathcal{L}$, for each pair of words $w, w' \in \mathcal{L}$: $w\!\downarrow_\mathsf{S} = w'\!\downarrow_\mathsf{S}$ *iff* $w = w'$. Now, if $w_1\,\alpha, w_2\,\alpha, w \in \mathcal{L}$ satisfy the required conditions for CUI then either $w_1\!\downarrow_\mathsf{S} = w\!\downarrow_\mathsf{S}$ or $w_2\!\downarrow_\mathsf{S} = w\!\downarrow_\mathsf{S}$, since $\mathsf{S} \in \mathsf{ptp}(\alpha)$. Hence cui($\mathcal{L}$) trivially holds.   ◇

The language in Example 3.11 is non-regular since it has the same structure of a language of well-balanced parenthesis. Remarkably, this implies that the g-language cannot be expressed in any other choreographic model we are aware of. The argument used to show cui($\mathcal{L}$) in Example 3.11 proves the following.

Proposition 3.12. *If there exists a participant involved in all the interactions of a g-language $\mathcal{L}$ then cui($\mathcal{L}$) holds.*

4   Communication Properties

Besides correctness and completeness, other properties could be of interest. For instance, one would like to ensure that participants eventually interact, if they are willing to. We consider a few properties, informally described as follows.

Harmonicity (HA): each sequence of communications that a participant is able to perform can be executed in some computation of the system.

Lock-freedom (LF): if a participant has pending communications to make on an ongoing computation, then there is a continuation of the computation involving that participant.

Strong lock-freedom (SLF): if a participant has pending communications to make on an ongoing computation, then each maximal continuation of the computation involves that participant.

Starvation-freedom (SF): if a participant has pending communications to make on an ongoing computation, then each infinite continuation of the computation involves that participant.

Deadlock-freedom (DF): in all completed computations each participant has no pending actions.

We now formalise the properties above.

Definition 4.1 (Communication properties). *Let S be a system on $\mathcal{P}$.*

HA *S is* harmonic *if $S(\mathsf{A}) \subseteq [\![S]\!] \downarrow_\mathsf{A}$ for each $\mathsf{A} \in \mathcal{P}$.*

LF *S is* lock free *if, for each finite word $w \in [\![S]\!]$ and participant $\mathsf{A} \in \mathcal{P}$, if $w \downarrow_\mathsf{A}$ is not maximal in $S(\mathsf{A})$ then there is a word w' such that $ww' \in [\![S]\!]$ and $w' \downarrow_\mathsf{A} \neq \varepsilon$.*

SLF *S is* strongly lock free *if, for each finite $w \in [\![S]\!]$ and participant $\mathsf{A} \in \mathcal{P}$, if $w \downarrow_\mathsf{A}$ is not maximal in $S(\mathsf{A})$ then for each word w' such that ww' is maximal in $[\![S]\!]$ we have $w' \downarrow_\mathsf{A} \neq \varepsilon$.*

SF *S is* starvation free *if, for each finite $w \in [\![S]\!]$ and participant $\mathsf{A} \in \mathcal{P}$, if $w \downarrow_\mathsf{A}$ is not maximal in $S(\mathsf{A})$ then $w' \downarrow_\mathsf{A} \neq \varepsilon$ for each infinite word w' such that $ww' \in [\![S]\!]$.*

DF *S is* deadlock free *if, for each finite and maximal word $w \in [\![S]\!]$ and participant $\mathsf{A} \in \mathcal{P}$, $w \downarrow_\mathsf{A}$ is maximal in $S(\mathsf{A})$.*

Barred for harmonicity, these properties appear in the literature under different names in various contexts. For instance, the notion of lock-freedom in [5] corresponds to ours, which in turn corresponds to the notion of liveness in [29,32] in a channel-based synchronous communication setting. Likewise, the notion of strong lock-freedom in [37] corresponds to ours and, under fair scheduling, to the notion of lock-freedom in [28]. As a final example, the definition of deadlock-freedom in its (equivalent) contrapositive form, coincides with the notion of progress as defined for synchronous processes in [23,35]. Harmonicity, introduced in the present paper, assures that no behaviour of a participant can be taken out from a system without affecting the overall behaviour of the system itself. Notice that the inverse of harmonicity, $[\![S]\!] \downarrow_\mathsf{A} \subseteq S(\mathsf{A})$, holds by construction.

The next proposition highlights the relations among our properties.

130   F. Barbanera et al.

Proposition 4.2. *The following relations hold among the properties in Defini-tion 4.1*

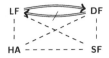

where implication does not hold in any direction between properties connected by dashed lines

Moreover, *DF* ∧ *SF* ⇔ *SLF*.

5 Communication Properties by Construction

Harmonicity is the only property in Definition 4.1 guaranteed by projection on any system. This can be obtained as a simple consequence of Corollary 3.2.

Corollary 5.1. *If $\mathcal{L}$ is a g-language then $\mathcal{L}{\downarrow}$ is harmonic.*

The other properties require some conditions on systems to be enjoyed by $\mathcal{L}{\downarrow}$. Basically, we will strengthen CUI which is too weak. For instance, cui($\mathcal{L}$) does imply neither deadlock-freedom nor lock-freedom for $\mathcal{L}{\downarrow}$.

Example 5.2 (CUI ⇏ DF). Consider the following words

$$w = \mathsf{A}{\to}\mathsf{C}{:}\mathsf{l}\cdot\mathsf{A}{\to}\mathsf{B}{:}\mathsf{m}\cdot\mathsf{A}{\to}\mathsf{C}{:}\mathsf{m} \qquad \text{and} \qquad w' = \mathsf{A}{\to}\mathsf{C}{:}\mathsf{r}\cdot\mathsf{A}{\to}\mathsf{B}{:}\mathsf{m}\cdot\mathsf{B}{\to}\mathsf{C}{:}\mathsf{m}$$

It is easy to check that the g-language $\mathcal{L} = \mathsf{pref}(\{\,w, w'\,\})$ is CUI. Informally, cui($\mathcal{L}$) holds because C can ascertain which of its last actions to execute from the first input. So, Corollary 3.2 and Theorem 3.7 ensure that $\mathcal{L} = [\![\mathcal{L}{\downarrow}]\!]$. However, $\mathcal{L}{\downarrow}$ is not deadlock-free. In particular, $w \in \mathcal{L} = [\![\mathcal{L}{\downarrow}]\!]$ is a deadlock since it is a finite maximal word whose projection on B, namely $w{\downarrow}_\mathsf{B} = \mathsf{A}\,\mathsf{B}?\mathsf{m}$, is not maximal in $\mathcal{L}{\downarrow}_\mathsf{B}$ because $w'{\downarrow}_\mathsf{B} = \mathsf{A}\,\mathsf{B}?\mathsf{m}\cdot\mathsf{B}\,\mathsf{C}!\mathsf{m} \in \mathcal{L}{\downarrow}_\mathsf{B}$.

By Proposition 4.2, the system above is also non lock-free.   ◇

In many models (cf. [25]) in order to ensure, besides other properties, also the correctness of $\mathcal{L}{\downarrow}$, a condition called *well-branchedness* is required. We iden-tify a notion weaker than well-branchedness, which by analogy we dub *branch-awareness* (BA for short).

Definition 5.3 (Branch-awareness). *A participant* X *distinguishes two g-words $w_1, w_2 \in \Sigma_{int}^\infty$ if*

$$w_1{\downarrow}_\mathsf{X} \neq w_2{\downarrow}_\mathsf{X} \qquad \text{and} \qquad w_1{\downarrow}_\mathsf{X} \not\prec w_2{\downarrow}_\mathsf{X} \qquad \text{and} \qquad w_2{\downarrow}_\mathsf{X} \not\prec w_1{\downarrow}_\mathsf{X}.$$

A g-language $\mathcal{L}$ on $\mathcal{P}$ is branch-aware *if each X ∈ $\mathcal{P}$ distinguishes all maximal words in $\mathcal{L}$ whose projections on X differ.*

Example 5.4. The language $\mathcal{L} = \mathsf{pref}(\{\,w, w'\,\})$ with $w = \mathsf{A}{\to}\mathsf{C}{:}\mathsf{l}\cdot\mathsf{A}{\to}\mathsf{B}{:}\mathsf{m}\cdot\mathsf{A}{\to}\mathsf{C}{:}\mathsf{m}$ and $w' = \mathsf{A}{\to}\mathsf{C}{:}\mathsf{r}\cdot\mathsf{A}{\to}\mathsf{B}{:}\mathsf{m}\cdot\mathsf{B}{\to}\mathsf{C}{:}\mathsf{m}$ from Example 5.2 is not branch-aware, since $w{\downarrow}_\mathsf{B} = \mathsf{A}\,\mathsf{B}?\mathsf{m}$ and $w'{\downarrow}_\mathsf{B} = \mathsf{A}\,\mathsf{B}?\mathsf{m}\cdot\mathsf{B}\,\mathsf{C}!\mathsf{m}$, hence $w{\downarrow}_\mathsf{B} \neq w'{\downarrow}_\mathsf{B}$ but $w{\downarrow}_\mathsf{B} \prec w'{\downarrow}_\mathsf{B}$.   ◇

Condition $w_1 \downarrow_X \neq w_2 \downarrow_X$ in Definition 5.3 is not strictly needed to define BA, but it makes the notion of 'distinguishes' more intuitive. Equivalently, as shown in Proposition 5.5 below, a participant X distinguishes two branches if, after a common prefix, X is actively involved in both branches, performing different interactions.

Proposition 5.5. *Participant* X *distinguishes two g-words* $w_1, w_2 \in \Sigma_{int}^{\infty}$ *iff there are* $w_1' \cdot \alpha_1 \preceq w_1$ *and* $w_2' \cdot \alpha_2 \preceq w_2$ *such that* $w_1' \downarrow_X = w_2' \downarrow_X$ *and* $\alpha_1 \downarrow_X \neq \alpha_2 \downarrow_X$.

The notions of well-branchedness in the literature [25] additionally impose that $\alpha_1 \downarrow_X$ and $\alpha_2 \downarrow_X$ in the above proposition are input actions, but for a (unique) participant (a.k.a., the *selector*) which is required to have different outputs.

In our case, BA is not needed for correctness, but it is nevertheless useful to prove the communication properties presented in Sect. 4.

Theorem 5.6 (Consequences of BA). *Let* $\mathcal{L}$ *be a branch-aware and CUI sc-language. Then* $\mathcal{L}\downarrow$ *satisfies all the properties in Definition 4.1.*

Example 5.7 (The task dispatching protocol is branch aware). In order to show that the g-language $\mathcal{L}$ in Example 3.11 is branch-aware, we first notice that each maximal word in $\mathcal{L}$ ends with the interactions S→D:s·S→H:s. If $\mathcal{L}$ were not branch-aware, there should be two maximal words w·S→D:s·S→H:s and w'·S→D:s·S→H:s and a participant X ∈ ptp($\mathcal{L}$) such that $(w$·S→D:s·S→H:s$) \downarrow_X \prec (w'$·S→D:s·S→H:s$) \downarrow_X$. This is impossible, since w and w' are both generated by the non terminal symbol S' and hence cannot contain the message s.   ◇

Proposition 4.2 refines as follows when restricting to projections of g-languages.

Proposition 5.8 *When considering only systems which are projections of g-languages the following relations hold among the properties in Definition 4.1*

where implication does
not hold in any direction
between properties con-
nected by dashed lines

Moreover, *DF* ∧ *SF* ⇔ *SLF*.

It is not difficult to show that branch-awareness actually characterises SLF for systems obtained by projecting CUI languages.

Proposition 5.9 (Branch-awareness characterises SLF). *A CUI g-language* $\mathcal{L}$ *is branch-aware iff* $\mathcal{L}\downarrow$ *is strongly lock-free.*

6   Global Types as Choreographic Languages

The global types of [37] are our first case study. We recall global types adapting some of the notation in [37] to our setting. Informally, a global type A → B :

$\{m_i.G_i\}_{1\leq i\leq n}$ specifies a protocol where participant A must send to B a message m_i for some $1 \leq i \leq n$ and then, depending on which m_i was chosen by A, the protocol continues as G_i. Global types and multiparty sessions are defined in [37] in terms of the following grammars:

$$G :: =^{co} \text{ end} \qquad\qquad P :: =^{co} \mathbf{0} \qquad\qquad \mathcal{M} :: = A \triangleright P$$
$$| \quad A \to B : \{m_i.G_i\}_{1\leq i\leq n} \qquad | \quad A?\{m_i.P_i\}_{1\leq i\leq n} \qquad | \quad \mathcal{M} \mid \mathcal{M}$$
$$| \quad A!\{m_i.P_i\}_{1\leq i\leq n}$$

respectively for *pre-global types*, *pre-processes*, and *pre-multiparty sessions*. The first two grammars are interpreted coinductively, that is their solutions are both minimal and maximal fixpoints (the latter corresponding to infinite trees) and all messages m_i are pairwise different. A pre-global type G (resp. pre-process P) is a *global type* (resp. *process*) if its tree representation is *regular*, namely it has finitely many distinct sub-trees. A *multiparty session* (MPS for short) is a pre-multiparty session such that (a) in $A \triangleright P$, participant A does not occur in process P and (b) in $A_1 \triangleright P_1 \mid \ldots \mid A_n \triangleright P_n$, participants A_i are pairwise different.

The semantics of global types is the LTS induced by

$$A \to B : \{m_i.G_i\}_{1\leq i\leq n} \xrightarrow{A\to B:m_i} G_i \qquad R \to S : \{m_i.G_i\}_{1\leq i\leq n} \xrightarrow{A\to B:m} R \to S : \{m_i.G_i'\}_{1\leq i\leq n}$$

where in the latter rule $\{A,B\} \cap \{R,S\} = \emptyset$ and for each $1 \leq i \leq n$, $G_i \xrightarrow{A\to B:m} G_i'$. A *branch* is a set $\{m_i.P_i\}_{1\leq i\leq n}$ where messages m_i are pairwise distinct.

The semantics for MPSs is the LTS defined by the following rule

$$A \triangleright B!(\{m.P\} \uplus \Lambda) \mid B \triangleright A?(\{m.P'\} \uplus \Lambda') \mid \mathcal{M} \xrightarrow{A\to B:m} A \triangleright P \mid B \triangleright P' \mid \mathcal{M} \qquad (1)$$

where $\_\uplus\_$ is the union of branches defined only on branches with disjoint sets of messages. Rule (1) applies only if the messages in Λ' include those in Λ, which is the case for MPSs obtained by projection, defined below.

Definition 6.1 (Projection *[37, Definition 3.4]*). *The projection of G on a participant X such that the depths of its occurrences in G are bounded is the partial function $G\upharpoonright_X$ coinductively defined by* $\text{end}\upharpoonright_X = \mathbf{0}$ *and, for a global type* $G = A \to B : \{m_i.G_i\}_{1\leq i\leq n}$, *by:*

$$G\upharpoonright_X = \begin{cases} \mathbf{0} & \text{if } X \text{ is not a participant of } G \\ B!\{m_i.G_i\upharpoonright_X\}_{1\leq i\leq n} & \text{if } X = A \\ A?\{m_i.G_i\upharpoonright_X\}_{1\leq i\leq n} & \text{if } X = B \\ G_1\upharpoonright_X & \text{if } X \notin \{A,B\} \text{ and } n = 1 \\ S?(\Lambda_1 \uplus \ldots \uplus \Lambda_n) & \text{if } X \notin \{A,B\}, \ n > 1, \text{ and } \forall 1 \leq i \leq n : \ G_i\upharpoonright_X = S?\Lambda_i \end{cases}$$

The global type G is projectable[2] if $G\upharpoonright_X$ is defined for all participants X of G, in which case $G\upharpoonright$ denotes the corresponding MPS.

The g-language $\mathcal{L}(G)$ associated to a global type G is the concurrency and prefix closure of $\mathcal{L}'(G)$, that is $\mathcal{L}(G) = \text{pref}(\{w \in \Sigma_{\text{int}}^{\infty} \mid \exists w' \in \mathcal{L}'(G) : w \sim w'\})$ where $\mathcal{L}'(G)$ is coinductively defined as follows:

$$\mathcal{L}'(\text{end}) = \{\varepsilon\} \qquad \text{and} \qquad \mathcal{L}'(A \to B : \{m_i.G_i\}_{1\leq i\leq n}) = \bigcup_{1\leq i\leq n}\{A\dashrightarrow B:m_i \cdot w \mid w \in \mathcal{L}'(G_i)\}$$

---

[2] In [37], projectability embeds well-branchedness.

We define the l-language $\mathbb{L}(\mathsf{B} \triangleright P)$ associated to a named process $\mathsf{B} \triangleright P$ as the prefix closure of $\mathbb{L}'(\mathsf{B} \triangleright P)$ which, letting $\star \in \{\,?,!\,\}$, is defined by

$$\mathbb{L}'(\mathsf{B} \triangleright \mathbf{0}) = \{\,\varepsilon\,\} \quad \text{and} \quad \mathbb{L}'(\mathsf{B} \triangleright \mathsf{A}\star\{\mathsf{m}_i.P_i\}_{1 \le i \le n}) = \bigcup_{1 \le i \le n}\{\,\mathsf{AB}\star\mathsf{m}_i\cdot w \mid w \in \mathbb{L}'(P_i)\,\}$$

The system associated to an MPS is defined as the following map:

$$S(\mathsf{A}_1 \triangleright P_1 \mid \ldots \mid \mathsf{A}_n \triangleright P_n) = \{\,\mathsf{A}_i \mapsto \mathbb{L}(\mathsf{A}_i \triangleright P_i) \mid 1 \le i \le n\,\}$$

Our constructions capture relevant properties of the global types in [37]. First, we relate projectability (cf. Definition 6.1) and our properties.

Proposition 6.2. *If* G *is a projectable global type then* $\mathcal{L}(\mathsf{G})$ *is a CUI and branch-aware sc-language.*

This yields the following correspondences between the two frameworks.

Proposition 6.3. *Given a projectable global type* G,

$$\mathcal{L}(\mathsf{G}) = \{\,w \mid \mathsf{G} \xrightarrow{w}\,\} \quad (2) \qquad\qquad [\![S(\mathsf{G}{\upharpoonright})]\!] = \{\,w \mid \mathsf{G}{\upharpoonright} \xrightarrow{w}\,\} \quad (3)$$

Projectable global types are proved strongly lock-free in [37]. The following result corresponds to [37, Theorem 4.7].

Corollary 6.4. $S(\mathsf{G}{\upharpoonright})$ *is strongly lock-free for any projectable* G.

The symmetry between senders and receivers in CUI and branch-awareness allows for an immediate generalisation of the projection in Definition 6.1 by extending the last case with the clause:

$$\mathsf{S}!(\varLambda_1 \uplus \ldots \uplus \varLambda_n) \qquad \text{if } \mathsf{X} \notin \{\mathsf{A}, \mathsf{B}\},\ n > 1,\ \text{and } \forall 1 \le i \le n\ :\ \mathsf{G}_i{\upharpoonright}_\mathsf{X} = \mathsf{S}!\varLambda_i$$

Corollary 6.4 still holds for this generalised definition of projection.

7 Choreography Automata

Recently we introduced *choreography automata* (c-automata) [6] as an expressive and flexible model of global specifications. A c-automaton $\mathbb{CA} = \langle S, q_0, \Sigma_{\mathrm{int}}, \rightarrow \rangle$ is a finite-state automaton whose transition relation is labelled in Σ_{int}, namely $\rightarrow \subseteq S \times \Sigma_{\mathrm{int}} \times S$ (cf. [7, Def. 8.2]: for the sake of space most of the technical details of this section are in [7]). Observe that the set $\mathcal{P}$ of participants of $\mathbb{CA}$ is necessarily finite. We have some immediate connection between c-automata and FCL by taking as the language $\mathcal{L}(\mathbb{CA})$ of $\mathbb{CA}$ the set of words obtained by concatenating the labels on any of its paths (including infinite paths, cf. [7, Def. 8.3]). In fact $\mathcal{L}(\mathbb{CA})$ is a continuous g-language, that is it is prefix-closed (cf. [7, Prop. 8.4]).

The local behaviour of a participant $\mathsf{A} \in \mathcal{P}$ can be straightforwardly obtained by projecting c-automata on *communicating finite-state machines* (CFSMs) [11].

Basically, a CFSM is a finite-state automaton whose transitions are labelled in Σ_{act} (cf. [7, Def. 8.1]). Formally, the *projection* of a c-automaton $\mathbb{CA}$ on A, written $\mathbb{CA}\downarrow_A$, is obtained by determinising up-to-language equivalence the *intermediate automaton*

$$A_A = \langle S, q_0, \Sigma_{act} \cup \{\varepsilon\}, \{q \xrightarrow{\lambda|_A} q' \mid q \xrightarrow{\lambda} q'\}\rangle$$

Finally, $\mathbb{CA}\downarrow = (\mathbb{CA}\downarrow_A)_{A\in\mathcal{P}}$ is the *projection of* $\mathbb{CA}$(cf. [7, Def. 8.5]).

By applying the definition of language of c-automaton to CFSMs we can associate an l-language $\mathbb{L}(M)$ to each CFSM M (cf. [7, Def. 8.3]). Projections of c-automata and of the corresponding g-languages are related: $\mathbb{L}(\mathbb{CA}\downarrow_A) = \mathcal{L}(\mathbb{CA})\downarrow_A$ (cf. [7, Prop. 8.8]).

The synchronous behaviour of a system of CFSMs $(M_A)_{A\in\mathcal{P}}$ can be given as an LTS where states are maps assigning a state in M_A to each $A \in \mathcal{P}$ and transitions are labelled by interactions (or by ε). Intuitively, given a configuration s, if M_A and M_B have respectively transitions $s(A) \xrightarrow{A\,B!m} q'_A$ and $s(B) \xrightarrow{A\,B?m} q'_B$ then $s \xrightarrow{A\rightarrow B:m} s[A \mapsto q'_A, B \mapsto q'_B]$, where $f[x \mapsto y]$ denotes the update of f on x with y. Likewise, $s(A) \xrightarrow{\varepsilon} q'_A$ in M_A implies $s \xrightarrow{\varepsilon} s[A \mapsto q'_A]$. Observing that $\mathbb{CA}\downarrow$ is ε-free, the LTS of $\mathbb{CA}\downarrow$ is a c-automaton and its language coincides with the g-language of the system $\{\mathbb{L}(\mathbb{CA}\downarrow_X)\}_{X\in\mathcal{P}}$ (cf. [7, Prop. 8.7]).

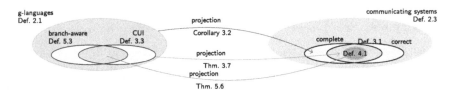

Fig. 1. Contributions of the paper

The communication properties of a system of CFSMs S on $\mathcal{P}$ considered in [6] are liveness, lock-freedom, and deadlock-freedom. We give an intuition of such properties (see [7, Def. 8.9] for a precise account).

- S is *live* when each reachable configuration where a participant $A \in \mathcal{P}$ can execute a communication has a continuation where A is involved;
- S is *lock-free* when in all computations starting from a reachable configuration where a participant $A \in \mathcal{P}$ can execute, A is involved;
- S is *deadlock-free* if in none of its reachable configurations s without outgoing transitions there exists $A \in \mathcal{P}$ willing to communicate.

A system of CFSMs $S = (M_X)_{X\in\mathcal{P}}$ is abstractly represented by the system $\hat{S} = (\mathbb{L}(M_X))_{X\in\mathcal{P}}$. It is the case that lock-freedom, strong lock-freedom, and deadlock-freedom of $\hat{S}$ (in the sense of Definition 4.1) respectively imply liveness, lock-freedom, and deadlock-freedom of S (cf. [7, Prop. 8.12]).

The conditions on c-automata devised in [6] in order to guarantee the above communication properties in the synchronous case turned out to be flawed. This is shown in [7, Sec. 8.3] (cf. [7, Ex. 8.10]).

Fortunately, the conditions given in the present paper can be applied also in the setting of c-automata. As shown in [7, Sec. 8.4], CUI and branch-awareness are decidable.

8   Concluding Remarks

We developed a general and abstract theory of choreographies based on formal languages, in which we recasted known properties and constructions such as projections from global to local specifications. We briefly recap our main contributions, synoptically depicted in Fig. 1.

One of our contributions is the characterisation of systems' correctness in terms of closure under unknown information (CUI). Other communication properties can be ensured by additionally requiring branch awareness (BA).

Finally, the versatility of FCL allows us to capture existing models. We considered two models chosen according to their "proximity" to FCL. The first model, the variant of MPSTs presented in [37], being based on behavioural types, radically differs from FCL. The second framework, the c-automata in [6], is closer to FCL given that it retraces the connection between automata and formal language theories.

Related Work. The use of formal language theories for the modelling of concurrent systems dates back to the theory of traces [33]. A trace is an equivalence class of words that differ only for swaps of independent symbols. Closure under concurrency corresponds on finite words to form traces, as we noted after Definition 2.8. An extensive literature has explored a notion of realisability whereby a language of traces is realisable if it is accepted by some class of finite-state automata. Relevant results in this respect are the characterisations in [16,39] (and the optimisation in [22]) for finite words and the ones in [19–21] for infinite ones. A key difference of our framework w.r.t. this line of work is that we aim to stricter notions of realisability: in our context it is not enough that the runs of the language may be faithfully executed by a certain class of finite-state automata. Rather we are interested in identifying conditions on the g-languages that guarantee well-behaved executions in "natural" realisations.

Other abstract models of choreographies, e.g. [6,18], have some relation with ours. Conversation protocols (CP) [18], probably the first automata-based model of choreographies, are non-deterministic Büchi automata whose alphabet resembles a constrained variant of our Σ_{int}. A comparison with the g-languages accepted by CPs is not immediate as CPs are based on asynchronous communications (although some connections are evident as noted below Definition 2.6).

Other proposals ascribable to choreographic settings (cf. [25]) define global views that can be seen as g-languages. We focus on synchronous approaches because our current theory needs to be extended to cope with asynchrony.

In [12, 31] the correctness of implementations of choreographies (called *choreography conformance*) is studied in a process algebraic setting. The other communication properties we consider here are not discussed there.

The notion of choreography implementation in [12] corresponds to our correctness plus a form of existential termination. It is shown that one can decide whether a system is an implementation of a given choreography, since both languages are generated by finite-state automata, hence language inclusion and existential termination are decidable.

In [31] three syntactic conditions (connectedness, unique points of choice and causality safety) ensure bisimilarity (hence trace equivalence) between a choreography and its projection. Connectedness rules out systems which are not c-closed, while we conjecture that unique points of choice and connectedness together imply our CUI and BA. Causality safety, immaterial in our case, is needed in [31] due to explicit parallel composition.

Many multiparty session type systems [25] have two levels of types (global and local) and one implementation level (local processes). This is the case also for synchronous session type systems such as [15, 30]. Our approach, like the session type systems in [5, 37], considers only (two) abstract descriptions, g-languages and l-languages. The literature offers several behavioural types featuring correctness-by-construction principles through conditions (known as projectability or well-branchedness) more demanding than ours. For instance, relations similar to those in Sect. 6 can be devised for close formalisms, such as [5] whose notion of projection is more general than the one in [37], yet its notion of projectability still implies CUI and BA.

There is a connection between CUI and the closure property CC2 [3] on message-sequence charts (MSCs) [26]. On finite words CC2 and CUI coincide. Actually, CUI can be regarded as a step-by-step way to ensure CC2 on finite words. The relations between our properties and CC3, also used in MSCs, are still under scrutiny.

Future Work. Our investigation proposes a new point of view for choreography formalisms and the related constructions. As such, a number of extensions and improvements need to be analysed, to check how they may fit in our setting. We list below the most relevant.

First, we need to extend our theory to cope with *asynchronous* communications. While the general approach should apply, it is not immediate how to extend CUI in order to characterize correctness for an asynchronous semantics. This is somehow confirmed by the results in [1, 2] on the realisability of MSCs showing that in the asynchronous setting this is a challenging problem.

A second direction is analysing how to drop prefix-closure, so allowing for specifications where the system (and single participants) may stop their execution at some points but not at others; a word would hence represent a complete computation, not only a partial one.

A further direction would unveil the correspondence between closure properties and subtyping relations used in many multiparty session types.

References

1. Alur, R.: The benefits of exposing calls and returns. In: Abadi, M., de Alfaro, L. (eds.) CONCUR 2005. LNCS, vol. 3653, pp. 2–3. Springer, Heidelberg (2005). https://doi.org/10.1007/11539452_2

2. Alur, R., Etessami, K., Yannakakis, M.: Realizability and verification of MSC graphs. In: Orejas, F., Spirakis, P.G., van Leeuwen, J. (eds.) ICALP 2001. LNCS, vol. 2076, pp. 797–808. Springer, Heidelberg (2001). https://doi.org/10.1007/3-540-48224-5_65

3. Alur, R., Etessami, K., Yannakakis, M.: Inference of message sequence charts. IEEE Trans. Softw. Eng. **29**(7), 623–633 (2003)

4. Autebert, J.-M., Beauquier, J., Boasson, L.: Langages sur des alphabets infinis. Discrete Appl. Math. **2**(1), 1–20 (1980). http://www.sciencedirect.com/science/article/pii/0166218X80900505. https://doi.org/10.1016/0166-218X(80)90050-5

5. Barbanera, F., Dezani-Ciancaglini, M., Lanese, I., Tuosto, E.: Composition and decomposition of multiparty sessions. J. Log. Algebraic Methods Program. **119**, 100620 (2021). http://www.sciencedirect.com/science/article/pii/S235222082030105X. https://doi.org/10.1016/j.jlamp.2020.100620

6. Barbanera, F., Lanese, I., Tuosto, E.: Choreography automata. In: Bliudze, S., Bocchi, L. (eds.) COORDINATION 2020. LNCS, vol. 12134, pp. 86–106. Springer, Cham (2020). https://doi.org/10.1007/978-3-030-50029-0_6

7. Barbanera, F., Lanese, I., Tuosto, E.: Formal choreographic languages (extended version). Technical report, GSSI (2022). https://emwww.github.io/home/tr/fcl.pdf

8. Basu, S., Bultan, T.: Choreography conformance via synchronizability. In: Srinivasan, S., Ramamritham, K., Kumar, A., Ravindra, M.P., Bertino, E., Kumar, R. (eds.) Proceedings of the 20th International Conference on World Wide Web, WWW 2011, Hyderabad, India, 28 March–1 April 2011, pp. 795–804. ACM (2011). https://doi.org/10.1145/1963405.1963516

9. Basu, S., Bultan, T., Ouederni, M.: Deciding choreography realizability. In: Proceedings of the 39th ACM SIGPLAN-SIGACT Symposium on Principles of Programming Languages, POPL 2012, Philadelphia, Pennsylvania, USA, 22–28 January 2012, pp. 191–202 (2012). https://doi.org/10.1145/2103656.2103680

10. Bonér, J.: Reactive Microsystems - The Evolution Of Microservices At Scale. O'Reilly (2018)

11. Brand, D., Zafiropulo, P.: On communicating finite-state machines. J. ACM **30**(2), 323–342 (1983)

12. Bravetti, M., Zavattaro, G.: Towards a unifying theory for choreography conformance and contract compliance. In: Lumpe, M., Vanderperren, W. (eds.) SC 2007. LNCS, vol. 4829, pp. 34–50. Springer, Heidelberg (2007). https://doi.org/10.1007/978-3-540-77351-1_4

13. Carbone, M., Honda, K., Yoshida, N.: Structured communication-centered programming for web services. ACM Trans. Program. Lang. Syst. **34**(2), 8:1–8:78 (2012). https://doi.org/10.1145/2220365.2220367

14. Coppo, M., Dezani-Ciancaglini, M., Yoshida, N., Padovani, L.: Global progress for dynamically interleaved multiparty sessions. Math. Struct. Comput. Sci. **26**(2), 238–302 (2016)

15. Dezani-Ciancaglini, M., Ghilezan, S., Jaksic, S., Pantovic, J., Yoshida, N.: Precise subtyping for synchronous multiparty sessions. In: Gay, S., Alglave, J. (eds.) Proceedings Eighth International Workshop on Programming Language Approaches

to Concurrency- and Communication-cEntric Software, PLACES 2015, London, UK, 18th April 2015, vol. 203. EPTCS, pp. 29–43 (2015). https://doi.org/10.4204/EPTCS.203.3

16. Duboc, C.: Mixed product and asynchronous automata. TCS **48**(3), 183–199 (1986). https://doi.org/10.1016/0304-3975(86)90094-0

17. Eilenberg, S.: Automata, Languages, and Machines., B. Pure and Applied Mathematics. Academic Press (1976). https://www.worldcat.org/oclc/310535259

18. Xiang, F., Bultan, T., Jianwen, S.: Conversation protocols: a formalism for specification and verification of reactive electronic services. TCS **328**(1–2), 19–37 (2004)

19. Gastin, P.: Infinite traces. In: Guessarian, I. (ed.) LITP 1990. LNCS, vol. 469, pp. 277–308. Springer, Heidelberg (1990). https://doi.org/10.1007/3-540-53479-2_12

20. Gastin, P.: Recognizable and rational languages of finite and infinite traces. In: Choffrut, C., Jantzen, M. (eds.) STACS 1991. LNCS, vol. 480, pp. 89–104. Springer, Heidelberg (1991). https://doi.org/10.1007/BFb0020790

21. Gastin, P., Petit, A., Zielonka, W.: A Kleene theorem for infinite trace languages. In: Albert, J.L., Monien, B., Artalejo, M.R. (eds.) ICALP 1991. LNCS, vol. 510, pp. 254–266. Springer, Heidelberg (1991). https://doi.org/10.1007/3-540-54233-7_139

22. Genest, B., Muscholl, A.: Constructing exponential-size deterministic Zielonka automata. In: Bugliesi, M., Preneel, B., Sassone, V., Wegener, I. (eds.) ICALP 2006. LNCS, vol. 4052, pp. 565–576. Springer, Heidelberg (2006). https://doi.org/10.1007/11787006_48

23. Ghilezan, S., Jaksic, S., Pantovic, J., Scalas, A., Yoshida, N.: Precise subtyping for synchronous multiparty sessions. J. Log. Algebraic Methods Program. **104**, 127–173 (2019). https://doi.org/10.1016/j.jlamp.2018.12.002

24. Honda, K., Yoshida, N., Carbone, M.: Multiparty asynchronous session types. J. ACM **63**(1), 9:1–9:67 (2016). Extended version of a paper presented at POPL08. https://doi.org/10.1145/2827695

25. Hüttel, H., et al.: Foundations of session types and behavioural contracts. ACM Comput. Surv. **49**(1), 3:1–3:36 (2016)

26. ITU Telecommunication Standardization Sector. ITU-T recommendation Z.120. Message Sequence Charts (MSC'96) (1996)

27. Kavantzas, N., Burdett, D., Ritzinger, G., Fletcher, T., Lafon, Y., Barreto, C.: Web services choreography description language version 1.0. Technical report, W3C (2005). http://www.w3.org/TR/ws-cdl-10/

28. Kobayashi, N.: A type system for lock-free processes. Inf. Comput. **177**, 122–159 (2002)

29. Kobayashi, N., Sangiorgi, D.: A hybrid type system for lock-freedom of mobile processes. ACM Trans. Program. Lang. Syst. **32**(5), 16:1–16:49 (2010). https://doi.org/10.1145/1745312.1745313

30. Kouzapas, D., Yoshida, N.: Globally governed session semantics. Log. Methods Comput. Sci. **10**(4) (2014). https://doi.org/10.2168/LMCS-10(4:20)2014

31. Lanese, I., Guidi, C., Montesi, F., Zavattaro, G.: Bridging the gap between interaction- and process-oriented choreographies. In: Software Engineering and Formal Methods, SEFM 2008, pp. 323–332 (2008)

32. Lange, J., Ng, N., Toninho, B., Yoshida, N.: Fencing off go: liveness and safety for channel-based programming. In: Castagna, G., Gordon, A.D. (eds.) Proceedings of the 44th ACM SIGPLAN Symposium on Principles of Programming Languages, POPL 2017, Paris, France, 18–20 January 2017, pp. 748–761. ACM (2017). http://dl.acm.org/citation.cfm?id=3009847

33. Mazurkiewicz, A.: Trace theory. In: Brauer, W., Reisig, W., Rozenberg, G. (eds.) ACPN 1986. LNCS, vol. 255, pp. 278–324. Springer, Heidelberg (1987). https://doi.org/10.1007/3-540-17906-2_30
34. OMG. Business Process Model and Notation (BPMN), Version 2.0, January 2011. https://www.omg.org/spec/BPMN
35. Padovani, L.: From lock freedom to progress using session types. In: Yoshida, N., Vanderbauwhede, W. (eds.) Proceedings 6th Workshop on Programming Language Approaches to Concurrency and Communication-cEntric Software, PLACES 2013, Rome, Italy, 23rd March 2013, vol. 137. EPTCS, pp. 3–19 (2013). https://doi.org/10.4204/EPTCS.137.2
36. Redziejowski, R.R.: Infinite-word languages and continuous mappings. TCS **43**, 59–79 (1986). https://doi.org/10.1016/0304-3975(86)90166-0
37. Severi, P., Dezani-Ciancaglini, M.: Observational equivalence for multiparty sessions. Fundam. Informaticae **170**(1–3), 267–305 (2019). https://doi.org/10.3233/FI-2019-1863
38. Staiger, L.: ω-languages. In: Rozenberg, G., Salomaa, A. (eds.) Handbook of Formal Languages, pp. 339–387. Springer, Heidelberg (1997). https://doi.org/10.1007/978-3-642-59126-6_6
39. Zielonka, W.: Notes on finite asynchronous automata. RAIRO Theor. Informatics Appl. **21**(2), 99–135 (1987). https://doi.org/10.1051/ita/1987210200991

A Model of Actors and Grey Failures

Laura Bocchi[1(✉)], Julien Lange[2(✉)], Simon Thompson[1(✉)],
and A. Laura Voinea[1(✉)]

[1] University of Kent, Canterbury, UK
{l.bocchi,s.j.thompson}@kent.ac.uk, laura.a.voinea@gmail.com
[2] Royal Holloway, University of London, Egham, UK
julien.lange@rhul.ac.uk

Abstract. Existing models for the analysis of concurrent processes tend to focus on fail-stop failures, where processes are either working or permanently stopped, and their state (working/stopped) is known. In fact, systems are often affected by grey failures: failures that are latent, possibly transient, and may affect the system in subtle ways that later lead to major issues (such as crashes, limited availability, overload). We introduce a model of actor-based systems with grey failures, based on two interlinked layers: an actor model, given as an asynchronous process calculus with discrete time, and a failure model that represents failure patterns to inject in the system. Our failure model captures not only fail-stop node and link failures, but also grey failures (e.g., partial, transient). We give a behavioural equivalence relation based on weak barbed bisimulation to compare systems on the basis of their ability to recover from failures, and on this basis we define some desirable properties of reliable systems. By doing so, we reduce the problem of checking reliability properties of systems to the problem of checking bisimulation.

1 Introduction

Many real-world computing systems are affected by non-negligible degrees of unpredictability, such as unexpected delays and failures, which are not straightforward to accurately capture. Several works contribute towards a better account of unpredictability, for example in the context of process calculi (also including session types) by extending calculi to model node failures [19,41], link failures [2], a combination of link and node failures [6], as well as programmatic constructs to deal with failures like escapes [15], interrupts [27], exceptions [20], and timeouts [7,31,32]. Most existing models assume a fail-stop model of failure, where processes are either working or permanently stopped, and their state either working or stopped is known. In fact, systems are often affected by grey failures: failures that are latent, possibly transient, and may affect the system in subtle

This work has been partially supported by EPSRC project EP/T014512/1 (STARDUST) and the BehAPI project funded by the EU H2020 RISE under the Marie Sklodowska-Curie action (No: 778233).

© IFIP International Federation for Information Processing 2022
M. H. ter Beek and M. Sirjani (Eds.): COORDINATION 2022, LNCS 13271, pp. 140–158, 2022.
https://doi.org/10.1007/978-3-031-08143-9_9

ways that later lead to major issues (such as crashes, limited availability, overload). Several kinds of grey failure have been studied in the last decade such as transient failure (e.g., a component is down at periodic intervals), partial failure (only some sub-components are affected), or slowdown [24]. The symptoms of grey failure tend to be ambiguous. In a distributed system, processes may have different perceptions as to the state of health of the system (aka *differential observation*) [28]. Grey failures tend to be behind many service incidents in cloud systems and traditional fault tolerance mechanisms tend to be ineffective or counterproductive [28]. Diagnosis is challenging and lengthy, for example the work in [33] estimates a median time for the diagnosis of partial failures to be 6 days and 5 h. One of the main causes of late diagnosis is ambiguity of the symptoms and hence difficulty in correlating failures with their effects.

In this paper we make a first step towards a better understanding of the correlation between failures and symptoms via static formal analysis. We focus on the distributed actor model of Erlang [45], which is known for its effectiveness in handling failures and has been emulated in many other languages, e.g., the popular Akka framework for Scala [48].

We define a formal model of actor-based systems with grey failures, which we call *'cursed systems'*. More precisely, we introduce two interlinked models: (1) a *model of systems*, which are networks of distributed actors; (2) a *model of (grey) failures* that allows us to characterise *'curses'* as patterns of grey failures to inject in the system. To capture the ambiguity of symptoms of grey failure we assume actors have no knowledge on the state of health of other actors. However, actors can observe the presence (or absence) of messages in their own mailboxes and hence the effects of failure in terms of missed communications. In Erlang, a key mechanism for detecting failure is the use of timeouts, which are one of the main ingredients of our system model.

Modelling failures as a separate layer allows us to compare systems recovery strategies with respect to specific failure patterns. This is a first step towards analysing the resilience of systems to failures, and assessing its effects on different parts of the system. We introduce a behavioural equivalence, based on weak barbed bisimulation, to compare systems affected by failures. We show that reliability properties of interest, namely resilience and recoverability, can be reduced to the problem of checking weak barbed bisimulation between systems with failures. Furthermore, we introduce a notion of augmentation, based on weak barbed bisimulation, to model and analyse the improvement of a system with respect to its recoverability against certain kinds of failure.

The paper is structured as follows. In Sect. 2, we give an informal overview of the system model, and compare it with related work. Next we introduce the models of failure (Sect. 3) and systems (Sect. 4). In Sect. 5 we give a behavioural equivalence between systems with failures, and show how it is used to model properties of interest. Section 6 discusses conclusions and related work.

2   Informal Overview

Actor-based systems are modelled using a process calculus with three key elements, following the actor model of Erlang: (1) time and timeouts, (2) asynchronous communication based on mailboxes with pattern-matching, and (3) actor nodes and injected failures.

Time and Timeouts. Timeouts are essential for an actor to decide when to trigger a recovery action. Time is also crucial to observe the effects of failure patterns including quantified delays or down-times of nodes and links. We based our model of time on the Temporal Process Language (TPL) [25], a well understood extension of CCS with discrete time and timeouts. Delays are processes of the form **sleep**.*P* that behave as *P* after one time unit. Timeouts are modelled after the idiomatic `receive..after` pattern in Erlang. Concretely, the Erlang pattern below (left) is modelled as the process below (right):

```
receive
    Pattern1 -> P1;
    ...
    PatternN -> PN
after
    m -> Q
end
```

$?\{p_1.P_1, \ldots, p_N.P_N\}$ **after** m Q

where $p_1, \ldots, p_N$ is a set of patterns, each associated with a continuation P_i, with $i \in \{1, \ldots, N\}$, and Q is the timeout handler, executed if none of the patterns can be matched with a message in the mailbox within m time units. Following TPL, an action can be either a time action or an instantaneous communication action, and time actions can happen only when communication actions are not possible (maximal progress [25]). Concretely, we define the systems behaviour as a reduction relation with two kinds of actions: communication actions $\rightharpoonup$ and time actions $\leadsto$. While TPL is synchronous and only prioritises synchronisations over delays, we model *asynchronous* communications and prioritise any send or receive action over time actions. Thus, in our model, by maximal progress, communications have priority over delays.

The state of an actor at a time t is modelled as $n[P](M)(t)$, where n is the actor identifier (unique in the system), M the mailbox, and P the process run by that actor. System $\mathbf{R}_t$ below is the parallel composition of actors n_1 and n_2:

$$\mathbf{R}_t = n_1[\,\mathbf{sleep}.!n_2\,a.0\,](\emptyset)(t) \parallel n_2[\,?a.P \text{ after } 1\ Q\,](\emptyset)(t)$$

Although each actor in $\mathbf{R}_t$ has its own local time t explicitly represented, which makes it easy to inject failures compositionally, our semantics keeps the time of parallel components synchronized (as in TPL). In $\mathbf{R}_t$, node n_1 is deliberately idling and n_2 is temporarily blocked on a receive/timeout action, so no communication can happen, and thus only a time action is possible, updating both actors' times and triggering the timeout in n_2:

$$\mathbf{R}_t \leadsto n_1[\,!n_2\,a.0\,](\emptyset)(t+1) \parallel n_2[\,Q\,](\emptyset)(t+1)$$

Mailboxes. Each pair of actors can communicate via two unidirectional links. For example, (n_1, n_2) denotes the link for communications from n_1 to n_2. An interaction involve three steps: (I) the sending actor sends the message by placing it in the appropriate link, (II) the message reaches the receiver's mailbox, and (III) the receiving actor processes the message. These three steps allows us to capture e.g., effects of failures in senders versus receivers, on nodes versus links, and to model latency. Consider the system $\mathbf{R}_c = n_1[\,!a.0\,](\emptyset)(t) \parallel n_2[\,?a.P\ \texttt{after}\ 2\ Q\,](b)(t)$. Step (I), the sending of a message, is illustrated below on $\mathbf{R}_c$:

$$\mathbf{R}_c \rightharpoonup n_1[\,0\,](\emptyset)(t) \parallel 1.(n_1, n_2, a) \parallel n_2[\,?a.P\ \texttt{after}\ 2\ Q\,](\emptyset)(t) = \mathbf{R}_c' \qquad (1)$$

$1.(n_1, n_2, a)$ models a latent message in link (n_1, n_2) with content a. Prefix 1 is the average network latency (assumed to be a constant). Due to latency, the message can only be added to the receiver's mailbox after one time step:

$$\mathbf{R}_c' \rightsquigarrow n_1[\,0\,](\emptyset)(t+1) \parallel (n_1, n_2, a) \parallel n_2[\,?a.P\ \texttt{after}\ 1\ Q\,](\emptyset)(t+1) \qquad (2)$$

These floating messages (n_1, n_2, a) with no latency are similar to messages in the ether [47], in the global mailbox [29], or to the floating messages in [30].

Step (II) is the reception of the message, and happens as illustrated below (omitting the idle actor n_1), where message a is added to the mailbox of n_2:

$$(n_1, n_2, a) \parallel n_2[\,?a.P\ \texttt{after}\ 1\ Q\,](\emptyset)(t+1) \rightharpoonup n_2[\,?a.P\ \texttt{after}\ Q\,](a)(t+1)$$

Step (III) is the processing of the message, as illustrated below:

$$n_2[\,?a.P\ \texttt{after}\ 1\ Q\,](a)(t+1) \rightharpoonup n_2[\,P\,](\emptyset)(t+1)$$

where message a in the mailbox matches the receive pattern (made up of a single atom a) and is therefore processed. Mailboxes give us an expressive model of communication for modern real-world systems. An alternative model of communication is peer-to-peer communication, used e.g., in Communicating Finite State Machines (CFSM) [13] and Multiparty Session Types [18, 26], where a receiver must specify from whom the message is expected. This makes it difficult to accurately capture interactions with public servers, or patterns like multiple producers-one consumer. Note that, in the interaction above, n_2 processes message a because it matches pattern a, although an older message b is present in the mailbox. Alternative models, like Mailbox CFSMs [5, 10], typically do not model the selective receive pattern (e.g., pattern-matching in Erlang) shown above. Without selective receive, participants can easily get stuck if messages are received in an unexpected order. One can encode peer-to-peer communication over FIFO unidirectional channels by using pattern matching with selective receive: using the sender's identifier in the message and in the receive pattern. A similar communication model to ours was proposed in [38].

Localities and Failures. The actor construct is similar to that used to model locality for processes [16], and also studied in relation to failures [6,21,22,42] but using a fail-stop untimed model. We use actor nodes to model the effects of injected failures on specific nodes and links.

Referring to system $\mathbf{R}'_c$ in (1), by placing floating messages into a link with latency before they reach the receiver's mailbox we can observe the effects of link failure as message loss. Assume link (n_1, n_2) is down at time t:

$$\mathbf{R}'_c \rightharpoonup n_1[\,0\,](\emptyset)(t) \parallel n_2[\,?a.P \text{ after } 2\ Q\,](\emptyset)(t)$$

the floating message gets lost which in turn would end up causing a timeout in n_2. Similarly, in case of node failure, node n_1 in system $\mathbf{R}_c$, seen earlier in (1), would go into a crashed node state before sending the message, hence triggering a timeout in n_2:

$$\mathbf{R}_c \rightharpoonup n_1[\,\downarrow\,](\emptyset)(t) \parallel n_2[\,?a.P \text{ after } 2\ Q\,](\emptyset)(t)$$

Assumptions. When a node crashes and comes back up again later on, it will come up with the same node identifier. We assume the behaviour within a node is sequential: actors can be composed in parallel but processes cannot, hence limiting communication to distributed communications between nodes. We choose to focus on inter-node communication on its own, because there already exist good strategies (e.g., in Erlang and Elixir) for dealing with in-node failure through the use of supervision hierarchy, supervision strategies, and let-it-crash philosophy. Messages in transit when a node goes down remain in transit and may enter the mailbox after this node is resumed. We allow a restricted (external) version of choice, based on the communication patterns found in Erlang. Free, or completely unrestricted choice, while central to many process algebras, for example CCS, tends to be less used in practice. For simplicity, we assume nodes are not created at run-time, focussing on fixed topologies. Extending the language with the capability of creating new nodes is relatively straightforward, and can be done in a similar way to π-calculus restriction.

3   A Model of Failures

Let $\mathcal{N}$ be the set of node identifiers in a system. The model of failures is defined to be the Δ function:

$$\Delta : \mathbb{N} \times (\mathcal{N} \cup (\mathcal{N} \times \mathcal{N})) \mapsto \{\downarrow, \uparrow, \circlearrowleft\}$$

mapping each discrete time $t \in \mathbb{N}$, node $n \in \mathcal{N}$, and link $(n_1, n_2) \in \mathcal{N} \times \mathcal{N}$ to a value representing the state of health of that node or link, at that time. The symbol $\uparrow$ denotes the "healthy" state, $\downarrow$ identifies the failure of a node or link, and $\circlearrowleft$ indicates a node or link slowdown. The failure scenarios covered by Δ include node crash, message loss, slow processes or slow networks. If *node* n *is*

Systems

$\mathbf{R} \ ::= \ \mathbf{n}[\,P\,](M)(t)$ node

     $| \ (\mathbf{n}_1, \mathbf{n}_2, m)(t)$ floating message

     $| \ u.(\mathbf{n}_1, \mathbf{n}_2, m)(t)$ latent message

     $| \ \mathbf{n}[\,\downarrow\,](\emptyset)(t)$ crashed node

     $| \ \emptyset$ empty

     $| \ \mathbf{R} \,\|\, \mathbf{R}$ parallel

Processes

$P \ ::= \ !\{\mathbf{n}_i \, m_i.P_i\}_{i \in I}$ send

     $| \ ?\{p_i.P_i\}_{i \in I} \ \textbf{after} \ P$ receive-timeout

     $| \ \textbf{sleep}.P$ sleep

     $| \ \mu t.P$ fixed-point

     $| \ t$ recursive variable

     $| \ \mathbf{0}$ inaction

Values

$V \ ::= \ a$ atom

     $| \ \mathbf{n}$ node id

     $| \ X$ variable

Message

$m \ ::= \ \widetilde{V}$ message tuple

Mailbox

$M \ ::= \ \emptyset \ | \ M \cdot m$

Receive Patterns

$E \ ::= \ X \ | \ a$ pattern element

$p \ ::= \ \widetilde{E}$ pattern tuple

Fig. 1. Syntax

down at time t, written $\Delta(t)(\mathbf{n}) = \downarrow$, then it will perform no action until it is resumed, if ever. If $\mathbf{n}$ is resumed at time t', then its state at time t' will be set to the initial state (see Definition 5 for the formal definition). If *link* $(\mathbf{n}_1, \mathbf{n}_2)$ *is down* at time t, written $\Delta(t)(\mathbf{n}_1, \mathbf{n}_2) = \downarrow$, then any message in transit on that link at time t will be lost. If *node* $\mathbf{n}$ *is slow* at time t, written $\Delta(t)(\mathbf{n}) = \circlearrowleft$, then any actions of the process running in $\mathbf{n}$ are delayed for one time step, and may resume at time $t+1$ if $\Delta(t+1)(\mathbf{n}) = \uparrow$. If *link* $(\mathbf{n}_1, \mathbf{n}_2)$ *is slow* at time t, written $\Delta(t)(\mathbf{n}_1, \mathbf{n}_2) = \circlearrowleft$, then the delivery of any message in transit on that link at time t will not happen at that time, and so will be delayed by at least one time unit. The delay is in effect added to the average network latency, which we model as a constant. Failures can be permanent or transient, as shown below by examples.

Example 1 (Permanent failures). Permanent node failure after a certain point in time, say $t = 10$, can be modelled by the Δ_1 definition below. Function Δ_2 shows a transient periodic structural failure of node $\mathbf{n}$, with each period having 100 time units of healthy state and 100 of down state. One could similarly model transient degrading failure by setting uptimes when $t = n^2$ for $(n \in \mathbb{N})$.

$$\Delta_1(\mathbf{n})(\mathbf{t}) = \begin{cases} \uparrow & \textit{if } t < 10 \\ \downarrow & \textit{otherwise} \end{cases} \qquad \Delta_2(\mathbf{n})(\mathbf{t}) = \begin{cases} \uparrow & \textit{if } t \textbf{ div } 100 \textbf{ mod } 2 \ = 0 \\ \downarrow & \textit{otherwise} \end{cases}$$

4   Calculus for Cursed Systems

This section presents the model for actor based systems. The syntax of the calculus is given in Fig. 1.

     Systems are nodes $\mathbf{n}[\,P\,](M)(t)$, messages (floating or latent), crashed nodes $\mathbf{n}[\,\downarrow\,](\emptyset)(t)$, empty systems $\emptyset$, and parallel compositions of systems $\mathbf{R} \,\|\, \mathbf{R}$. Term

$\mathbf{n}[P](M)(t)$ denotes the state of node $\mathbf{n} \in \mathcal{N}$ where P is the process running in $\mathbf{n}$, and M is the mailbox of $\mathbf{n}$. A mailbox is a (possibly empty) list of messages. A message m is a tuple of values, which can be atoms a, node ids $\mathbf{n}$ or variables X. Messages are read from a mailbox via pattern matching. We define the pattern matching function in the style of [38] through the derivations in Fig. 2.

$$[\textsc{Var1}]\ (X, a) \vdash_{\text{match}} [a/X] \qquad [\textsc{Var2}]\ (X, \mathbf{n}) \vdash_{\text{match}} [\mathbf{n}/X]$$

$$[\textsc{Tuple}]\ \frac{(E, V) \vdash_{\text{match}} \underline{\sigma} \qquad (\widetilde{E}, \widetilde{V}) \vdash_{\text{match}} \sigma}{(E\widetilde{E}, V\widetilde{V}) \vdash_{\text{match}} \underline{\sigma}\sigma}$$

$$[\textsc{Atom}]\ (a, a) \vdash_{\text{match}} [a/a]$$

$$[\textsc{Mbox1}]\ \frac{(E, m) \vdash_{\text{match}} \sigma}{(E, m \cdot M) \vdash_{\text{match}} \sigma} \qquad [\textsc{Mbox2}]\ \frac{(E, m) \nvdash_{\text{match}} \qquad (E, M) \vdash_{\text{match}} \sigma}{(E, m \cdot M) \vdash_{\text{match}} \sigma}$$

Fig. 2. Matching rules

Given a pattern $\widetilde{E}$ and a message (tuple) $\widetilde{V}$, $(\widetilde{E}, \widetilde{V}) \vdash_{\text{match}} \sigma$ the match function returns a substitution σ. Note that the matching is only defined if $\widetilde{E}$ and $\widetilde{V}$ have the same size, and if the pattern and message match. We write $(E, m) \nvdash_{\text{match}}$ when message m does *not* match pattern E.

A floating message $(\mathbf{n_1}, \mathbf{n_2}, m)(t)$ represents a message m in link $(\mathbf{n_1}, \mathbf{n_2})$. Latent messages $u.(\mathbf{n_1}, \mathbf{n_2}, m)(t)$ are floating messages which can only reach the receiver's mailbox after a latency u. We assume all sent messages have a latency defined as a constant L, which abstracts the average network latency.

Looking at processes, a term of the form $!\{\mathbf{n_i}\ m_i.P_i\}_{i \in I}$ chooses to send to node $\mathbf{n_i}$ a message m_i and continues as P_i. Term $?\{p_i.P_i\}_{i \in I}$ **after** P tries to pattern match a message from the mailbox against one of the patterns p_i, and continues as P_i given that the matching succeeds for p_i, timing out **after** one time unit if no message matches and executing P. Process **sleep**.P consumes a time unit and then continues as P. Process $\mu t.P$ is for recursion, and t is recursion call. Finally, $\mathbf{0}$ is the idle process.

Remark 1. We use notation $?\{p_i.P_i\}_{i \in I}$ **after** $u\,P$ as syntactic sugar for nesting u timeouts[1] and **sleep** $u.P$ for the sequential composition of u delays with continuation P.

Recall (Sect. 3) that we fix the set of system's nodes $\mathcal{N}$, and the domain of Δ is $\mathcal{N} \cup (\mathcal{N} \times \mathcal{N})$, that is the set of nodes and links between pairs of nodes. Our unit of analysis is a *cursed system* defined below.

Definition 1 (Cursed system). *A cursed system is a pair* $(\mathbf{R}, \Delta)$ *where* $\mathbf{R}$ *is a system,* Δ *is a curse.*

The semantics of cursed systems is given in Definition 2 as a reduction relation over systems that is parametric on Δ. We write $\mathbf{R}_1 \equiv \mathbf{R}_2$ to mean that the

---

[1] As $Q(u)$ where $Q(0) = ?\{p_i.P_i\}_{i \in I}$ **after** P and $Q(i+1) = ?\{p_i.P_i\}_{i \in I}$ **after** $Q(i)$.

systems $\mathbf{R}_1$ and $\mathbf{R}_2$ are the same up-to associativity and commutativity of $\|$, plus $0.(\mathbf{n}_1, \mathbf{n}_2, m)(t) \equiv (\mathbf{n}_1, \mathbf{n}_2, m)(t)$ and $\mathbf{R} \parallel \emptyset \equiv \mathbf{R}$.

Definition 2 (Operational semantics for cursed systems). *Reduction is the smallest relation on cursed systems over communication actions denoted by* $\rightarrowtail$, *and time actions denoted by* $\rightsquigarrow$, *that satisfies the rules in Fig. 3. We use* $\rightarrow$ *when* $\rightarrow \in \{\rightarrowtail, \rightsquigarrow\}$. *For readability, in the rules we assume* Δ *fixed and write* $\mathbf{R} \rightarrow \mathbf{R}'$ *instead of* $(\mathbf{R}, \Delta) \rightarrow (\mathbf{R}', \Delta)$.

The first set of rules in Fig. 3a is for actors actions, happening at a time t, when the nodes and links are in a healthy state i.e. $\Delta(t)(\mathbf{n}) = \uparrow$. In rule [SND], $\mathbf{n}$ chooses to send a message m_j to node $\mathbf{n}_j$, and continues as P_j. Modelling asynchronous communication, a latent message $L.(\mathbf{n}, \mathbf{n}_j, m_j)(t)$ is introduced in the system, where L is the network latency constant. Rule [SCHED] delivers a floating message to the receiver's mailbox. Rule [RCV], retrieves the first message m in the mailbox that matches one of the receive patterns p_j. The match function returns a substitution σ that is applied to the continuation process P_j associated with pattern p_j; and m is removed from the mailbox. Finally, Rule [REC] allows a node with a recursive process to proceed with a communication or a time action.

The second set of rules, in Fig. 3b, is for time-passing reduction in absence of failures. Rules [SLEEP] and [TIMEOUT] model reduction of time consuming and receiving with timeout processes, respectively. Rule [TIMEOUT] can only be applied if none of the messages in the mailbox is matching any of the patterns $\{p_i\}_{i \in I}$ yielding an urgent receive semantics [39] reflecting the receive primitive in Erlang. Rule [LATENCY] allows time passing for latent messages. Note that, by setting $u' = \max(u - 1, 0)$, if a receiver node crashes, all latent/floating messages remain in the link until the node is able to receive them, i.e. in a healthy state. We omit the rules for state-preserving time passing for idle nodes and $\mathbf{n}[\mathbf{0}](M)(t)$.

The third set of rules, in Fig. 3c, models the effects of failures injected at time t. Rule [NLATE] models a delay, injected by $\Delta(t)(\mathbf{n}) = \circlearrowright$, in the execution of the process P in a node $\mathbf{n}$: a time unit elapses without any action in P. Rule [MSGLOSS] models a lossy link at time t, injected by $\Delta(t)(\mathbf{n}_1, \mathbf{n}_2) = \downarrow$, and permanently deletes a message $u.(\mathbf{n}_1, \mathbf{n}_2, m)(t)$ in transit. Rule [MSGLATE] models a slow link, injected by $\Delta(t)(\mathbf{n}_1, \mathbf{n}_2) = \circlearrowright$, by allowing time to pass but without decreasing the latency u of the message. Rule [NDOWN] models an instantaneous node that crash injected by $\Delta(t)(\mathbf{n}) = \downarrow$, and erases the process and mailbox of the node. Rule [DOWNLATE] allows time to pass for a crashed node. In rule [NUP] a crashed node is restarted with its initial process P and empty mailbox. Σ is a mapping from $\mathcal{N}$ to processes, that gives the initial process of each actor node. We assume that the node identifier is unchanged when restarting the node.

The last set of rules given in Fig. 3d models system actions. In rule [PARCOM] a communication action of system part $\mathbf{R}_1$ is reflected in the composite system $\mathbf{R}_1 \parallel \mathbf{R}_2$. In rule [PARTIME] time actions need to be reflected in all the parts of a system. A whole system can have a time action only if all parts of the system have no communication or failure actions to perform at the current time ($\mathbf{R}_i \nrightarrow$). [STR] is for communication and time actions of structurally equivalent systems.

$$[\textsc{Snd}] \; \frac{\Delta(t)(\mathbf{n}_1) = \uparrow \qquad j \in I}{\mathbf{n}[\,!\{\mathbf{n}_1 \, m_i.P_i\}_{i \in I}\,](M)(t) \rightharpoonup \mathbf{n}[\,P_j\,](M)(t) \parallel L.(\mathbf{n}, \mathbf{n}_j, m_j)(t)}$$

$$[\textsc{Sched}] \; \frac{\Delta(t)(\mathbf{n}_1) = \uparrow \qquad \Delta(t)(\mathbf{n}_2, \mathbf{n}_1) = \uparrow}{(\mathbf{n}_2, \mathbf{n}_1, m)(t) \parallel \mathbf{n}_1[\,P\,](M)(t) \rightharpoonup \mathbf{n}_1[\,P\,](M \cdot m)(t)}$$

$$[\textsc{Rcv}] \; \frac{\Delta(t)(\mathbf{n}) = \uparrow \qquad j \in I, \; (p_j, m) \vdash_{\text{match}} \sigma \qquad \forall i \in I, \; (p_i, M_1) \nvdash_{\text{match}}}{\mathbf{n}[\,?\{p_i.P_i\}_{i \in I} \, \textbf{after} \, P\,](M_1 \cdot m \cdot M_2)(t) \rightharpoonup \mathbf{n}[\,P_j \sigma\,](M_1 \cdot M_2)(t)}$$

$$[\textsc{Rec}] \; \frac{\Delta(t)(\mathbf{n}) = \uparrow \qquad \mathbf{n}[\,P[\mu \mathbf{t}.P/\mathbf{t}]\,](M)(t) \rightharpoonup \mathbf{n}[\,P'\,](M)(t')}{\mathbf{n}[\,\mu \mathbf{t}.P\,](M)(t) \rightharpoonup \mathbf{n}[\,P'\,](M)(t')}$$

(a) Actor/Node actions

$$[\textsc{Sleep}] \; \frac{\Delta(t)(\mathbf{n}) = \uparrow}{\mathbf{n}[\,\textbf{sleep}.P\,](M)(t) \rightsquigarrow \mathbf{n}[\,P\,](M)(t+1)}$$

$$[\textsc{Latency}] \; \frac{\Delta(t)(\mathbf{n}_1, \mathbf{n}_2) = \uparrow \qquad u' = \max(u - 1, 0)}{u.(\mathbf{n}_1, \mathbf{n}_2, m)(t) \rightsquigarrow u'.(\mathbf{n}_1, \mathbf{n}_2, m)(t+1)}$$

$$[\textsc{Timeout}] \; \frac{\Delta(t)(\mathbf{n}) = \uparrow \qquad \forall i \in I, \; (p_i, M) \nvdash_{\text{match}}}{\mathbf{n}[\,?\{p_i.P_i\}_{i \in I} \, \textbf{after} \, P\,](M)(t) \rightsquigarrow \mathbf{n}[\,P\,](M)(t+1)}$$

(b) Time actions

$$[\textsc{NLate}] \; \frac{\Delta(t)(\mathbf{n}) = \circlearrowleft}{\mathbf{n}[\,P\,](M)(t) \rightsquigarrow \mathbf{n}[\,P\,](M)(t+1)} \qquad [\textsc{MsgLoss}] \; \frac{\Delta(t)(\mathbf{n}_1, \mathbf{n}_2) = \downarrow \qquad u \geq 0}{u.(\mathbf{n}_1, \mathbf{n}_2, m)(t) \rightharpoonup \emptyset}$$

$$[\textsc{MsgLate}] \; \frac{\Delta(t)(\mathbf{n}_1, \mathbf{n}_2) = \circlearrowleft \qquad u \geq 0}{u.(\mathbf{n}_1, \mathbf{n}_2, m)(t) \rightsquigarrow u.(\mathbf{n}_1, \mathbf{n}_2, m)(t+1)} \qquad [\textsc{NDown}] \; \frac{\Delta(t)(\mathbf{n}) = \downarrow}{\mathbf{n}[\,P\,](M)(t) \rightharpoonup \mathbf{n}[\,\downarrow\,](\emptyset)(t)}$$

$$[\textsc{DownLate}] \; \frac{\Delta(t)(\mathbf{n}) = \downarrow}{\mathbf{n}[\,\downarrow\,](\emptyset)(t) \rightsquigarrow \mathbf{n}[\,\downarrow\,](\emptyset)(t+1)} \qquad [\textsc{NUp}] \; \frac{\Delta(t)(\mathbf{n}) = \uparrow \qquad \Sigma(\mathbf{n}) = P}{\mathbf{n}[\,\downarrow\,](\emptyset)(t) \rightharpoonup \mathbf{n}[\,P\,](\emptyset)(t)}$$

(c) Failure actions

$$[\textsc{ParCom}] \; \frac{\mathbf{R}_1 \rightharpoonup \mathbf{R}_1'}{\mathbf{R}_1 \parallel \mathbf{R}_2 \rightharpoonup \mathbf{R}_1' \parallel \mathbf{R}_2} \qquad [\textsc{Str}] \; \frac{\mathbf{R}_1 \equiv \mathbf{R}_1' \qquad \mathbf{R}_1 \rightarrow \mathbf{R}_2 \qquad \mathbf{R}_2 \equiv \mathbf{R}_2'}{\mathbf{R}_1' \rightarrow \mathbf{R}_2'}$$

$$[\textsc{ParTime}] \; \frac{\mathbf{R}_1 \rightsquigarrow \mathbf{R}_1' \qquad \mathbf{R}_2 \rightsquigarrow \mathbf{R}_2' \qquad \forall i \in \{1, 2\}. \, \mathbf{R}_i \nrightarrow}{\mathbf{R}_1 \parallel \mathbf{R}_2 \rightsquigarrow \mathbf{R}_1' \parallel \mathbf{R}_2'}$$

(d) System actions

Fig. 3. Reduction and structural equivalence

4.1   Basic Properties of Systems Reductions

In the remainder of this section we discuss two properties of cursed systems: time-coherence (the semantics keeps clocks synchronized) and non-zenoness. We start by defining the time of a system. All definitions below apply straightforwardly to cursed systems by fixing a Δ.

Definition 3 (Time of a system). *Let $\underline{t}$ range over $\mathbb{N} \cup \{*\}$. We define the synchronization (partial) function δ:*

$$\delta(*, \underline{t}) = \delta(\underline{t}, *) = \underline{t} \quad \delta(*, *) = * \quad \delta(\underline{t}, \underline{t}) = \underline{t}$$

$\delta(\underline{t}_1, \underline{t}_2)$ returns a time or a wildcard $*$, and is undefined if $\underline{t}_1 \neq \underline{t}_2$ and neither $\underline{t}_1$ nor $\underline{t}_2$ is a wildcard. We define $\texttt{time}(\mathbf{R})$ as a partial function over systems:

$$\texttt{time}(\mathbf{R}) = \begin{cases} * & \mathbf{R} = \emptyset \\ t & \mathbf{R} = \mathtt{n}[\,P\,](M)(t) \ or \ \mathbf{R} = \mathtt{n}[\,\downarrow\,](M)(t) \ or \\ & \mathbf{R} = (\mathtt{n}_1, \mathtt{n}_2, m)(t) \ or \ \mathbf{R} = u.(\mathtt{n}_1, \mathtt{n}_2, m)(t) \\ \delta(\texttt{time}(\mathbf{R}_1), \texttt{time}(\mathbf{R}_2)) & \mathbf{R} = \mathbf{R}_1 \,||\, \mathbf{R}_2 \end{cases}$$

We can now define time-coherence of a system, holding when all its components have the same time.

Definition 4 (Time coherence). $\mathbf{R}$ *is* time coherent *if $\texttt{time}(\mathbf{R})$ is defined.*

For example, system $\mathtt{n}_1[\,P\,](M)(t) \,||\, (\mathtt{n}_1, \mathtt{n}_2, m)(t) \,||\, \emptyset$ is time-coherent, while system $\mathtt{n}_1[\,P\,](M)(t) \,||\, (\mathtt{n}_1, \mathtt{n}_2, m)(t+1) \,||\, \emptyset$ is not.

The time function is also useful to characterise systems where all actors are coherently at time 0 and in their initial state.

Definition 5 (Initial system). *Let Σ be a mapping from $\mathcal{N}$ to processes such that $\Sigma(\mathtt{n})$ is the initial process of $\mathtt{n}$. A system $\mathbf{R}$ is* initial *if $\texttt{time}(\mathbf{R}) = 0$ and*

$$\mathbf{R} \equiv \mathtt{n}_1[\,\Sigma(\mathtt{n}_1)\,](\emptyset)(0) \,||\, \ldots \,||\, \mathtt{n}_m[\,\Sigma(\mathtt{n}_m)\,](\emptyset)(0)$$

with $\{1, \ldots, m\} = \mathcal{N}$. A cursed system $(\mathbf{R}, \Delta)$ is initial *if $\mathbf{R}$ is initial.*

Next we show that the reduction over systems preserves time-coherence, hence all reachable systems are coherent.

Lemma 1 (Time-coherence invariant) *If $\mathbf{R}$ is time-coherent and $\mathbf{R} \to \mathbf{R}'$ then $\mathbf{R}'$ is time-coherent.*

The proof of the lemma is straightforward, by induction on the derivation. In fact, the only rule that updates the time of a parallel composition is [PARTIME] which requires time passing for all parallel processes. The fact that if $\mathbf{R}$ is initial then $time(\mathbf{R})$ is defined (as 0) yields the following property. We let $\to^*$ be the transitive closure of the reduction relation.

Property 1. Let **R** be initial, if **R** →* **R**′ then **R**′ is time-coherent.

We assume any system **R** to start off as initial and hence, by Property 1, to be time-coherent.

Next, we give a desirable property for timed models: non-zenoness. This prevents an infinite number of communication actions at any given time (Zeno behaviours). Besides yielding a more natural abstraction of a real world system, non-zenoness simplifies analysis, for example, we can assume the set of reachable states from system to be finite. We start by defining a non-instantaneous process.

Definition 6 (Non-instantaneous process). *We define function* ninst(P) *inductively as follows:*

$$
\text{ninst}(P) = \begin{cases} \bigwedge_{i \in I} \text{ninst}(P_i) & \textit{if } P = !\{\mathtt{n_i}\, m_i.P_i\}_{i \in I} \textit{ or } P = ?\{p_i.P_i\}_{i \in I} \textbf{ after } Q \\ \text{ninst}(Q) & \textit{if } P = \mu X.Q \\ \texttt{true} & \textit{if } P = \textbf{sleep}.Q \\ \texttt{false} & \textit{if } P = X \textit{ or } P = 0 \end{cases}
$$

We say that P is non-instantaneous if ninst(P) = true. *We say that* **R** *is non-instantaneous if all nodes in* **R** *run non-instantaneous processes.*

Property 2 (Non-zenoness). Let **R** be non-instantaneous. If **R** →* **R**′ then there is a finite number of **R**″ such that **R**′ ⇀ **R**″.

The proof is straightforward by induction on the structure of **R**′. Hereafter we assume systems to be non-instantaneous, and hence non-Zeno.

5 Properties of Cursed Systems

In this section we define a behavioural relation between cursed systems, as a weak barbed bisimulation [44]. The aim is to compare the systems' abilities to preserve 'normal' functionality when they are affected by failures. We abstract from the fact that some parts of the system may be deadlocked, as long as healthy actors keep receiving the messages they expect. Mailbox-based (rather than point-to-point) communication and pattern matching allow us to capture e.g., multiple-producers scenarios where a consumer can receive the expected feeds as long as *some* producers are healthy. Our behavioural relation also abstracts from time, to disregard the delays introduced by recovering actions, and only observe the effects of such delays (we do not focus on efficiency). Essentially, two systems are equivalent when actors receive the same messages, abstracting from senders, in a time-abstract way. On the basis of this equivalence we define *recoverability* and *augmentation*.

We start by defining weak barbed bisimulation for cursed systems.

Definition 7 (Barb). *The ready actions of P are defined inductively as follows:*

$$\text{rdy}(!\{n_i\, m_i.P_i\}_{i\in I} = \{!\, n_i\, m_i\}_{i\in I} \qquad \text{rdy}?\{p_i.P_i\}_{i\in I} \; \textit{after}\; P) = \{?\, p_i\}_{i\in I}$$
$$\text{rdy}(0) = \text{rdy}(t) = \text{rdy}(\textbf{sleep}.P) = \emptyset \qquad \text{rdy}(\mu t.P) = \text{rdy}(P)$$

Let $\mathbf{R} \downarrow x$ be the least relation satisfying the rules below.

$$n[\,P\,](M)(t) \downarrow x \qquad \textit{if}\; !\, n'm \in \text{rdy}(P) \wedge x = !\, n'm \;\vee\; ?\, p \in \text{rdy}(P) \wedge x = ?\, n\, p$$
$$(n_1, n_2, m) \downarrow !\, n_2\, m$$
$$(\mathbf{R}_1 \parallel \mathbf{R}_2) \downarrow x \qquad \textit{if}\; \mathbf{R}_1 \downarrow x\; \textit{or}\; \mathbf{R}_2 \downarrow x$$

If $\mathbf{R} \downarrow x$ we say that $\mathbf{R}$ has a barb *on x.*

Barbs abstract from the sender of a message. This allows us to disregard the identity of the senders, following mailbox-based communications in actor-based systems. Scenarios where the identity of the sender is important can be encoded by using node identifiers as message content. We observe m and p to retain expressiveness with respect to channel-based scenarios, as discussed in Sect. 5.3.

Definition 8 (Weak barbed bisimulation). *Recall $\rightarrow \in \{\rightarrow, \rightsquigarrow\}$. A weak (time-abstract) barbed bisimulation is a symmetric binary relation $\mathcal{S}$ between cursed systems such that $(\mathbf{R}_1, \Delta_1)\, \mathcal{S}\, (\mathbf{R}_2, \Delta_2)$ implies:*

1. *If $(\mathbf{R}_1, \Delta_1) \rightarrow (\mathbf{R}_1', \Delta_1)$ then $(\mathbf{R}_2, \Delta_2) \rightarrow^* (\mathbf{R}_2', \Delta_2)$ and $(\mathbf{R}_1', \Delta_1)\, \mathcal{S}\, (\mathbf{R}_2', \Delta_2)$.*
2. *If $\mathbf{R}_1 \downarrow x$ for some x, then $(\mathbf{R}_2, \Delta_2) \rightarrow^* (\mathbf{R}_2', \Delta_2)$ and $\mathbf{R}_2' \downarrow x$.*

and the symmetric of (1) and (2). $(\mathbf{R}_1, \Delta_1)$ is barbed bisimilar to $(\mathbf{R}_2, \Delta_2)$, written $(\mathbf{R}_1, \Delta_1) \approx (\mathbf{R}_2, \Delta_2)$, if there exists some weak barbed bisimulation $\mathcal{S}$ such that $(\mathbf{R}_1, \Delta_1)\, \mathcal{S}\, (\mathbf{R}_2, \Delta_2)$.

5.1 Resilience and Recoverability

We define resilience as the ability of a system to behave 'normally' despite failures injection. Let $\uparrow$ be the function that assigns $\uparrow$ to all nodes and links at any time.

Definition 9 (Resilience). *Initial $(\mathbf{R}, \Delta)$ is resilient if $(\mathbf{R}, \uparrow) \approx (\mathbf{R}, \Delta)$.*

The definition of resilience sets the behaviour of a system without curses as a model of the *expected behaviour*. In some cases, e.g. when looking at retry strategies, while the system may be affected by failures, one may want to observe that it *eventually* recovers. To this aim, we define n-recoverability as the ability of a system to display the expected behaviour after time n.

Definition 10 (n-Recoverability). *Let $n \in \mathbb{N}$ and $(\mathbf{R}, \Delta)$ initial. $(\mathbf{R}, \Delta)$ is n-recoverable if $(\mathbf{R}, \Delta) \rightarrow^* (\mathbf{R}', \Delta)$ and $time(\mathbf{R}') = n$ implies $(\mathbf{R}, \uparrow) \approx (\mathbf{R}', \Delta)$.*

Basically, a system is resilient if it is 0-recoverable. We give some examples of resilience and n-recoverability, where we fix the latency $L = 1$.

Example 2 (Resilience). Consider the cursed system $(\mathbf{R}, \Delta)$ with:

$$\mathbf{R} = \mathbf{n}_1[\,\mathbf{sleep}.\,!\,\mathbf{n}_2\,a.0\,](\emptyset)(0)\,||\,\mathbf{n}_2[\,?\,a.\mathbf{sleep}.0\;\mathtt{after}\;5\,](\emptyset)(0)$$

and $\Delta(\mathbf{n}_1, \mathbf{n}_2)$ injecting network delays at time 1 and 2 and $\uparrow$ otherwise. $(\mathbf{R}, \Delta)$ is resilient; the timeout of 5 is good for networks delays of 2 time units. However, $(\mathbf{R}, \Delta)$ would not be resilient for longer networks delays.

Example 3 (n-recoverability). Consider cursed system $(\mathbf{R}, \Delta)$ with:

$$\mathbf{R} = \mathbf{n}_1[\,\mathbf{sleep}.!\mathbf{n}_2\,a.0\,](\emptyset)(0)\,||\,\mathbf{n}_2[\,\mu t.?a.\mathbf{sleep}.0\;\mathtt{after}\;4\,\mathtt{t}\,](\emptyset)(0)$$

and $\Delta(\mathbf{n}_1, \mathbf{n}_2)$ injecting network delays at time 1, 2, and 3 (and $\uparrow$ otherwise). $(\mathbf{R}, \Delta)$ is 5-resilient. Note that any behaviour by $\mathbf{n}_1$ before 5 is disregarded, even in cases where some communication occurred.

By Definition 10, checking resilience and n-recoverability is reduced to the problem of checking weak barbed bisimulation. Note that, in Definition 10, the number of $\mathbf{R}'$ that can be reached from $\mathbf{R}$ is finite, because the execution up to $\mathbf{R}'$ lasts for n time units and, by Property 2, a system can perform only a finite number of actions at any given time.

5.2 Augmentation of Cursed Systems

Augmentation of a cursed system is the result of adding or modifying some behaviour in the initial system to improve the system's ability of handling failures.

Definition 11 (Augmentation). *System* $\mathbf{R}_{\mathrm{I}}$ *is an augmentation of* $\mathbf{R}$ *if* $time(\mathbf{R}_{\mathrm{I}}) = time(\mathbf{R})$ *and: (i)* $(\mathbf{R}, \uparrow) \approx (\mathbf{R}_{\mathrm{I}}, \uparrow)$ *(transparency); (ii) there exist* Δ *and* n *such that* $(\mathbf{R}_{\mathrm{I}}, \Delta)$ *is* n-*recoverable and* $(\mathbf{R}, \Delta)$ *is not* n-*recoverable (improvement). Moreover, we say that an augmentation is* preserving *if, for all* n *and* Δ, $(\mathbf{R}, \Delta)$ *is* n-*recoverable implies* $(\mathbf{R}_{\mathrm{I}}, \Delta)$ *is* n-*recoverable.*

Example 4 (Augmentation). Consider the small producer-consumer system $\mathbf{R}$ below, composed of a producer node $\mathbf{n}_p$, a queue node $\mathbf{n}_q$, and a consumer node $\mathbf{n}_c$. The producer recursively sends items to the queue and sleeps for a time unit. The queue expects to receive an item within three time units that then gets sent to the consumer. In case of a timeout the queue loops back to the beginning and awaits an item from the producer. The consumer recursively receives items from the queue. We fix the latency of the system to $L = 1$.

$$\mathbf{R} = \mathbf{n}_q[\,\mu t.\,?\,item.\mathbf{sleep}.\,!\,\mathbf{n}_c\,item.\mathbf{t}\;\mathtt{after}\;3\,\mathtt{t}\,](\emptyset)(0)\,||$$
$$\quad \mathbf{n}_p[\,\mu t.\,!\,\mathbf{n}_q\,item.\mathbf{sleep}.\mathbf{t}\,](\emptyset)(0)\,||\,\mathbf{n}_c[\,\mu t.\,?\,item.\mathbf{sleep}.\mathbf{t}\;\mathtt{after}\;4\,\mathtt{t}\,](\emptyset)(0)$$

$$\mathbf{R}_{\mathrm{I}} = \mathbf{R}\,||\,\mathbf{n}_{p'}[\,\mu t.\,!\,\mathbf{n}_q\,item.\mathbf{sleep}.\mathbf{t}\,](\emptyset)(0)$$

The augmented producer-consumer $\mathbf{R}_\mathbf{I}$ adds behaviour to the system by having a second producer node $\mathbf{n}_{p'}$. $\mathbf{R}_\mathbf{I}$ improves the resilience to a producer node or its link failing or being slow. For example the curse function $\Delta(\mathbf{n}_p)$ injecting node delay for the producer node between time 1 and 3 and $\uparrow$ otherwise impacts the first system $\mathbf{R}$ but not its augmented counterpart $\mathbf{R}_\mathbf{I}$. $\mathbf{R}$ is 4-recoverable while $\mathbf{R}_\mathbf{I}$ is 0-recoverable. Moreover, $\mathbf{R}_\mathbf{I}$ preserving augmentation of system $\mathbf{R}$.

5.3   Augmentation with Scoped Barbs

Augmentations often need to introduce additional behaviour into actors. One may want to disregard part of 'behind the scenes' augmentation when comparing the behaviour of cursed systems using the relation in Definition 8. For simplicity, instead of adding scope restriction to the calculus, we extend barbs with scopes to hide behaviour of some nodes or links. With mailboxes, all interactions to a node are directed to the one mailbox. Defining scope restriction only on node identifiers would be less expressive than scope restriction based on channels, e.g., it would not be possible to hide specific communications to a node, while in channel-based calculi one can use ad-hoc hidden channels. To retain expressiveness, we define scope restriction that takes into account *patterns* in the communication between nodes.

Definition 12 (Scoped barb). *Let N be a finite set of elements of the form* ! n p *or* ? n p *where* n $\in \mathcal{N}$ *and p is a pattern.* $\mathbf{R} \downarrow_N x$ *if: (1)* $\mathbf{R} \downarrow x$, *(2)* $x \notin N$, *and (3) if $x =$! n m then for all* ! n $p \in N$, $(p, m) \not\vdash_{\text{match}}$. *If* $\mathbf{R} \downarrow_N x$ *we say that* $\mathbf{R}$ *has a N-scoped barb on x.*

We extend Definition 8 using $\downarrow_N$ instead of $\downarrow$, obtaining scoped weak-barbed bisimulation $\approx_N$, and Definition 11 to use $\approx_N$. This setting allow us to analyse producer consumer scenarios, or more complex ones, like the Circuit Breaker pattern [40] widely used in distributed systems.

Example 5 (Circuit breaker). Consider system $(\mathbf{R}, \Delta)$ with a client $\mathbf{n}_c$ and a service $\mathbf{n}_s$, and its augmentation $\mathbf{R}_\mathbf{I}$ with a circuit breaker running on node $\mathbf{n}_s$:

$\mathbf{R} = \; \mathbf{n}_c[\, \mu t. \,! \mathbf{n}_s \, request. \,? \, reply.\mathbf{sleep}.t \; \mathtt{after}\; 4\,0\,](\emptyset)(0) \,\|$
$\qquad \mathbf{n}_s[\, \mu t. \,? \, request.\mathbf{sleep}. \,! \mathbf{n}_c \, reply.t \; \mathtt{after}\; 4\,t\,](\emptyset)(0)$

$\mathbf{R}_\mathbf{I} = \mathbf{n}_c[\, \mu t. \,! \mathbf{n}_s \, request. \,?\{reply.\mathbf{sleep}.t,\, ko.P_f\} \; \mathtt{after}\; 8\,0\,](\emptyset)(0) \,\|$
$\qquad \mathbf{n}_s[\, \mu t. \,? \, X_1.! \mathbf{n}_1 \, X_1. \,? \, X_2.! \mathbf{n}_c \, X_2.t \; \mathtt{after}\; 4\,P'_f \; \mathtt{after}\; 4\,t\,](\emptyset)(0) \,\|$
$\qquad \mathbf{n}_1[\, \mu t. \,?\{request.\mathbf{sleep}.! \mathbf{n}_s \, reply.t,\, ruok.\mathbf{sleep}.! \mathbf{n}_s \, imok.t\} \; \mathtt{after}\; 6\,t\,](\emptyset)(0)$

$P_f = \mu t'. \,? \, retry.\mathbf{sleep}.t \; \mathtt{after}\; 5\,t'$
$P'_f = \,! \mathbf{n}_c \, ko.\mathbf{sleep}.\mu t'. \,! \mathbf{n}_s \, ruok. \,? \, imok.\mathbf{sleep}. \,! \mathbf{n}_c \, retry.t \; \mathtt{after}\; 3\,t'$

with a $\Delta(\mathbf{n}_c, \mathbf{n}_s)$ injecting link slow $\circlearrowleft$ at times 1, 2, and 3 and healthy otherwise, and latency to $L = 1$. The impact of failure on the $\mathbf{R}$ makes it unrecoverable, as the link delay cascades to node $\mathbf{n}_c$. We augment $\mathbf{R}$ with a circuit breaker process which runs on the previous server node $\mathbf{n}_s$ that monitors for failure, prevents faults in one part of the system and controls the retries to the service node now n_1. The node n_s forwards messages between nodes n_c and n_1, and in case of a timeout checks the health of n_s and tells node n_c when it can safely retry the request. When comparing $\mathbf{R}$ and $\mathbf{R_I}$ for resilience, recoverability or transparency we wish to abstract from the additional behaviour introduced by the circuit breaker pattern for which we use Definition 12 with: $N = \{!\,n_s\,ruok,\ ?\,n_s\,imok,\ ?\,n_s\,reply,\ ?\,n_1\,request,\ !\,n_s\,reply,\ ?\,n_1\,ruok,\ !\,n_s\,imok,\ !\,n_c\,ko,\ !\,n_c\,retry,\ ?\,n_c\,ko,\ ?\,n_c\,retry\}$. This effectively hides the entire behaviour of n_1 and node n_s's health checking behaviour. Using the extended definition we find that for the same curse function system $\mathbf{R_I}$ is 0-recoverable. Similarly, for the curse function delays link (n_s, n_1) at times 1, 2, and 3, $\mathbf{R_I}$ is 0-recoverable.

6   Conclusion and Related Work

We introduced a model for actor-based systems with grey failures and investigated the definition of behavioural equivalence for it. We used weak barbed bisimulation to compare systems on the basis of their ability to recover from faults, and defined properties of resilience, recoverability and augmentation. We reduced the problem of checking reliability properties of systems to a problem of checking bisimulation. We introduced scope restriction for mailboxes based on patterns, which allows us to model relatively complex real-world scenarios like the Circuit Breaker.

As further work we plan to extend the recovery function Σ to model checkpointing of intermediate node states. Note that Σ can already be set as an arbitrary process, but a more meaningful extension would account for the way in which checkpoints are saved. Moreover, we plan to add a notion of intermittent correctness, to model recovery with partial checkpoints rather than re-starting from the initial state, or intermittent expected/unexpected behaviour. Another area of future work is to use the characteristic formulae approach [23,46], a method to compute simulation-like relations in process algebras, to generate formulae for the properties introduced and reduce them to a model checking problem that can be offloaded to a model checker.

A related formalism to our model is Timed Rebeca [1], which is actor-based and features similar constructs for deadlines and delays. Timed Rebeca actors can also use a 'now' function to get their local times. Extending our calculus with 'now' and allowing messages to have time as data sort, would allow us to model scenarios e.g., where a node calculates the return-trip time to another node and changes its behaviour accordingly. While Timed Rebeca can encode network delays (adding delays to receive actions – using a construct called 'after'), it does not model links explicitly. Explicit links and separation between curses and systems make it easier in our calculus to compare systems with respect to recoverability. Rebeca was encoded in McErlang [1] and Real-Time Maude [43] for verification. We have ongoing work on encoding our model in UPPAAL. Our main challenge in this respect is to formalise a meaningful and manageable set of curses to verify the model against.

In [21], Francalanza and Hennessy introduced a behavioural theory for DπF, a distributed π-calculus with with nodes and links failures. For a subset of DπF, they also developed a notion of fault-tolerance up to n-faults [22], which is preserved by contexts, and which is related to our notion of resilience. The behavioural theory in [21] is based on reduction barbed congruence. The idea is to use a contextual relation to abstract from the behaviour of hidden nodes/links, while still observing their effects on the network, e.g., as to accessibility and reachability of other nodes. The scoped barbs in Sect. 5.3 have the similar purpose of hiding augmentations while observing their effects on recoverability. However, because of asynchronous communication over mailboxes (while DπF is based on synchronous message passing), our notion of hiding is less structural (i.e., based on nodes and links) and more application-dependent (i.e., based on patterns). At present, we have left pattern hiding out of the semantics, but further investigation towards a contextual relation that works for hidden patterns is promising future work. DπF studies partial failures but does not consider transient failures and time. On the other hand, DπF features mobility which we do not support. In fact, we rely on the assumption of fixed networks: since our observation is based on patterns (and ignores senders) we opted for relying on a stable structure to simplify our reasoning on what augmentation vs recoverability means, leaving mobility issues for future investigation.

Most ingredients of the given model (e.g., timeouts [7,31,32], mailboxes [38], localities [6,16,41]) have been studied in literature, often in isolation. We investigated the inter-play of these ingredients, focussing on reliability properties. One of the first papers dealing with asynchronous communication in process algebra is by de Boer et al. [9], where different observation criteria are studied (bisimulation, traces and abstract traces) following the axiomatic approach typical of the process algebra ACP [8]. An alternative approach has been followed by Amadio et al. [4] who defined asynchronous bisimulation for the π-calculus [36]. They started from operational semantics (expressed as a standard labelled transition system), and then considered the largest bisimulation defined on internal steps that equates processes only when they have the same observables, and which is closed under contexts. The equivalence obtained in this way is called barbed congruence [37]. Notably, when asynchronous communication is considered, barbed congruence is defined assuming as observables the messages that are ready to be delivered to a potential external observer. Merro and Sangiorgi [34] have subsequently studied barbed congruence in the context of the Asynchronous Localised π-calculus (ALπ), a fragment of the asynchronous π-calculus in which only output capabilities can be transmitted, i.e., when a process receives the name of a channel, it can only send messages along it, but cannot receive on it. Another line of research deals with applying the testing approach to asynchronous communication; this has been investigated by Castellani and Hennessy [17] and by Boreale et al. [11,12]. These papers consider an asynchronous variant of CCS [35]. Testing discriminates less than our equivalence, concerning choice, and observes divergent behaviours which we abstract from. Lanese et al. [30] look at bisimulation for Erlang, focussing on the management of process ids. Besides the aforementioned work by Francalanza and Hennessy [21,22], several works look at distributed process algebras with unreliable communication due to faults in the underlying network. Riely and Hennessy [41] study behavioural equivalence over process calculi with locations. Amadio [3] extends the π-calculus with located actions, in the context of a higher-order distributed programming language. Fournet et al. [19] look at locations, mobility and the possibility of location failure in the distributed join calculus. The failure of a location can be detected and recovered from. Berger and Honda [6] augment the asynchronous π-calculus with a timer, locations, message-loss, location failure and the ability to save process state. They define a notion of weak bisimulation over networks. Their model however does not include timeout, link delays, or a way of injecting faults. Cano et al. [14] develop a calculus and type system for multiparty reactive systems that models time dependent interactions. Their setting is synchronous and their focus is on proving properties as types safety or input timeliness, while ours is comparing asynchronous systems with faults.

References

1. Aceto, L., Cimini, M., Ingolfsdottir, A., Reynisson, A.H., Sigurdarson, S.H., Sirjani, M.: Modelling and simulation of asynchronous real-time systems using timed Rebeca. EPTCS **58**, 1–19 (2011). https://doi.org/10.4204/eptcs.58.1
2. Adameit, M., Peters, K., Nestmann, U.: Session types for link failures. In: Bouajjani, A., Silva, A. (eds.) FORTE 2017. LNCS, vol. 10321, pp. 1–16. Springer, Cham (2017). https://doi.org/10.1007/978-3-319-60225-7_1
3. Amadio, R.M.: An asynchronous model of locality, failure, and process mobility. In: Garlan, D., Le Métayer, D. (eds.) COORDINATION 1997. LNCS, vol. 1282, pp. 374–391. Springer, Heidelberg (1997). https://doi.org/10.1007/3-540-63383-9_92
4. Amadio, R.M., Castellani, I., Sangiorgi, D.: On bisimulations for the asynchronous pi-calculus. Theor. Comput. Sci. **195**(2), 291–324 (1998). https://doi.org/10.1016/S0304-3975(97)00223-5
5. Basu, S., Bultan, T., Ouederni, M.: Deciding choreography realizability. Proc. ACM Program. Lang. **47**(POPL), 191–202 (2012). https://doi.org/10.1145/2103656.2103680
6. Berger, M., Honda, K.: The two-phase commitment protocol in an extended π-calculus. ENTCS **39**(1), 21–46 (2003). https://doi.org/10.1016/S1571-0661(05)82502-2
7. Berger, M., Yoshida, N.: Timed, distributed, probabilistic, typed processes. In: Shao, Z. (ed.) APLAS 2007. LNCS, vol. 4807, pp. 158–174. Springer, Heidelberg (2007). https://doi.org/10.1007/978-3-540-76637-7_11
8. Bergstra, J.A., Klop, J.W.: Process algebra for synchronous communication. Inf. Control. **60**(1–3), 109–137 (1984). https://doi.org/10.1016/S0019-9958(84)80025-X
9. de Boer, F.S., Klop, J.W., Palamidessi, C.: Asynchronous communication in process algebra. In: Proceedings LICS, pp. 137–147. IEEE Computer Society (1992). https://doi.org/10.1109/LICS.1992.185528
10. Bollig, B., Giusto, C.D., Finkel, A., Laversa, L., Lozes, É., Suresh, A.: A unifying framework for deciding synchronizability. In: Proceedings CONCUR. LIPIcs, vol. 203, pp. 14:1–14:18. Schloss Dagstuhl - Leibniz-Zentrum für Informatik (2021). https://doi.org/10.4230/LIPIcs.CONCUR.2021.14

11. Boreale, M., De Nicola, R., Pugliese, R.: A theory of "May" testing for asynchronous languages. In: Thomas, W. (ed.) FoSSaCS 1999. LNCS, vol. 1578, pp. 165–179. Springer, Heidelberg (1999). https://doi.org/10.1007/3-540-49019-1_12
12. Boreale, M., Nicola, R.D., Pugliese, R.: Trace and testing equivalence on asynchronous processes. Inf. Comput. **172**(2), 139–164 (2002). https://doi.org/10.1006/inco.2001.3080
13. Brand, D., Zafiropulo, P.: On communicating finite-state machines. J. ACM **30**(2), 323–342 (1983). https://doi.org/10.1145/322374.322380
14. Cano, M., Castellani, I., Di Giusto, C., Pérez, J.A.: Multiparty Reactive Sessions. Research Report 9270, INRIA, April 2019. https://hal.archives-ouvertes.fr/hal-02106742
15. Capecchi, S., Giachino, E., Yoshida, N.: Global escape in multiparty sessions. MSCS **26**(2), 156–205 (2016). https://doi.org/10.1017/S0960129514000164
16. Castellani, I.: Process algebras with localities. In: Handbook of Process Algebra, pp. 945–1045. North-Holland/Elsevier (2001). https://doi.org/10.1016/b978-044482830-9/50033-3
17. Castellani, I., Hennessy, M.: Testing theories for asynchronous languages. In: Arvind, V., Ramanujam, S. (eds.) FSTTCS 1998. LNCS, vol. 1530, pp. 90–101. Springer, Heidelberg (1998). https://doi.org/10.1007/978-3-540-49382-2_9
18. Coppo, M., Dezani-Ciancaglini, M., Yoshida, N., Padovani, L.: Global progress for dynamically interleaved multiparty sessions. MSCS **26**(2), 238–302 (2016). https://doi.org/10.1017/S0960129514000188
19. Fournet, C., Gonthier, G., Levy, J.-J., Maranget, L., Rémy, D.: A calculus of mobile agents. In: Montanari, U., Sassone, V. (eds.) CONCUR 1996. LNCS, vol. 1119, pp. 406–421. Springer, Heidelberg (1996). https://doi.org/10.1007/3-540-61604-7_67
20. Fowler, S., Lindley, S., Morris, J.G., Decova, S.: Exceptional asynchronous session types: session types without tiers. Proc. ACM Program. Lang. **3**(POPL), 1–29 (2019). https://doi.org/10.1145/3290341
21. Francalanza, A., Hennessy, M.: A theory for observational fault tolerance. JLAMP **73**(1–2), 22–50 (2007). https://doi.org/10.1007/11690634_2
22. Francalanza, A., Hennessy, M.: A theory of system behaviour in the presence of node and link failure. Inf. Comput. **206**(6), 711–759 (2008). https://doi.org/10.1016/j.ic.2007.12.002
23. Graf, S., Sifakis, J.: A modal characterization of observational congruence on finite terms of CCS. Inf. Control. **68**(1–3), 125–145 (1986). https://doi.org/10.1016/S0019-9958(86)80031-6
24. Gunawi, H.S., et al.: Fail-slow at scale: evidence of hardware performance faults in large production systems. ACM Trans. Storage **14**(3), 23:1–23:26 (2018). https://doi.org/10.1145/3242086
25. Hennessy, M., Regan, T.: A process algebra for timed systems. Inf. Comput. **117**(2), 221–239 (1995). https://doi.org/10.1006/inco.1995.1041
26. Honda, K., Yoshida, N., Carbone, M.: Multiparty asynchronous session types. J. ACM **63**(1), 9:1–9:67 (2016). https://doi.org/10.1145/2827695
27. Hu, R., Neykova, R., Yoshida, N., Demangeon, R., Honda, K.: Practical interruptible conversations. In: Legay, A., Bensalem, S. (eds.) RV 2013. LNCS, vol. 8174, pp. 130–148. Springer, Heidelberg (2013). https://doi.org/10.1007/978-3-642-40787-1_8
28. Huang, P., et al.: Gray failure: the Achilles' heel of cloud-scale systems. In: Proceedings HotOS, pp. 150–155. Association for Computing Machinery, New York (2017). https://doi.org/10.1145/3102980.3103005
29. Lanese, I., Nishida, N., Palacios, A., Vidal, G.: A theory of reversibility for Erlang. JLAMP **100**, 71–97 (2018). https://doi.org/10.1016/j.jlamp.2018.06.004

30. Lanese, I., Sangiorgi, D., Zavattaro, G.: Playing with bisimulation in Erlang. In: Boreale, M., Corradini, F., Loreti, M., Pugliese, R. (eds.) Models, Languages, and Tools for Concurrent and Distributed Programming. LNCS, vol. 11665, pp. 71–91. Springer, Cham (2019). https://doi.org/10.1007/978-3-030-21485-2_6

31. Laneve, C., Zavattaro, G.: Foundations of web transactions. In: Sassone, V. (ed.) FoSSaCS 2005. LNCS, vol. 3441, pp. 282–298. Springer, Heidelberg (2005). https://doi.org/10.1007/978-3-540-31982-5_18

32. López, H.A., Pérez, J.A.: Time and exceptional behavior in multiparty structured interactions. In: Carbone, M., Petit, J.-M. (eds.) WS-FM 2011. LNCS, vol. 7176, pp. 48–63. Springer, Heidelberg (2012). https://doi.org/10.1007/978-3-642-29834-9_5

33. Lou, C., Huang, P., Smith, S.: Understanding, detecting and localizing partial failures in large system software. In: NDSI, pp. 559–574. USENIX Association (2020). https://www.usenix.org/conference/nsdi20/presentation/lou

34. Merro, M., Sangiorgi, D.: On asynchrony in name-passing calculi. In: Larsen, K.G., Skyum, S., Winskel, G. (eds.) ICALP 1998. LNCS, vol. 1443, pp. 856–867. Springer, Heidelberg (1998). https://doi.org/10.1007/BFb0055108

35. Milner, R.: Communication and Concurrency. PHI Series in Computer Science. Prentice Hall, Upper Saddle River (1989)

36. Milner, R., Parrow, J., Walker, D.: A calculus of mobile processes. I. Inf. Comput. **100**(1), 1–40 (1992). https://doi.org/10.1016/0890-5401(92)90008-4

37. Milner, R., Sangiorgi, D.: Barbed bisimulation. In: Kuich, W. (ed.) ICALP 1992. LNCS, vol. 623, pp. 685–695. Springer, Heidelberg (1992). https://doi.org/10.1007/3-540-55719-9_114

38. Mostrous, D., Vasconcelos, V.T.: Session typing for a featherweight Erlang. In: De Meuter, W., Roman, G.-C. (eds.) COORDINATION 2011. LNCS, vol. 6721, pp. 95–109. Springer, Heidelberg (2011). https://doi.org/10.1007/978-3-642-21464-6_7

39. Murgia, M.: Input urgent semantics for asynchronous timed session types. JLAMP **107**, 38–53 (2019). https://doi.org/10.1016/j.jlamp.2019.04.001

40. Nygard, M.T.: Release It!: Design and Deploy Production-Ready Software. Pragmatic Bookshelf (2018)

41. Riely, J., Hennessy, M.: Distributed processes and location failures. In: Degano, P., Gorrieri, R., Marchetti-Spaccamela, A. (eds.) ICALP 1997. LNCS, vol. 1256, pp. 471–481. Springer, Heidelberg (1997). https://doi.org/10.1007/3-540-63165-8_203

42. Riely, J., Hennessy, M.: Distributed processes and location failures. Theor. Comput. Sci. **266**(1–2), 693–735 (2001). https://doi.org/10.1016/S0304-3975(00)00326-1

43. Sabahi-Kaviani, Z., Khosravi, R., Ölveczky, P.C., Khamespanah, E., Sirjani, M.: Formal semantics and efficient analysis of timed Rebeca in real-time Maude. Sci. Comput. Program. **113**, 85–118 (2015). https://doi.org/10.1016/j.scico.2015.07.003

44. Sangiorgi, D., Walker, D.: The π-Calculus: A Theory of Mobile Processes. Cambridge University Press, Cambridge (2001)

45. Sankar, K.: Programming Erlang - Software for a Concurrent World by Joe Armstrong, p. 536. Pragmatic Bookshelf (2007). ISBN-10: 193435600x. J. Funct. Program. **19**(2), 259–261 (2009). https://doi.org/10.1017/S0956796809007163

46. Steffen, B.: Characteristic formulae. In: Ausiello, G., Dezani-Ciancaglini, M., Della Rocca, S.R. (eds.) ICALP 1989. LNCS, vol. 372, pp. 723–732. Springer, Heidelberg (1989). https://doi.org/10.1007/BFb0035794

47. Svensson, H., Fredlund, L., Earle, C.B.: A unified semantics for future Erlang. In: Proceedings ACM SIGPLAN Workshop on Erlang, pp. 23–32. ACM (2010). https://doi.org/10.1145/1863509.1863514

48. Wyatt, D.: Akka Concurrency. Artima Incorporation, Sunnyvale (2013)

Soft Concurrent Constraint Programming with Local Variables

Laura Bussi[1], Fabio Gadducci[1(✉)], and Francesco Santini[2]

[1] Dipartimento di Informatica, Università di Pisa, Pisa, Italy
laura.bussi@phd.unipi.it, fabio.gadducci@unipi.it
[2] Dipartimento di Matematica e Informatica, Università degli Studi di Perugia, Perugia, Italy
francesco.santini@unipg.it

Abstract. We extend Soft Concurrent Constraint languages with the possibility to manage variables that are local (i.e., private) to some of the agents. Being constraints soft, it is possible to represent preferences as a partially ordered set. With respect to the related literature using an idempotent operator for constraint composition, a soft language requires a revision of the hiding operator, which is used to locally keep the computation effect on a variable, and conceal it from the global store. We provide the language with labelled and unlabelled reduction semantics as well as bisimulation equivalences, further proving their correspondence.

Keywords: Soft concurrent constraint programming · residuated monoids · local variables · bisimulation equivalences

1 Introduction

Concurrent Constraint Programming (CCP) is a declarative model for concurrency where agents interact on a common store of information by telling and asking constraints [22]. In general terms, a constraint is a relationship on a set of variables: an assignment of (some of) the variables in the store needs to be found so to satisfy a given goal. A constraint system provides a signature from which the constraints are built; it is formalised as an algebra with operators to express conjunction of constraints, absent and inconsistent information, hiding of information and parameter passing.

The *polyadic* and *cylindric algebras* are two algebraisation of the first-order calculus [16], which have been widely adopted in the literature to provide the semantics of constraint formulas [17,25]. A cylindric algebra is formed by enhancing a Boolean algebra by means of a family of unary operations called *cylindrifications*. Technically, the cylindrification operation $\exists_x(c)$ is used to project out the information about a variable x from a constraint c: for example, because it is

Research partially supported by the MIUR PRIN 2017FTXR7S "IT-MaTTerS" and by GNCS-INdAM ("Gruppo Nazionale per il Calcolo Scientifico").

© IFIP International Federation for Information Processing 2022
M. H. ter Beek and M. Sirjani (Eds.): COORDINATION 2022, LNCS 13271, pp. 159–177, 2022.
https://doi.org/10.1007/978-3-031-08143-9_10

important to focus only on the variables that appear in the goal of a constraint logic program.

While polyadic algebras are the algebraic version of the pure first-order calculus, cylindric algebras yield an algebraisation of the first-order calculus with *equality*. However, equality can be also achieved in polyadic algebras via additional axioms that specify which terms are to be considered equal under the abstract interpretation.

While most of the solutions in the literature adopt a cylindric algebra to represent constraints [25], other proposals take advantage of polyadic algebras: in [17] the motivation is to allow projections on infinite sets, while in [8] replacing diagonals (used to perform parameters passing [25], borrowed from cylindric algebras) with polyadic operators allows for a compact - *polynomial* - representation of soft constraints. Moreover, in case it is necessary to use preferences beside hard constraints, i.e. *Soft Concurrent Constraint Programming* (SCCP) [3,15], algebra operators interact with a residuated monoid structure of values [14]: while the semi-lattice of such preferences must be complete for cylindric algebras, it is not necessary so for polyadic ones [8].

The soft CCP language we present in this paper is a further generalisation of what can be found in the literature, in particular [1] (see also Sect. 7). More precisely, it allows for a more general algebraic structure than the absorptive and idempotent monoid used there, and it covers also bipolar (i.e., positive/negative) preferences, thus generalising [6]; secondly, polyadic algebras can model many problems using a polynomial representation of constraints. In fact, polynomial constraints play an important role in program analysis and verification (e.g. when synthesising program invariants and analysing the reachability of hybrid systems), and they have been recently used in SAT modulo theories [9]. Moreover, the language allows an agent to perform operations on variables (in particular, adding and asking constraints) that are local, i.e., visible only to the agent itself: for this reason, the *hiding* operator needs to consider the effect of local steps with respect to the global store, which is seen by all the agents participating to a concurrent computation. In this way, it is possible to distinguish between local and global knowledge of agents, in the form of a local and a global store of constraints.

Beside the language syntax, we provide a reduction semantics and a saturated bisimulation relation, again taking inspiration from and generalising [1]. In order for two computation states to be *saturated bisimilar*, it is required that *i)* they should expose the same barbs, *ii)* whenever one of them moves then the other should reply and arrive at an equivalent state, *iii)* they should be equivalent under all the possible stores. Intuitively, barbs are basic observations (i.e., predicates) on the system states; in the case of CCP languages, barbs are represented by the constraint store. In addition, we show a labelled bisimulation to (partially) overcome the need to check the store closure (i.e., item *iii*). As a final step, we show that the labelled and unlabelled reduction semantics correspond, and we advance a labelled bisimulation relation.

This paper is a continuation of [8], exploiting the polyadic formalism to define a concurrent constraint language. Section 2 and Sect. 3 present the necessary background on the algebraic structure needed to model polyadic constraints. The following sections are focused on the semantics of a concurrent constraint-based language using local variables and polyadic constraints, on the correspondence between different semantics, and on the equivalence relations among processes. Section 4 presents the syntax and a reduction semantics for the language, while Sect. 5 presents a labelled reduction for the same language. Section 6 shows further formal results on the correspondence between the two semantics, and a bisimilarity relation to compare processes with the labelled semantics. In Sect. 7 we summarise the most related work about CCP-based languages with the notion of local and global variables. In Sect. 8 we finally wrap up the paper with conclusive thoughts and ideas about future works.

2   An Introduction to Residuated Monoids

This section reports some results on residuated monoids, which are the algebraic structure adopted for modelling soft constraints in the following of the paper. These background results are mostly drawn from [15], where also proofs can be found.

2.1   Preliminaries on Ordered Monoids

The first step is to define an algebraic structure for modelling preferences, where it is possible to compare values and combine them. Our choice falls into the range of *bipolar* approaches, in order to represent both positive and negative preferences: we refer to [14] for a detailed introduction and a comparison with other proposals.

Definition 1 (Orders). *A partial order (PO) is a pair $\langle A, \leq \rangle$ such that A is a set and $\leq \subseteq A \times A$ is a reflexive, transitive, and anti-symmetric relation. A semi-lattice (SL) is a PO such that any finite subset of A has a least upper bound (LUB).*

The LUB of a (possibly infinite) subset $X \subseteq A$ is denoted $\bigvee X$, and it is clearly unique. Note that $\bigvee \emptyset$ is the bottom, denoted as $\bot$, of the PO. Should it exist, $\bigvee A$ is the top, denoted as $\top$, of the PO.

Definition 2 (Ordered monoids). *A (commutative) monoid is a triple $\langle A, \otimes, 1 \rangle$ such that $\otimes : A \times A \to A$ is a commutative and associative function and $1 \in A$ is its identity element, i.e., $\forall a \in A.a \otimes 1 = a$. A partially ordered monoid (POM) is a 4-tuple $\langle A, \leq, \otimes, 1 \rangle$ such that $\langle A, \leq \rangle$ is a PO and $\langle A, \otimes, 1 \rangle$ a monoid. A semi-lattice monoid (SLM) is a POM such that their underlying PO is a SL.*

As usual, we use the infix notation: $a \otimes b$ stands for $\otimes(a, b)$.

Example 1 (Power set). Given a (possibly infinite) set S, a key example is represented by the POM $\mathbb{P}(S) = \langle 2^S, \subseteq, \cap, S \rangle$ of subsets of S, with the partial order given by subset inclusion and the (idempotent) monoidal operator by intersection. In fact, $\mathbb{P}(S)$ is a continuous lattice, since all LUBs exist, and S is both the top and the identity element.

In general, the partial order $\leq$ and the multiplication operator $\otimes$ can be unrelated. This is not the case for distributive SLMs (such as $\mathbb{P}(S)$ above).

Definition 3 (Distributivity). *Let $\langle A, \leq, \otimes, 1 \rangle$ be an SLM. It is distributive if for any finite $X \subseteq A$ it holds $\forall a \in A. a \otimes \bigvee X = \bigvee \{a \otimes x \mid x \in X\}$.*

Note that distributivity implies that $\otimes$ is monotone with respect to $\leq$.

Remark 1. It is almost straightforward to show that our proposal encompasses many other formalisms in the literature. Indeed, distributive semi-lattice monoids are *tropical* semirings (also known as dioids), namely, semirings with an idempotent sum operator $a \oplus b$, which in our formalism is obtained as $\bigvee \{a, b\}$. If 1 is the top of the SL we end up in *absorptive* semirings [19], which are known as c-semirings in the soft constraint jargon [3] (see [4] for a brief survey on residuation for such semirings). Note that requiring the monotonicity of $\otimes$ and imposing 1 to be the top of the partial order means that preferences are negative, i.e., that it holds $\forall a, b \in A. a \otimes b \leq a$.

2.2 Remarks on Residuation

It is often needed to be able to "remove" part of a preference, due e.g. to the non-monotone nature of the language at hand for manipulating constraints. The structure of our choice is given by residuated monoids [19]. They introduce a new operator $\ominus$, which represents a "weak" (due to the presence of partial orders) inverse of $\otimes$.

Definition 4 (Residuation). *A residuated POM is a 5-tuple $\langle A, \leq, \otimes, \ominus, 1 \rangle$ such that $\langle A, \leq, \otimes, 1 \rangle$ is a POM and $\ominus : A \times A \to A$ is a function satisfying $\forall a, b, c \in A. b \otimes c \leq a \iff c \leq a \ominus b$. A residuated SLM is a residuated POM such that the underlying PO is a SL.*

In order to confirm the intuition about weak inverses, Lemma 1 below precisely states that residuation conveys the meaning of an approximated form of subtraction.

Lemma 1. *Let $\langle A, \leq, \otimes, \ominus, 1 \rangle$ be a residuated POM. Then $a \ominus b = \bigvee \{c \mid b \otimes c \leq a\}$ for all $a, b \in A$.*

In words, the LUB of the (possibly infinite) set $\{c \mid b \otimes c \leq a\}$ exists and is equal to $a \ominus b$. In fact, residuation implies distributivity (see [14, Lemma 2.2]).

Lemma 2. *Let $\langle A, \leq, \otimes, \ominus, 1 \rangle$ be a residuated POM. Then $\otimes$ is monotone. If additionally it is a SLM, then it is distributive.*

Example 2. Consider again the SLM $\mathbb{P}(S)$ from Example 1. It is clearly residuated, with $X \ominus Y = (S \setminus Y) \cup X$. In fact, the residuated operator plays the role of classical logical implication $Y \implies X$. Note also that $S \setminus Y = \emptyset \ominus Y$, so algebraically we have that $X \ominus Y = X \vee (\bot \ominus Y)$ holds in $\mathbb{P}(S)$.

In any residuated POM the $\ominus$ operator is also monotone on the first argument and anti-monotone on the second one, i.e., $\forall a, b, c \in A. a \leq b \implies c \ominus b \leq c \ominus a$. The definition below identifies sub-classes of residuated monoids that are suitable for an easier manipulation of constraints (see e.g. [4]).

Definition 5 (Families of POMs). *A residuated POM $\langle A, \leq, \otimes, \ominus, 1 \rangle$ is*

- *localised if $\forall a \in A. a \notin \{\bot, \top\} \implies a \ominus a = 1;$*
- *invertible if $\forall a, b \in A. a \leq b < \top \implies b \otimes (a \ominus b) = a;$*
- *cancellative if $\forall a, b, c \in A. a \notin \{\bot, \top\} \wedge a \otimes b = a \otimes c \implies b = c.$*

Remark 2. When introduced in [14, Def. 2.4], localisation was equivalently stated as $\forall a, b \in A. \bot < a \leq b < \top \implies a \ominus b \leq 1$. Indeed, the latter implies $a \ominus a \leq 1$, while $1 \leq a \ominus a$ by definition. Now, assuming $a \ominus a = 1$ and $a \leq b$, by anti-monotonicity $a \ominus b \leq a \ominus a = 1$. Note the constraint on $a \notin \{\bot, \top\}$: indeed, a residuated POM always has a top element and moreover $a \ominus \bot = \top \ominus a = \top$ for any a.

Note that being cancellative is a strong requirement. It implies e.g. some uniqueness of invertibility, that is, for any a, b there exists at most a c such that $b \otimes c = a$. It is moreover equivalent to what we could call strong locality, that is, $\forall a, b \in A. a \notin \{\bot, \top\} \implies (a \otimes b) \ominus a = b$. Indeed, this property implies cancellativeness, since if $a \otimes b = a \otimes c$ then $b = (a \otimes b) \ominus a = (a \otimes c) \ominus a = c$. On the other side, it is implied, since $((a \otimes b) \ominus a) \otimes a = a \otimes b$ holds in residuated POMs.

As a final remark, note that $\mathbb{P}(S)$ is localised and invertible, yet it is not cancellative.

3   A Polyadic Approach to Constraint Manipulation

This section presents our personal take on polyadic algebras for ordered monoids: the standard axiomatisation of e.g. [24] has been completely reworked, in order to be adapted to the constraints formalism. It extends our previous description in [8] by further elaborating on the laws for the polyadic operators in residuated monoids.

3.1   Cylindric and Polyadic Operators for Ordered Monoids

We introduce two families of operators that will be used for modelling variables hiding and substitution, which are key features in languages for manipulating constraints. One is a well-known abstraction for existential quantifiers, the other one an axiomatisation of the notion of substitution, and it is proposed as a weaker alternative to diagonals [25], the standard tool for modelling equivalence in constraint programming.[1]

Cylindric Operators. We fix a POM $\mathbb{S} = \langle A, \leq, \otimes, \mathbf{1} \rangle$ and a set V of variables, and we define a family of cylindric operators axiomatising existential quantifiers.

Definition 6 (Cylindric ops). *A cylindric operator $\exists$ for $\mathbb{S}$ and V is a family of monotone functions $\exists_x : A \to A$ indexed by elements in V such that for all $a, b \in A$ and $x, y \in V$*

1. $a \leq \exists_x a$,
2. $\exists_x \exists_y a = \exists_y \exists_x a$,
3. $\exists_x (a \otimes \exists_x b) = \exists_x a \otimes \exists_x b$.

Let $a \in A$. The support *of a is the set of variables $sv(a) = \{x \mid \exists_x a \neq a\}$.*

In other words, $\exists$ fixes a monoid action which is monotone and increasing.

Polyadic Operators. We now move to define a family of operators axiomatising substitutions. They interact with quantifiers, thus, beside a partially ordered monoid $\mathbb{S}$ and a set V of variables, we fix a cylindric operator $\exists$ over $\mathbb{S}$ and V.

Let $F(V)$ be the set of functions with domain and codomain V. For a function σ its support is $sv(\sigma) = \{x \mid \sigma(x) \neq x\}$ and, for a set $X \subseteq V$, $\sigma \mid_X : X \to V$ denotes the restriction of σ to X and $\sigma^c(X) = \{y \mid \sigma(y) \in X\}$ the counter-image of X along σ.

Definition 7 (Polyadic ops). *A polyadic operator s for a cylindric operator $\exists$ is a family of monotone functions $s_\sigma : A \to A$ indexed by elements in $F(V)$ such that for all $a, b \in A$, $x \in V$, and $\sigma, \tau \in F(V)$*

1. $sv(\sigma) \cap sv(a) = \emptyset \implies s_\sigma a = a$,
2. $s_\sigma(a \otimes b) = s_\sigma a \otimes s_\sigma b$,
3. $\sigma \mid_{sv(a)} = \tau \mid_{sv(a)} \implies s_\sigma a = s_\tau a$,
4. $\exists_x s_\sigma a = \begin{cases} s_\sigma \exists_y a & \text{if } \sigma^c(\{x\}) = \{y\} \\ s_\sigma a & \text{if } \sigma^c(\{x\}) = \emptyset \end{cases}$.

A polyadic operator offers enough structure for modelling variable substitution. In the following, we fix a cylindric operator $\exists$ and a polyadic operator s for it.

3.2 Cylindric and Polyadic Operators for Residuated Monoids

We now consider the interaction of previous structures with residuation. To this end, in the following we assume that $\mathbb{S}$ is a residuated POM (see Definition 4).

---

[1] "Weaker alternative" here means that diagonals allow for axiomatising substitutions at the expenses of working with complete partial orders: see e.g. [15, Definition 11].

Lemma 3. *Let $x \in V$ and $a, b \in A$. Then it holds $\exists_x(a \oplus \exists_x b) \leq \exists_x a \oplus \exists_x b \leq \exists_x(\exists_x a \oplus b)$.*

Remark 3. It is easy to check that $\exists_x(a \oplus \exists_x b) \leq \exists_x a \oplus \exists_x b$ is actually equivalent to state that $\exists_x(a \otimes \exists_x b) \geq \exists_x a \otimes \exists_x b$.

We can show that $\oplus$ does not substantially alter the free variables of its arguments.

Lemma 4. *Let $a, b \in A$. Then it holds $sv(a \oplus b) \subseteq sv(a) \cup sv(b)$.*

A result similar to Lemma 3 relates residuation and polyadic operators.

Lemma 5. *Let $a, b \in A$ and $\sigma \in F(V)$. Then it holds $s_\sigma(a \oplus b) \leq s_\sigma a \oplus s_\sigma b$. Furthermore, if σ is invertible, then the equality holds.*

3.3 Polyadic Soft Constraints

Our key example comes from the soft constraints literature: our presentation generalises [5], whose underlying algebraic structure is of absorptive and idempotent semirings.

Definition 8 (Soft constraints). *Let V be a set of variables, D a finite domain of interpretation and $\mathbb{S} = \langle A, \leq, \otimes, \oplus, 1 \rangle$ a residuated SLM. A (soft) constraint $c : (V \to D) \to A$ is a function associating a value in A with each assignment $\eta : V \to D$ of the variables.*

The set of constraints forms a residuated SLM $\mathbb{C}$, with the structure lifted from $\mathbb{S}$. Denoting the application of a constraint function $c : (V \to D) \to A$ to a variable assignment $\eta : V \to D$ as $c\eta$, we have that $c_1 \leq c_2$ if $c_1\eta \leq c_2\eta$ for all $\eta : V \to D$.

Lemma 6 (Cylindric and polyadic operators for (soft) constraints). *The residuated SLM of constraints $\mathbb{C}$ admits cylindric and polyadic operators, defined as*

- $(\exists_x c)\eta = \bigvee\{c\rho \mid \eta \mid_{V\setminus\{x\}} = \rho \mid_{V\setminus\{x\}}\}$ *for all $x \in V$,*
- $(s_\sigma c)\eta = c(\eta \circ \sigma)$ *for all $\sigma \in F(V)$.*

Remark 4. Note that $sv(c)$ coincides with the classical notion of support for soft constraints. Indeed, if $x \notin sv(c)$, then two assignments $\eta_1, \eta_2 : V \to D$ differing only for the image of x coincide (i.e., $c\eta_1 = c\eta_2$). The cylindric operator is called *projection* in the soft framework, and $\exists_x c$ is denoted $c \Downarrow_{V\setminus\{x\}}$.

Example 3. For the sake of simplicity, and to better illustrate the differences of our proposal with respect to [1], our running example will be the SLM of soft constraints where D is a finite initial segment of the naturals and $\mathbb{S}$ is the residuated SLM $\langle \{\bot, \top\}, \{\bot \leq \top\}, \wedge, \top \rangle$ of booleans. That SLM coincide with the SLM $\mathbb{P}(F)$, for F the family of functions $V \to D$: it is localised and invertible, and the top and the identity element coincides with F, i.e., the constraint c such that $c\eta = \top$ for all η. We will then usually express a constraint in $\mathbb{P}(F)$ as a SAT formula with inequations like $x \leq 1$, intended as $(x \leq 1)\eta = \top$ if $\eta(x) \leq 1$ and $\bot$ otherwise. The support of $x \leq 1$ is of course $\{x\}$. As expected, $\exists_x$ behaves as an existential quantifier, so that $\exists_x(x \leq 1) = \top$ and $\exists_x((x \leq 1) \wedge (y \leq 3)) = y \leq 3$. Similarly, for a substitution σ we have that $s_\sigma(x \leq 1) = \sigma(x) \leq 1$.

4   Polyadic Soft CCP: Syntax and Reduction Semantics

This section introduces our language. We fix a set of variables V, ranged over by x, y, ..., and a residuated POM $\mathbb{S} = \langle \mathscr{C}, \leq, \otimes, \ominus, 1 \rangle$, which is cylindric and polyadic over V and whose elements are ranged over by c, d, ...

Definition 9 (Agents). *The set $\mathscr{A}$ of agents, parametric with respect to a set $\mathscr{P}$ of (unary) procedure declarations $p(x) = A$, is given by the following grammar*

$$A ::= \mathbf{stop} \mid \mathbf{tell}(c) \mid \mathbf{ask}(c) \mapsto A \mid A \parallel A \mid p(x) \mid \exists_x A$$

Hence, the syntax includes a termination agent **stop**, and the two typical operations of CCP languages [25]: $\mathbf{tell}(c)$ adds the constraint c to a common store through which all agents interact, and $\mathbf{ask}(c) \mapsto A$ continues as agent A only when c is entailed by such a store (otherwise its execution is suspended). The other operators respectively express the parallel composition between two agents (i.e., $A \parallel A$), the hiding of a variable x in the computation of A ($\exists_x A$), and, finally, the calling of a procedure $p \in \mathscr{P}$ (whose body is an agent A) with an actual parameter identified by variable x.

In the following we consider a set $\mathscr{E}$ of extended agents that uses the existential operator $\exists_x^\pi A$, where $\pi \in \mathscr{C}^*$ is meant to represent the sequence of updates performed on the local store. More precisely, the extended agent may carry some information about the hidden variable x in an incremental way. We will often write $\exists_x A$ for $\exists_x^{[]} A$ and π_i for the i-th element of $\pi = [\pi_0, \ldots, \pi_n]$.

We denote by $fv(A)$ the set of free variables of an (extended) agent, defined in the expected way by structural induction, assuming that $fv(\mathbf{tell}(c)) = sv(c)$, $fv(\mathbf{ask}(c) \mapsto A) = sv(c) \cup fv(A)$, and $fv(\exists_x^\pi A) = (fv(A) \cup \bigcup_i sv(\pi_i)) \setminus \{x\}$. In the following, we restrict our attention to procedure declarations $p(x) = A$ such that $fv(A) = \{x\}$.

Definition 10 (Substitutions). *Let $[^y/_x] : V \to V$ be the substitution defined as*

$$[^y/_x](w) = \begin{cases} y & \text{if } w = x \\ w & \text{otherwise} \end{cases}.$$

It induces an operator $[^y/_x] : \mathscr{E} \to \mathscr{E}$ on extended agents as expected, in particular

$$(\exists_w^\pi A)[^y/_x] = \begin{cases} \exists_w^{(s_{[^y/_x]}\pi)} A[^y/_x] & \text{if } w \notin \{x, y\} \\ (\exists_z^{(s_{[^z/_w]}\pi)} A[^z/_w])[^y/_x] & \text{for } z \notin fv(\exists_w^\pi A) \text{ otherwise} \end{cases}$$

where $s_{[y/x]} : \mathscr{C} \to \mathscr{C}$ is the function associated with $[y/x]$ and $s_{[y/x]}[\pi_1, \ldots, \pi_n]$ is a shorthand for $[s_{[y/x]}\pi_1, \ldots, s_{[y/x]}\pi_n]$.

Note that the choice of z in the rule above is immaterial, since for the polyadic operator it holds $\exists_x c = \exists_y s_{[y/x]}(c)$ if $y \notin sv(c)$. In the following we consider terms to be equivalent up-to α-conversion, meaning that terms differing only for hidden variables are considered equivalent, i.e., $\exists_w^\pi A = \exists_z^{(s_{[z/w]}\pi)} A[z/w]$ for $z \notin fv(\exists_w^\pi A)$.

Lemma 7. *Let $A \in \mathscr{E}$ and $x \notin fv(A)$. Then $A[y/x] = A$.*

Table 1. Axioms of the reduction semantics for SCCP.

A1 $\langle \mathbf{tell}(c), \sigma \rangle \to \langle \mathbf{stop}, \sigma \otimes c \rangle$ **Tell**

A2 $\dfrac{\sigma \leq c}{\langle \mathbf{ask}(c) \mapsto A, \sigma \rangle \to \langle A, \sigma \rangle}$ **Ask**

A3 $\dfrac{p(x) = A \in \mathcal{P}}{\langle p(y), \sigma \rangle \to \langle A[y/x], \sigma \rangle}$ **Rec**

Example 4. Consider the SLM $\mathbb{P}(F)$ illustrated in Example 3. We can specify agents such as $\mathbf{ask}(y \leq 5) \mapsto \mathbf{stop}$, i.e., an agent asking the store about the possible values of y, then terminating. Or $\exists_x(\mathbf{tell}(x \leq 1) \parallel \mathbf{tell}(y \leq 3))$ with $x \neq y$, meaning that the constraint $x \leq 1$ is local: indeed, thanks to α-conversion it coincides with $\exists_z(\mathbf{tell}(z \leq 1) \parallel \mathbf{tell}(y \leq 3))$ for any $z \neq y$. As we are going to see, the execution of $\mathbf{tell}(z \leq 1)$ will take the latter agent to $\exists_z^{[z \leq 1]}\mathbf{tell}(y \leq 3)$, which in turn coincides with $\exists_x^{[x \leq 1]}\mathbf{tell}(y \leq 3)$.

4.1 Reduction Semantics

We now move to the reduction semantics of our calculus. Given a sequence $\pi = [\pi_1, \ldots, \pi_n]$, we will use $\pi_\otimes$ and $\exists_x \pi$ as shorthands for $\pi_1 \otimes \ldots \otimes \pi_n$ and $[\exists_x \pi_1, \ldots, \exists_x \pi_n]$, respectively, sometimes combining them as in $(\exists_x \pi)_\otimes$, with $[]_\otimes = 1$.

Definition 11 (Reductions). *Let $\Gamma = \mathscr{E} \times \mathscr{C}$ be the set of configurations. The direct reduction semantics for SCCP is the pair $\langle \Gamma, \to \rangle$ such that $\to \, \subseteq \, \Gamma \times \Gamma$ is the binary relations obtained by the axioms in Table 1.*

The reduction semantics for SCCP is the pair $\langle \Gamma, \to \rangle$ such that $\to \, \subseteq \, \Gamma \times \Gamma$ is the binary relation obtained by the rules in Table 1 and Table 2.

Table 2. Contextual rules of the reduction semantics for SCCP.

R1
$$\frac{\langle A, \sigma \rangle \to \langle A', \sigma' \rangle}{\langle A \parallel B, \sigma \rangle \to \langle A' \parallel B, \sigma' \rangle}$$
Par1

R2
$$\frac{\langle A, \pi_0 \otimes \sigma \rangle \to \langle B, \sigma_1 \rangle \text{ with } \pi_0 = \pi_\otimes \ominus (\exists_x \pi)_\otimes}{\langle \exists_x^\pi A, \sigma \rangle \to \langle \exists_x^{\pi\rho} B, \sigma \otimes \exists_x \rho \rangle \text{ with } \rho = \sigma_1 \ominus (\pi_0 \otimes \sigma)} \text{ for } x \notin sv(\sigma) \quad \textbf{Hide}$$

The split distinguishes between the axioms and the rules guaranteeing the closure with respect to the parallel and existential operators. Indeed, rule **R1** models the interleaving of two agents in parallel, assuming for the sake of simplicity that the parallel operator is associative and commutative, as well as satisfying **stop** $\parallel A = A$. In **A1** a constraint c is added to the store σ. **A2** checks if c is entailed by σ: if not, the computation is blocked. Axiom **A3** replaces a procedure identifier with the associated body, renaming the formal parameter with the actual one.

Let us instead discuss in some details the rule **R2**. The intuition is that if we reach an agent $\langle \exists_x^\pi A, \sigma \rangle$, then during the computation a sequence π of updates has been performed by the local agent, and $(\exists_x \pi)_\otimes$ has been added to the global store. The chosen store for the configuration in the premise is $\pi_0 \otimes \sigma$ for $\pi_0 = \pi_\otimes \ominus (\exists_x \pi)_\otimes$: the effect $(\exists_x \pi)_\otimes$ of the sequence of updates is removed from the local store $\pi_\otimes$, which may carry information about x, since that effect had been previously added to the global store. Now, $\rho = \sigma_1 \ominus (\pi_0 \otimes \sigma)$ is precisely the information added by the step originating from A, which is then restricted and added to σ. On the local store we simply add that effect ρ to the sequence of updates, with $\pi\rho = [\pi_0, \ldots, \pi_n, \rho]$.

Lemma 8 (On monotonicity). *Let* $\langle A, \sigma \rangle \to \langle B, \rho \rangle$ *be a reduction. Then* $\rho = (\rho \ominus \sigma) \otimes \sigma$ *and* $fv(\langle B, \rho \rangle) \subseteq fv(\langle A, \sigma \rangle)$.

Example 5. Consider the agents $A_1 = \textbf{ask}(y \leq 5) \mapsto \textbf{stop}$ and $A_2 = \exists_x(\textbf{tell}(x \leq 1) \parallel \textbf{tell}(y \leq 3))$ with $x \neq y$ discussed in Example 4, and the configuration $\langle A_1 \parallel A_2, \top \rangle$. Starting from the configuration $\langle A_2, \top \rangle$ we have the reductions

$$\langle A_2, \top \rangle \to \langle \exists_x^{[y \leq 3]} \textbf{tell}(x \leq 1), y \leq 3 \rangle \to \langle \exists_x^{[y \leq 3, y > 3 \vee x \leq 1]} \textbf{stop}, y \leq 3 \rangle$$

In both cases, first we apply **A1**, then **R1** and finally **R2**. Looking at the application of **R2** to the first reduction, we have that $\pi_\otimes = \top = (\exists_x \pi)_\otimes$, thus $\pi_0 = \top$, $\rho = (y \leq 3) \ominus \top = y \leq 3 = \exists_x(y \leq 3)$. Now, consider the second reduction. In that case we have $\pi_0 = (y \leq 3) \ominus (y \leq 3) = \top$ and $\rho = ((y \leq 3) \wedge (x \leq 1)) \ominus (y \leq 3) = y > 3 \vee x \leq 1$ and $\exists_x \rho = \top$. Note that in both the second and third state, agent A_1 could be executed.

Remark 5. With respect to the crisp language with local variables introduced in [1], which can be recast in our framework as absorptive POMs where the monoidal operator is idempotent, our proposal differs mostly for the structure of rule **R2**, which could be presented as shown below

$$\frac{\langle A, \pi_0 \otimes \sigma \rangle \to \langle B, \xi \otimes \pi_0 \otimes \sigma \rangle \text{ with } \pi_0 = \pi_\otimes \ominus (\exists_x \pi)_\otimes}{\langle \exists_x^\pi A, \sigma \rangle \to \langle \exists_x^{\pi\xi} B, \sigma \otimes \exists_x \xi \rangle} \text{ for } x \notin sv(\sigma)$$

The proposals coincide for cancellative monoids, since inverses are unique. However, this is not so if the monoidal operator is idempotent, thus the crisp rule represents in fact a schema, giving rise to a possibly infinite family of reductions departing from an agent. Our choice of the witness $\exists_x \sigma_1 \ominus (\pi_0 \otimes \sigma)$ avoids such non-determinism.

Let $\gamma = \langle A, \sigma \rangle$ be a configuration. We denote by $fv(\gamma)$ the set $fv(A) \cup sv(\sigma)$ and by $\gamma[^z/_w]$ the component-wise application of the substitution $[^z/_w]$.

Definition 12. *A configuration $\langle A, \sigma \rangle$ is initial if $A \in \mathscr{A}$ and $\sigma = 1$; it is reachable if it can be reached by an initial configuration via a sequence of reductions.*

Lemma 9 (On monotonicity, II). *Let $\langle A \parallel \exists_x^\pi B, \sigma \rangle$ be a reachable configuration. Then $\sigma = (\sigma \ominus (\exists_x \pi)_\otimes) \otimes (\exists_x \pi)_\otimes$.*

Remark 6. An alternative solution for the structure of rule **R2** would have been

$$\frac{\langle A, \pi_\otimes \otimes \sigma_0 \rangle \to \langle B, \sigma_1 \rangle \text{ with } \sigma_0 = \sigma \ominus (\exists_x \pi)_\otimes}{\langle \exists_x^\pi A, \sigma \rangle \to \langle \exists_x^{\pi\rho} B, \sigma \otimes \exists_x \rho \rangle \text{ with } \rho = \sigma_1 \ominus (\pi_\otimes \otimes \sigma_0)} \text{ for } x \notin sv(\sigma)$$

Indeed, in the light of Lemma 9, the proposals coincide for invertible semirings, since $\pi_0 \otimes \sigma = (\pi_\otimes \ominus (\exists_x \pi)_\otimes) \otimes (\exists_x \pi)_\otimes \otimes (\sigma \ominus (\exists_x \pi)_\otimes) \leq \pi_\otimes \otimes (\sigma \ominus (\exists_x \pi)_\otimes)$, and the equality holds for invertible semirings since $\pi_\otimes \leq (\exists_x \pi)_\otimes$.

4.2   Saturated Bisimulation

As proposed in [1] for crisp languages, we define a barbed equivalence between two agents [21]. Intuitively, barbs are basic observations (predicates) on the states of a system, and in our case they correspond to the constraints in $\mathscr{C}$.

Definition 13 (Barbs). *Let $\langle A, \sigma \rangle$ be a configuration and $c \in \mathscr{C}$. We say that $\langle A, \sigma \rangle$ verifies c, or that $\langle A, \sigma \rangle \downarrow_c$ holds, if $\sigma \leq c$.*

Satisfying a barb c means that the agent $\mathbf{ask}(c) \mapsto A$ can be executed in the store σ, i.e., the reduction $\langle \mathbf{ask}(c) \mapsto A, \sigma \rangle \to \langle A, \sigma \rangle$ is allowed. We now move to equivalences: along [1], we propose the use of *saturated bisimilarity* to obtain a congruence.

Definition 14 (Saturated bisimilarity). *A saturated bisimulation is a symmetric relation R on configurations such that whenever $(\langle A, \sigma \rangle, \langle B, \rho \rangle) \in R$*

1. if $\langle A, \sigma \rangle \downarrow_c$ then $\langle B, \rho \rangle \downarrow_c$;
2. if $\langle A, \sigma \rangle \to \gamma_1$ then there is γ_2 such that $\langle B, \rho \rangle \to \gamma_2$ and $(\gamma_1, \gamma_2) \in R$;
3. $(\langle A, \sigma \otimes d \rangle, \langle B, \rho \otimes d \rangle) \in R$ for all d.

We say that γ_1 and γ_2 are saturated bisimilar ($\gamma_1 \sim_s \gamma_2$) if there exists a saturated bisimulation R such that $(\gamma_1, \gamma_2) \in R$. We write $A \sim_s B$ if $\langle A, 1 \rangle \sim_s \langle B, 1 \rangle$.

Note that $\langle A, \sigma \rangle \sim_s \langle B, \rho \rangle$ implies that $\sigma = \rho$. Moreover, it is also a congruence. Indeed, a context $C[\cdot]$, i.e., an agent with a placeholder $\cdot$, can modify the behaviour of a configuration only by adding constraints to its store.

Proposition 1. *Let $A \sim_s B$ and $C[\cdot]$ a context. Then $C[A] \sim_s C[B]$.*

5   Labelled Reduction Semantics

The definition of $\sim_s$ is unsatisfactory because of the store closure, i.e., the quantification in condition *3* of Definition 14. This section presents a labelled version of the reduction semantics that allows for partially avoiding such drawback.

Definition 15 (Labelled reductions). *Let $\Gamma = \mathscr{A} \times \mathscr{C}$ be the set of configurations. The labelled direct reduction semantics for SCCP is the pair $\langle \Gamma, \rightarrow \rangle$ such that $\rightarrow \subseteq \Gamma \times \mathscr{C} \times \Gamma$ is the ternary relation obtained by the axioms in Table 3.*
The labelled reduction semantics for SCCP is the pair $\langle \Gamma, \rightarrow \rangle$ such that $\rightarrow \subseteq \Gamma \times \mathscr{C} \times \Gamma$ is the ternary relation obtained by the rules in Table 3 and Table 4.

Table 3. Axioms of the labelled semantics for SCCP.

$$\textbf{LA1} \quad \langle \textbf{tell}(c), \sigma \rangle \xrightarrow{1} \langle \textbf{stop}, \sigma \otimes c \rangle \qquad \textbf{Tell}$$

$$\textbf{LA2} \quad \frac{\alpha \leq c \ominus \sigma}{\langle \textbf{ask}(c) \mapsto A, \sigma \rangle \xrightarrow{\alpha} \langle A, \alpha \otimes \sigma \rangle} \qquad \textbf{Ask}$$

$$\textbf{LA3} \quad \frac{p(x) = A \in \mathcal{P}}{\langle p(y), \sigma \rangle \xrightarrow{1} \langle A[^y/_x], \sigma \rangle} \qquad \textbf{Rec}$$

Table 4. Contextual rules of the labelled semantics for SCCP.

$$\textbf{LR1} \quad \frac{\langle A, \sigma \rangle \xrightarrow{\alpha} \langle A', \sigma' \rangle}{\langle A \parallel B, \sigma \rangle \xrightarrow{\alpha} \langle A' \parallel B, \sigma' \rangle} \qquad \textbf{Par}$$

$$\textbf{LR2} \quad \frac{\langle A, \pi_0 \otimes \sigma \rangle \xrightarrow{\alpha} \langle B, \sigma_1 \rangle \text{ with } \pi_0 = \pi_\otimes \oplus (\exists_x \pi)_\otimes}{\langle \exists_x^\pi A, \sigma \rangle \xrightarrow{\alpha} \langle \exists_x^{\pi\rho} B, \alpha \otimes \sigma \otimes \exists_x \rho \rangle \text{ with } \rho = \sigma_1 \oplus (\alpha \otimes \pi_0 \otimes \sigma)} \quad \text{for } x \notin sv(\sigma) \cup sv(\alpha) \quad \textbf{Hide}$$

In Table 3 and Table 4 we refine the notion of transition (respectively given in Table 1 and Table 2) by adding a label that carries additional information about the constraints that cause the reduction. Indeed, rules in Table 3 and Table 4 mimic those in Table 1 and Table 2, except for a constraint α that represents the additional information that must be combined with σ in order to fire an action from $\langle A, \sigma \rangle$ to $\langle A', \sigma' \rangle$.

For the rules in Table 3, as well as for rule **LR1**, we can restate the intuition given for their unlabelled counterparts. The difference concerns the axioms for **ask**(c): if c is not entailed from σ, then some additional information is imported from the environment, ensuring that the state $\alpha \otimes \sigma \leq c$ allows the execution of **ask**(c).

Once again, the more complex axiom is **LR2**. With respect to **R2**, the additional intuition is that α should not contain the restricted variable x: additional information can be obtained from the environment, as long as it does not interact with data that are private to the local agent. Note that by choosing $\rho = \sigma_1 \oplus (\alpha \otimes \pi_0 \otimes \sigma)$, we are removing α from the update to be memorised in the local store. However, since α is added to the global store, it will not be necessary to receive it again in the future.

Example 6. Consider the agent $A = \exists_x (\textbf{tell}(x \leq 1) \parallel \textbf{ask}(y \leq 5) \mapsto \textbf{stop})$, with the same SLM as in Example 5. We now have the labelled reductions

$$\langle A, \top \rangle \xrightarrow{1} \langle \exists_x^{[x \leq 1]} \textbf{ask}(y \leq 5) \mapsto \textbf{stop}, \top \rangle \xrightarrow{\alpha} \langle \exists_x^{[x \leq 1, x > 1 \vee \alpha]} \textbf{stop}, \top \rangle$$

for every $\alpha \leq (y \leq 5) \oplus (x \leq 1) = (x > 1) \vee (y \leq 5)$ such that $x \notin sv(\alpha)$, e.g., $y \leq 5$. Indeed, for the first reduction we first apply **LA1**, then **LR1**, and finally **LR2**, while for the second reduction we first apply **LA2** and then **LR2**. Looking at the application of **LR2** to the first reduction, we have that $\pi_\otimes = \top = (\exists_x \pi)_\otimes$, thus $\pi_0 = \top$, $\rho = (x \leq 1) \oplus \top = x \leq 1$ and $\exists_x \rho = \top$. Now, consider the second reduction. In that case we have $\pi_0 = (x \leq 1) \oplus \top = x \leq 1$, $\rho = (\alpha \wedge (x \leq 1)) \oplus (x \leq 1) = x > 1 \vee \alpha$ and $\exists_x \rho = \top$.

Remark 7. Concerning rule **LA2**, an alternative solution would have been to restrict the possible reductions to the one with the maximal label, that is, $\langle \textbf{ask}(c) \mapsto A, \sigma \rangle \xrightarrow{c \ominus \sigma} \langle A, (c \ominus \sigma) \otimes \sigma \rangle$. However, as hinted at in Example 6, this might have been restrictive in combination with rule **LR2**. Selecting $\alpha = (x > 1) \vee (y \leq 5)$ is problematic, since x occurs free. Instead, the choice of $\alpha = y \leq 5$, or any other value such as $y \leq 4$, $y \leq 3$, ..., fits the intuition of information from the environment triggering the reduction.

Note instead that the choice of removing the requirement $x \notin sv(\alpha)$ and put $\exists_x \alpha$ as label in the conclusion of rule **LR2** would be too liberal. Once again, it would be counterintuitive for the previous example, since $\exists_x ((x > 1) \vee (y \leq 5)) = \top$. Or consider the configuration $\gamma = \langle \exists_x^{[x \leq 1]} \textbf{ask}(x = 0) \mapsto \textbf{stop}, \top \rangle$: such a configuration should intuitively be deadlocked. However, we have that $\langle \textbf{ask}(x = 0) \mapsto \textbf{stop}, x \leq 1 \rangle \xrightarrow{\alpha} \langle \textbf{stop}, \alpha \wedge x \leq 1 \rangle$ for $\alpha \leq (x = 0) \oplus (x \leq 1) = (x > 1) \vee (x = 0) = x \neq 1$, thus allowing the reduction $\gamma \xrightarrow{\top} \langle \exists_x^{[x \leq 1, \alpha \vee x \leq 1]} \textbf{stop}, \top \rangle$, which clashes with the intuition that receiving information should not enable reductions involving (necessarily) the restricted variable.

Lemma 10 (On labelled monotonicity). *Let $\langle A, \sigma \rangle \xrightarrow{\alpha} \langle B, \rho \rangle$ be a labelled reduction. Then $\rho = (\rho \oplus (\alpha \otimes \sigma)) \otimes \alpha \otimes \sigma$ and $fv(\langle B, \rho \rangle) \subseteq fv(\langle A, \sigma \rangle) \cup sv(\alpha)$.*

Remark 8. We will later prove that if $\mathbb{S}$ is localised and $\alpha \neq \mathbf{1}$ then $\rho \oplus (\alpha \otimes \sigma) = \mathbf{1}$. In other terms, if $\langle A, \sigma \rangle \xrightarrow{\alpha} \langle B, \rho \rangle$ is a labelled reduction and $\alpha \neq \mathbf{1}$, then $\rho = \alpha \otimes \sigma$. Indeed, since $\alpha \neq \mathbf{1}$ its derivation must use the axiom **LA2**. Consider e.g. a labelled reduction $\langle \exists_x^\pi A, \sigma \rangle \xrightarrow{\alpha} \langle \exists_x^{\pi\rho} B, \alpha \otimes \sigma \otimes \exists_x \rho \rangle$. If $\alpha \neq \mathbf{1}$, then $\rho = \mathbf{1}$. Indeed, this is the expected behaviour: if an input from the context is needed, there is no contribution by the agent to the local store, hence the update is correctly $\mathbf{1}$.

Definition 16. *A configuration is l-reachable if it can be reached by an initial configuration via a sequence of labelled reductions.*

Lemma 11 (On labelled monotonicity, II). *Let $\langle B \parallel \exists_x^\pi C, \sigma \rangle$ be an l-reachable configuration. Then $\sigma = (\sigma \oplus (\exists_x \pi)_\otimes) \otimes (\exists_x \pi)_\otimes$.*

6 Semantics Correspondence and Labelled Bisimilarity

We collect further formal results in two different subsections: Sect. 6.1 proves the correspondence between the unlabelled and the labelled semantics, while Sect. 6.2 proposes a bisimilarity reduction for the labelled semantics.

6.1 On the Correspondence Between Reduction Semantics

This section shows the connection between labelled and unlabelled reduction semantics.

Proposition 2 (Soundness). *If $\langle A, \sigma \rangle \xrightarrow{\alpha} \langle B, \sigma' \rangle$ then $\langle A, \alpha \otimes \sigma \rangle \rightarrow \langle B, \sigma' \rangle$.*

The theorem above can be easily reversed, saying that if a configuration $\langle A, \sigma \rangle$ is reachable, then it is also l-reachable via a sequence of reductions labelled with $\mathbf{1}$.

Lemma 12. *If $\langle A, \sigma \rangle \rightarrow \langle B, \sigma' \rangle$ then $\langle A, \sigma \rangle \xrightarrow{\mathbf{1}} \langle B, \sigma' \rangle$.*

These results also ensure that a configuration is reachable iff it is l-reachable. However, we are interested in a more general notion of completeness, possibly taking into account reductions needing a label. For this, we first need some technical lemmas.

Now, note that the proof of every (labelled) reduction is given by the choice of an axiom and a series of applications of the rules **LR1** and **LR2**. Also, note that if $\langle A, \sigma \rangle \xrightarrow{\alpha} \langle B, \sigma' \rangle$ is a reduction via the axiom **LA1**, then $\alpha = \mathbf{1}$.

Proposition 3 (Completeness, I). *Let $\langle A, \tau \rangle \xrightarrow{\mathbf{1}} \langle B, \tau' \rangle$ be a reduction via the axiom **LA1** for $\tau \notin \{\bot, \top\}$. If $\mathscr{C}$ is cancellative then $\langle A, \sigma \rangle \xrightarrow{\mathbf{1}} \langle B, \sigma' \rangle$ and $\tau' \oplus \tau = \sigma' \oplus \sigma$ for every $\sigma \notin \{\bot, \top\}$.*

Proposition 4 (Completeness, II). *Let* $\langle A, \tau \rangle \xrightarrow{\beta} \langle B, \tau' \rangle$ *be a reduction via the axiom* **LA2** *for* $\tau \notin \{\bot, \top\}$. *If* $\mathscr{C}$ *is localised then* $\tau' = \beta \otimes \tau$ *and if* $\alpha \leq (\beta \otimes \tau) \oplus \sigma$ *then* $\langle A, \sigma \rangle \xrightarrow{\alpha} \langle B, \alpha \otimes \sigma \rangle$ *for every* $\sigma \notin \{\bot, \top\}$.

Clearly $\alpha = (\beta \otimes \tau) \oplus \sigma$ is a possible witness. Note however that it might be that $\beta \otimes \tau \nleq \alpha \otimes \sigma$ if $\sigma = \bot$, in which case $\alpha = \top$.

6.2   Labelled Bisimulation

We now exploit the labelled reductions in order to define a suitable notion of bisimilarity without the upward closure condition. As it occurs with the crisp language [1] and the soft variant with global variables [15], barbs cannot be removed from the definition of bisimilarity because they cannot be inferred by the reductions.

Definition 17 (Strong bisimilarity). *A strong bisimulation is a symmetric relation* R *on configurations such that whenever* $(\langle A, \sigma \rangle, \langle B, \rho \rangle) \in R$

1. *if* $\langle A, \sigma \rangle \downarrow_c$ *then* $\langle B, \rho \rangle \downarrow_c$;
2. *if* $\langle A, \sigma \rangle \xrightarrow{\alpha} \gamma_1$ *then there is* γ_2 *such that* $\langle B, \alpha \otimes \rho \rangle \rightarrow \gamma_2$ *and* $(\gamma_1, \gamma_2) \in R$;
3. $(\langle A, \sigma \otimes d \rangle, \langle B, \rho \otimes d \rangle) \in R$ *for all* d *such that* $d \nleq \mathbf{1}$.

We say that γ_1 *and* γ_2 *are strongly bisimilar* ($\gamma_1 \sim \gamma_2$) *if there exists a strong bisimulation* R *such that* $(\gamma_1, \gamma_2) \in R$. *We write* $A \sim B$ *if* $\langle A, \mathbf{1} \rangle \sim \langle B, \mathbf{1} \rangle$.

Note that $\langle A, \sigma \rangle \sim \langle B, \rho \rangle$ implies $\sigma = \rho$, as for saturated bisimilarity. We improved on the feasibility of $\sim$ by requiring that the equivalence is upward closed only whenever the store does not decrease. Note that in some cases, e.g. when $\mathscr{C}$ is absorptive (as in [1]), the clause is vacuous. However, thanks to the correspondence results in Sect. 6.1, it can be proved upward-closed for all d, and thus it is also a congruence.

Proposition 5. *Let* $\langle A, \sigma \rangle \sim \langle B, \rho \rangle$ *and* $d \in \mathscr{C}$. *If* $\mathscr{C}$ *is cancellative then* $\langle A, \sigma \otimes d \rangle \sim \langle B, \rho \otimes d \rangle$.

As for the unlabelled case (Proposition 1), strong bisimilarity is a congruence.

Proposition 6. *Let* $A \sim B$ *and* $C[\cdot]$ *a context. If* $\mathscr{C}$ *is cancellative then* $C[A] \sim C[B]$.

Finally, we can state the correspondence between our bisimilarity semantics.

Theorem 1. $\sim_s \subseteq \sim$. *Moreover, if* $\mathscr{C}$ *is cancellative, then the equality holds.*

7   Related Works

As it is possible to appreciate from the survey in [22], the literature on CCP languages is quite ample. In the following of this section we briefly summarise proposals that consider both local and global stores, and information mobility.

The work that is most related to ours is represented by [1]. Anyhow, the differences are significant: in that work the underlying constraint system is crisp, as it can only deal with hard constraints (which indeed we can do as well). Furthermore, the authors of [1] adopt a cylindric algebra instead of a polyadic one, as introduced in Sect. 1. Finally, as already noted in Remark 5 in this paper, the use of the local store is different with respect to our approach. Since the monoidal operator is idempotent, in [1] the semantics of the hiding operator is simply presented as $\langle \exists_x^e A, \sigma \rangle \rightarrow \langle \exists_x^{e'} B, \sigma \otimes \exists_x e' \rangle$ if $\langle A, e \otimes \exists_x \sigma \rangle \rightarrow \langle B, e' \otimes \exists_x \sigma \rangle$. Since we have introduced polyadic operators, with their simpler representation of substitutions, and thus we consider agents up-to α-conversion, we can replace $\exists_x \sigma$ with σ by requiring that $x \notin sv(\sigma)$. Most importantly, in [1] the local store e is used to fire a step that only changes the local store to e', and this change is visible in the global store except for the effect on variable x. However, this rule is intrinsically non-deterministic, since many such e' can exist. Moreover, since we are not idempotent we cannot add the whole e' to both the local and the global stores, but only the "difference" between e' and e at each step.

In [20] the authors describe a *spatial* constraint system with operators to specify information and processes moving from a space to another. Such a language provides for the specification of spatial mobility and epistemic concepts such as belief, utterance and lies: besides local stores for agents (representing belief), it can express the epistemic notion of knowledge by means of a derived spatial operator that specifies global shared information. Differently from this work, our approach focuses on preferences, on the concurrent language on top of the system, and on process equivalences.

The process calculi in [2,12] provide to agents the use of assertions within π-like processes. A soft language is adopted in [12]: from a variant of π-calculus it inherits *explicit fusions*, i.e. simple constraints expressing name equalities, in order to pass constraints from an agent to another. However, the algebraic structure is neither residuated nor polyadic; in addition, no process-equivalence relation is proposed. In [13,23] processes can send constraints using communication channels much like in the π-calculus.

A further language that uses π-calculus features to exchange constraints between agents, but this time with a probabilistic semantics, is shown in [10]. A congruence relation and a labelled transition system are also shown in the paper.

In [18] the authors propose an extension of the CCP language with the purpose to model process migration within a hierarchical network. Agents bring their local store when they migrate. In [11] the authors enrich a CCP language with the possibility to share (read/write) the information in the global store, and communicate with other agents (via multi-party or handshake).

All the systems described in this section are based on hard constraints, and they do not consider preferences associated with constraints (except [12], whose algebraic structure is however less general). In addition, a very few proposals formalise process equivalences by providing a deeper investigation of the semantics.

8 Conclusions and Further Works

With the language we presented in this paper, our goal was to further extend and generalise the family of CCP-based languages. In fact, *i)* with respect to crisp languages we can represent preferences, and thus both hard and soft constraints. Then, *ii)* polyadic operators make it possible to have a compact representation of soft constraints (about this, we point the interested reader to [8]), which in turn can be used in several applications, as in hybrid systems, loop invariant generation, and parameter design of control [9]. Furthermore, *iii)* the polyadic algebra we adopted takes advantage of a residuated POM which allows any partially ordered set of preference values, while $\oplus$ permits to easily compute barbs and remove one constraint (store) from another. The use of a non idempotent operator $\otimes$ for combining constraints led us to redesign the local stores proposed in [1], to add to the global store the information added at each computation step only.

An important issue we are currently working on is to remove the requirement of cancellativeness on the first completeness result between the reduction semantics, hence in the correspondence between the barbed and strong bisimilarities, as well as to remove the closure of the store with $d \not\leq 1$ in the definition of strong bisimilarity. Instead, our proposal could be easily extended in order to describe the weak variant of our bisimulation equivalences, which is the main reason why we introduced barbs directly in this paper. Indeed, in such semantics equivalent configurations may have different stores, and barbs were introduced to address this kind of issues [21].

In the case of "soft languages", the removal of constraints can also be partial, while in case of "crisp languages", constraint tokens can only be entirely removed or left in the store. A *retract* operation could also be directly included in the language syntax, in the style of [7,12], even if it is not in the scope of this paper.

For the future, we conceive more applicative extensions of the language we designed: while in this paper we focused on its formal definition, semantics, and process equivalence, we can think of application fields concerning epistemic concepts or process migration from node to node, as some of the proposals in Sect. 7 offer.

Separately from the process algebra focus we developed in this paper, we can also think of defining the class of Polynomial *Soft* Constraint Satisfaction Problems (PSCSPs), as accomplished in [26] with crisp constraints, in order to achieve a similar generalisation with respect to CSPs. Hence, we can implement polynomial constraint satisfaction as a SMT module, where agents can tell constraints and ask for their satisfaction.

References

1. Aristizábal, A., Bonchi, F., Palamidessi, C., Pino, L., Valencia, F.: Deriving labels and bisimilarity for concurrent constraint programming. In: Hofmann, M. (ed.) FoSSaCS 2011. LNCS, vol. 6604, pp. 138–152. Springer, Heidelberg (2011). https://doi.org/10.1007/978-3-642-19805-2_10
2. Bengtson, J., Johansson, M., Parrow, J., Victor, B.: Psi-calculi: mobile processes, nominal data, and logic. In: LICS 2009, pp. 39–48. IEEE Computer Society (2009)
3. Bistarelli, S., Montanari, U., Rossi, F.: Semiring-based constraint satisfaction and optimization. J. ACM 44(2), 201–236 (1997)
4. Bistarelli, S., Gadducci, F.: Enhancing constraints manipulation in semiring-based formalisms. In: Brewka, G., Coradeschi, S., Perini, A., Traverso, P. (eds.) ECAI 2006. FAIA, vol. 141, pp. 63–67. IOS Press (2006)
5. Bistarelli, S., Montanari, U., Rossi, F.: Soft concurrent constraint programming. ACM Trans. Comput. Log. 7(3), 563–589 (2006)
6. Bistarelli, S., Pini, M.S., Rossi, F., Venable, K.B.: From soft constraints to bipolar preferences: modelling framework and solving issues. Exp. Theor. Artif. Intell. 22(2), 135–158 (2010)
7. Bistarelli, S., Santini, F.: A nonmonotonic soft concurrent constraint language to model the negotiation process. Fund. Inform. 111(3), 257–279 (2011)
8. Bonchi, F., Bussi, L., Gadducci, F., Santini, F.: Polyadic soft constraints. In: Alvim, M.S., Chatzikokolakis, K., Olarte, C., Valencia, F. (eds.) The Art of Modelling Computational Systems: A Journey from Logic and Concurrency to Security and Privacy. LNCS, vol. 11760, pp. 241–257. Springer, Cham (2019). https://doi.org/10.1007/978-3-030-31175-9_14
9. Borralleras, C., Lucas, S., Oliveras, A., Rodríguez-Carbonell, E., Rubio, A.: SAT modulo linear arithmetic for solving polynomial constraints. J. Automed Reasoning 48(1), 107–131 (2012)
10. Bortolussi, L., Wiklicky, H.: A distributed and probabilistic concurrent constraint programming language. In: Gabbrielli, M., Gupta, G. (eds.) ICLP 2005. LNCS, vol. 3668, pp. 143–158. Springer, Heidelberg (2005). https://doi.org/10.1007/11562931_13
11. Brim, L., Kretínský, M., Jacquet, J., Gilbert, D.R.: Modelling multi-agent systems as synchronous concurrent constraint processes. Comput. Artif. Intell. 21(6) (2002)
12. Buscemi, M.G., Montanari, U.: Open bisimulation for the concurrent constraint pi-calculus. In: Drossopoulou, S. (ed.) ESOP 2008. LNCS, vol. 4960, pp. 254–268. Springer, Heidelberg (2008). https://doi.org/10.1007/978-3-540-78739-6_20
13. Díaz, J.F., Rueda, C., Valencia, F.D.: Pi+- calculus: a calculus for concurrent processes with constraints. CLEI Electron. J. 1(2) (1998)
14. Gadducci, F., Santini, F.: Residuation for bipolar preferences in soft constraints. Inf. Process. Lett. 118, 69–74 (2017)
15. Gadducci, F., Santini, F., Pino, L.F., Valencia, F.D.: Observational and behavioural equivalences for soft concurrent constraint programming. J. Log. Algebraic Methods Program. 92, 45–63 (2017)
16. Galler, B.A.: Cylindric and polyadic algebras. Proc. Am. Math. Soc. 8(1), 176–183 (1957)
17. Giacobazzi, R., Debray, S.K., Levi, G.: A generalized semantics for constraint logic programs. In: FGCS 1992, pp. 581–591. IOS Press (1992)
18. Gilbert, D., Palamidessi, C.: Concurrent constraint programming with process mobility. In: Lloyd, J., et al. (eds.) CL 2000. LNCS (LNAI), vol. 1861, pp. 463–477. Springer, Heidelberg (2000). https://doi.org/10.1007/3-540-44957-4_31

19. Golan, J.: Semirings and Affine Equations over Them. Kluwer (2003)
20. Guzmán, M., Haar, S., Perchy, S., Rueda, C., Valencia, F.D.: Belief, knowledge, lies and other utterances in an algebra for space and extrusion. J. Log. Algebraic Methods Program. **86**(1), 107–133 (2017)
21. Milner, R., Sangiorgi, D.: Barbed bisimulation. In: Kuich, W. (ed.) ICALP 1992. LNCS, vol. 623, pp. 685–695. Springer, Heidelberg (1992). https://doi.org/10.1007/3-540-55719-9_114
22. Olarte, C., Rueda, C., Valencia, F.D.: Models and emerging trends of concurrent constraint programming. Constraints **18**(4), 535–578 (2013)
23. Réty, J.: Distributed concurrent constraint programming. Fund. Inform. **34**(3), 323–346 (1998)
24. Sági, G.: Polyadic algebras. In: Andréka, H., Ferenczi, M., Németi, I. (eds.) Cylindric-like Algebras and Algebraic Logic. BSMS, vol. 22, pp. 367–389. Springer, Heidelberg (2013). https://doi.org/10.1007/978-3-642-35025-2_18
25. Saraswat, V.A., Rinard, M.C., Panangaden, P.: Semantic foundations of concurrent constraint programming. In: Wise, D.S. (ed.) POPL 1991, pp. 333–352. ACM Press (1991)
26. Scott, A.D., Sorkin, G.B.: Polynomial constraint satisfaction problems, graph bisection, and the Ising partition function. ACM Trans. Algorithms **5**(4), 45:1–45:27 (2009)

Runtime Verification and Monitor Synthesis

A Synthesis Tool for Optimal Monitors in a Branching-Time Setting

Antonis Achilleos[1], Léo Exibard[1], Adrian Francalanza[2],
Karoliina Lehtinen[3], and Jasmine Xuereb[1,2(✉)]

[1] Reykjavik University, Reykjavík, Iceland
jasmine.xuereb.15@um.edu.mt
[2] University of Malta, Msida, Malta
[3] CNRS, Aix-Marseille University and University of Toulon, LIS,
Toulon, France

Abstract. Monitorability is a characteristic that delineates between the properties that can be runtime verified by a monitor and those that cannot. Existing notions of monitorability for branching-time specifications are quite restrictive, limiting the set of monitorable properties to a small logical fragment. A recent study has enlarged the set of monitorable branching-time properties by weakening the requirements expected of the monitors effecting the verification: it defines a novel notion of optimal monitor that carries out the maximum number of detections that can be effected for any property, thereby turning a branching-time property into a monitorable one. The study also outlines a method for obtaining a unique optimal monitor from any branching-time property but falls short of providing an automation for this procedure. In this paper, we present a prototype tool that generates monitorable properties for branching-time properties expressed in a variant of the modal μ-calculus, based on this procedure. We also assess the performance of the prototype tool by evaluating its performance against several specifications.

Keywords: Runtime Verification · Monitor Synthesis ·
Branching-time specifications

1 Introduction

Runtime Verification (RV) is a lightweight verification technique that checks whether a system satisfies some correctness property [11]. This is achieved using monitors [18], which are computational entities that run alongside the system to incrementally observe its behaviour, flagging acceptance or rejection verdicts whenever they detect property satisfactions or violations. When compared to other verification techniques, RV is constrained by the fact that monitors base their analysis on the current system execution being observed. This complicates

This research was supported by the project'Mode(l)s of Verification and Monitorability (MoVeMnt)' (no. 217987-051) of the Icelandic Research Fund.

© IFIP International Federation for Information Processing 2022
M. H. ter Beek and M. Sirjani (Eds.): COORDINATION 2022, LNCS 13271, pp. 181–199, 2022.
https://doi.org/10.1007/978-3-031-08143-9_11

the verification of correctness properties describing aspects such as infinite executions or alternative execution paths, the evidence of which is hard to represent in a (finite) execution trace.

These monitorability limits were extensively studied in [19] for branching-time properties expressed in RECHML [5], a variant of the modal μ−calculus. There, the authors describe what should be demanded of monitors to adequately runtime verify properties. The first monitor requirement is *soundness*, meaning that whenever a monitor flags an acceptance or a rejection verdict, the system must respectively satisfy or violate the property. Since monitors that may flag both acceptance and rejection verdicts (called *multi-verdict* monitors) are generally inconsistent in the branching-time setting [19], the second monitor requirement is a weaker form of the dual of soundness, termed *partial completeness*. This means that monitors must be able to either reach a verdict for *all* property satisfactions or *all* property violations.

In this study, we focus on monitors that can only flag rejections. The properties for which such monitors can reject all violations are called *rejection-monitorable* (hereafter simply called *monitorable*), and they are precisely the known class of *safety properties* [6] as all of their violations can be detected within a finite sequence of events. This set of monitorable properties is characterised by a maximally expressive syntactic fragment of RECHML, termed sHML [19]. In other words, a formula is semantically equivalent to another one in this fragment *if and only if* it can be runtime verified.

Example 1. A system operating a coffee machine produces three events; insert money (m), output coffee (c), and grind more coffee beans (g). Suppose that this system is expected to satisfy the following specification:

> *"The coffee machine cannot produce event g (grind) immediately* (S_1)
> *after event c (coffee)."*

Specification S_1 can only be violated if the system can exhibit event c followed by event g. Such a violation can *always* be witnessed by a finite execution, which, in turn, implies that S_1 is monitorable.

> *"In all executions, the coffee machine eventually produces event c,* (S_2)
> *but not before m (money)."*

Consider specification S_2 above. It can be violated either *(i)* if the system never generates event c or *(ii)* it generates c before m. Suppose the monitor observes the sequence of events mgmgmg $\cdots$. Although event c will *never* be generated, a monitor runtime verifying this property *cannot* flag a violation because despite not having observed c yet, it cannot tell whether it might observe it in the future. Put otherwise, observing a finite execution does *not* provide the monitor with enough information to detect the violation in *(i)*. This implies that S_2 is not monitorable since no monitor can detect *all* violating systems. ■

As indicated by the limited syntax of sHML, restricting RV to monitorable properties severely limits its applicability. Indeed, many properties (such as S_2

above) still fall outside of this scope as *some* violations cannot be determined from finite system executions. Two possible approaches to extend these monitorability limits are weakening the correctness requirements expected of the monitors effecting the verification or increasing the monitors' observational power. We focus on the first approach, which was studied in [4]. In that work, the authors define a novel notion of *optimal monitors*, which flag all possible violations that can be determined with a finite sequence of events. More concretely, these monitors runtime verify the part of the property that is monitorable, termed the *strongest monitorable consequence*.

Example 2. Although specification S_2 from Example 1 is not monitorable, it turns out that *some* of its violations can be detected. In particular, a violation can be flagged from a finite execution whenever a sequence of events with prefix g $\cdots$ gc is observed since c occurs before m. Rather than ruling out S_2 as not monitorable and disregarding its runtime verification altogether, we extract its strongest monitorable consequence, informally described by specification S_3.

$$\textit{"In all executions, the coffee machine never produces c before m."} \qquad (S_3)$$

Clearly, specification S_3 is weaker than S_2, but it gives the best monitorable approximation of the original specification. ∎

The work in [4] outlines a two-step procedure to effectively construct an optimal monitor for branching-time RECHML properties, expressed in disjunctive form [30]. This procedure first extracts the strongest monitorable consequence, which is formulated in sHML, then synthesises a sound and complete monitor to effect the runtime verification. However, the work in [4] falls short of providing an automation for this procedure.

In this study, we investigate whether the procedure in [4] is amenable to mechanisation. To date, there are several automated monitor synthesis procedures that generate sound and complete monitors: one such tool is detectEr [7]. However, like all known synthesis procedures [7,8,19], this tool is only defined for sHML, and thus fails to generate monitors for properties that are either unmonitorable or not expressed in this fragment. To this end, our final aim is to build a toolchain that takes an arbitrary RECHML formula φ, generates its disjunctive form φ', and after extracting its strongest monitorable consequence φ'', synthesises an optimal monitor m, as outlined in Fig. 1. We leave the first phase for future work and focus on the second one, represented by the component labelled SMC. The third phase will be handled by the detectEr tool. Our contributions are two-fold:

1. In Sect. 3, we present a prototype tool that generates the strongest monitorable consequence for arbitrary branching-time properties expressed in disjunctive RECHML, based on the procedure proposed in [4].
2. In Sect. 5, we assess the performance of the implemented prototype tool against several specifications.

Fig. 1. Toolchain

2 Preliminaries

We assume a finite set of *actions* $a, b, \ldots \in$ ACT and *processes* $p, q \ldots \in$ PRC. The triple $\langle$PRC, ACT, $\longrightarrow\rangle$ forms a Labelled Transition System (LTS), where $\longrightarrow \subseteq$ (PRC, ACT, PRC) is a transition relation and $(p, a, q) \in \longrightarrow$ is denoted by the suggestive notation $p \xrightarrow{a} q$. Traces are finite or infinite sequences of actions, $t, u \in$ ACT$^* \cup$ ACT^w, and we say that process p *produces trace* t if there exists a sequence of transitions $p \xrightarrow{a} q \xrightarrow{b} \cdots$ for $t = ab\cdots$. *Specifications* (or *properties*) are defined as sets of processes, $P, Q, R \in \mathcal{P}($PRC$)$, where P is a *consequence* of Q when $Q \subseteq P$.

2.1 The Specification Logic

In this RV set-up, we presuppose a specification logic to unambiguously describe the behaviour expected from the system under scrutiny, *i.e.*, the properties of states in the respective LTS. Properties are formulated in RECHML, allowing a good level of generality of the obtained results. This set of formulae assumes a countably infinite supply of recursion variables $X, Y, \ldots \in$ LVAR and is built using the actions in ACT, as described in Fig. 2. On the other hand, the semantics of RECHML is given by the set of processes that satisfy each formula. We write $[\![\varphi, \rho]\!]$ to denote the set of processes that satisfy φ given an interpretation ρ of the free variables of the formula φ where $\rho : $ LVAR $\rightharpoonup \mathcal{P}(PRC)$. The notation $\rho[X \mapsto P]$ represents an interpretation ρ' such that $\rho'(X) = P$ and $\rho'(Y) = \rho(Y)$ for all $Y \neq X$. A process satisfies the universal modality $[a]\varphi$ if *all* the states that it *can* reach after performing an a-labelled transition satisfy φ. Conversely, the existential modality $\langle a \rangle \varphi$ is satisfied by the processes that can perform *at least one* a-labelled transition and reach a state that satisfies φ. The fixed point in min $X.\varphi$ and max $X.\varphi$ binds all the free occurrences of X in φ, and we assume that for each recursion variable, there is only one such formula binding it. We call the subformula φ the *binding formula* of X and denote it as φ_X. Intuitively, these least and greatest fixed points allow for recursion, whereby they can be respectively interpreted as *reachability* and *invariance*.

Example 3. Specification S_2 from Example 1 for ACT $= \{c, g, m\}$ is formalised as formula φ_2 below.

$$\varphi_2 = \min Y.[c]\mathsf{ff} \wedge [g]Y \wedge [m]\varphi_1$$
$$\text{where } \varphi_1 = \min X.([m]X \wedge [g]X) \vee \langle c \rangle \mathsf{tt}$$

While the inner least fixed point in φ_2 (*i.e.*, formula φ_1) ensures that the system eventually produces a c event, the outermost least fixed point prohibits it from happening before the first occurrence of m. ∎

RECHML Syntax

$\varphi, \psi \in \text{RECHML} ::=$ tt   (truth) | ff   (falsehood)

$\quad | \; \varphi \vee \psi$ (disjunction) | $\varphi \wedge \psi$ (conjunction)

$\quad | \; \langle a \rangle \varphi$ (existential modality) | $[a]\varphi$ (universal modality)

$\quad | \; \min X.\varphi$ (least fixed point) | $\max X.\varphi$ (greatest fixed point)

$\quad | \; X$ (recursion variable)

Branching-Time Semantics

$$\llbracket \text{tt}, \rho \rrbracket \stackrel{\text{def}}{=} \text{PRC} \qquad\qquad\qquad \llbracket \text{ff}, \rho \rrbracket \stackrel{\text{def}}{=} \emptyset$$

$$\llbracket [a]\varphi, \rho \rrbracket \stackrel{\text{def}}{=} \{p \mid \forall q \cdot p \stackrel{a}{\rightarrow} q \text{ implies } q \in \llbracket \varphi, \rho \rrbracket\} \quad \llbracket \varphi \vee \psi, \rho \rrbracket \stackrel{\text{def}}{=} \llbracket \varphi, \rho \rrbracket \cup \llbracket \psi, \rho \rrbracket$$

$$\llbracket \langle a \rangle \varphi, \rho \rrbracket \stackrel{\text{def}}{=} \{p \mid \exists q \cdot p \stackrel{a}{\rightarrow} q \text{ and } q \in \llbracket \varphi, \rho \rrbracket\} \quad \llbracket \varphi \wedge \psi, \rho \rrbracket \stackrel{\text{def}}{=} \llbracket \varphi, \rho \rrbracket \cap \llbracket \psi, \rho \rrbracket$$

$$\llbracket \min X.\varphi, \rho \rrbracket \stackrel{\text{def}}{=} \bigcap \{P \mid \llbracket \varphi, \rho[X \mapsto P] \rrbracket \subseteq P\} \quad \llbracket X, \rho \rrbracket \stackrel{\text{def}}{=} \rho(X)$$

$$\llbracket \max X.\varphi, \rho \rrbracket \stackrel{\text{def}}{=} \bigcup \{P \mid P \subseteq \llbracket \varphi, \rho[X \mapsto P] \rrbracket\}$$

Fig. 2. The syntax and semantics of RECHML in the branching-time setting.

2.2 Monitorability in RecHML

A translation procedure known as *monitor synthesis* generates computational entities, termed *monitors*, from correctness specifications. These monitors are then instrumented to run alongside the system and flag a verdict once they have observed sufficient runtime behaviour: an *acceptance* if the system satisfies the specification and a *rejection* if it violates it. These monitoring outcomes are assumed to be definite and irrevocable. In the branching-time setting, multi-verdict monitors (*i.e.*, monitors that may output both acceptance and rejection verdicts) are inconsistent [19, Theorem 2]. Therefore, we restrict our study to single-verdict monitors. To simplify the exposition, we focus on rejection monitors, *i.e.*, monitors that can only flag rejections. Monitors $m, n \in \text{MON}$ can be described as suffix-closed sets of traces $m, n \subseteq \text{ACT}^*$ that witness property violations [3,15], where MON is the set of all possible monitors. More concretely, monitor m rejects process p, denoted as $\textbf{rej}(m, p)$, if p produces a trace in m.

Definition 1 (Monitorability [19]). *A specification P is monitorable if there exists some $m \in \text{MON}$ that is:*

1. sound *for specification P, i.e., for all $p \in \text{PRC}$, $\textbf{rej}(m, p)$ implies $p \notin P$;*
2. complete *for specification P, i.e., for all $p \in \text{PRC}$, $p \notin P$ implies $\textbf{rej}(m, p)$.*

Since monitors can only observe finite prefixes of a trace, several logical formulae from Fig. 2, such as property φ_2 in Exmaple 3, are not monitorable. Indeed, the work in [19] shows that the subset of formulae in RECHML that is monitorable is characterised by the syntactic fragment sHML.

Theorem 1 (Safety Fragment [19]**).** *Formula* $\varphi \in$ RECHML *is monitorable iff it is equivalent to a formula in the syntactic fragment* sHML *defined as below:*

$$\varphi, \psi \in \text{sHML} ::= tt \quad | \quad ff \quad | \quad [a]\varphi \quad | \quad \varphi \wedge \psi \quad | \quad max\,X.\varphi \quad | \quad X \qquad \square$$

2.3   Extending the Limits of Monitorability

The syntax of sHML is restricted and, indeed, many RECHML formulae are not monitorable [19]. However, this should not deter our efforts, since, in general, a part of those properties could be amenable to monitoring. For instance, although specification S_2 from Example 2 is not monitorable, specification S_3 (which is its consequence) is monitorable. Following a best-effort strategy, the work in [4] defines the notion of an *optimal monitor* that aims at capturing the best monitor among all possible sound monitors for a given property. There, the authors also show that such a monitor actually runtime verifies the *strongest monitorable consequence* of that property. In the rest of this section, we give an overview of those results as they form the theoretical foundation of our prototype tool.

Definition 2 (Optimal Monitor [4]**).** *Monitor* m *is* optimal *for property* P *whenever:*

1. *it is sound for* P*;*
2. *for all* $n \in$ MON*, if* n *is sound for* P *then* $n \subseteq m$*.*

Optimal monitors can be characterised in terms of the strongest monitorable consequence of the specification for which they are monitoring. In turn, this allows us to establish a correspondence between the two.

Definition 3 (Strongest Monitorable Consequence [4]**).** *The* strongest monitorable consequence *of specification* P *is a property* Q *that is monitorable such that:*

1. *it is a consequence of* P*, i.e.,* $P \subseteq Q$*;*
2. *for any* R *that is monitorable, if* $P \subseteq R$ *then* $Q \subseteq R$*.*

Example 4. Properties φ_1 and φ_2 from Example 3 are not monitorable, and thus cannot be expressed in sHML. However, their strongest monitorable consequences can be respectively formalised as $\varphi_3 = tt$ and $\varphi_4 = max\,Y.[c]ff \wedge [g]Y$. In such cases where the strongest monitorable consequence of a property is tt, then it is impossible to detect any violations from a finite prefix.   ∎

Theorem 2 ([4]**).** *A monitor* $m \in M$ *that is sound for* P *is optimal for* P *iff it is sound and complete for the strongest monitorable consequence of* P*.* $\square$

From Theorem 2, we elaborate a two-step procedure to construct the optimal monitor for a property that first extracts its strongest monitorable consequence and then synthesises a sound and complete monitor for it. In this study, we focus on the former as the latter will be handled by the detectEr tool.

3 Design and Implementation

In this section, we give a detailed overview of the algorithm that constructs the strongest monitorable consequence of arbitrary RECHML formulae, following closely the procedure laid out in [4]. This construction consists of three steps: eliminating existential modalities, eliminating least fixed points, and eliminating disjunctions. Since these constructs are sources of non-monitorability, removing them from a RECHML formula yields a formula which can be shown to be the strongest monitorable consequence. This procedure relies on two crucial assumptions, namely that formulae are in *disjunctive form* and all subformulae are *satisfiable*, with the exception of ff. We thus proceed to give all the necessary technical developments before delving into the implementation details.

3.1 Disjunctive Form

For a finite set of formulae Γ, we use the standard notation $\bigwedge \Gamma$ to denote the conjunction of all the formulae in Γ. Similarly, $\bigvee \Gamma$ denotes the disjunction of all the formulae in Γ. As usual, $\bigwedge \varnothing$ denotes tt and $\bigvee \varnothing$ denotes ff.

Definition 4 (Disjunctive Form [30]). *The set of* RECHML *formulae in disjunctive form is given by the following grammar:*

$$\varphi, \psi \in \text{DISHML} ::= tt \quad | \quad ff \quad | \quad \varphi \vee \psi \quad | \quad \bigwedge_{a \in A} \left((\bigwedge_{\varphi \in \mathcal{B}_a} \langle a \rangle \varphi) \wedge [a] \bigvee_{\varphi \in \mathcal{B}_a} \varphi \right)$$

$$| \quad min\, X.\varphi \quad | \quad max\, X.\varphi \quad | \quad X$$

where $A \subseteq$ ACT and $\mathcal{B}_a \subseteq$ DISHML is a finite set of formulae, where $a \in A$.

The conjunctions in disjunctive form denote that for each action $a \in A$, all formulae in $\mathcal{B}_a$ are satisfied by some a-successor, and all a-successors satisfy a formula in $\mathcal{B}_a$. The intuition behind this representation is to push conjunctions as far as possible towards the modalities to explicitly describe the interaction between conjuncts. As will be demonstrated in Sect. 3.2, this is crucial for constructing the strongest monitorable consequence.

Example 5. Consider formula $\varphi_5 = [c][g]\text{ff} \wedge [c](\langle g \rangle \text{tt} \vee [c]\text{ff})$, whereby the subformula $\langle g \rangle \text{tt} \vee [c]\text{ff}$ represents the implication $[g]\text{ff} \implies [c]\text{ff}$. The conjuncts in φ_5 respectively describe the specifications "*g cannot occur immediately after c*" and "*if after c, g cannot occur, then c cannot occur either.*" This property is not in disjunctive form, but it is equivalent to the disjunctive formula φ_6 below, which describes the local behaviour "*after c, neither c nor g can occur.*"

$$\varphi_6 = [c]\text{ff} \vee \big(\langle c \rangle ([g]\text{ff} \wedge [c]\text{ff}) \wedge [c]([g]\text{ff} \wedge [c]\text{ff}) \big) \qquad \blacksquare$$

Walukiewicz [30] presents a procedure for constructing an equivalent DISHML formula from any RECHML one. However, in this paper, we focus on the computation of the strongest monitorable consequence and leave the conversion to disjunctive form for future work. The work in [30] also shows that satisfiability checking is linear; in our tool, all unsatisfiable subformulae are reduced to ff in a single pass.

Example 6. For the rest of this section, we use the following running example. Assume that $\mathrm{ACT} = \{c, m\}$ and consider $\varphi_7 = (\max X.[c]X \wedge [m]\mathsf{ff}) \wedge (\langle c \rangle \mathsf{tt} \vee [m]\mathsf{ff})$. This formula describes the property *"m never occurs, and if c cannot occur, then m cannot occur either."* Its equivalent disjunctive form is given by φ_8 below.

$$\varphi_8 = ([c]\mathsf{ff} \wedge [m]\mathsf{ff}) \vee ([m]\mathsf{ff} \wedge \langle c \rangle \varphi_8' \wedge [c]\varphi_8')$$
$$\text{where } \varphi_8' = \max X.([c]\mathsf{ff} \wedge [m]\mathsf{ff}) \vee (\langle c \rangle X \wedge [c]X \wedge [m]\mathsf{ff}) \qquad \blacksquare$$

3.2 Step 1: Eliminating Existential Modalities

In the first step, all occurrences of the existential modalities in the disjunctive formula are eliminated by replacing them with tt. Intuitively, this step is necessary since the non-existence of an a-successor, which would violate formulae of the form $\langle a \rangle \varphi$, cannot be identified by observing a single execution.

Remark 1. Disjunctive form is crucial for this step. Applying this transformation to φ_5 from Example 5 yields $[c]([g]\mathsf{ff} \wedge (\mathsf{tt} \vee [c]\mathsf{ff}))$, which can be simplified to $[c][g]\mathsf{ff}$. However, this is *not* the best approximation as the strongest monitorable consequence obtained from its disjunctive form, φ_6, is $[c][c]\mathsf{ff} \wedge [c][g]\mathsf{ff}$. $\blacksquare$

Example 7. Given formula φ_8 from Exmaple 6, the algorithm automating this step returns the formula φ_9 below.

$$\varphi_9 = ([c]\mathsf{ff} \wedge [m]\mathsf{ff}) \vee ([m]\mathsf{ff} \wedge \mathsf{tt} \wedge [c]\max X.([c]\mathsf{ff} \wedge [m]\mathsf{ff}) \vee (\mathsf{tt} \wedge [c]X \wedge [m]\mathsf{ff}))$$

It is not hard to see that this induces several redundant terms. However, we ignore them for now as they will be handled in the ensuing step. $\blacksquare$

3.3 Step 2: Eliminating Least Fixed Points

The second step consists of transforming all least fixed points into greatest fixed points. Indeed, the only way to detect a violation of a least fixed point at runtime is to find a violation with a finite sequence of events, which is equivalent to detecting a violation of a greatest fixed point. We directly automate this by replacing all subformulae of the form $\min X.\varphi$ with $\max X.\varphi$.

This step, together with the previous one, induces several redundant subformulae, which, in turn, introduce a significant amount of unnecessary computation in the ensuing step. To this end, our algorithm recursively simplifies the resulting formula based on the axioms below, where $A \subseteq \mathrm{ACT}$, in the following order of precedence: $(A1), (A2), \ldots, (A6)$.

(A1) $\varphi \vee \mathsf{tt} \Rrightarrow \mathsf{tt}$ (A2) $\varphi \wedge \mathsf{tt} \Rrightarrow \varphi$ (A3) $[a]\mathsf{tt} \Rrightarrow \mathsf{tt}$

(A4) $\max X.\mathsf{tt} \Rrightarrow \mathsf{tt}$ (A5) $\max X.X \Rrightarrow \mathsf{tt}$ (A6) $\max X. \bigwedge_{a \in A}[a]X \Rrightarrow \mathsf{tt}$

$$\frac{\Gamma \cup \{\psi \vee \varphi\}}{\Gamma \cup \{\psi, \varphi\}} \, (\vee) \qquad \frac{\Gamma \cup \{\psi \wedge \varphi\}}{\Gamma \cup \{\psi\} \quad \Gamma \cup \{\varphi\}} \, (\wedge) \qquad \frac{\Gamma \cup \{\max X.\varphi\}}{\Gamma \cup \{\varphi\}} \, (\max) \qquad \frac{\Gamma \cup \{X\}}{\Gamma \cup \{\varphi_X\}} \, (X)$$

$$\frac{\Gamma}{\{\psi \mid [a]\psi \in \Gamma\}} \, ([a]) \qquad \frac{\Gamma \cup \{\mathsf{ff}\}}{\Gamma} \, (\mathsf{ff}) \qquad \frac{\Gamma \cup \{\mathsf{tt}\}}{\{\mathsf{tt}\}} \, (\mathsf{tt}) \qquad \frac{\Gamma \cup \{[a]\psi, [b]\varphi\}, a \neq b}{\{\mathsf{tt}\}} \, ([a, b])$$

Fig. 3. Tableau rules where Γ is a formula set.

Example 8. Formula φ_9 from Exmaple 7 does not have any least fixed points. Therefore, during the first pass, the algorithm automating this transformation leaves the formula unchanged. The second pass then returns the simplified formula with respect to the axioms $(A1)$ to $(A6)$, resulting in φ_{10} below.

$$\varphi_{10} = \big([c]\mathsf{ff} \wedge [m]\mathsf{ff}\big) \vee \big([m]\mathsf{ff} \wedge [c]\max X.([c]\mathsf{ff} \wedge [m]\mathsf{ff}) \vee ([c]X \wedge [m]\mathsf{ff})\big) \qquad \blacksquare$$

3.4   Step 3: Eliminating Disjunctions

The final and most challenging step is to obtain a disjunction-free formula. This can be decomposed into two parts: apply the tableau rules in Fig. 3 to obtain a tree with back edges (*i.e.*, edges from leaves to inner nodes), and relabel the nodes of the tree. These are respectively automated by Algorithms 1 and 2.

Definition 5 (Tableau for Disjunction Elimination [4]). *Given a formula φ, its tableau is a pair $\langle T, L \rangle$, where T is a tree with back edges and L is a labelling function such that:*

1. *the root of T is labelled as $\{\varphi\}$, and*
2. *each internal node and its children are labelled according to a rule in Fig. 3. Internal nodes are labelled with the premise, while their children are labelled with the conclusion. Additionally, rule $[a]$ is applied only when $L(n)$ matches the premise of no other rule and it contains at least one $[a]\varphi'$ for some φ'.*

The interpretation of the tableau in Definition 5 is that the formulae in Γ are disjuncted, whereas the branches are conjuncted. The rules are read top-down to form a tree, with the topmost premise being the root and the conclusions being the branches. Since formulae might not have unique tableaux, rule $([a])$ must be left for last to synchronises the different tableaux of the same formula. This means that irrespective of the order of rule application, all children derived using rule $([a])$ are identical. Additionally, although all the rules except for regenerations, *i.e.*, rule (X), reduce the formula size, the order of application directly influences the size of the tableau, which, in turn, affects the tool's performance.

Example 9. Consider the set of formulae $\{[a]\varphi_1 \wedge [a]\varphi_2, \mathsf{tt}\}$ for some φ_1, φ_2. This set pattern matches with the premise of two rules, namely (tt) and $(\wedge)$. Applying the former, the formula set is immediately reduced to $\{\mathsf{tt}\}$. However, if the latter rule is applied, the tree branches into $\{[a]\varphi_1, \mathsf{tt}\}$ and $\{[a]\varphi_2, \mathsf{tt}\}$, both of which induce further proof obligations. $\qquad \blacksquare$

```
 1  def CREATETABLEAU(F, V, count)
 2    if F = {tt} then
 3      return Leaf(F, −1)
 4    else if F = {ff} then
 5      return Leaf(F, −1)
 6    else
 7      ⟨children, rule⟩ ← APPLYRULE(F)
 8      if children = [c] and ∃⟨c, x⟩ ∈ V for some x then
 9        return Leaf(F, x)
10      else
11        V ← V ++ [⟨F, count⟩]
12        c_trees ← CREATETABLEAU(c, V, count+1) for each c in children
13        return Node(count, F, c_trees, rule, false)
14  def SETBACKEDGETARGETS(t)
15    targets ← [ ]
16    for each Leaf l in t where l.backedge_target ≠ −1 do
17      targets ← targets ++ [l.backedge_target]
18    for each Node n in t where n.node_id ∈ targets do
19      n.backedge ← true
20    return t
```

Alg. 1. Pseudocode for Building the Tableau

Our implementation circumvents the unnecessary computation steps induced by the application order of the rules by assuming the following order of priorities: (tt), ([a, b]), (ff), (max), (∨), (∧), (X), ([a]). We chose this ordering based on the fact that the first two rules simplify the formula set, rule (∨) increases the size of the formula set and thus the chance of applying (tt) or ([a, b]), whereas rules (∧) and (X) respectively increase the width and depth of the tree.

We implement the tableau in Definition 5 as a polymorphic tree: this allows us to use the same tree structure albeit with different implementations. Nodes are composed of (i) a node_id, (ii) a node_label, (iii) a list of children, where each child is a tree, (iv) a rule of type string, and (v) a boolean value, backedge, indicating whether that node is the target of some back edge. Leaves have two elements: (i) a leaf_label, and (ii) an integer value, backedge_target, to store the node_id of the back edge target; when there is no back edge, this is set to −1. For convenience, we use the suggestive dot notation (.) to access specific elements. E.g., the rule applied at node n is accessed via the field n.rule.

The algorithm automating the tableau construction is described in Algorithm 1. The procedure starts from the root of the tableau, which is the singleton element $\{\varphi\}$, applies the rule with a matching premise, and then repeats this procedure for each resulting child. Since each node is a set of formulae, our algorithm implements the tableau as a tree of formula sets. The algorithm uses a set $\mathcal{F}$ and a list $\mathcal{V}$. The former is initialised to $\{\varphi\}$ and stores the formula set waiting to be analysed. The latter, initialised to empty, stores pairs $\langle S, x \rangle$, where S is a formula set that has been already generated and x is its identifier. When each set S in $\langle S, x \rangle \in \mathcal{V}$ can reach some other set S' in $\langle S', x' \rangle \in \mathcal{V}$ via some rule, the algorithm terminates as no new leaves or nodes can be created.

Function CREATETABLEAU( ) is the main function. If $\mathcal{F}$ is the singleton element {tt} or {ff}, a leaf with no back edges is created on lines 3 and 5. Otherwise, the algorithm checks whether it needs to create a new node or add a back edge to some previous node in the tree by calling APPLYRULE( ) on line 7. This function returns a pair containing a list of formula sets, which represent the current node's children, and the rule applied to derive them. If there is only one child c and $\langle c, x \rangle$ is in $\mathcal{V}$, then some node n with label c has already been generated. Thus, a leaf with a back edge to n is created on line 9 by setting backedge_target to x. Otherwise, the tree for each resulting child is constructed on line 12. Once the entire tree is constructed, SETBACKEDGETARGETS( ) on line 14 performs two passes: it first retrieves the list of identifiers of the back edge targets from the leaves (lines 16, 17), then traverses the tree again to update n.backedge to *true* for all nodes n that are target of some back edges (lines 18, 19).

Example 10. Recall property φ_{10} in Example 8. Since tableaux tend to grow relatively in size, we focus on subformula $\varphi_{11} = \max X.([c]\mathsf{ff} \wedge [m]\mathsf{ff}) \vee ([c]X \wedge [m]\mathsf{ff})$, whose tableau is depicted by the left tree in Fig. 4 and forms a subgraph of the tableau for φ_{10}. We omit the outer curly brackets denoting that the formulae form a set and only include specific elements for better readability.

Starting with the initial formula, Algorithm 1 creates a node with identifier 0 and a child with label $\{([c]\mathsf{ff} \wedge [m]\mathsf{ff}) \vee ([c]X \wedge [m]\mathsf{ff})\}$, obtained via rule max. Since the latter formula set has not been generated yet, its tree is created via a recursive call to CREATETABLEAU( ) on line 12. This tree generation continues until the fifth recursive call, where a node with label $\{\mathsf{ff}, X\}$ and identifier 5 is created, whose child is the tree for formula set $\{X\}$. The latter has not been generated yet, but its child, obtained via rule X, has label $\{\varphi_X\}$ where φ_X is given by $([c]\mathsf{ff} \wedge [m]\mathsf{ff}) \vee ([c]X \wedge [m]\mathsf{ff})$: this is precisely the same as that of the node with identifier 1. Therefore, a leaf with backedge_target 1 is created (line 9).

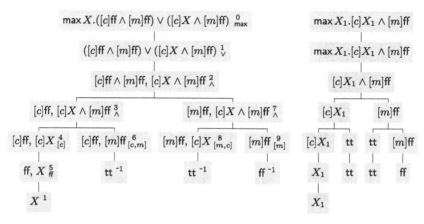

Fig. 4. The tableau for formula φ_{11} before and after relabelling.

```
 1  def RELABELTABLEAU(t)
 2  if t = Leaf l then
 3    m ← l.backedge_target
 4    if m ≠ −1 then return Leaf(X_m, m)
 5    else if tt ∈ l.leaf_label then return Leaf(tt, −1)
 6    else return Leaf(ff, −1)
 7  else t = Node n
 8    children ← RELABELTABLEAU(c) for c in n.children
 9    if n.rule = (∧) then
10      [c_1, c_2] ← children
11      f ← LABEL(c_1) ∧ LABEL(c_2)
12    else if n.rule = [a] for some a then
13      [c] ← children
14      f ← [a]LABEL(c)
15    else
16      [c] ← children
17      f ← LABEL(c)
18    if n.backedge then
19      m ← n.id
20      return Node(m, max X_m.f, children, n.rule, true)
21    else
22      return Node(m, f, children, n.rule, false)
```

Alg. 2. Pseudocode for Relabelling the Tableau

Once the entire tree is generated, SETBACKEDGETARGETS( ) then updates the field backedge of the node with identifier 1 to *true*. ∎

The algorithm implementing the tableau relabelling is described in Algorithm 2. Given a tree of formula sets, RELABELTABLEAU( ) recursively constructs a new tree of the same shape, whose root label is the strongest monitorable consequence. Each leaf of the inputted tree is relabelled to either X_m (where m is the identifier of the back edge target), tt or ff (lines 4, 5, 6). Each node is relabelled in two steps: the algorithm first relabels its children via a recursive call to RELABELTABLEAU( ) on line 8, then it relabels the node according to which rule was applied to derive its children. For rule (∧), the new label is the conjunction of its two children c_1 and c_2, whereas for rule ([a]), it is that of its child prefixed by [a] (lines 11, 14). Otherwise, the label is identical to that of its child (line 17). Before creating a node with these values, line 18 checks whether it is the target of a back edge: if it is, the label is turned into a greatest fixed point by prefixing it with max X_m where m is the node's identifier. The function LABEL( ) retrieves the value of node_label or leaf_label, depending on the node type.

Remark 2. Implementing line 11 naively results in formulae with several redundant terms, where one of the conjuncts (or both) is tt. Our implementation sidesteps this by conjuncting c_1 and c_2 only if both are different from tt, and sets the label to c_1 when c_2 is equivalent to tt and vice versa. Also, all labels in the relabelled tableau consist a single formula. Arguably, such a tableau still can be implemented as a tree of formula sets, but it would impinge on the tool's performance as the algorithm would repeatedly have to retrieve the formula from the set. To this end, we implement the relabelled tableau as a tree of formulae, justifying why we opted to define the tree structure as a polymorphic type. □

Example 11. The relabelled tableau for formula φ_{11} from Example 10 is depicted by the right tree in Fig. 4. Since its internal structure is analogous to that of the left tree, we omit the node identifiers and rules used to derive the children.

Starting from the root of the left tree, Algorithm 2 creates a new node with label $\max X_1.[c]X_1 \wedge [m]\mathsf{ff}$ on line 17. This is obtained by inheriting the label of its child, generated via a recursive call to RELABELTABLEAU( ) on line 8. Since the node with identifier 1 is the target of a back edge, a new node is created on line 18 where its label is obtained in two steps. First, it retrieves the label of its child on line 17, and then transforms it into a greatest fixed point label by prefixing it with $\max X_1$. This tree generation continues until the leaves of the tree are reached: for the leaf with label $\{X\}$ and a back edge to node 1, a new leaf with label X_1 is created, whereas all the other leaves are left untouched. ∎

Once Algorithm 2 returns the relabelled tableau, our prototype tool outputs its root label, which describes the strongest monitorable consequence of the initial formula.

4   The Tool

The previous section presented a thorough overview of the algorithms for constructing the strongest monitorable consequence. In this section, we give more details on the tool's internal architecture and how it can be used in practice.

4.1   Internal Architecture

The algorithms in Sect. 3 are implemented in OCaml (version 4.08.0) in a straightforward fashion, resulting in a prototype tool that takes as input a formula and outputs its strongest monitorable consequence. This is achieved by first building a parse tree for the inputted formula, using the *Menhir* parser generator, and then successively calling the functions automating the three steps in Sect. 3. The OCaml code is organised into several modules in the src/ directory, which can be further decomposed into three folders; definitions, parsing and utils. The first directory stores two modules, strongestMonCons.ml and SMCTableau-Rules.ml. The former implements the first two steps in Sects. 3.2 and 3.3, while the latter implements Algorithms 1 and 2 and the tableau rules as the functions create_tableau(), relabel_tableau(), and apply_rules() respectively, preserving the naming conventions from Sect. 3.4. The second directory then contains the modules that handle the parsing, whereas the last stores all modules containing user-defined types and helper functions.

4.2   Usage

The tool can be invoked from the terminal, where the formula is inputted either by passing it as a command line argument or by providing the path of the file containing the formula when prompted. For instance, in the first approach, the strongest monitorable consequence of φ_8 from Example 6 is generated by executing the command below, where the logical or's and and's are respectively substituted by the | and & operators.

```
./main.native "([c]ff & [m]ff) | ([m]ff & <c>(max X.([c]ff & [m]ff) |
    (<c>X & [c]X & [m]ff)) & [c](max X.([c]ff & [m]ff) | (<c>X & [c]X
    & [m]ff)))"
```

Conversely, the second approach involves omitting the formula altogether: this is especially appealing when formulae are more complex, while facilitating integration with the first component in the toolchain of Fig. 1 once it is realized. The output returned by both methods can be decomposed into four parts; (i) the parse tree of the inputted formula, (ii) elimination of existential modalities, (iii) elimination of least fixed points, and (iv) elimination of disjunctions. Inputting formula φ_8 from Example 6, our tool returns the following, where the formulae outputted in (ii) and (iii) respectively correspond to φ_9 and φ_{10} from Examples 7 and 8.

```
================================ STEP 1 ================================

The formula after eliminating existential modalities is:
[c]ff & [m]ff | [m]ff & tt & [c](max X.[c]ff & [m]ff | tt & [c]X & [m]ff)

================================ STEP 2 ================================

The formula after eliminating minimal fixed points is:
[c]ff & [m]ff | [m]ff & tt & [c](max X.[c]ff & [m]ff | tt & [c]X & [m]ff)

The simplified formula is:
[c]ff & [m]ff | [m]ff & [c](max X.[c]ff & [m]ff | [c]X & [m]ff)
```

The fourth part of the output consists of two trees, representing the tableau of the formula returned in (iii) before and after relabelling. In our example, the output below shows a subtree of the tableau for φ_{10} before the relabelling, which corresponds to the tableau for φ_{11} from Example 10, depicted in Fig. 4. We omit the output after the relabelling as it possesses a similar format.

```
   └ (max)6 ── max X.[c]ff & [m]ff | [c]X & [m]ff;
     └ (or)7 ── [c]ff & [m]ff | [c]X & [m]ff; back edge target
       └ (and)8 ── [c]ff & [m]ff; [c]X & [m]ff;
         ├ (and)9 ── [c]X & [m]ff; [c]ff;
         │ ├ ([c])10 ── [c]ff; [c]X;
         │ └ (ff)11 ── ff; X;
         │   └ (X)12 ── X;
```

```
          ⌐ [c]ff & [m]ff | [c]X & [m]ff; back edge to 7
      ⌐ ([a,b])13 ── [c]ff; [m]ff;
       ⌐ tt;
  ⌐ (and)14 ── [c]X & [m]ff; [m]ff;
   ⌐ ([a,b])15 ── [c]X; [m]ff;
   ⌐ tt;
  ⌐ ([m])16 ── [m]ff;
   ⌐ (ff)17 ── ff;
```

Our tool can also export the computed strongest monitorable consequence to the format expected by detectEr tool and write it to file. This functionality can be triggered using the keyword **save**, as shown below. In turn, this allow us to input the file to detectEr, which will then synthesise the optimal monitor.

```
./main.native "([c]ff & [m]ff) | ([m]ff & <c>(max X.([c]ff & [m]ff) |
   (<c>X & [c]X & [m]ff)) & [c](max X.([c]ff & [m]ff) | (<c>X & [c]X
   & [m]ff)))" save
```

5   Evaluation

Sections 3 and 4 demonstrate that the procedure in [4] for computing the strongest monitorable consequence of RECHML formulae can be automated, albeit with an exponential worst-case complexity upper bound. However, it remains unclear whether this is fully-representative of the implemented prototype. In this section, we evaluate the scalability our tool; in the absence of standard benchmarks, we devise two strategies for our empirical evaluation. All experiments were carried out on a Quad-Core Intel Core i5 64-bit machine with 16 GB memory, running OCaml version 4.08.0 on OSX Catalina. They can be *reproduced* using the sources provided at https://github.com/jasmine97xuereb/optimal-monitor.

Parametrisable Formulae. Since eliminating the existential modalities and least fixed points is linear, the disjunction elimination step is responsible for the overall complexity of the algorithm. We thus construct a family of DISHML formulae aimed at maximizing the width and depth of the tableau that is constructed in Algorithm 1. More concretely, $P_1(k)$ below defines a family of formulae with a high branching-factor, resulting in a high level of branching in the tableau. The formulae generated by the skeleton $P_2(k)$ consist of several disjunctions and modalities over the same action, which blow-up the size of the formula sets. Additionally, several of these sets are composed of recursion variables $X_1, \ldots, X_n$, inducing further iterations in Algorithms 1 and 2. We contend that these skeletons adequately stress test our tool since the tableau construction of the generated formulae heavily relies on the application of rules $(\wedge)$, $(\vee)$, and (X), which induce the highest increase in tableaux size and complexity.

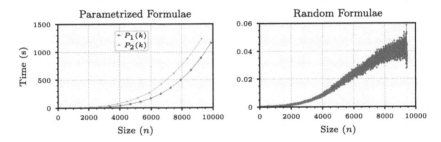

Fig. 5. Performance of the tool against different formulae

$$P_1(k) = \max X. \bigwedge_{i \in k} \left(\bigwedge_{\varphi \in \mathcal{B}_{a_i}} \langle a \rangle \varphi \wedge [a] \bigvee_{\varphi \in \mathcal{B}_{a_i}} \varphi \right) \text{ where } \mathcal{B}_a = \{[a]\mathsf{ff}, X\}$$

$$P_2(k) = \bigvee_{i \in k} \max X_i. \left(\bigwedge_{j \in k} \langle a_j \rangle X_i \wedge [a_j] X_i \right) \wedge [b_i]\mathsf{ff}$$

We evaluate the mean running time (over 5 repeated runs) for these property instances over an increasing parameter k. The results, reported in the left graph of Fig. 5, show that for this set of properties, our implementation runs in quadratic time. We remark that, at this point, it is open to investigation whether the exponential worst-case complexity can be reached.

Random Formulae. Since the parametrised instances only target specific features of the algorithm, we also evaluate it against formulae that are randomly generated following a uniform distribution on the grammar of DISHML for better coverage. The plotted results in the right graph of Fig. 5, which show the mean running time (over 500 repeated runs) of random formulae with increasing size, indicate that the average running time remains considerably lower than that for the family of formulae generated by the parameterised instances. Indeed, formulae are drastically simplified before reaching the third step, and modalities rarely interact in a way that make the tableau grow. We note that it is not clear how close the distribution adopted here is to the one obtained from uniformly chosen RECHML formulae that are *then* converted to disjunctive form.

Although there is no guarantee that the results obtained in this section carry over to the toolchain in Fig. 1, they give preliminary evidence that our prototype tool scales well in the general case.

6   Conclusion

This paper investigates the implementability aspects of the procedure outlined in [4]. In particular, our prototype tool takes arbitrary branching-time properties expressed in disjunctive RECHML and constructs their best monitorable approximation according to [1,20]. This enables us to extend the known synthesis tools to generate optimal monitors for arbitrary branching-time properties. The tool and the accompanying demo video can be found at https://zenodo.org/badge/latestdoi/420058357 and https://youtu.be/XI6GoG4MaNk.

6.1   Future Work

We plan to automate the translation from RECHML formulae to their equivalent disjunctive form as presented in [30] to complete the toolchain of Fig. 1. In turn, this will allow us to investigate possible optimisations based on a more precise evaluation of our tool. Finally, we note that the detectEr tool can handle actions that carry data from an infinite domain. We plan to investigate to what extent the techniques in [4] generalise to this setting. This is a challenging endeavour as the automata-logic correspondence they rely on is far more complex in the presence of data [13, 16].

6.2   Related Work

Linear- vs Branching-Time. In linear-time monitoring, we are interested in a property of the current execution, rather than the system as a whole. This is particularly useful for checking in deployed systems whether the output of a third-party component is safe to use in a critical component, for example. Then, whether the non-trusted component can also produce unsafe executions is largely irrelevant. Finding optimal monitors corresponds to computing the good and bad prefixes of a linear-time property, that is, the prefixes of which either all or no continuation satisfies the property, as done by Kupferman and Vardi [24] or by Havelund and Peled [20]. In contrast, when RV is used as a best-effort alternative to model-checking, we are trying to work out whether the *system*, rather than the current execution, is correct. Since monitors still only observe one execution, the proportion of monitorable properties is, unavoidably, smaller [2]. As a result, the benefit of using optimal monitors is even greater, as it expands the realm of properties that monitors can be used for. Note that the complexity of finding optimal monitors is double-exponential already in the linear-time setting [24], so the difficulty added by the branching-time setting is mostly conceptual.

Monitoring with Prior Knowledge. One of the use-cases for optimal monitors is the incorporation of prior knowledge (assumptions) into the monitor, which allows more violations to be identified. As argued in [4], computing the optimal monitor is also an optimal way to incorporate prior knowledge into the monitor. This problem has been studied in the linear-time setting (with linear-time assumptions) by Henzinger and Saraç [22], by Cimatti *et al.* [14], and by Leucker [25], and for hyperproperties by Stucki *et al.* [29].

Monitoring Tools. Among many RV tools, let us mention MaC [23], PathExplorer [21], Eagle [9], and RuleR [10], Temporal Rover [17], and Java-MOP [26], all runtime verification tools based on various specification languages. Blech *et al.* [27], Schneider *et al.* [28] and Basin *et al.* [12] aim to generate *verified*

monitors from specifications. The former uses proof assistant Coq and targets
regular properties, while the latter two use Isabelle/HOL and target metric first
order temporal logics; both produce executable monitors in OCaml. Typically,
these tools focus on linear-time specifications, which makes them harder to adapt
to properties generated primarily for model-checking rather than RV, and does
not lend them to incorporating prior knowledge of the system, expressed as
branching time properties, into the monitoring set-up.

References

1. Aceto, L., Achilleos, A., Francalanza, A., Ingólfsdóttir, A.: Monitoring for silent
   actions. In: FSTTC. LIPIcs, vol. 93, pp. 7:1–7:14. Schloss Dagstuhl - Leibniz-
   Zentrum für Informatik (2017)
2. Aceto, L., Achilleos, A., Francalanza, A., Ingólfsdóttir, A., Lehtinen, K.: Adventures in monitorability: from branching to linear time and back again. PACMPL
   3(POPL), 52:1–52:29 (2019)
3. Aceto, L., Achilleos, A., Francalanza, A., Ingólfsdóttir, A., Lehtinen, K.: An operational guide to monitorability. In: Ölveczky, P.C., Salaün, G. (eds.) SEFM 2019.
   LNCS, vol. 11724, pp. 433–453. Springer, Cham (2019). https://doi.org/10.1007/
   978-3-030-30446-1_23
4. Aceto, L., Achilleos, A., Francalanza, A., Ingólfsdóttir, A., Lehtinen, K.: The best a
   monitor can do. In: CSL. LIPIcs, vol. 183, pp. 7:1–7:23. Schloss Dagstuhl - Leibniz-
   Zentrum für Informatik (2021)
5. Aceto, L., Ingólfsdóttir, A., Larsen, K.G., Srba, J.: Reactive Systems: Modelling,
   Specification and Verification. Cambridge U.P. (2007)
6. Alpern, B., Schneider, F.B.: Recognizing safety and liveness. Distributed Comput.
   2(3), 117–126 (1987)
7. Attard, D.P., Aceto, L., Achilleos, A., Francalanza, A., Ingólfsdóttir, A., Lehtinen,
   K.: Better late than never or: verifying asynchronous components at runtime. In:
   Peters, K., Willemse, T.A.C. (eds.) FORTE 2021. LNCS, vol. 12719, pp. 207–225.
   Springer, Cham (2021). https://doi.org/10.1007/978-3-030-78089-0_14
8. Attard, D.P., Francalanza, A.: A monitoring tool for a branching-time logic. In:
   Falcone, Y., Sánchez, C. (eds.) RV 2016. LNCS, vol. 10012, pp. 473–481. Springer,
   Cham (2016). https://doi.org/10.1007/978-3-319-46982-9_31
9. Barringer, H., Goldberg, A., Havelund, K., Sen, K.: Rule-based runtime verification. In: Steffen, B., Levi, G. (eds.) VMCAI 2004. LNCS, vol. 2937, pp. 44–57.
   Springer, Heidelberg (2004). https://doi.org/10.1007/978-3-540-24622-0_5
10. Barringer, H., Rydeheard, D., Havelund, K.: Rule systems for run-time monitoring:
    from Eagle to RuleR. J. Log. Comput. 20(3), 675–706 (2008)
11. Bartocci, E., Falcone, Y., Francalanza, A., Reger, G.: Introduction to runtime
    verification. In: Bartocci, E., Falcone, Y. (eds.) Lectures on Runtime Verification.
    LNCS, vol. 10457, pp. 1–33. Springer, Cham (2018). https://doi.org/10.1007/978-
    3-319-75632-5_1
12. Basin, D., et al.: A formally verified, optimized monitor for metric first-order
    dynamic logic. In: Peltier, N., Sofronie-Stokkermans, V. (eds.) IJCAR 2020. LNCS
    (LNAI), vol. 12166, pp. 432–453. Springer, Cham (2020). https://doi.org/10.1007/
    978-3-030-51074-9_25
13. Björklund, H., Schwentick, T.: On notions of regularity for data languages. Theor.
    Comput. Sci. 411(4–5), 702–715 (2010)

14. Cimatti, A., Tian, C., Tonetta, S.: Assumption-based runtime verification with partial observability and resets. In: Finkbeiner, B., Mariani, L. (eds.) RV 2019. LNCS, vol. 11757, pp. 165–184. Springer, Cham (2019). https://doi.org/10.1007/978-3-030-32079-9_10
15. d'Amorim, M., Roşu, G.: Efficient monitoring of ω-languages. In: Etessami, K., Rajamani, S.K. (eds.) CAV 2005. LNCS, vol. 3576, pp. 364–378. Springer, Heidelberg (2005). https://doi.org/10.1007/11513988_36
16. D'Antoni, L.: In the Maze of Data Languages. CoRR abs/1208.5980 (2012)
17. Drusinsky, D.: The temporal rover and the ATG rover. In: Havelund, K., Penix, J., Visser, W. (eds.) SPIN 2000. LNCS, vol. 1885, pp. 323–330. Springer, Heidelberg (2000). https://doi.org/10.1007/10722468_19
18. Francalanza, A.: A theory of monitors. Inf. Comput. **281**, 104704 (2021)
19. Francalanza, A., Aceto, L., Ingólfsdóttir, A.: Monitorability for the Hennessy-Milner logic with recursion. FMSD **51**(1), 87–116 (2017)
20. Havelund, K., Peled, D.: Runtime verification: from propositional to first-order temporal logic. In: Colombo, C., Leucker, M. (eds.) RV 2018. LNCS, vol. 11237, pp. 90–112. Springer, Cham (2018). https://doi.org/10.1007/978-3-030-03769-7_7
21. Havelund, K., Roşu, G.: Monitoring Java programs with Java PathExplorer. Electron. Notes Theor. Comput. Sci. **55**(2), 200–217 (2001)
22. Henzinger, T.A., Saraç, N.E.: Monitorability under assumptions. In: Deshmukh, J., Ničković, D. (eds.) RV 2020. LNCS, vol. 12399, pp. 3–18. Springer, Cham (2020). https://doi.org/10.1007/978-3-030-60508-7_1
23. Kim, M., Viswanathan, M., Ben-Abdallah, H., Kannan, S., Lee, I., Sokolsky, O.: Formally specified monitoring of temporal properties. In: ECRTS, pp. 114–122. IEEE (1999)
24. Kupferman, O., Vardi, M.Y.: Model checking of safety properties. Formal Methods Syst. Des. **19**(3), 291–314 (2001)
25. Leucker, M.: Sliding between model checking and runtime verification. In: Qadeer, S., Tasiran, S. (eds.) RV 2012. LNCS, vol. 7687, pp. 82–87. Springer, Heidelberg (2013). https://doi.org/10.1007/978-3-642-35632-2_10
26. Meredith, P.O., Jin, D., Griffith, D., Chen, F., Roşu, G.: An overview of the MOP runtime verification framework. Int. J. Softw. Tools Technol. Transfer **14**(3), 249–289 (2012)
27. Blech, J.O., Falcone, Y., Becker, K.: Towards certified runtime verification. In: Aoki, T., Taguchi, K. (eds.) ICFEM 2012. LNCS, vol. 7635, pp. 494–509. Springer, Heidelberg (2012). https://doi.org/10.1007/978-3-642-34281-3_34
28. Schneider, J., Basin, D., Krstić, S., Traytel, D.: A formally verified monitor for metric first-order temporal logic. In: Finkbeiner, B., Mariani, L. (eds.) RV 2019. LNCS, vol. 11757, pp. 310–328. Springer, Cham (2019). https://doi.org/10.1007/978-3-030-32079-9_18
29. Stucki, S., Sánchez, C., Schneider, G., Bonakdarpour, B.: Gray-box monitoring of hyperproperties with an application to privacy. FMSD **58**, 1–34 (2021)
30. Walukiewicz, I.: Completeness of Kozen's Axiomatisation of the propositional mu-calculus. In: Proceedings, 10th Annual IEEE Symposium on Logic in Computer Science, pp. 14–24. IEEE (1995)

A Monitoring Tool for Linear-Time μHML

Luca Aceto[2,3], Antonis Achilleos[2], Duncan Paul Attard[1,2(✉)],
Léo Exibard[2], Adrian Francalanza[1], and Anna Ingólfsdóttir[2]

[1] University of Malta, Msida, Malta
{duncan.attard.01,afra1}@um.edu.mt
[2] Reykjavik University, Reykjavik, Iceland
{luca,antonios,duncanpa17,
leoe,annai}@ru.is
[3] Gran Sasso Science Institute,
L'Aquila, Italy
luca.aceto@gssi.it

Abstract. We present the implementation of a prototype tool that runtime checks specifications written in a maximally-expressive safety fragment of the linear-time modal μ-calculus called MAXHML. Our technical development is founded on previous results that give a compositional synthesis procedure for generating monitors from MAXHML formulae. This paper instantiates this synthesis to a first-order setting, where systems produce executions containing events that carry data. We augment the logic with predicates over data, and extend the synthesis procedure to generate executable monitors for Erlang, a general-purpose programming language. These monitors are instrumented via inlining to induce minimal runtime overhead. Our monitoring algorithm also maintains information, which it uses to explain how verdicts are reached.

Keywords: Runtime verification · Linear-time specifications · Monitor synthesis

1 Introduction

Runtime Verification (RV) [13,17,36,52] is a lightweight verification technique that dynamically checks the *current execution* to determine whether a System under Scrutiny (SuS) satisfies or violates some correctness stipulation. These stipulations are generally expressed using a specification logic to formally describe the behaviour the SuS should observe. RV synthesises specifications

Supported by the doctoral student grant (No: 207055) and the MoVeMnt project (No: 217987) of the Icelandic Research Fund, the BehAPI project funded by the EU H2020 RISE of the Marie Skłodowska-Curie action (No: 778233), the ENDEAVOUR Scholarship Scheme (Group B, national funds), and the MIUR project PRIN 2017FTXR7S IT MATTERS.

© IFIP International Federation for Information Processing 2022
M. H. ter Beek and M. Sirjani (Eds.): COORDINATION 2022, LNCS 13271, pp. 200–219, 2022.
https://doi.org/10.1007/978-3-031-08143-9_12

into *monitors*: computational entities that are instrumented with the SuS to analyse its execution (expressed as a trace of events) *incrementally*, and reach *verdicts* that cannot be retracted when observing future events. Figure 1 depicts this set-up.

The vast majority of existing work and tooling efforts on RV focus on checking specifications that describe properties of *system executions* (Fig. 1a). Most of these studies are conducted in the context of temporal logics that are based on LTL (*e.g.*, [19,21,23–25,41,58–60]). Despite its widespread use, LTL has limited expressiveness. For instance, it cannot express properties such as *'every even position in the execution satisfies some proposition p'* [4,62].

The modal μ-calculus with a linear-time interpretation [49] has been shown to embed several other standard logics, including LTL, making it suitable to express a wider range of properties. Recent work [3,4] studies monitors for μHML [7,51], a reformulation of the μ-calculus. One aspect that sets that work apart from the ones cited above is the modular approach the authors adopt in their technical development. Rather than redefining the semantics of the logic to assimilate the notion of monitoring verdicts, their study identifies *runtime monitorable* syntactic fragments of μHML, delineating between its semantics on the one hand, and the operational semantics of monitors on the other. The authors define a synthesis procedure that generates *correct* monitors from these fragments. They also establish a correspondence between monitor acceptance (resp. rejection) verdicts and satisfactions (resp. violations) in the logic, and show that the fragments identified are *maximally-expressive*, *i.e.*, characterise all monitorable properties. This separation of concerns provides a principled approach to RV tool construction.

This paper presents the implementation of a prototype tool that builds on the theoretical foundations of [3,4]. It adopts the fragment MAXHML of μHML that is used to specify safety properties on the *current system execution*. The study in [3,4] considers regular properties, which arguably limits its applicability to a broader setting where executions contain events that carry data [17,35]. We, therefore, lift the results of that study to a first-order setting, and extend the logic and synthesis procedure with predicates *over data*. Our adaptation of the monitor synthesis closely follows the one of [3,4], giving us high assurances that the corresponding monitors are correct. A facet that is often overlooked in RV is *verdict explainability*, where tools justify how monitoring judgements are reached [39]. Instantiations of this concept are commonplace in related fields. For example, model checking tools [48] produce diagnostic traces that explain why a model fails to satisfy some specification; in the same spirit, programming language frameworks capture runtime information and present it in the form of stack traces or core dumps. We take a first step in this direction, and engineer our monitoring algorithm to derive an explanation that is constructed using the monitor operational semantics of [3,4]. Since our prototype tool does not yet perform space optimisations for the purposes of explainable verdicts, this feature is intended for debugging or offline use.

In a parallel research direction, we study other monitorable μHML fragments in a *branching-time* setting [1,2,37,38], where the logic describes prop-

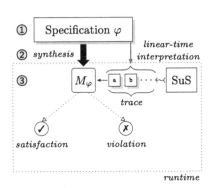
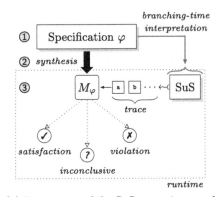

(a) Property φ of the SuS execution *trace*   (b) Property φ of the SuS execution *graph*

Fig. 1. RV of linear- and branching-time property φ by analysing the SuS trace

erties about the *computation graph* of programs (Fig. 1b). Much of this body of work is concretised as detectEr [12–14,26], a runtime monitoring tool for concurrent Erlang programs. The material we propose in this paper complements the one in detectEr, contributing towards one tool that can runtime check specifications under their linear- and branching-time interpretations. Our contributions are:

(i) We extend the logic MAXHML with data support, and show how this is used to specify properties on the current system execution, Sect. 2;

(ii) adapt the monitor synthesis and operational semantics of [3,4] to enable monitors to reach verdicts based on the data carried by trace events, Sect. 3;

(iii) discuss the challenges encountered when instantiating the synthesis in Sect. 3 to a general-purpose programming language, and overview the technique we use to instrument monitors that induce minimal runtime overhead, Sect. 4.

2 The Logic

We overview our chosen logic, MAXHML, a *maximally-expressive* syntactic fragment of μHML used to describe safety properties of system executions [3]. It assumes a set of *external* actions $\alpha, \beta \in$ ACT, together with a distinguished internal action $\tau \notin$ ACT that represents one *internal* step of computation. External actions range over values taken from some (potentially infinite) data domain, $\mathbb{D}$. Executions, also referred to as traces, are *infinite* sequences of external system actions that abstractly represent *complete* system runs. We reserve the metavariables $t, u \in$ ACT$^\omega$ to represent infinite traces, and use αt to denote an infinite trace that starts with α and continues with t.

MAXHML^d Syntax

$$\varphi, \psi \in \text{MAXHML}^d ::= \text{tt} \mid \text{ff} \mid \langle \boldsymbol{x}, e \rangle \varphi \mid [\boldsymbol{x}, e] \varphi \mid \varphi \vee \psi \mid \varphi \wedge \psi \mid \max X.(\varphi) \mid X$$

MAXHML^d Semantics

$$[\![\text{tt}, \sigma]\!] \triangleq \text{ACT}^\omega \qquad\qquad\qquad [\![\text{ff}, \sigma]\!] \triangleq \emptyset$$

$$[\![\langle \boldsymbol{x}, e \rangle \varphi, \sigma]\!] \triangleq \{ t \mid (\exists u. \exists \alpha. \, t = \alpha u \text{ and } e[^\alpha/_x] \Downarrow \text{true and } u \in [\![\varphi[^\alpha/_x], \sigma]\!]) \}$$

$$[\![[\boldsymbol{x}, e] \varphi, \sigma]\!] \triangleq \{ t \mid (\forall u. \forall \alpha. \, (t = \alpha u \text{ and } e[^\alpha/_x] \Downarrow \text{true}) \text{ implies } u \in [\![\varphi[^\alpha/_x], \sigma]\!]) \}$$

$$[\![\varphi \vee \psi, \sigma]\!] \triangleq [\![\varphi, \sigma]\!] \cup [\![\psi, \sigma]\!] \qquad\qquad [\![\varphi \wedge \psi, \sigma]\!] \triangleq [\![\varphi, \sigma]\!] \cap [\![\psi, \sigma]\!]$$

$$[\![\max X.(\varphi), \sigma]\!] \triangleq \bigcup \{ S \mid S \subseteq [\![\varphi, \sigma[X \mapsto S]]\!] \} \qquad [\![X, \sigma]\!] \triangleq \sigma(X)$$

Fig. 2. Syntax and linear-time semantics for the logic MAXHML^d

Figure 2 shows our extension of MAXHML, called MAXHML^d, with predicates over data. Its syntax assumes a denumerable set of logical variables, $X, Y \in \text{LVAR}$. In addition to the standard Boolean constructs, the logic can express recursive properties as greatest fixed point formulae, $\max X.(\varphi)$, that bind the free occurrences of X in φ. The existential and universal modalities $\langle \boldsymbol{x}, e \rangle \varphi$ and $[\boldsymbol{x}, e] \varphi$ express the dual notions of *possibility* and *necessity* respectively. We augment these two modal constructs with *symbolic actions*, $(\boldsymbol{x}, e)$, to enable the reasoning on the data carried by external actions. Symbolic actions are pairs consisting of data variables, $x, y \in \text{DVAR}$, and *decidable* Boolean constraint expressions, $e, f \in \text{BEXP}$. Data variables range over the domain $\mathbb{D}$ of data values, and bind the free occurrences of x in the expression e of the modality *and* in the continuation formula φ. The set BEXP, defined over $\mathbb{D}$ and DVAR, consists of the usual Boolean operators $\neg$ and $\wedge$, together with a set of relational operators that depends on $\mathbb{D}$, which we leave unspecified. For clarity, we omit writing the Boolean constraint expression e in modalities when $e = \text{true}$, and use **bold** lettering to identify binders in symbolic actions. In the sequel, the standard notions of open and closed expressions, and formula equality up to alpha-conversion are used. A formula is said to be *guarded* if every fixed point variable X appears within the scope of a modality that is itself in the scope of X. For example, $\max X.([\boldsymbol{x}]\text{ff} \wedge [\boldsymbol{y}]X)$ is guarded, as is $\max X.([\boldsymbol{x}]([\boldsymbol{y}]\text{ff} \wedge X))$, while $[\boldsymbol{x}]\max X.([\boldsymbol{y}]\text{ff} \wedge X)$ is not. Without loss of expressiveness [50], we assume all formulae to be guarded.

The linear-time interpretation of MAXHML^d is given by the denotational semantic function $[\![-]\!]$ that maps a formula to a *set* of traces. The function $[\![-]\!]$ uses valuations, $\sigma : \text{LVAR} \to 2^{\text{ACT}^\omega}$, to define the semantics inductively on the structure of formulae. The value $\sigma(X)$ is the set of traces that are assumed to satisfy X. In $[\![-]\!]$, modal formulae are interpreted w.r.t. symbolic actions. A symbolic action $(\boldsymbol{x}, e)$ describes a *set* of external system actions. An action α is in this set when the data value it carries satisfies the Boolean constraint expression e that is instantiated with the *applied substitution* $[^\alpha/_x]$, i.e., $e[^\alpha/_x] \Downarrow \text{true}$ (see Fig. 2). The possibility formula $\langle \boldsymbol{x}, e \rangle \varphi$ denotes all the traces αu where α is in the action set $(\boldsymbol{x}, e)$ *and* u satisfies the continuation $\varphi[^\alpha/_x]$. Dually, $[\boldsymbol{x}, e]\varphi$ denotes all the traces αu that, *if* prefixed by some α from the action set $(\boldsymbol{x}, e)$, u *then* satisfies $\varphi[^\alpha/_x]$. The set of traces satisfying the greatest fixed point formula $\max X.(\varphi)$ is the union of all the post-fixed point solutions, $S \subseteq \mathrm{ACT}^\omega$, of the function induced by the formula φ. Since the interpretation of *closed* formulae does not depend on the environment σ, we may use $\llbracket\varphi\rrbracket$ in lieu of $\llbracket\varphi, \sigma\rrbracket$. A trace t satisfies (the closed) formula φ when $t \in \llbracket\varphi\rrbracket$, and violates φ when $t \notin \llbracket\varphi\rrbracket$.

To facilitate our exposition in this section and Sect. 3, we let $\mathbb{D} = \mathbb{Z}$, and fix the set of operators used in BEXP to $\neg$, $\wedge$ and $=$. Sect. 4 considers the general case where the data carried by external actions can consist of *composite* data types. Henceforth, the terms *action* and *event* are used synonymously.

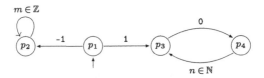

Fig. 3. Token server that issues integer identifier tokens to client programs

2.1 Trace Properties

Consider the model of a reactive token server, p_1 in Fig. 3, that issues client programs with identifier tokens that they use as an alias to write logs to a remote logging service. Clients request an identifier by sending the command 0, which the server then fulfils by replying with a new token, $n \in \mathbb{N}$. Since the server is itself a program that also uses the remote logging service, it is launched with its (reserved) identifier token 1. Figure 3 shows that from its initial state p_1, the token server either: *(i)* starts up with the token 1 and transitions to p_3, where it waits for incoming client requests, or, *(ii)* fails to start and transitions with a status of -1 to the sink p_2, thereafter exhibiting *undefined behaviour*. There are a number of properties we want *executions* of this token server to observe.

Example 1. One rudimentary property the current execution of server p_1 should uphold is that '*no failure occurs at start up*'. This safety requirement is expressed in terms of the MAXHML^d formula:

$$[\boldsymbol{x}, x = -1]\mathsf{ff} \qquad\qquad (\varphi_1)$$

The symbolic action $(\boldsymbol{x}, x = -1)$ defines the singleton set $\{-1\} \subset \mathbb{Z}$ of external system actions. Necessity modal formulae $[\boldsymbol{x}, e]\varphi$ state that, for *any* trace prefix α in the set defined by $(\boldsymbol{x}, e)$, the trace continuation u must then satisfy φ. However, *no* trace satisfies ff. This means that, in order for server traces *not* to violate formula φ_1, they must start with actions $\alpha \notin \{-1\}$. The set of traces $1 . (0 . \mathbb{N})^\omega$ exhibited by p_1 satisfies this property, whereas $-1 . \mathbb{Z}^\omega$ does not. ∎

Example 2. Further to the stipulation of Example 1, we require that *'the server is initialised with the identifier token 1'*, expressed as:

$$[\boldsymbol{x}, x = -1]\mathsf{ff} \wedge \langle \boldsymbol{x}, x = 1\rangle\mathsf{tt} \qquad\qquad (\varphi_2)$$

The conjunct $[\boldsymbol{x}, x = -1]\mathsf{ff}$ guards against traces of p_1 exhibiting failure when loading; $\langle \boldsymbol{x}, x = 1\rangle\mathsf{tt}$ asserts that the trace exhibits 1 at start up, indicating a successful initialisation of the server. Formula φ_2 is satisfied exactly by server traces of the form $1 . \mathbb{N}^\omega$. Note that the binders $\boldsymbol{x}$ in $[\boldsymbol{x}, x = -1]$ and $\langle \boldsymbol{x}, x = 1\rangle$ of φ_2 bind the variables x in *different* scopes. ∎

The symbolic actions of Examples 1 and 2 define sets of external actions w.r.t. literal values (*e.g.* $-1, 1$). More generally, action sets can be defined using constraint expressions that refer to other data variables within the same scope.

Example 3. Amongst the executions satisfying φ_2 are those where the server accidentally returns its identifier token 1 in reply to client requests. We therefore demand that *'the server private token 1 is not leaked in client replies'*. Formula φ_3 expresses this recursive property in a general way (note that Boolean constraint expressions $e = \mathsf{true}$ are elided):

$$[\boldsymbol{x}]\mathsf{max}\,X.\big([\boldsymbol{y}]([\boldsymbol{z}, x = z]\mathsf{ff} \wedge [\boldsymbol{z}, x \neq z]X)\big) \qquad\qquad (\varphi_3)$$

The symbolic action $(\boldsymbol{x}, \mathsf{true})$ in the first necessity defines the set of actions $\mathbb{Z}$. Its binder, $\boldsymbol{x}$, binds the variable x in $\mathsf{max}\,X.\big([\boldsymbol{y}]([\boldsymbol{z}, x = z]\mathsf{ff} \wedge [\boldsymbol{z}, x \neq z]X)\big)$. For some initial server action $\alpha \in \mathbb{Z}$, applying the substitution $[^\alpha/_x]$ to this continuation and unfolding the recursion variable once, gives the residual formula:

$$[\boldsymbol{y}]\Big([\boldsymbol{z}, \alpha = z]\mathsf{ff} \wedge [\boldsymbol{z}, \alpha \neq z]\mathsf{max}\,X.\big([\boldsymbol{y}]([\boldsymbol{z}, \alpha = z]\mathsf{ff} \wedge [\boldsymbol{z}, \alpha \neq z]X)\big)\Big) \qquad (\varphi_3')$$

The necessity $[\boldsymbol{y}]$ maps $\boldsymbol{y}$ to the second server action β in the trace, *i.e.*, $[^\beta/_y]$. Applying $[^\beta/_y]$ to $[\boldsymbol{z}, \alpha = z]\mathsf{ff}$ and $[\boldsymbol{z}, \alpha \neq z]\mathsf{max}X\big([\boldsymbol{y}]([\boldsymbol{z}, \alpha = z]\mathsf{ff} \wedge [\boldsymbol{z}, \alpha \neq z]X)\big)$ leaves both sub-formulae unchanged, since $\boldsymbol{y}$ binds no variables. For the third server action γ, the modalities $[\boldsymbol{z}, \alpha = z]$ and $[\boldsymbol{z}, \alpha \neq z]$ map $\boldsymbol{z}$ to γ. Formula φ_3 is violated, ff, when the constraint $\alpha = z[^\gamma/_z]$ holds, *i.e.*, $\alpha \in \{n \in \mathbb{Z} \mid \alpha = \gamma\}$.

Crucially, a *fresh* scope for data variables is created upon each unfolding of X, such that $\boldsymbol{y}$ and $\boldsymbol{z}$ can be mapped to new values. By contrast, the value in $\boldsymbol{x}$ is substituted for *once* in φ_3' and remains fixed when X is unfolded. Concretely, formula φ_3 compares actions at *every* odd position in the trace against the one at the head. Interpreting φ_3 over traces that the token sever exhibits on *successful* initialisation ensures that in particular, $1 . (0 . \{n \in \mathbb{N} \mid n \neq 1\})^* . (0 . 1) . \mathbb{N}^\omega$ are violating. We remark that this property is *not* expressible in LTL. ∎

3 Monitor Synthesis

The logic MAXHML^d is interpreted over infinite traces that represent *complete* system runs (refer to Sect. 2). In (online) RV where the SuS is *reactive*, obtaining complete runs is typically not possible [17,52], since the current trace corresponds to a prefix that is incrementally extended as the system execution unfolds. The notions of *good* and *bad prefixes* for monitorable properties provide sufficient evidence to determine acceptance or rejection. Informally, a good (resp. bad) prefix is a finite trace for which *every* extension satisfies (resp. violates) a property φ [10,24]. Monitors capture this principle through *irrevocable verdicts* that, once reached, cannot be retracted when observing future events.

Monitors may be viewed as processes via the syntax given in Fig. 4. This syntax differs from its regular counterpart of [3,4] in that it augments the prefixing construct with symbolic actions, $(\boldsymbol{x}, e)$. Besides the prefixing, external choice, and recursion constructs of CCS [54], the syntax of Fig. 4 includes disjunctive, $\oplus$, and conjunctive, $\otimes$, *parallel composition*. We use the symbol $\odot$ to refer to both $\oplus$ and $\otimes$ when needed. Monitor verdict states, $v \in \text{VRD}$, are expressed as yes and no, respectively denoting *acceptance* and *rejection*.

Monitor Syntax

$$m, n \in \text{MON} ::= v \quad | \quad (\boldsymbol{x}, e).m \quad | \quad m{+}n \quad | \quad m{\oplus}n \quad | \quad m{\otimes}n \quad | \quad \text{rec}\,X.m \quad | \quad X$$
$$v \in \text{VRD} ::= \text{yes} \quad | \quad \text{no}$$

Monitor Small-Step Semantics

$$\text{MVRD} \frac{}{v \xrightarrow{\alpha} v} \qquad \text{MACT} \frac{e[^{\alpha}/_{x}] \Downarrow \text{true}}{(\boldsymbol{x}, e).m \xrightarrow{\alpha} m[^{\alpha}/_{x}]} \qquad \text{MCHS}_{\text{L}} \frac{m \xrightarrow{\alpha} m'}{m{+}n \xrightarrow{\alpha} m'}$$

$$\text{MTAU}_{\text{L}} \frac{m \xrightarrow{\tau} m'}{m{\odot}n \xrightarrow{\tau} m'{\odot}n} \qquad \text{MPAR} \frac{m \xrightarrow{\alpha} m' \quad n \xrightarrow{\alpha} n'}{m{\odot}n \xrightarrow{\alpha} m'{\odot}n'} \qquad \text{MDIS}Y_{\text{L}} \frac{}{\text{yes}{\oplus}m \xrightarrow{\tau} \text{yes}}$$

$$\text{MDIS}N_{\text{L}} \frac{}{\text{no}{\oplus}m \xrightarrow{\tau} m} \qquad \text{MCON}Y_{\text{L}} \frac{}{\text{yes}{\otimes}m \xrightarrow{\tau} m} \qquad \text{MCON}N_{\text{L}} \frac{}{\text{no}{\otimes}m \xrightarrow{\tau} \text{no}}$$

$$\text{MREC} \frac{}{\text{rec}\,X.m \xrightarrow{\tau} m[^{\text{rec}\,X.m}/_{x}]}$$

Monitor Synthesis

$$(\!| \text{tt} |\!) = \text{yes} \qquad\qquad\qquad (\!| \text{ff} |\!) = \text{no}$$
$$(\!| \langle \boldsymbol{x}, e \rangle \varphi |\!) = (\boldsymbol{x}, e).(\!| \varphi |\!) + (\boldsymbol{x}, \neg e).\text{no} \qquad (\!| [\boldsymbol{x}, e] \varphi |\!) = (\boldsymbol{x}, e).(\!| \varphi |\!) + (\boldsymbol{x}, \neg e).\text{yes}$$
$$(\!| \varphi \vee \psi |\!) = (\!| \varphi |\!) \oplus (\!| \psi |\!) \qquad\qquad (\!| \varphi \wedge \psi |\!) = (\!| \varphi |\!) \otimes (\!| \psi |\!)$$
$$(\!| \max X.(\varphi) |\!) = \text{rec}\,X.(\!| \varphi |\!) \qquad\qquad (\!| X |\!) = X$$

Fig. 4. Syntax, synthesis, and small-step semantics for parallel monitors

Figure 4 outlines the behaviour of monitors, where the transitions rules MREC, MCHS$_\text{L}$, and its symmetric case MCHS$_\text{R}$ (omitted), are standard. Rule MACT describes the analysis monitors perform, where the binder x in the symbolic action (x, e) is mapped to an external system action α, yielding the substitution $[^\alpha/_x]$ that is applied to the Boolean constraint expression e. The monitor $(x, e).m$ analyses α *only if* the instantiated constraint $e[^\alpha/_x]$ is satisfied, whereupon α is substituted for the *free* variable x in the body m. Verdict irrevocability is modelled by MVRD, where once in a verdict state v, any action can be analysed by monitors without altering v. Rule MPAR enables parallel sub-monitors to transition in lock-step when they analyse the *same* action α. The rest of the rules (omitting the obvious symmetric cases) cater for the internal reconfiguration of monitors. For instance, rules MDISY_L and MDISN_L state that in disjunctive parallelism, **yes** supersedes the verdicts of other monitors, whilst **no** does not affect the verdicts of other monitors; MCONY_L and MCONN_L express the dual case for parallel conjunctions. Finally, MTAU$_\text{L}$ and its symmetric analogue permit sub-monitors to execute internal reconfigurations independently.

Our adaptation $(\!|-|\!)$ of the compositional synthesis procedure for regular monitors [3, 4] is also given in Fig. 4. It generates monitors for $\varphi \in \text{MAXHML}^d$, following the inductive structure of formulae. The translation for truth and falsehood, and the greatest fixed point and recursion variable constructs is direct; disjunction and conjunction are transformed to their parallel counterparts. Modal constructs are mapped to *deterministic* external choices, where the left summand handles the case where a system action α is in the set described by the symbolic action (x, e), and the right summand, the case where α is *not* in this set. This embodies the duality of possibility and necessity: when α is not in the action set (x, e), the formula $\langle x, e \rangle \varphi$ is violated, whereas $[x, e]\varphi$ is trivially satisfied.

Example 4. The monitor m_2 synthesised from formula φ_2 is:

$$\begin{aligned}
(\!|\varphi_2|\!) &= (\!|[x, x = -1]\text{ff} \wedge \langle x, x = 1 \rangle \text{tt}|\!) = (\!|[x, x = -1]\text{ff}|\!) \otimes (\!|\langle x, x = 1\rangle \text{tt}|\!) \quad (m_2) \\
&= \big((x, x = -1).\text{no} + (x, x \neq -1).\text{yes}\big) \otimes \big((x, x = 1).\text{yes} + (x, x \neq 1).\text{no}\big)
\end{aligned}$$

When analysing the server traces $-1 . \mathbb{Z}^\omega$, monitor m_2 reduces to $\text{no} \otimes \text{no}$ via the rule MPAR. Its premises are obtained by applying the MCHS$_\text{L}$ and MACT to the left sub-monitor, and MCHS$_\text{R}$ and MACT to the right sub-monitor, giving:

$$(x, x = -1).\text{no} + (x, x \neq -1).\text{yes} \xrightarrow{-1} \text{no} \quad \text{and} \quad (x, x = 1).\text{yes} + (x, x \neq 1).\text{no} \xrightarrow{-1} \text{no}$$

Monitor $\text{no} \otimes \text{no}$ afterwards transitions internally, $\text{no} \otimes \text{no} \xrightarrow{\tau} \text{no}$, via either rule MCON$N_\text{L}$ or MCONN_R. Analogously, m_2 reaches the verdict **yes** when analysing the server traces $1 . \mathbb{N}^\omega$. Recall that when in a verdict state, the monitor can *always* analyse future events by virtue of MVRD, flagging the *same* outcome. The behaviour of monitor m_2 corresponds to the property that φ_2 describes (refer to [3, 4] for details). ∎

Example 5. Consider the recursive monitor m_3 synthesised from formula φ_3:

$$(x).\mathsf{rec}\, X.\, (y).\Big(\big((z, x = z).\mathsf{no} + (z, x \neq z).\mathsf{yes}\big) \otimes \big((z, x \neq z).X + (z, x = z).\mathsf{yes}\big)\Big) \quad (m_3)$$

For the server traces $1.0.2.0.1.(0.\mathbb{N})^{\omega}$, m_3 instantiates x to the value 1 at the head, and applies the substitution $[^1/_x]$ to the residual monitor, giving:

$$\mathsf{rec}\, X.\, (y).\Big(\big((z, 1 = z).\mathsf{no} + (z, 1 \neq z).\mathsf{yes}\big) \otimes \big((z, 1 \neq z).X + (z, 1 = z).\mathsf{yes}\big)\Big) \quad (m_3')$$

Hereafter, m_3' unfolds continually, ensuring that no event carries the value 1 observed at the head of the trace. At every even position, y is instantiated with 0, whereas the binders z in each of the sub-monitors composed in parallel compare the value carried by events occurring at odd trace positions against 1. Monitor m_3' reaches the verdict no via these reductions:

$$m_3' \xrightarrow{\tau} (y).\Big(\big((z, 1 = z).\mathsf{no} + (z, 1 \neq z).\mathsf{yes}\big) \otimes \big((z, 1 \neq z).m_3' + (z, 1 = z).\mathsf{yes}\big)\Big) \quad (m_3'')$$

$$\xrightarrow{0} \big((z, 1 = z).\mathsf{no} + (z, 1 \neq z).\mathsf{yes}\big) \otimes \big((z, 1 \neq z).m_3' + (z, 1 = z).\mathsf{yes}\big) \quad (m_3''')$$

$$\xrightarrow{2} \mathsf{yes} \otimes m_3' \xrightarrow{\tau} m_3'' \xrightarrow{\tau} m_3''' \xrightarrow{0} m_3''' \xrightarrow{1} \mathsf{no} \otimes \mathsf{yes} \xrightarrow{\tau} \mathsf{no} \xrightarrow{n} \mathsf{no} \xrightarrow{n} \dots$$

For the non-rejecting server traces $1.(0.\{n \in \mathbb{N} \mid n \neq 1\})^{\omega}$, monitor m_3' visits the state $\mathsf{yes} \otimes m_3'$ indefinitely, where m_3' supersedes the uninfluential verdict yes following the rule MCONY$_L$. ∎

4   Implementation

We implement our tool in Erlang [11,27], a general-purpose programming language that adopts the *actor model* of concurrency [8,44]. In this model, processes communicate exclusively by addressing *asynchronous messages* to one another via their uniquely-assigned Process ID (PID). Besides sending and receiving messages, processes can also fork other processes. This concurrency paradigm is tailored to reactive systems, making it ideal for our study.

4.1   Refining the Model

We refine the logic of Sect. 2 and monitor model of Sect. 3 to fit the Erlang use-case, where data can consist of composite types, such as tuples and lists. Accordingly, we generalise our definition of external actions as follows. Let $l \in \mathcal{L}$ be a finite set of *action labels*, and $d_1, d_2, \dots$ be data values taken from a set of data domains $\mathcal{D} = \bigcup_{i \in \mathbb{N}} \mathbb{D}_i$ (*e.g.* integers, PIDs, tuples, *etc.*). An external action

α is a tuple, $(l, d_1, \ldots, d_n)$, where the first element is the label, and $d_1, \ldots, d_n$ is the *data payload* carried by α. We use the notation $l(d_1, \ldots, d_n)$ to write α.

Patterns, $p \in \mathrm{PAT}$, are counterparts to external system actions. These are defined as tuples, $(l, \boldsymbol{x_1}, \ldots, \boldsymbol{x_n})$, where $x_1, x_2, \ldots$ are data variables ranging over $\mathcal{D}$. Our revised definition of symbolic actions in the modal constructs $\langle p, e \rangle \varphi$ and $[p, e]\varphi$ uses these patterns instead of variables (*cf.* Sect. 2). The binders $\boldsymbol{x_1}, \ldots, \boldsymbol{x_n}$ in p bind the free occurrences of $x_1, \ldots, x_n$ in the Boolean constraint e, and in the continuation φ. We define the function, $\mathsf{match}(p, \alpha)$, to handle *pattern matching*. This function returns a substitution, $\pi : \mathrm{DVAR} \rightharpoonup \mathcal{D}$, that maps the variables in p to the corresponding data values in the payload carried by α, when the shape of the pattern matches that of the action, or $\perp$ if the match is unsuccessful. Analogous to the symbolic actions of Sect. 2, (p, e) describes a set of actions: an action α is in this set if *(i)* the patten match succeeds, *i.e.,* $\mathsf{match}(p, \alpha) = \pi$, and, *(ii)* the *instantiated* Boolean constraint expression $e\pi$ holds.

To instantiate our tool to Erlang, we use the action label set $\mathcal{L} = \{\rightarrow, \leftarrow, \star, !, ?\}$, that captures the lifecycle of, and interaction between processes. The *fork* action, $\rightarrow$, is exhibited by a process when it creates a child; its dual, $\leftarrow$, is exhibited by the child process upon *initialisation*. An *error* action, $\star$, signals abnormal process behaviour; *send* and *receive*, respectively ! and ?, denote interaction. Table 1 details the actions related to these labels, and the data payload they carry.

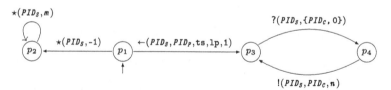

Fig. 5. Client-server interaction of the Erlang token server implementation

Our token server of Fig. 3 is readily translatable to Erlang, as shown in Fig. 5. The server starts when its main function, $\mathtt{lp}$, in the Erlang module $\mathtt{ts}$ is invoked, state p_1. From p_1, it transitions to p_3, exhibiting the initialisation event $\leftarrow(PID_S, PID_P, \mathtt{ts}, \mathtt{lp}, 1)$; the placeholders PID_S and PID_P respectively denote the PID values of the token server process and of the parent process forking the server. At p_3, the server accepts client requests, consisting of the tuple $\{PID_C, 0\}$, where PID_C denotes the PID of the client, and 0 is the command requesting a new token. From state p_4, the server replies with n, and transitions back to p_3. This client-server interaction results in the server events $?(PID_S, \{PID_C, 0\})$ and $!(PID_S, PID_C, n)$. When the server fails at startup, it exhibits abnormal behaviour, shown as the error events $\star(PID_S, \mathtt{-1})$ and $\star(PID_S, m)$.

Example 6. Formula φ_2 w.r.t. the Erlang server of Fig. 5 is expressed as follows:

$$[\star(x_1, x_2), x_2 = \mathtt{-1}]\mathsf{ff} \wedge \langle \leftarrow(x_1, x_2, x_3, x_4, x_5), x_5 = 1 \rangle \mathsf{tt} \qquad (\varphi_4)$$

Table 1. Actions capturing the behaviour exhibited by Erlang processes

Action α	Action pattern p	Variables	Description
fork	$\rightarrow(x_1,x_2,y_1,y_2,y_3)$	x_1	PID of the parent process forking x_2
initialise	$\leftarrow(x_2,x_1,y_1,y_2,y_3)$		
		x_2	PID of the child process forked by x_1
		y_1,y_2,y_3	Function signature forked by x_1
error	$\star(x_1,y_1)$	x_1	PID of the erroneous process
		y_1	Error datum, *e.g.* error reason, *etc.*
send	$!(x_1,x_2,y_1)$	x_1	PID of the process sending the message
		x_2	PID of the recipient process
		y_1	Message datum, *e.g.* integer, tuple, *etc.*
receive	$?(x_2,y_1)$	x_2	PID of the recipient process
		y_1	Message datum, *e.g.* integer, tuple, *etc.*

The patterns in the left and right conjuncts of φ_4 match the error and initialisation events. When p_1 exhibits an error at start up, $\mathsf{match}(\star(x_1,x_2),\star(\mathit{PID_S},\text{-}1))$, yields the substitution $\pi = [^{\mathit{PID_S}}/x_1, ^{\text{-}1}/x_2]$, and the instantiated Boolean constraint $(x_2 = \text{-}1)\pi$ holds. For the same event, $\mathsf{match}(\leftarrow(x_1,x_2,x_3,x_4,x_5),\star(\mathit{PID_S},\text{-}1)) = \bot$ in the right conjunct, leading to a violation of formula φ_4. The reverse argument applies for when p_1 loads successfully, where φ_4 is satisfied. In φ_4, the pattern variables x_1 in $\star(x_1,x_2)$, and x_1,x_2,x_3,x_4 in $\leftarrow(x_1,x_2,x_3,x_4,x_5)$ are *redundant*.

$$[\leftarrow(\_,\_,\_,\_,x_5)]\mathsf{max}\,X\Big([\_]\big([!(\_,\_,z_3),x_5 = z_3]\mathsf{ff} \wedge [!(\_,\_,z_3),x_5 \neq z_3]X\big)\Big) \qquad (\varphi_5)$$

Formula φ_5 restates φ_3 with pattern matching. It uses the 'don't care' pattern $\_$, that matches *arbitrary* values, eliding redundant patterns and variables. ∎

4.2   The Monitor Synthesis

Our synthesis from MAXHML^d specifications to executable Erlang monitors follows that of Fig. 4. Figure 6 omits the cases for the falsity, necessity and conjunction constructs, as these are analogous to the ones for tt, $\langle p, e \rangle \varphi$ and $\varphi \vee \psi$. The translation from specifications to monitors is executed in three stages. First, a formula is parsed into its equivalent Abstract Syntax Tree (AST). This is then

$$(\!|\text{tt}|\!) = \text{yes} \qquad\qquad (\!|\varphi \vee \psi|\!) = \{\text{or}, (\!|\varphi|\!), (\!|\psi|\!)\}$$

$$(\!|\max X.(\varphi)|\!) = \{\text{rec}, \text{fun } X() \to (\!|\varphi|\!) \text{ end}\} \qquad (\!|X|\!) = \{\text{rec}, X\}$$

$$(\!|\langle p,e\rangle\varphi|\!) = \begin{cases} \{\text{chs}, & \overbrace{}^{predicate} \\ \quad \{\text{act}, \text{fun}(p) \text{ when } e \to \text{true}; (\_) \to \text{false end}, \\ \quad \text{fun}(p) \to (\!|\varphi|\!) \text{ end}\}, \\ \quad \{\text{act}, \text{fun}(p) \text{ when } e \to \text{false}; (\_) \to \text{true end}, \\ \quad \underbrace{\text{fun}(\_) \to \text{no end}\}}_{monitor\ body} \\ \} \end{cases} \begin{array}{l} \\ \left.\rule{0pt}{3ex}\right\} {\ left\ action} \\ \\ \left.\rule{0pt}{3ex}\right\} {\ right\ action} \end{array}$$

Fig. 6. Translation from MAXHML^d formulae to Erlang code (excerpt)

passed to the code generator that visits each of its nodes, mapping it to a *monitor description* as per the rules of Fig. 6. The monitor description is encoded as an Erlang AST to simplify its handling. In the final stage, this AST is processed by the Erlang compiler to emit the monitor source code or a BEAM [27] executable.

In this definition of $(\!|-|\!)$, tt (resp. ff) is translated to the Erlang *atom* yes (resp. no) that indicates acceptance (resp. rejection). The remaining cases generate Erlang tuples whose first element, called the *tag*, is an atom that identifies the kind of monitor. Disjunctions (resp. conjunctions) are translated to the tuple tagged with or (resp. and), combining two sub-monitor descriptions. Greatest fixed point constructs, $\max X.(\varphi)$, are mapped to rec tuples consisting of *named* functions, fun X() $\to (\!|\varphi|\!)$ end, that can be referenced by $(\!|X|\!)$. Modal constructs are synthesised as a choice with *left* and *right* actions. An action tuple, act, combines a *predicate* function and an associated *monitor body* that is unfolded when the predicate is true. The predicate function encodes the pattern matching *and* Boolean constraint evaluation as one operation, using two *clauses*. Its first clause, fun(p) when e, tests the constraint e w.r.t. the variables in the pattern p that become *dynamically* instantiated with the data values carried by an action α at runtime. The second catch-all clause (_) covers the remaining cases, namely when: *(i)* either the action under analysis fails to match the pattern, or, *(i)* the pattern matches *but* the Boolean constraint does *not* hold. For the left action, the predicate clause fun(p) when e returns true when the pattern match and guard test succeed, and false otherwise, *i.e.*, (_). This condition is inverted for the right action, modelling cases *(i)* and *(ii)* just described. Our encoding of the aforementioned predicate in terms of Erlang function clauses spares us from implementing the pattern matching and constraint evaluation mechanism. It also enables monitors to support most of the Erlang data types and its full range of Boolean constraint expression syntax [11]. For similar reasons, $(\!|\langle p,e\rangle\varphi|\!)$ encodes the monitor body as fun(p) $\to (\!|\varphi|\!)$ end to delegate scoping to the Erlang language. This facilitates our synthesis and optimises the memory management of monitors by offloading this aspect onto the language runtime.

```
 1 def DERIVEACT(α, mon)              22 def DERIVETAU(mon)
 2 match mon do                       23 match mon do
 3   case yes ∨ no                     24   case {or, yes, m} return yes
 4     print 'Verdict reached'         25   case {or, no, m} return m
 5   case {act, Pred, m}               26   case {and, yes, m} return m
 6     return m(α) # Apply m to event α 27   case {and, no, m} return no
 7   case {chs, m, n}                  28   case {rec, m} return m() # Unfold
 8     if HOLDS(α, m) ∧ ¬HOLDS(α, n)   29   case {Op, m, n} ∧ Op ∈ {or, and}
 9       return DERIVEACT(α, m)        30     if m' = DERIVETAU(m) ∧ m' ≠ ⊥
10     else                       if  31       return m'
       ¬HOLDS(α, m)∧HOLDS(α, n)        32     else
11       return DERIVEACT(α, n)        33       return DERIVETAU(n)
12     end if                          34     end if
13   case {Op, m, n} ∧ Op ∈ {or, and}  35   case Otherwise return ⊥
14     m' = DERIVEACT(α, m)            36 end def
15     n' = DERIVEACT(α, n)
16     return {Op, m', n'}            ─────────────────────────────────
17 end def                             37 def REDUCETAU(m)
─────────────────────────────────     38   if m' = DERIVETAU(m) ∧ m' ≠ ⊥
Expect: Monitor must be in ready state 39     return REDUCETAU(m')
18 def ANALYSEACT(α, m)                40   else
19   m' = DERIVEACT(α, m)              41     return m # No more τ reductions
20   return REDUCETAU(m')              42   end if
21 end def                             43 end def
```

Alg. 1. Algorithm that reduces monitors following the small-step rules of Fig. 4

4.3   The Monitoring Algorithm

The synthesis procedure of Fig. 4 generates monitors that can runtime check formulae in parallel against the same position in the trace via disjunctive and conjunctive parallel composition. Our tool is however engineered to *emulate* parallel monitors, rather than forking processes and delegate their execution to the Erlang runtime. While the latter method tends to simplify the synthesis and runtime monitoring, we adopt the *former* approach for two reasons:

(i) Previous empirical evidence suggests that parallelising via processes may induce high overhead when the RV set-up is considerably scaled [15]. A process-free design may render this overhead more manageable [5,6].
(ii) Emulating parallel monitors requires us to tease apart the synthesised monitor description from its operational semantics. By separating these two aspects, our monitoring algorithm can track the operational rules it applies to reduce the monitor state, and use these to justify how verdicts are reached.

Our monitoring algorithm (Algorithm 1) takes a monitor description m generated by $(\!-\!)$, and performs successive reductions by applying m to events from the trace until a verdict is reached. Simultaneously, the algorithm maintains all the possible *active* states of the monitor as this is evolved from one state to the next. Algorithm 1 encodes this reduction strategy using a series of **case** state-ments (lines 2–16 and 23–35), following the operational semantics of Fig. 4. Each **case** maps the first part of a rule conclusion to a *pattern*, enabling the monitor-ing algorithm to unambiguously **match** the rule to apply. The body of **cases** consists of a **return** statement that corresponds to the outcome dictated by the rule. Rules with premises (*e.g.* MCHS$_L$, MPAR, *etc.*) are reduced *recursively* by reapplying rules until an axiom is met, whereas axioms (*e.g.* MVRD, MDIS$_L$, *etc.*) reduce immediately. For example, the pattern $\{$chs$, m, n\}$ on line 7 speci-fies that MCHS$_L$ and MCHS$_R$ only apply to monitors of the form $m + n$. Selecting whether to reduce the left or right sub-monitor by analysing α is delegated to the function HOLDS. This instantiates the predicate encoded in **act** tuples with the data from α (see Fig. 6), returning the result of the predicate test. When the condition HOLDS$(\alpha, m) \wedge \neg$HOLDS(α, n) is **true**, $m + n$ is reduced to m, equivalent to the application of MCHS$_L$; the argument for MCHS$_R$ is symmetric.

The function ANALYSEACT of Algorithm 1 conducts the runtime analysis. It ensures that once an action is analysed, the monitor is left in a state where it is *ready* to analyse the next action. We implement this logic by organising the application of the operational rules of Fig. 4 into two functions, DERIVEACT and DERIVETAU, according to the kind of action used to reduce the monitor. DERIVEACT on line 19 reduces the monitor *once* by applying it to the action under analysis, yielding m'. Subsequently, REDUCETAU reapplies the function DERIVETAU until all the internal transitions of the monitor are exhausted (lines 38–42). The cases on lines 24–27, corresponding to the axioms MDISY_L, MDISN_L, MCONY_L, MCONN$_L$, terminate redundant monitor states, and may be seen as a form of *garbage collection*. Due to space constraints, DERIVETAU omits the cases symmetric to those of lines 24–27.

Every single application of DERIVEACT and DERIVETAU results in a deriva-tion that shows how a monitor evolves from one state to the next according to the operational rules of Fig. 4. The function ANALYSEACT keeps a complete his-tory of these derivations internally. Derivations are represented as trees, rooted at the conclusion and terminating at the axiom nodes, that for each step: *(i)* maintain the monitor state consisting of the substitution π, and, *(ii)* the name of the rule used to derive the step. Maintaining the variable-value mapping in π across derivation steps demands that we track the changes in these variables for every active monitor state. This includes accounting for different binding scopes, variable shadowing, and the creation of fresh scopes when recursion variables, X, are unfolded. Our Erlang implementation of the functions listed in Algorithm 1 in the tool incorporate this described logic. We are aware that storing the com-plete history ultimately impacts the performance of the runtime analysis. Our tool compromises by offering two operating modes, normal and debug, where in the latter, the full derivation history is stored in memory for the purpose of explainability.

4.4   Monitor Instrumentation

Our tool leverages the existing inlining [34] mechanism implemented in detectEr to instrument the SuS with monitors. While this approach assumes access to the source code of the SuS, it has been shown to induce lower overhead, by contrast to its outline counterpart [5,32,33]. The tool provides the meta keyword with, to identify the SuS components against which MAXHML^d specifications are runtime checked. Readers are referred to [12] for more details.

5   Case Study

We show the usability of our tool by applying it to an off-the-shelf Erlang web-server called Cowboy [45]. Cowboy delegates its socket management to Ranch (a socket acceptor pool for TCP protocols [46]), but forwards incoming HTTP client requests to *protocol handlers* that are forked dynamically by the webserver to service requests independently. We use our tool to runtime check MAXHML^d specifications describing fragments of the interaction protocol between the Cowboy and Ranch components. Our aim is to: *(i)* demonstrate the *expressiveness* of our logic by capturing properties of real-world software, *(ii)* validate the *applicability* of our monitoring and instrumentation techniques to third-party code, namely to applications built on top of the Erlang OTP middleware libraries, and, *(iii)* explore the *utility* of explainable verdicts for diagnosing software issues.

We redesign the token server of Fig. 5 as a REST web service deployed on Cowboy. The server generates identifier tokens using one of two formats, UUIDs, or short alphanumeric strings. Clients request tokens by issuing a GET request with parameter, type=uuid or type=short, specifying the token format required. The web service offers a standard interface: *(i)* it returns HTTP 400 when the type parameter is omitted from the request, and, *(ii)* HTTP 500 when an unsupported type is used. We also simulate intermittent faults in the Cowboy components by *injecting* process crashes based on a fair Bernoulli trial [55].

For our case study, we consider a selection of properties describing the Cowboy-Ranch interaction protocol. One such property, φ_{rp}, concerns Cowboy *request processes* that service client requests. It states that in its (current) execution, '*a request process does not issue HTTP responses with code 500, nor does it crash*'.

$$\max X. \left(\begin{array}{l} [!(\textbf{\textit{rprc}}, \_, \{\textbf{\textit{tag}}, \textbf{\textit{code}}, \ldots\}), tag = \texttt{resp} \wedge code = 200]X \wedge \\ [!(\textbf{\textit{rprc}}, \_, \{\textbf{\textit{tag}}, \textbf{\textit{code}}, \ldots\}), tag = \texttt{resp} \wedge code = 500]\text{ff} \wedge \\ [\star(\textbf{\textit{rprc}}, \textbf{\textit{stat}}), stat = \texttt{crash}]\text{ff} \end{array} \right) \quad (\varphi_{\text{rp}})$$

In φ_{rp}, the binders *tag* and *code* become instantiated with the atom resp designating a response message, and the HTTP code of the response returned to requesting clients. Besides ensuring that response messages sent by request processes do not contain the code 500, *i.e.*, $tag = \texttt{resp} \wedge code = 500$, formula φ_{rp} also asserts that these processes do not crash, *i.e.*, $stat = \texttt{crash}$. The binder *rprc*, referring to the request process PID, is included in φ_{rp} for clarity.

While the monitor synthesised from φ_{rp} flags the corresponding rejection, the verdict (alone) does not indicate the source of the error. This may suffice for verifying small-scale systems where errors are manually-trackable, but becomes impractical in realistic settings such as this case study. Our algorithm addresses this shortcoming by giving a justification showing how a monitor reaches its verdict.

6   Conclusion

This paper presents the implementation of a RV tool that runtime checks specifications written in a safety-fragment of the linear-time modal μ-calculus, called MAXHML, augmented with predicates over data. Our work builds on previous theoretical results for the regular setting [3,4] that give a compositional synthesis procedure which generates monitors from MAXHML formulae. We extend the logic, synthesis, and monitor operational semantics of [3,4] to enable the tool to handle events that carry data. We discuss the implementability of this synthesis procedure, and overview the approach our monitoring algorithm takes towards providing justifiable monitoring verdicts. Our tool is validated via a realistic case study that uses an off-the-shelf, third-party Erlang webserver. We show how our augmented logic flexibly expresses properties involving data, and argue for the utility of explainable verdicts for diagnosing software issues.

Related Work. The synthesis procedure in this paper contrasts with another by a line of work that investigates the monitorable safety fragment of the branching-time modal μ-calculus, called sHML [37,38]. The latter synthesis generates monitors with non-deterministic behaviour that, while sufficient for the theoretical results required in *op. cit.*, may lead to missed detections in practice. An early materialisation of [37,38] as the tool detectEr [13,14,26,40] addresses this shortcoming by parallelising monitors using processes, enabling them to reach verdicts along all possible paths. While effective, this approach scales poorly [15]. Ongoing work on detectEr [12] indicates that a process-free approach could lead to more efficient runtime monitoring that scales considerably better [5,6].

There are other ways to monitoring systems with events that carry data besides the ones cited in Sect. 1 (see *e.g.*, [18,20,22,41–43,61]). One work that shares characteristics with ours is Parametric Trace Slicing (PTS) [29,57], where the global trace is projected into local sub-traces called *slices*, based on parametric specifications. These are properties specified in terms of *symbolic events* whose parameters are instantiated to values from events in the global trace. We use similar means to identify the SuS components to be instrumented, thus filtering out events and obtain trace slices (see Sect. 4.4). PTS is adopted by a number of RV tools that handle data (see *e.g.*, [9,28,31,47,53]), notably MarQ [16,56] for Java, and Elarva [30] for Erlang. Elarva takes a naïve strategy to PTS, relying on a central process to collect trace events that are demultiplexed between monitors to obtain slices. This makes it susceptible to single point of failures, and does not scale in practice. The design we use is more robust, as it directly instruments components of the SuS, giving us a modicum of fault containment when monitoring independently-executing components that can fail in isolation.

References

1. Aceto, L., Achilleos, A., Francalanza, A., Ingólfsdóttir, A.: A framework for parameterized monitorability. In: Baier, C., Dal Lago, U. (eds.) FoSSaCS 2018. LNCS, vol. 10803, pp. 203–220. Springer, Cham (2018). https://doi.org/10.1007/978-3-319-89366-2_11

2. Aceto, L., Achilleos, A., Francalanza, A., Ingólfsdóttir, A., Kjartansson, S.Ö.: Determinizing monitors for HML with recursion. JLAMP **111** (2020)

3. Aceto, L., Achilleos, A., Francalanza, A., Ingólfsdóttir, A., Lehtinen, K.: Adventures in monitorability: from branching to linear time and back again. Proc. ACM Program. Lang. **3**(POPL), 52:1–52:29 (2019)

4. Aceto, L., Achilleos, A., Francalanza, A., Ingólfsdóttir, A., Lehtinen, K.: An operational guide to monitorability with applications to regular properties. Softw. Syst. Model. **20**(2), 335–361 (2021)

5. Aceto, L., Attard, D.P., Francalanza, A., Ingólfsdóttir, A.: A Choreographed outline instrumentation algorithm for asynchronous components. CoRR **abs/2104.09433** (2021)

6. Aceto, L., Attard, D.P., Francalanza, A., Ingólfsdóttir, A.: On benchmarking for concurrent runtime verification. In: FASE 2021. LNCS, vol. 12649, pp. 3–23. Springer, Cham (2021). https://doi.org/10.1007/978-3-030-71500-7_1

7. Aceto, L., Ingólfsdóttir, A., Larsen, K.G., Srba, J.: Reactive Systems: Modelling, Specification and Verification. Cambridge University Press, Cambridge (2007)

8. Agha, G., Mason, I.A., Smith, S.F., Talcott, C.L.: A foundation for actor computation. JFP **7**(1), 1–72 (1997)

9. Allan, C., et al.: Adding trace matching with free variables to AspectJ. In: OOPSLA, pp. 345–364. ACM (2005)

10. Alpern, B., Schneider, F.B.: Defining liveness. Inf. Process. Lett. **21**(4), 181–185 (1985)

11. Armstrong, J.: Programming Erlang: Software for a Concurrent World. Pragmatic Bookshelf (2007)

12. Attard, D.P., Aceto, L., Achilleos, A., Francalanza, A., Ingólfsdóttir, A., Lehtinen, K.: Better late than never or: verifying asynchronous components at runtime. In: Peters, K., Willemse, T.A.C. (eds.) FORTE 2021. LNCS, vol. 12719, pp. 207–225. Springer, Cham (2021). https://doi.org/10.1007/978-3-030-78089-0_14

13. Attard, D.P., Cassar, I., Francalanza, A., Aceto, L., Ingólfsdóttir, A.: Introduction to Runtime Verification. In: Behavioural Types: From Theory to Tools, pp. 49–76. Automation, Control and Robotics, River (2017)

14. Attard, D.P., Francalanza, A.: A monitoring tool for a branching-time logic. In: Falcone, Y., Sánchez, C. (eds.) RV 2016. LNCS, vol. 10012, pp. 473–481. Springer, Cham (2016). https://doi.org/10.1007/978-3-319-46982-9_31

15. Attard, D.P., Francalanza, A.: Trace partitioning and local monitoring for asynchronous components. In: Cimatti, A., Sirjani, M. (eds.) SEFM 2017. LNCS, vol. 10469, pp. 219–235. Springer, Cham (2017). https://doi.org/10.1007/978-3-319-66197-1_14

16. Barringer, H., Falcone, Y., Havelund, K., Reger, G., Rydeheard, D.: Quantified event automata: towards expressive and efficient runtime monitors. In: Giannakopoulou, D., Méry, D. (eds.) FM 2012. LNCS, vol. 7436, pp. 68–84. Springer, Heidelberg (2012). https://doi.org/10.1007/978-3-642-32759-9_9
17. Bartocci, E., Falcone, Y., Francalanza, A., Reger, G.: Introduction to runtime verification. In: Bartocci, E., Falcone, Y. (eds.) Lectures on Runtime Verification. LNCS, vol. 10457, pp. 1–33. Springer, Cham (2018). https://doi.org/10.1007/978-3-319-75632-5_1
18. Basin, D.A., Klaedtke, F., Müller, S., Zalinescu, E.: Monitoring metric first-order temporal properties. J. ACM **62**(2), 15:1–15:45 (2015)
19. Basin, D.A., Klaedtke, F., Zalinescu, E.: Failure-aware runtime verification of distributed systems. In: FSTTCS. LIPIcs, vol. 45, pp. 590–603. Schloss Dagstuhl - Leibniz-Zentrum für Informatik (2015)
20. Basin, D., Klaedtke, F., Zǎlinescu, E.: Runtime verification of temporal properties over out-of-order data streams. In: Majumdar, R., Kunčak, V. (eds.) CAV 2017. LNCS, vol. 10426, pp. 356–376. Springer, Cham (2017). https://doi.org/10.1007/978-3-319-63387-9_18
21. Bauer, A., Falcone, Y.: Decentralised LTL monitoring. FMSD **48**(1–2), 46–93 (2016)
22. Bauer, A., Küster, J., Vegliach, G.: The ins and outs of first-order runtime verification. Formal Methods Syst. Des. **46**(3), 286–316 (2015)
23. Bauer, A., Leucker, M., Schallhart, C.: Comparing LTL semantics for runtime verification. J. Log. Comput. **20**(3), 651–674 (2010)
24. Bauer, A., Leucker, M., Schallhart, C.: Runtime verification for LTL and TLTL. ACM Trans. Softw. Eng. Methodol. **20**(4), 14:1–14:64 (2011)
25. Bonakdarpour, B., Fraigniaud, P., Rajsbaum, S., Rosenblueth, D.A., Travers, C.: Decentralized asynchronous crash-resilient runtime verification. In: CONCUR. LIPIcs, vol. 59, pp. 16:1–16:15. Schloss Dagstuhl - Leibniz-Zentrum für Informatik (2016)
26. Cassar, I., Francalanza, A., Attard, D.P., Aceto, L., Ingólfsdóttir, A.: A suite of monitoring tools for Erlang. In: RV-CuBES. Kalpa Publications in Computing, vol. 3, pp. 41–47 (2017)
27. Cesarini, F., Thompson, S.: Erlang Programming: A Concurrent Approach to Software Development. O'Reilly Media (2009)
28. Chen, F., Rosu, G.: MOP: an efficient and generic runtime verification framework. In: OOPSLA, pp. 569–588 (2007)
29. Chen, F., Roşu, G.: Parametric trace slicing and monitoring. In: Kowalewski, S., Philippou, A. (eds.) TACAS 2009. LNCS, vol. 5505, pp. 246–261. Springer, Heidelberg (2009). https://doi.org/10.1007/978-3-642-00768-2_23
30. Colombo, C., Francalanza, A., Gatt, R.: Elarva: a monitoring tool for Erlang. In: Khurshid, S., Sen, K. (eds.) RV 2011. LNCS, vol. 7186, pp. 370–374. Springer, Heidelberg (2012). https://doi.org/10.1007/978-3-642-29860-8_29
31. Decker, N., Harder, J., Scheffel, T., Schmitz, M., Thoma, D.: Runtime monitoring with union-find structures. In: Chechik, M., Raskin, J.-F. (eds.) TACAS 2016. LNCS, vol. 9636, pp. 868–884. Springer, Heidelberg (2016). https://doi.org/10.1007/978-3-662-49674-9_54
32. Erlingsson, Ú.: The inlined reference monitor approach to security policy enforcement. Ph.D. thesis, Cornell University (2004)
33. Erlingsson, Ú., Schneider, F.B.: SASI enforcement of security policies: a retrospective. In: NSPW, pp. 87–95 (1999)

34. Falcone, Y., Krstić, S., Reger, G., Traytel, D.: A taxonomy for classifying runtime verification tools. In: Colombo, C., Leucker, M. (eds.) RV 2018. LNCS, vol. 11237, pp. 241–262. Springer, Cham (2018). https://doi.org/10.1007/978-3-030-03769-7_14

35. Francalanza, A.: A theory of monitors. Inf. Comput. **281**, 104704 (2021)

36. Francalanza, A., et al.: A foundation for runtime monitoring. In: Lahiri, S., Reger, G. (eds.) RV 2017. LNCS, vol. 10548, pp. 8–29. Springer, Cham (2017). https://doi.org/10.1007/978-3-319-67531-2_2

37. Francalanza, A., Aceto, L., Ingolfsdottir, A.: On verifying Hennessy-Milner logic with recursion at runtime. In: Bartocci, E., Majumdar, R. (eds.) RV 2015. LNCS, vol. 9333, pp. 71–86. Springer, Cham (2015). https://doi.org/10.1007/978-3-319-23820-3_5

38. Francalanza, A., Aceto, L., Ingólfsdóttir, A.: Monitorability for the Hennessy-Milner logic with recursion. FMSD **51**(1), 87–116 (2017)

39. Francalanza, A., Cini, C.: Computer says no: verdict explainability for runtime monitors using a local proof system. J. Log. Algebraic Methods Program. **119**, 100636 (2021)

40. Francalanza, A., Seychell, A.: Synthesising correct concurrent runtime monitors. FMSD **46**(3), 226–261 (2015)

41. Havelund, K., Peled, D.: Runtime verification: from propositional to first-order temporal logic. In: Colombo, C., Leucker, M. (eds.) RV 2018. LNCS, vol. 11237, pp. 90–112. Springer, Cham (2018). https://doi.org/10.1007/978-3-030-03769-7_7

42. Havelund, K., Peled, D.: BDDs for representing data in runtime verification. In: Deshmukh, J., Ničković, D. (eds.) RV 2020. LNCS, vol. 12399, pp. 107–128. Springer, Cham (2020). https://doi.org/10.1007/978-3-030-60508-7_6

43. Havelund, K., Reger, G., Thoma, D., Zălinescu, E.: Monitoring events that carry data. In: Bartocci, E., Falcone, Y. (eds.) Lectures on Runtime Verification. LNCS, vol. 10457, pp. 61–102. Springer, Cham (2018). https://doi.org/10.1007/978-3-319-75632-5_3

44. Hewitt, C., Bishop, P.B., Steiger, R.: A universal modular ACTOR formalism for artificial intelligence. In: IJCAI, pp. 235–245. William Kaufmann (1973)

45. Hoguin, L.: Cowboy (2020). https://ninenines.eu

46. Hoguin, L.: Ranch (2020). https://ninenines.eu

47. Jin, D., Meredith, P.O., Lee, C., Rosu, G.: JavaMOP: efficient parametric runtime monitoring framework. In: ICSE, pp. 1427–1430 (2012)

48. Clarke Jr., E.M., Grumberg, O., Peled, D.A.: Model Checking. MIT Press, Cambridge (1999)

49. Kozen, D.: Results on the propositional μ-calculus. In: Nielsen, M., Schmidt, E.M. (eds.) ICALP 1982. LNCS, vol. 140, pp. 348–359. Springer, Heidelberg (1982). https://doi.org/10.1007/BFb0012782

50. Kupferman, O., Vardi, M.Y., Wolper, P.: An automata-theoretic approach to branching-time model checking. J. ACM **47**(2), 312–360 (2000)

51. Larsen, K.G.: Proof systems for satisfiability in Hennessy-Milner logic with recursion. TCS **72**(2&3), 265–288 (1990)

52. Leucker, M., Schallhart, C.: A brief account of runtime verification. JLAP **78**(5), 293–303 (2009)

53. Meredith, P.O., Jin, D., Griffith, D., Chen, F., Rosu, G.: An overview of the MOP runtime verification framework. STTT **14**(3), 249–289 (2012)

54. Milner, R.: Communication and Concurrency. Prentice Hall (1989)

55. Papoulis, A.: Probability, Random Variables, and Stochastic Processes. McGraw Hill (1991)

56. Reger, G., Cruz, H.C., Rydeheard, D.: MARQ: monitoring at runtime with QEA. In: Baier, C., Tinelli, C. (eds.) TACAS 2015. LNCS, vol. 9035, pp. 596–610. Springer, Heidelberg (2015). https://doi.org/10.1007/978-3-662-46681-0_55

57. Reger, G., Rydeheard, D.: From first-order temporal logic to parametric trace slicing. In: Bartocci, E., Majumdar, R. (eds.) RV 2015. LNCS, vol. 9333, pp. 216–232. Springer, Cham (2015). https://doi.org/10.1007/978-3-319-23820-3_14

58. Scheffel, T., Schmitz, M.: Three-valued asynchronous distributed runtime verification. In: MEMOCODE, pp. 52–61 (2014)

59. Sen, K., Vardhan, A., Agha, G., Rosu, G.: Efficient decentralized monitoring of safety in distributed systems. In: ICSE, pp. 418–427 (2004)

60. Sen, K., Vardhan, A., Agha, G., Rosu, G.: Decentralized runtime analysis of multithreaded applications. In: IPDPS. IEEE (2006)

61. Stolz, V.: Temporal assertions with parametrized propositions. J. Log. Comput. **20**(3), 743–757 (2010)

62. Wolper, P.: Temporal logic can be more expressive. Inf. Control. **56**(1/2), 72–99 (1983)

Microservices

Model-Driven Generation of Microservice Interfaces: From LEMMA Domain Models to Jolie APIs

Saverio Giallorenzo[1,2], Fabrizio Montesi[3], Marco Peressotti[3],
and Florian Rademacher[4(✉)]

1 Università di Bologna, Bologna, Italy
saverio.giallorenzo2@unibo.it
2 INRIA, Sophia Antipolis, France
3 University of Southern Denmark,
Odense, Denmark
{fmontesi,peressotti}@imada.sdu.dk
4 University of Applied Sciences and Arts
Dortmund, Dortmund, Germany
florian.rademacher@fh-dortmund.de

Abstract. We formally define and implement a translation from domain models in the LEMMA modelling framework to microservice APIs in the Jolie programming language. Our tool enables a software development process whereby microservice architectures can first be designed with the leading method of Domain-Driven Design (DDD), and then corresponding data types and service interfaces (APIs) in Jolie are automatically generated. Developers can extend and use these APIs as guides in order to produce compliant implementations. Our tool thus contributes to enhancing productivity and improving the design adherence of microservices.

1 Introduction

Microservice Architecture (MSA) is one of the current leading patterns in distributed software architectures [22]. While widely adopted, MSA comes with specific challenges regarding architecture design, development, and operation [5,29]. To cope with this complexity, researchers in software engineering and programming languages started proposing linguistic approaches to MSA: language frameworks that ease the design and development of MSAs with high-level constructs that make microservice concerns in the two different stages syntactically manifest.

Concerning development, Ballerina and Jolie are examples of programming languages [21,23] with new linguistic abstractions for effectively programming

Work partially supported by Independent Research Fund Denmark, grant no. 0135-00219.

© IFIP International Federation for Information Processing 2022
M. H. ter Beek and M. Sirjani (Eds.): COORDINATION 2022, LNCS 13271, pp. 223–240, 2022.
https://doi.org/10.1007/978-3-031-08143-9_13

the configuration and coordination of microservices. Concerning design, Model-Driven Engineering (MDE) [3] has gained relevance as a method for the specification of service architectures [1], crystallised in MDE-for-MSA modelling languages such as MicroBuilder, MDSL, LEMMA, and JHipster [15,16,26,32]. Jolie's abstractions have been found to offer a productivity boost in industry [13]. LEMMA provides linguistic support for the application of concepts from Domain-Driven Design [6,26], and has been validated in real-world use cases [27,30].

Recently, it has been observed that the metamodels of LEMMA's modelling languages and the Jolie programming language have enough contact points to consider their integration [11]. In the long term, such an integration could bring (quoting from [11])

> "*an ecosystem that coherently combines MDE and programming abstractions to offer a tower of abstractions [19] that supports a step-by-step refinement process from the abstract specification of a microservice architecture to its implementation*".

The aim is to provide a toolchain that enables people to apply MDE to the design of microservices in LEMMA, and then seamlessly switch to a programming language with dedicated support for microservices like Jolie in order to develop an implementation of the design. To this end, three important parts of the metamodels of LEMMA and Jolie need to be covered and integrated [11]:

1. *Application Programming Interfaces* (API), describing what functionalities (and their data types) a microservice offers to its clients;
2. *Access Points*, capturing where and how clients can interact with the API;
3. *Behaviours*, defining the internal business logic of a microservice.

Since the API is the layer the other two build upon, in this paper we focus on concretising the relationship between LEMMA and Jolie API layers. To this end, we contribute a formal encoding between a meaningful subset of LEMMA's Domain Data Modelling Language (DDML) and Jolie types and interfaces. This encoding enables systematic translation of LEMMA domain models, which, following Domain-Driven Design (DDD) [6] principles, capture domain-specific types including operation signatures, to Jolie APIs. Our second contribution, LEMMA-2Jolie implements our encoding as a code generator that allows automatic translation of LEMMA domain models to Jolie APIs. Specifically, LEMMA2Jolie not only shows the encoding's feasibility and practicability, but also constitutes a crucial contribution towards improving the adoption of DDD in microservice design, which in practice is often perceived complex given the lack of formal guidelines on how to map DDD domain models to microservice code [2]. We have evaluated LEMMA2Jolie in the context of a nontrivial microservice architecture that had previously been used to validate LEMMA [27], which covers all the aspects of the formal encoding. The generated Jolie code is as expected, in the sense that it is faithful to the formal encoding and the model defined in LEMMA. We use snippets of this code to exemplify our method throughout the paper.

$$CTX ::= \textbf{context } id \textbf{ \{}\overline{CT}\textbf{\}}$$

$$CT \quad ::= STR \mid COL \mid ENM$$

$$STR \quad ::= \textbf{structure } id \; [\langle\overline{STRF}\rangle] \textbf{ \{}\overline{FLD \; OPS}\textbf{\}}$$

$$STRF ::= \textbf{aggregate} \mid \textbf{domainEvent} \mid \textbf{entity} \mid \textbf{factory}$$
$$\qquad\qquad \mid \text{service} \mid \text{repository} \mid \textbf{specification} \mid \textbf{valueObject}$$

$$FLD \quad ::= id \; id \; [\langle\overline{FLDF}\rangle] \mid S \; id \; [\langle\overline{FLDF}\rangle]$$

$$FLDF ::= \textbf{identifier} \mid \textbf{part}$$

$$OPS \quad ::= \textbf{procedure } id \; [\langle\overline{OPSF}\rangle] \; (\overline{FLD}) \mid \textbf{function } (id \mid S) \; id \; [\langle\overline{OPSF}\rangle] \; (\overline{FLD})$$

$$OPSF ::= \text{closure} \mid \textbf{identifier} \mid \text{sideEffectFree} \mid \textbf{validator}$$

$$COL \quad ::= \textbf{collection } id \textbf{ \{}(S \mid id)\textbf{\}}$$

$$ENM \quad ::= \textbf{enum } id \textbf{ \{}\overline{id}\textbf{\}}$$

$$S \qquad ::= \textbf{int} \mid \textbf{string} \mid \textbf{unspecified} \mid \ldots$$

Fig. 1. Simplified grammar of LEMMA's DDML. Greyed out features are out of the scope of this paper and subject to future work.

In general, LEMMA2Jolie is a concrete proof that the work started in [11] constitutes a bridge between the two communities of programming language and MDE research, converging on linguistic approaches to MSA—for instance, one can take our insights and apply them to integrate other MSA modelling and programming languages.

The remainder of the paper is organised as follows. Section 2 introduces and exemplifies the encoding between LEMMA's DDML and Jolie APIs. Section 3 describes the architecture and implementation of LEMMA2Jolie. Section 4 presents future work and concludes the paper.

2   Encoding LEMMA Domain Modelling Concepts in Jolie

This section describes and exemplifies domain modelling with LEMMA (cf. Sect. 2.1), and the development of types and interfaces with Jolie (cf. Sect. 2.2). Next, it reports a formal encoding from LEMMA domain models to Jolie APIs and illustrates its application (cf. Sects. 2.3 and 2.4).

2.1   LEMMA Domain Modelling Concepts

LEMMA's DDML supports domain experts and service developers in the construction of models that capture domain-specific types of microservices. Figure 1 shows the core rules of the DDML grammar[1].

The DDML follows DDD to capture domain concepts. DDD's Bounded Context pattern [6] is crucial in MSA design as it makes the boundaries of coherent

---

[1] The complete grammar can be found at https://github.com/SeelabFhdo/lemma/blob/main/de.fhdo.lemma.data.datadsl/src/de/fhdo/lemma/data/DataDsl.xtext.

domain concepts explicit, thereby defining their scope and applicability [22]. A LEMMA domain model defines named bounded **contexts** (rule CTX in Fig. 1). A **context** may specify domain concepts in the form of complex types (CT), which are either structures (STR), collections (COL), or enumerations (ENM).

A **structure** gathers a set of data fields (FLD). The type of a data field is either a complex type from the same bounded context (id) or a built-in primitive type, e.g., **int** or **string** (S). The **unspecified** keyword enables continuous domain exploration according to DDD [6]. That is, it supports the construction of underspecified models and their subsequent refinement as one gains new domain knowledge [25]. Next to fields, **structures** can comprise operation signatures (OPS) to reify domain-specific behaviour. An operation is either a **procedure** without a return type, or a **function** with a complex or primitive return type.

LEMMA's DDML supports the assignment of DDD patterns, called *features*, to structured domain concepts and their components. For instance, the **entity** feature (rule $STRF$ in Fig. 1) expresses that a structure comprises a notion of domain-specific identity. The **identifier** feature then marks the data fields ($FLDF$) or operations ($OPSF$) of an **entity** which determine its identity. For compactness, we defer the detailed presentation of the considered DDD features to Sect. 2.4, when discussing their relationship with our encoding to Jolie.

The DDML also enables the modelling of **collections** (rule COL in Fig. 1), which represent sequences of primitives (S) or complex (id) values, as well as **enumerations** (ENM), which gather sets of predefined literals.

The following listing shows an example of a LEMMA domain model constructed with the grammar of the DDML [27].

```
context BookingManagement {
 structure ParkingSpaceBooking⟨entity⟩ {
  long bookingID⟨identifier⟩,
  double priceInEuro,
  function double priceInDollars
 }
}                                                          LEMMA
```

The domain model defines the bounded **context** *BookingManagement* and its **structured** domain concept *ParkingSpaceBooking*. It is a DDD **entity** whose *bookingID* field holds the **identifier** of an entity instance. The entity also clusters the field *priceInEuro* to store the price of a parking space booking, and the **function** signature *priceInDollars* for currency conversion of a booking's price.

2.2 Jolie Types and Interfaces

Jolie interfaces and types define the functionalities of a microservice and the data types associated with those functionalities i.e., the API of a microservice. Figure 2 shows a simplified variant of the grammar of Jolie APIs, taken from [21] and updated to Jolie 1.10 (the latest major release at the time of writing).

An **interface** is a collection of named operations (**RequestResponse**), where the sender delivers its message of type TP_1 and waits for the receiver

$$I \quad ::= \textbf{interface } id \ \{\overline{\textbf{RequestResponse } id(TP_1)(TP_2)}\}$$

$$TP ::= id \mid B$$

$$TD ::= \textbf{type } id : \ T$$

$$T \quad ::= B \ [\{\overline{id \ C : \ T}\}] \mid \textbf{undefined}$$

$$C \quad ::= [min, max] \mid * \mid ?$$

$$B \quad ::= \textbf{int}[(R)] \mid \textbf{string}[(R)] \mid \textbf{void} \mid \ \dots$$

$$R \quad ::= \textbf{range}([min, max]) \mid \textbf{length}([min, max]) \mid \textbf{enum}(\dots) \mid \ \dots$$

Fig. 2. Simplified syntax of Jolie APIs (types and interfaces)

to reply with a response of type TP_2—although Jolie also supports **oneWay**s, where the sender delivers its message to the receiver, without waiting for the latter to process it (fire-and-forget), we omit them here because they are not used in the encoding (cf. Sect. 2.3). Operations have types describing the shape of the data structures they can exchange, which can either define custom, named types (id) or basic ones (B) (**integer**s, **string**s, etc.).

Jolie **type** definitions (TD) have a tree-shaped structure. At their root, we find a basic type (B)—which can include a refinement (R) to express constraints that further restrict the possible inhabitants of the type [9]. The possible branches of a **type** are a set of nodes, where each node associates a name (id) with an array with a range length (C) and a type T.

Jolie data types and interfaces are technology agnostic: they model Data Transfer Objects (DTOs) built on native types generally available in most architectures [4].

Based on the grammar in Fig. 2, the following listing shows the Jolie equivalent of the example LEMMA domain model from Sect. 2.1.

```
///@beginCtx(BookingManagement)
///@entity
type ParkingSpaceBooking {
 ///@identifier
 bookingID: long
 priceInEuro: double
}
interface ParkingSpaceBooking_interface {
 RequestResponse:
  priceInDollars(ParkingSpaceBooking)(double)
}
///@endCtx
                                                Jolie
```

Structured LEMMA domain concepts like *ParkingSpaceBooking* and their data fields, e.g., *bookingID*, are directly translatable to corresponding Jolie **type**s.

To map LEMMA DDD information to Jolie, we use Jolie documentation comments (///) together with an @-sign. It is followed by (i) the string *begin-Ctx* and the parenthesised name of a modelled bounded context, e.g., *Booking-*

Management; (ii) the DDD feature name, e.g., *entity*; or (iii) the string *endCtx* to conclude a bounded context. This approach enables to preserve semantic DDD information for which Jolie currently does not support native language constructs. The comments serve as documentation to the programmer who will implement the API. In the future, we plan on leveraging these special comments also in automatic tools (see Sects. 2.4 and 4).

LEMMA operation signatures are expressible as **RequestResponse** operations within a Jolie **interface** for the LEMMA domain concept that defines the signatures. For example, we mapped the domain concept *ParkingSpaceBooking* and its operation signature *priceInDollars* to the Jolie interface *ParkingSpaceBooking_interface* with the operation *priceInDollars*.

2.3 Encoding LEMMA Domain Models as Jolie APIs

In the following, we report an encoding from LEMMA domain models to Jolie APIs that formalises and extends the mapping exemplified in Sect. 2.2. Figure 3 shows the encoding.

The encoding is split in three encoders: the *main* encoder $[\![\,\cdot\,]\!]$ walks through the structure of LEMMA domain models to generate Jolie APIs using the encoders for *operations* $(\!(\,\cdot\,)\!)$ and for *structures* $([\![\,\cdot\,]\!])$, respectively.

The operations encoder $(\!(\,\cdot\,)\!)$ generates Jolie interfaces based on **procedures** and **functions** in the given models by translating structure-specific operations into Jolie operations. This translation requires some care. On one hand, LEMMA's **procedures** and **functions** recall object methods in the sense that they operate on data stored in their defining structure. On the other hand, Jolie separates data from code that can operate on it (operations). Therefore, the encoding needs to decouple **procedures** and **functions** from their defining structures as illustrated in Sect. 2.2 by the mapping of the LEMMA domain concept *ParkingSpaceBooking* and its operation signature *priceInDollars* to the Jolie interface *ParkingSpaceBooking_interface* with the operation *priceInDollars* .

Given a structure X, we extend the signature of its **procedures** with a parameter for representing the structure they act on and a return type X for the new state of the structure, essentially turning them into functions that transform the enclosing structure. For instance, we regard a procedure with signature $(Y \times \cdots \times Z)$ in X as a function with type $X \times Y \times \cdots \times Z \to X$. This approach is not new and can be found also in modern languages like Rust [18,33] and Python [24]. The operation synthesised by the $(\!(\,\cdot\,)\!)$ encoder accepts the *id_type* generated by the $[\![\,\cdot\,]\!]$ encoder that, in turn, has a *self* leaf carrying the enclosing data structure (id_s). The encoding of **functions** follows a similar path. Note that, when encoding *self* leaves, we do not impose the constraint of providing one such instance (represented by the ? cardinality), but rather allow clients to provide it (and leave the check of its presence to the API implementer).

The main encoder $[\![\,\cdot\,]\!]$ and the structure encoder $([\![\,\cdot\,]\!])$ transform LEMMA types into Jolie types. **context**s translate into pairs of *///@beginCtx(context_name)* and *///@endCtx* Joliedoc comment annotations.

All the other constructs translate into **types** and their subparts. When translating **procedures** and **functions**, the two encoders follow the complementary scheme of $(\!(\,\cdot\,)\!)$ and synthesise the types for the generated operations. The other rules are straightforward.

$$\llbracket \textbf{context } id \ \{\overline{CT}\} \rrbracket \quad = ///@beginCtx(id)$$
$$\overline{\llbracket CT \rrbracket}$$
$$///@endCtx$$

$$(\!(\textbf{structure } id \ [\langle \overline{STRF} \rangle] \ \{\overline{FLD} \ \overline{OPS}\})\!) \quad = \overline{\lfloor ///@STRF \rfloor} \textbf{ interface } id\_interface \ \{\overline{(\!(OPS)\!)_{id}}\}$$

$$(\!(\textbf{procedure } id \ [\langle \overline{OPSF} \rangle] \ (\overline{FLD}))\!)_{id_s} \quad = \textbf{RequestResponse}: \ \overline{\lfloor ///@OPSF \rfloor} \ id(id\_type)(id_s)$$

$$(\!(\textbf{function } (S \mid id_r) \ id \ [\langle \overline{OPSF} \rangle] \ (\overline{FLD}))\!)_{id_s} = \textbf{RequestResponse}: \ \overline{\lfloor ///@OPSF \rfloor} \ id(id\_type)((\llbracket S \rrbracket \mid id_r))$$

$$\llbracket \textbf{structure } id \ [\langle \overline{STRF} \rangle] \ \{\overline{FLD} \ \overline{OPS}\} \rrbracket \quad = \textbf{type } \llbracket \textbf{structure } id \ [\langle \overline{STRF} \rangle] \ \{\overline{FLD}\} \rrbracket$$
$$\overline{\llbracket OPS \rrbracket_{id}} \ (\!(\textbf{structure } id \ [\langle \overline{STRF} \rangle] \ \{\overline{OPS}\})\!)_{id}$$

$$\llbracket \textbf{procedure } id \ [\langle \overline{OPSF} \rangle] \ (\overline{FLD}) \rrbracket_{id_s} \quad = \textbf{type } id\_type: \ \textbf{void } \{self?: \ id_s \ \overline{\llbracket FLD \rrbracket}\}$$

$$\llbracket \textbf{function } (id_r \mid S) \ id \ [\langle \overline{OPSF} \rangle] \ (\overline{FLD}) \rrbracket_{id_s} = \textbf{type } id\_type: \ \textbf{void } \{self?: \ id_s \ \overline{\llbracket FLD \rrbracket}\}$$

$$\llbracket \textbf{collection } id \ \{(S \mid id_r)\} \rrbracket \quad = \textbf{type } id: \ \textbf{void } \{ \llbracket \textbf{collection } id \ \{(S \mid id_r)\} \rrbracket \}$$

$$\llbracket \textbf{enum } id \ \{\overline{id}\} \rrbracket \quad = \textbf{type } \llbracket \textbf{enum } id \ \{\overline{id}\} \rrbracket$$

$$\llbracket \textbf{structure } id \ [\langle \overline{STRF} \rangle] \ \{\overline{FLD}\} \rrbracket \quad = \overline{\lfloor ///@STRF \rfloor} \ id: \ \textbf{void } \{ \overline{\llbracket FLD \rrbracket} \}$$

$$\llbracket S \ id \ [\langle \overline{FLDF} \rangle] \rrbracket \quad = \overline{\lfloor ///@FLDF \rfloor} \ id: \ \llbracket S \rrbracket$$

$$\llbracket id_r \ id \ [\langle \overline{FLDF} \rangle] \rrbracket \quad = \overline{\lfloor ///@FLDF \rfloor} \ id: \ id_r$$

$$\llbracket \textbf{collection } id \ \{S\} \rrbracket \quad = id*: \ \llbracket S \rrbracket$$

$$\llbracket \textbf{collection } id \ \{id_r\} \rrbracket \quad = id*: \ id_r$$

$$\llbracket \textbf{enum } id \ \{\overline{id}\} \rrbracket \quad = id: \ \textbf{string}(enum(``id"))$$

$$\llbracket \textbf{int} \rrbracket \quad = \textbf{int}$$

$$\llbracket \textbf{unspecified} \rrbracket \quad = \textbf{undefined}$$

Fig. 3. Salient parts of the Jolie encoding for LEMMA's domain modelling concepts.

2.4 Applying the Encoding

This subsection illustrates the application of the encoding from Sect. 2.3 using the Booking Management Microservice (BMM) of a microservice-based Park and Charge Platform (PACP) modelled with LEMMA [27]. The PACP enables drivers of electric vehicles to offer their charging stations for use by others. Its BMM manages the corresponding bookings based on domain concepts that were designed following DDD principles [6] and expressed in LEMMA's DDML.

In the following paragraphs, unless indicated, the encoded Jolie APIs respect the DDD constraints expressed by the considered features.

Aggregate and Part. In DDD, aggregates prescribe object graphs, whose parts must maintain a consistent state [6]. Aggregates are always loaded from and stored to a database in a consistent state and within one transaction. A DDD aggregate consists of at least an entity or value object (see below). The following left listing shows the *PSB* aggregate in the LEMMA domain model for the BMM.

structure PSB
⟨ **aggregate** ⟩ {
  TimeSlot timeSlot ⟨ **part** ⟩,
  double priceInEuro
}
structure TimeSlot { ... }
<div align="right">LEMMA</div>
	///@aggregate
	type PSB {
	  ///@part
	  timeSlot: TimeSlot
	  priceInEuro: **double**
	}
	type TimeSlot { ... }
	<div align="right">Jolie</div>

PSB is a **structure**d domain concept with the **aggregate** feature (cf. Sect. 2.1) and it clusters the field *timeSlot*, which has a structured type and is a **part** of the aggregate. Notice that for this domain model, LEMMA's DDML would emit warnings, because (i) a DDD aggregate must specify a root entity; and (ii) a part should either be an entity or value object [6]. We extend the *PSB* aggregate below to gradually fix these issues, thereby explaining the semantics of DDD entities and value objects.

In the Jolie encoding (on the right), we have as many **type** definitions as we have **structure**s in the LEMMA model.

Entity and Identifier. Instances of DDD entities are distinguishable by a domain-specific identity [6], e.g., a unique ID. The following left listing extends the *PSB* aggregate with the **entity** feature and an **identifier** field.

structure PSB
⟨ **aggregate, entity** ⟩ {
  long bookingID ⟨ **identifier** ⟩,
  TimeSlot timeSlot ⟨ **part** ⟩,
  double priceInEuro
}
<div align="right">LEMMA</div>
	///@aggregate
	///@entity
	type PSB {
	  ///@identifier
	  bookingID: **long**
	  ///@part
	  timeSlot: TimeSlot
	  priceInEuro: **double**
	}
	<div align="right">Jolie</div>

LEMMA's DDML requires the **entity** feature on an aggregate to signal that its fields prescribe the structure of its root entity. The **identifier** feature can be used to mark those fields that determine the identity of an entity instance. In the example above, the value of *bookingID* is marked to identify *PSB*s.

The Jolie encoding of **entity** and **identifier** fields is straightforward.

Next to fields, DDML supports the **identifier** feature on a single **function** of an entity to enable identity calculation at runtime. To illustrate this approach, the following listing models the *bookingID* of the *PSB* root entity as a function.

structure PSB ⟨ **entity** ⟩ {
  function long bookingID
  ⟨ **identifier** ⟩ (),
  ...
}
 	
LEMMA
	///*@entity*
	type PSB { ... }
	type bookingID_type { self?: PSB }
	interface PSB_interface {
	  RequestResponse:
	    ///*@identifier*
	    bookingID(bookingID_type)(**long**)
	}
	Jolie

Following our encoding (cf. Sect. 2.3), we create the Jolie **type** *bookingID_type* for the *bookingID* **identifier** function. The **type**'s *self* leaf enables implementers to access the fields of the *PSB* and define how to compute the identifier.

Factory. DDD factories make the creation of objects with complex consistency requirements explicit [6]. LEMMA's DDML considers factories to constitute **functions** that return instances of aggregates, entities, or value objects. The following left listing illustrates the usage of factories by specifying the **factory** function *create* as part of the *PSB* aggregate. This function shall create *PSB* instances for a given time slot *timeSlot* and a *priceInEuro*.

structure PSB ⟨ ... ⟩{
  TimeSlot timeSlot,
  double priceInEuro,
  function PSB create⟨**factory**⟩(
    TimeSlot timeSlot,
    double priceInEuro
)
 	
}
LEMMA
	type PSB { ... }
	///*@factory*
	type create_type {
	  timeSlot: TimeSlot
	  priceInEuro: **double**
	}
	interface PSBFactory_interface {
	  RequestResponse:
	    create(create_type)(PSB)
	}
	Jolie

As opposed to the encoding for LEMMA **identifier functions** (see above), we do not encode a *self* leaf in Jolie **types** such as *create_type* for LEMMA **factory** functions. Since the semantics of factories is that of generating an instance of the enclosing **structure**, it would not make sense to pass to it one of those instances as a *self* leaf. Consequently, we could include a rule in Fig. 3 which avoids the generation of said *self* leaf (this is more an issue of minimality of the generated code, since we set the leaf as optional (**?**)). Additionally, we can enforce a check on Jolie operations like *create* following immediately after ///*@factory*-commented **types** by making sure their input **types** do not contain the produced **type**, e.g., *PSB*. Complementary, we can also check that the response type of Jolie-encoded factory operations coincides with the produced **type**.

Specification and Validator. DDD specifications are domain concepts that make business rules, policies, or consistency specifications for aggregates explicit [6]. A specification must comprise one or more validators, which are functions with a boolean return type that reify the specification's predicates.

LEMMA's DDML provides the features **specification** and **validator** to mark structures as specifications and identify their validators. Below we extend the BMM's domain model with the *BookingExpiration* specification. Its *isExpired* validator returns **true** if a parking space booking *PSB* instance has expired.

structure PSB ⟨ ... ⟩ { ... }
structure BookingExpiration
⟨ **specification** ⟩ {
  function boolean isExpired
  ⟨ **validator** ⟩ (PSB p)
}
 	
LEMMA
	type PSB { ... }
	///*@specification*
	type isExpired_type { p: PSB }
	interface BookingExpiration_interface {
	  RequestResponse:
	    ///*@validator*
	    isExpired(isExpired_type)(**bool**)
	}
	Jolie

Since the specification is a field-less **structure**, we do not create a corresponding **type** *BookingExpiration* as it would be empty. Instead, and as per our encoding (cf. Sect. 2.3), we create the ///*@specification*-annotated **type** *isExpired_type* for the *isExpired* **validator** within the **interface** *BookingExpiration_interface*. From the point of view of the consistency of the annotations, following the namespace convention from Fig. 3, we can check that the ///*@validator* actually accepts the related **structure**. To do this, we follow the "breadcrumbs" left by our encoders. First, we find a ///*@validator*-commented **RequestResponse** (e.g., *isExpired*) and we make sure its response type is **bool**. Then, we follow the request type (e.g., *isExpired_type*) to make sure that: *i*) the ///*@validator* has an associated ///*@specification* (e.g., *isExpired_type*) **type** and *ii*) the **type** has one leaf, which is the **structure** the **validator** validates.

Value Object. As opposed to entities, DDD value objects cluster data and logic, which are not dependent on objects' identity [6]. Thus, value objects serve as DTOs for data exchange between microservices [22]. In asynchronous communication scenarios, value objects can model *domain events* emitted by a bounded context during runtime [7]. For example, all PACP microservices interact with each other via domain events [27].

LEMMA's DDML supports the **valueObject** and **domainEvent** features to mark structured domain concepts as value objects and possibly as domain events. The following left listing illustrates the usage of the **valueObject** feature.

```
context BookingManagement {              ///@beginCtx(BookingManagement)
  structure PSB ⟨ ... ⟩ {                type PSB {
    TimeSlot timeSlot,                     timeSlot: TimeSlot
    double priceInEuro                     priceInEuro: double
  }                                      }
  structure PSB_VO⟨ valueObject ⟩ {      ///@valueObject
    TimeSlot timeSlot,                   type PSB_VO {
    double price,                          timeSlot: TimeSlot
    string currency                        price: double
  }                                        currency: string
  structure TimeSlot⟨ valueObject ⟩ {    }
    ...                                  ///@valueObject
  }                                      type TimeSlot { ... }
}                          LEMMA         ///@endCtx                        Jolie
```

Above, we extend the BMM's domain model with the *PSB_VO* value object: a DTO for the *PSB* aggregate that slightly changes it type to make its representation more general. Namely, *PSB_VO* separates the *currency* from the value of the *price*. The *timeSlot* field remains the same, but we make sure it is also a **valueObject**.

The LEMMA domain model also shows the definition of bounded **context**s in the DDML. All three structures *PSB*, *PSB_VO*, and *TimeSlot* are enclosed by the *BookingManagement* **context** on which the BMM operates exclusively.

The encoding from LEMMA to Jolie follows Fig. 3 without exceptions. Notice, in particular, the "opening" *///@beginCtx(BookingManagement)* and "closing" *///@endCtx* comments for the context. With those comments, we are declaring that the types (and interfaces) that appear between them belong to the context *BookingManagement*. In LEMMA, contexts indicate a boundary within which (complex) types belonging in the same context can co-exist and interact (e.g., by being part of the inputs and output of **procedure**s and **function**s). Then, as seen above, **valueObject**s exist to allow data to cross boundaries, by defining data types (e.g., **structure**s) purposed to act as DTOs.

While the encoding from LEMMA's DDML ensures that, at the API level, the coherence defined by **context**s and **valueObject**s is preserved, e.g., there exists no **type** with leaves whose types belong in different contexts nor **interface**s belonging in a context that accept types from another context, unless *///@valueObject*s. However, behaviours that users write can arbitrarily combine data structures and operators and possibly break the coherence of contexts.

In the future, we would like to devise static checks able to enforce the coherence of LEMMA's DDML contexts also in behaviours, e.g., by tracing the contexts in which values belong—from the types of the operations that generated them, via receptions—and prohibit mixing values that belong in different contexts (e.g., by forbidding to use them with operations belonging in different contexts, although their types might be compatible). This static check would also handle the exception of values whose types are annotated as *///@valueObject*s, which are the only ones allowed to be used in a mixed way (i.e., in operations that take or produce *///@valueObject*-annotated types.).

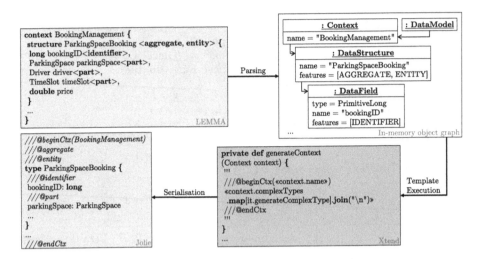

Fig. 4. LEMMA2Jolie phases to generate Jolie APIs from LEMMA domain models.

Additional Features. Our encoding captures the **repository** and **closure** features of LEMMA's DDML (cf. Fig. 1). Checks regarding the **sideEffectFree** feature follow the same considerations of the **valueObject** feature: we need to inspect a service behaviour to make sure its does not modify the values obtained from ///@*sideEffectFree*-commented operations. **services** are a generalisation of the **specification** feature, where we have a structure that contains only **functions** and **procedures**—LEMMA further specialises **services** into, **domainServices**, **infrastructureServices**, **applicationServices**, which are subject to future works.

3 LEMMA2Jolie: A Code Generator to Derive Jolie APIs from LEMMA Domain Models

This section presents our LEMMA2Jolie tool, which implements the encoding presented in Sect. 2. In the sense of MDE, LEMMA2Jolie is a *model-to-text transformation* [3] that generates Jolie APIs from LEMMA domain models.

Architecture. As depicted in Fig. 4, LEMMA2Jolie consists of three phases to derive Jolie APIs from LEMMA domain models.

In the Parsing phase, LEMMA2Jolie instantiates an in-memory object graph conforming to the metamodel of the DDML [26] from a given LEMMA domain model. The object graph allows systematic traversal of the model elements to map them to the corresponding Jolie code (cf. Sect. 2.3) in the following Template Execution phase. As the phase name indicates, LEMMA2Jolie relies on *template-based code generation* [3] to transform in-memory LEMMA domain models to

Jolie. That is, we prescribe the target blocks of a Jolie program as strings involving static Jolie statements and dynamic variables which are evaluated at runtime to complement the prescribed target blocks with context-dependent information, e.g., the name of a bounded context in a specific LEMMA domain model. After template execution, the Serialisation phase stores the evaluated templates to physical files with valid Jolie code.

Implementation Overview. We implemented LEMMA2Jolie in Xtend[2], which is a Java dialect that integrates a sophisticated templating language (see below). Furthermore, LEMMA2Jolie relies on LEMMA's Java-based Model Processing Framework[3], which aims to facilitate the development of model processors such as code generators. To this end, the framework provides built-in support for parsing models constructed with languages that are based on the Eclipse Modelling Framework [31]—as is the case for all LEMMA modelling languages including the DDML. Additionally, the framework prescribes a certain workflow for model processing and enables implementers to integrate with it using Java annotations.

Listing 1 describes the implementation of LEMMA2Jolie's code generation module which integrates with the Code Generation phase of LEMMA's Model Processing Framework. The module is responsible for template execution and the eventual serialisation of Jolie code.

A code generation module is a Java class with the @CodeGenerationModule annotation that extends the AbstractCodeGenerationModule class (Lines 1 and 2). LEMMA's Model Processing Framework delegates to a code generation module after it parsed an input model in the modelling language supported by the module. To specify the supported language, a code generation module overrides the inherited getLanguageNamespace method to return the language's namespace, which in the case of LEMMA2Jolie is that of LEMMA's DDML (Line 4).

The entrypoint for code generation is the execute method of a code generation module. It can access the in-memory object graph of a parsed model via the resource attribute. Lines 6 to 13 show the execute method of LEMMA2-Jolie's code generation module. In Line 7, we retrieve the root of the model as an instance of the DataModel concept of the DDML's metamodel (cf. Fig. 4). Next, we call the template method generateContext (see Listing 1) for each parsed Context instance and gather the generated Jolie code in the generatedContexts variable (Line 8). In Lines 9 and 10, we determine the path of the generated Jolie file, which will be created in the given target folder and with the same base name as the input LEMMA domain model but with Jolie's extension "ol". Line 11 triggers the serialisation of the generated Jolie code via the inherited withCharset method.

Lines 15 to 19 show the implementation of the template method generateContext. It expects an instance of the metamodel concept Context as input

---

[2] https://www.eclipse.org/xtend
[3] https://github.com/SeelabFhdo/lemma/tree/main/de.fhdo.lemma. model_processing

Listing 1. Xtend excerpt of LEMMA2Jolie's code generation module.

```
1   @CodeGenerationModule(name="main")
2   class GenerationModule extends AbstractCodeGenerationModule {
3     ...
4     override getLanguageNamespace() { return DataPackage.eNS_URI }
5
6     override execute(...) {
7       val model = resource.contents.get(0) as DataModel
8       val generatedContexts = model.contexts.map[it.generateContext]
9       val baseFileName = FilenameUtils.getBaseName(modelFile)
10      val targetFile = '''«targetFolder»«File.separator»«baseFileName».ol'''
11      return withCharset(#{targetFile -> generatedContexts.join("\n")},
12        StandardCharsets.UTF_8.name)
13    }
14
15    private def generateContext(Context context) {'''
16    ///@beginCtx(«context.name»)
17    «context.complexTypes.map[it.generateComplexType].join("\n")»
18    ///@endCtx
19    '''}
20
21    private def dispatch generateComplexType(DataStructure structure) {'''
22    «structure.generateType»
23    «IF !structure.operations.empty»
24      «structure.generateInterface»
25    «ENDIF»
26    '''}
27  }
```

(cf. Fig. 4) and represents the starting point of each template execution since bounded contexts are the top-level elements in LEMMA domain models. An Xtend template is realized between a pair of three consecutive apostrophes within which it is whitespace-sensitive and preserves indentation. Within opening and closing guillemets, Xtend templates enable access to variables and computing operations, whose evaluation shall replace a certain template portion. Consequently, the expression «context.name» in the template string in Line 16 is at runtime replaced by the name of the bounded context passed to generateContext. For a bounded context with name "BookingManagement", Line 16 of the template will thus result in the generated Jolie code ///@beginCtx(BookingManagement) (cf. Fig. 4).

To foster its overview and maintainability, we decomposed our template for Jolie APIs into several template methods following the specification of our encoding (cf. Sect. 2.3). As a result, the generation of Jolie code covering the internals of modelled bounded contexts happens in overloaded methods called generateComplexType. Each of these methods derives Jolie code for a certain kind of LEMMA complex type, i.e., data structure, list, or enumeration. In Line 17, the template delegates to the version of generateComplexType for LEMMA data structures. Following our encoding, the method implements a template to map data structures to Jolie types (Line 22) and interfaces in case the LEMMA data structure exhibits operation signatures (Lines 23 to 25).

The LEMMA2Jolie source code is available as a Software Heritage archive [10]. In addition, we provide a publicly downloadable video illustrating LEMMA2-Jolie's practical capabilities[4].

4   Related and Future Work

Related Work. The maturity of MDE in research and practice as well as its ability to effectively support the engineering of complex software systems [8] has fostered the development of a variety of tools similar to LEMMA2Jolie [15–17,28,32]. That is, they constitute code generators in the sense of MDE [3] and are capable to generate artefacts relevant to MSA engineering. For this purpose, the tools process models constructed in a certain modelling language.

By contrast to LEMMA2Jolie, the majority of related code generators focuses on Java as target technology [15,28,32] and thus not on a programming language specifically tailored to the challenges of microservice implementation. Reducing the semantic gap between the concepts of microservices and implementation languages is the reason for which new service-oriented languages like Ballerina and Jolie have been developed. Furthermore, the modelling languages supported by related tools and hence the generated code address only single concerns in MSA engineering, i.e., domain modelling [17,28] or the implementation and provisioning of service APIs [15,16,32]. By contrast, LEMMA's modelling languages offer an integrated solution to multi-concern modelling in MSA engineering, by providing modelling languages for various viewpoints on microservice architectures [26].

Future Work. The specified encoding (cf. Sect 2.3) and its implementation (cf. Sect. 3) show the feasibility to integrate the LEMMA and Jolie ecosystems. Future works include extending our results to other languages, studying the maturity of LEMMA2Jolie, proving formal guarantees on the correctness of the encoding, and extending the presented integration in several ways.

We plan to evaluate the maturity and stability of LEMMA2Jolie by investigating its application in real-world use cases [27,30].

To obtain correctness guarantees on our encoding, first we would need to formalise the semantics of LEMMA's DDML and of Jolie APIs, and then prove that the encoding generates Jolie APIs that preserve the semantics of input DDML models. This work is in progress, e.g., parts of Jolie have been already formalised [12,20,21] and LEMMA implements context conditions [14] to constrain the well-formedness of DDML models w.r.t. their intended semantics [26].

We also aim to investigate the possibility of round-trip engineering (RTE), i.e., the bidirectional synchronisation of changes between LEMMA models and Jolie code. This would enable, for example, domain experts and microservice

---

[4] https://bit.ly/3rTGysX

developers to interact by using their views of interest (model vs implementation) but without risking that they fall out of sync. While domain experts could continue to capture domain knowledge about a microservice architecture in conceptual DDD domain models, developers could adapt data types and APIs derived from those models using Jolie as their primary language. Based on RTE, changes in Jolie code could then automatically be reflected in DDD domain models and vice versa, with the option to immediately resolve potential conflicts in domain understanding. Furthermore, we see potential for LEMMA2Jolie to cover all phases in MSA engineering, from domain-driven service design to implementation and deployment. For example, we would like to extend LEMMA2Jolie to deal also with the definition of access points (communication endpoints that define how APIs can be accessed), behaviours (implementations of services written in Jolie that accompany LEMMA models), and the generation of deployment configurations (e.g., configuration of infrastructural services, containerisation, and deployment plans for Kubernetes). This potential is specifically fostered by both LEMMA and Jolie constituting *language-based approaches to MSA engineering*, which facilitates their integration. For example, we could extend LEMMA to include Jolie implementation code in service models.

References

1. Ameller, D., Burgués, X., Collell, O., Costal, D., Franch, X., Papazoglou, M.P.: Development of service-oriented architectures using model-driven development: a mapping study. Inf. Softw. Technol. **62**, 42–66 (2015)
2. Bogner, J., Fritzsch, J., Wagner, S., Zimmermann, A.: Microservices in industry: insights into technologies, characteristics, and software quality. In: 2019 IEEE International Conference on Software Architecture Companion (ICSA-C), pp. 187–195. IEEE (2019). https://doi.org/10.1109/ICSA-C.2019.00041
3. Combemale, B., France, R.B., Jézéquel, J.-M., Rumpe, B., Steel, J., Vojtisek, D.: Engineering Modeling Languages: Turning Domain Knowledge into Tools. CRC Press (2017)
4. Daigneau, R.: Service Design Patterns. Addison-Wesley (2012)
5. Dragoni, N., et al.: Microservices: yesterday, today, and tomorrow. In: Present and Ulterior Software Engineering, pp. 195–216. Springer, Cham (2017). https://doi.org/10.1007/978-3-319-67425-4_12
6. Evans, E.: Domain-Driven Design. Addison-Wesley (2004)
7. Evans, E.: Domain-Driven Design Reference. Dog Ear Publishing (2015)
8. France, R., Rumpe, B.: Model-driven development of complex software: a research roadmap. In: 2007 Future of Software Engineering, pp. 37–54. IEEE (2007)
9. Freeman, T., Pfenning, F.: Refinement types for ML. In: Proceedings of the 1991 Conference on Programming Language Design and Implementation, pp. 268–277 (1991)
10. Giallorenzo, S., Montesi, F., Peressotti, M., Rademacher, F., LEMMA2Jolie: a tool to generate Jolie APIs from LEMMA domain models 2022. Università di Bologna et al. vcs: https://github.com/frademacher/lemma2jolie. SWHID: https://swh:1:dir:05b245d8a132648eefffd8aaac5cc35ae945637b;origin=github.com/frademacher/lemma2jolie;visit=swh:1:snp:5f1f9cd4eca3af22d943302e8ab593c92b1d59ef;anchor=swh:1:rev:bae07adfaa0acdf7841c8295cc62d03e894a6bc1

11. Giallorenzo, S., Montesi, F., Peressotti, M., Rademacher, F., Sachweh, S.: Jolie and LEMMA: model-driven engineering and programming languages meet on microservices. In: Damiani, F., Dardha, O. (eds.) COORDINATION 2021. LNCS, vol. 12717, pp. 276–284. Springer, Cham (2021). https://doi.org/10.1007/978-3-030-78142-2_17

12. Guidi, C., Lucchi, R., Gorrieri, R., Busi, N., Zavattaro, G.: SOCK: a calculus for service oriented computing. In: International Conference on Service-Oriented Computing, pp. 327–338 (2006)

13. Guidi, C., Maschio, B.: A Jolie based platform for speeding-up the digitalization of system integration processes. In: Proceedings of the Second International Conference on Microservices (Microservices 2019) (2019). https://www.conf-micro. services/2019/papers/Microservices_2019_paper_6.pdf

14. Harel, D., Rumpe, B.: Meaningful modeling: what's the semantics of "semantics"? Computer 37(10), 64–72 (2004). https://doi.org/10.1109/MC.2004.172

15. JHipster: JHipster Domain Language (JDL), 14 February 2022. https://www. jhipster.tech/jdl

16. Kapferer, S., Zimmermann, O.: Domain-driven service design. In: Dustdar, S. (ed.) SummerSOC 2020. CCIS, vol. 1310, pp. 189–208. Springer, Cham (2020). https:// doi.org/10.1007/978-3-030-64846-6_11

17. Kapferer, S., Zimmermann, O.: Domain-specific language and tools for strategic domain-driven design, context mapping and bounded context modeling. In: Proceedings of the 8th International Conference on Model-Driven Engineering and Software Development - Volume 1: MODELSWARD, pp. 299–306. SciTePress (2020). https://doi.org/10.5220/0008910502990306

18. Klabnik, S., Nichols, C.: The Rust Programming Language (Covers Rust 2018). No Starch Press (2019)

19. Milner, R.: The tower of informatic models. From semantics to Computer Science (2009)

20. Montesi, F., Carbone, M.: Programming services with correlation sets. In: Kappel, G., Maamar, Z., Motahari-Nezhad, H.R. (eds.) ICSOC 2011. LNCS, vol. 7084, pp. 125–141. Springer, Heidelberg (2011). https://doi.org/10.1007/978-3-642-25535-9_9

21. Montesi, F., Guidi, C., Zavattaro, G.: Service-oriented programming with Jolie. In: Web Services Foundations. In: Bouguettaya, A., Sheng, Q.Z., Daniel, F. (eds.) Web Services Foundations, pp. 81–107. Springer, New York (2014). https://doi. org/10.1007/978-1-4614-7518-7_4

22. Newman, S.: Building Microservices: Designing Fine-Grained Systems. O'Reilly (2015)

23. Oram, A.: Ballerina: A Language for Network-Distributed Applications. O'Reilly (2019)

24. Python Software Foundation: The Python Language Reference (2021). https:// docs.python.org/3/reference/index.html

25. Rademacher, F., Sachweh, S., Zündorf, A.: Deriving microservice code from under-specified domain models using DevOps-enabled modeling languages and model transformations. In: 2020 46th Euromicro Conference on Software Engineering and Advanced Applications (SEAA), pp. 229–236. IEEE (2020)

26. Rademacher, F., Sorgalla, J., Wizenty, P., Sachweh, S., Zündorf, A.: Graphical and textual model-driven microservice development. In: Microservices, pp. 147–179. Springer, Cham (2020). https://doi.org/10.1007/978-3-030-31646-4_7

27. Rademacher, F., Sorgalla, J., Wizenty, P., Trebbau, S.: Towards holistic modeling of microservice architectures using LEMMA. In: Companion Proceedings of the 15th European Conference on Software Architecture. CEUR-WS (2021)
28. Sculptor Team: Sculptor-Generating Java code from DDD-inspired textual DSL, 14 February 2022. https://www.sculptorgenerator.org
29. Soldani, J., Tamburri, D.A., Heuvel, W.-J.V.D.: The pains and gains of microservices: a systematic grey literature review. J. Syst. Softw. **146**, 215–232 (2018)
30. Sorgalla, J., Wizenty, P., Rademacher, F., Sachweh, S., Zündorf, A.: Applying model-driven engineering to stimulate the adoption of DevOps processes in small and medium-sized development organizations. SN Comput. Sci. **2**(6), 1–25 (2021). https://doi.org/10.1007/s42979-021-00825-z
31. Steinberg, D., Budinsky, F., Paternostro, M., Merks, E.: EMF: Eclipse Modeling Framework. Addison-Wesley (2008)
32. Terzić, B., Dimitrieski, V., Kordić, S., Milosavljević, G., Luković, I.: Development and evaluation of MicroBuilder: a model-driven tool for the specification of REST microservice software architectures. Enterprise Inf. Syst. **12**(8–9), 1034–1057 (2018)
33. The Rust Foundation: The Rust Reference (2021). https://doc.rust-lang.org/reference/

Author Index

Printed in the United States
by Baker & Taylor Publisher Services